Family scene at the turn of the century.
In the privacy of the courtyards of Moorish houses,
the women prepare food and spin wool.

Gateway leading to Berrima,
the business quarter of the medina (old city) of Meknès
which is today occupied by ironmongers' shops.

"Morocco is like a tree nourished by roots deep in the soil of Africa,
which breathes through foliage rustling to the winds of Europe."
King Hassan II of Morocco

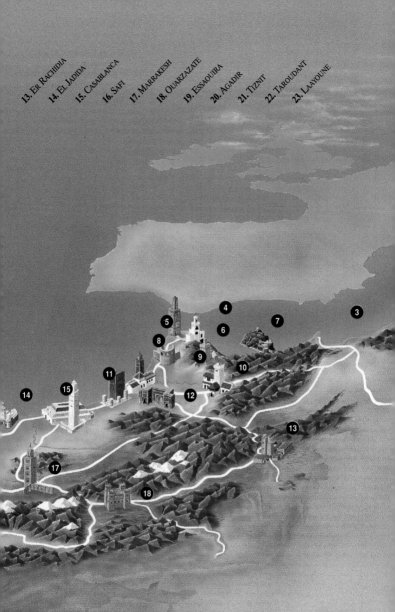

13. Er Rachidia
14. El Jadida
15. Casablanca
16. Safi
17. Marrakesh
18. Ouarzazate
19. Essaouira
20. Agadir
21. Tiznit
22. Taroudant
23. Laayoune

13

HOW TO USE THIS GUIDE

(Sample page shown from the guide to Venice)

The symbols at the top of each page refer to the different parts of the guide.

■ NATURAL ENVIRONMENT

● KEYS TO UNDERSTANDING

▲ ITINERARIES

◆ PRACTICAL INFORMATION

The itinerary map shows the main points of interest along the way and is intended to help you find your bearings.

The mini-map locates the particular itinerary within the wider area covered by the guide.

Immediately outside the railway station lies Cannaregio, the first of the six sextiers of Venice. Situated at the north-west end of the city, this is the second largest sestier after Castello ▲ 155, covering an area of 450 hectares. Nearly a third of the population of Venice is concentrated here, amounting to more than twenty thousand people. There are two theories about the origin of the name Cannaregio, meaning the the it comes from Canal regio (the Royal Canal), meaning the broad waterway which once provided convenient access to the city from the mainland, by prolonging the lagoon canal of San Secondo (which runs parallel to the railway bridge). The other hypothesis is that the words for reeds and canes, used to abound in this area. In any case, as a of straight, parallel canals, with long fondamenta abutting southwards and linked to the palaces of the Grand Canal. To workmen's houses interspersed with magnificent palaces the south, behind the palaces of the Grand Canal was built at the street known as the Strada Nuova was built at the end of the last century. Now pedestrianized, this Apostoli, and crossing the sestiere from one side to the Apostoli, and crossing the sestiere from one side to the other and adopting a number of different names as it goes. Few people lived in this sestiere until the 11th century, and it seems to have taken form only gradually, as the process of draining and consolidating the theories progressed. From the 15th century onwards, Cannaregio was a definable quarter. Before the 15th it was still peripheral to Venice proper, despite attempting was the bridge and the Strada Nuova built, manufacturing was the principal industry in the district. The draining of the Sacca della new area of growth within the Fondamenta Nuove. A similar project in the 16th century, the draining of the Sacca della Misericordia, was also never realized

The gateway to Venice, after all, is under the Piazzale near the station but the Grand Canal before us, churned by propellers, profaned as a great river.
Fernand Braudel, *Venise*

Santa Lucia Station.

THE GATEWAY TO VENICE ★

PONTE DELLA LIBERTA. Built by the Austrians 50 years after the Treaty of Campo Formio in 1797 ● *34,* to link Venice with Milan. The bridge ended the thousand-year separation from the mainland and shook the city's economy to its roots as Venice, already in the throes of the industrial revolution, saw its dependence on the mainland grow out of all recognition. **SANTA LUCIA STATION.** The present station dates from 1955, but still bears the name of the Renaissance church demolished in 1861 to make way for it. Opposite is the green dome of the Church of San Simeone Piccolo

🚶 Half a day

BRIDGES TO VENICE
The Austrians conceived a project for a bridge to connect Mestre and Venice as early as 1814. Work was not until 1846 that construction of the Ponte della liberta was finally begun. The new viaduct was soon swollen almost 3,500 feet, and it included 222 stone arches. On April 25, 1933, the Ponte della Liberta was opened. Built by the engineer Umberto Fantucci, this bridge was intended for use by motor cars.

★ The star symbol signifies that a particular site has been singled out by the publishers for its special beauty, atmosphere or cultural interest.

● ▲ ■ ◆
The symbols alongside a title or within the text itself provide cross-references to a theme or place dealt with elsewhere in the guide.

At the beginning of each itinerary, the suggested means of transport to be used and the time it will take to cover the area are indicated:

🚤 By boat
🚶 On foot
🚲 By bicycle
⊙ Duration

THE GATEWAY TO VENICE ★

PONTE DELLA LIBERTA. Built by the Austrians 50 years after the Treaty of Campo Formio in 1797 ● *34,* to link Venice with Milan. The bridge ended the thousand-year separation from the mainland and shook the city's economy to its roots as Venice, already in the throes of the industrial revolution, saw

🚶 Half a day

BRIDGES TO VENICE

NATURE

"A cold country with a hot sun" is how the Moroccans describe their land. Because of its coastline, which borders both the Atlantic and the Mediterranean, and the high barriers formed by its mountain ranges, Morocco has the widest range of climates of all the North African countries. Precipitation falls mainly in spring and autumn and the summers are hot and dry. Although this subtropical climate is similar to that of the maritime regions of California and southern Europe, it varies considerably according to latitude and altitude (sea level, desert and high mountain ranges) and to the effects of winds and currents.

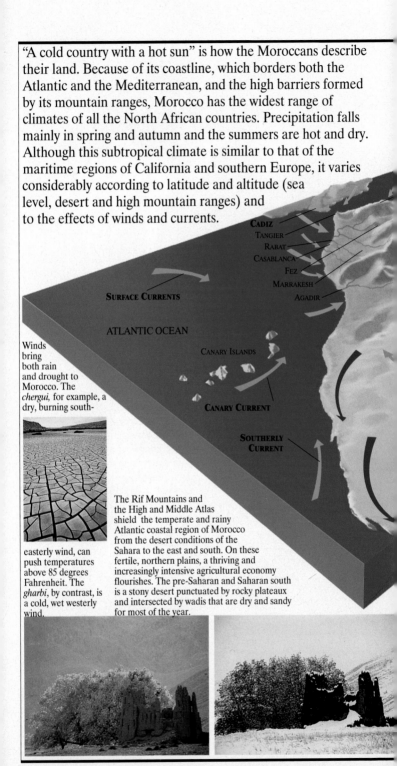

CADIZ
TANGIER
RABAT
CASABLANCA
FEZ
MARRAKESH
AGADIR

SURFACE CURRENTS

ATLANTIC OCEAN

CANARY ISLANDS

CANARY CURRENT

SOUTHERLY CURRENT

Winds bring both rain and drought to Morocco. The *chergui*, for example, a dry, burning south-easterly wind, can push temperatures above 85 degrees Fahrenheit. The *gharbi*, by contrast, is a cold, wet westerly wind.

The Rif Mountains and the High and Middle Atlas shield the temperate and rainy Atlantic coastal region of Morocco from the desert conditions of the Sahara to the east and south. On these fertile, northern plains, a thriving and increasingly intensive agricultural economy flourishes. The pre-Saharan and Saharan south is a stony desert punctuated by rocky plateaux and intersected by wadis that are dry and sandy for most of the year.

For a relatively small country, Morocco has a strikingly varied landscape. Many different types of local climate have produced such contrasting scenery as mountain valleys carpeted with flowers, the sun-scorched dunes of the Sahara, moist cedar forests and wadis swollen with spring rains. You can quite easily travel from the snows of the High Atlas to the sands of the Sahara in the space of a day.

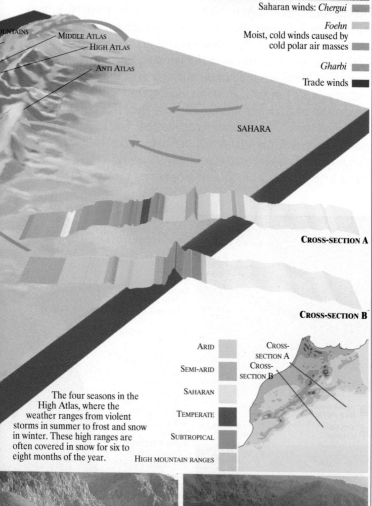

Saharan winds: *Chergui*

Foehn

Moist, cold winds caused by cold polar air masses

Gharbi

Trade winds

OUNTAINS
MIDDLE ATLAS
HIGH ATLAS
ANTI ATLAS

SAHARA

CROSS-SECTION A

CROSS-SECTION B

ARID

SEMI-ARID

SAHARAN

TEMPERATE

SUBTROPICAL

HIGH MOUNTAIN RANGES

CROSS-SECTION A
CROSS-SECTION B

The four seasons in the High Atlas, where the weather ranges from violent storms in summer to frost and snow in winter. These high ranges are often covered in snow for six to eight months of the year.

FOSSILIZED SHARK'S TOOTH
From the secondary period, found in phosphate deposits.

Morocco's geological structure is the result of the movement of tectonic plates. This movement takes the form of divergence (causing the creation of oceans) and of compression (causing oceans to close and continental mountain chains to form, creating faults and volcanoes). The geological history of Morocco can be summarized in three stages. More than two billion years ago the Anti Atlas and part of the western Sahara were formed. During the primary period the sea engulfed the land, bringing about the appearance of marine life. At the end of this period, the collision of the African, European and American plates resulted in the formation of the central plateau and of granite ranges such as the Zaërs. During the tertiary period the western and eastern Meseta, the High and Middle Atlas and the Rif Mountains were formed. The legacy of this geological activity is a land rich in fossils and a wide variety of minerals. Today, Morocco is not only the world's third-largest phosphate producer but also possesses vast reserves of silver.

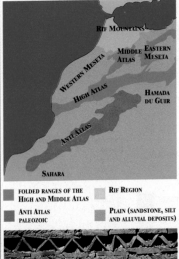

RIF MOUNTAINS

MIDDLE ATLAS — EASTERN MESETA

WESTERN MESETA

HIGH ATLAS

HAMADA DU GUIR

ANTI ATLAS

SAHARA

- FOLDED RANGES OF THE HIGH AND MIDDLE ATLAS
- ANTI ATLAS PALEOZOIC
- RIF REGION
- PLAIN (SANDSTONE, SILT AND ALLUVIAL DEPOSITS)

The inhabitants of southern Morocco build their houses with bricks made of clay (kaolinite) and straw, which are both weatherproof and provide some protection against the heat. Using bricks also saves wood.

MINERALS

1 BARYTES
There are several deposits of this brown barium oxide in southern Morocco.

2 GALENA
Lead sulfide. Deposits in the Middle Atlas.

3 FIBROUS GYPSUM
Calcium sulfide.

4 GYPSUM FLOWER OR GYPSUM
Calcium sulfate, widely found in the Sahara.

5 ARAGONITE
Calcium carbonate. Colors range from pink to red. Deposits at Bou Azzer and Salghef.

6 AND 9 WULFENITE
Consists of lead molybdate. Colors range from orange to red. Deposits found on Jebel Mansour.

7 VANADINITE
Contains lead, chlorine and vanadium. Colors range from yellow to reddish brown. Deposits at Mibladen and on Jebel Nasser.

8 AMETHYST GEODE
Purple quartz found in southern Morocco.

11

12

▲ Houses built from local clay. The shade of red depends on the clay's iron content.

FOSSILS

10 TRILOBITES

Unrolled Phacops. Trilobites are also found in rolled-up form. Typical of the primary era and found in the Erfoud, Er Rachidia and Agadir regions.

Outcrops of rock rich in Nautiloidea.

11 AMMONITES

Hildoceras fossil dating from the secondary period and very common in the Middle Atlas.

12 NAUTILOIDEA

Group of Orthoceras fossils from the middle of the primary period. Found in the Erfoud and Er Rachidia regions.

The Moroccan coastline extends over 2,200 miles. The Mediterranean coast consists of rocky scree and mountains dropping steeply to the sea, while the low sandstone cliffs of the Atlantic shoreline, which become higher towards the south, are punctuated by beaches. The stretch of level coast between Tangier and the Oued Draa, much of which backs onto exposed limestone, looks like a flat terrace with shallow, flat-bottomed pools within a tracery of ridges. Seaweed grows in abundance, and fish and shellfish marooned in the pools when the terrace is uncovered at low tide are a rich source of food for sea birds.

TURNSTONE
The turnstone turns over small stones, seaweed and empty shells in its search for worms.

RINGED PLOVER AND OYSTERCATCHER
These birds feed on worms, molluscs and other invertebrates and pass the winter on the Moroccan coast.

At low tide, sea birds scour the pools for prawns, blennies, mudskippers, sea urchins, limpets and small octopus.

BLACK-BELLIED PLOVER

COASTAL TERRACE
Mussels abound on the ridges surrounding shallow

pools, which are often lined with sea anemones and harbor

the rare microscopic Botryllus (above) and Glossodoris.

MOROCCAN CORMORANT
Nests on the cliffs of the Atlantic coast.

DEAD CLIFFS
Some way inland and surrounded by compacted dunes, these cliffs are the vestiges of a shifting coastline.

As it advanced and retreated, each quaternary sea left a layer of relatively soft silt that was broken down by wind and spray and deposited on the living cliffs.

WHITE-EYED GULL
Found usually around the Red Sea and the Gulf of Aden, it nests mainly on rocky islets and cliffs. It feeds on fish and shellfish, and also scavenges dead fish in the fishing ports.

DUNLIN **REDSHANK** **WHIMBREL** **OYSTER-CATCHER** **TURNSTONE** **SANDWICH TERN**

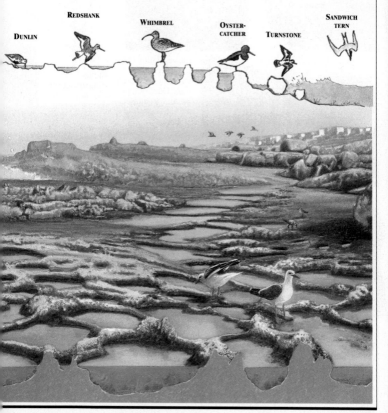

OUED MASSA

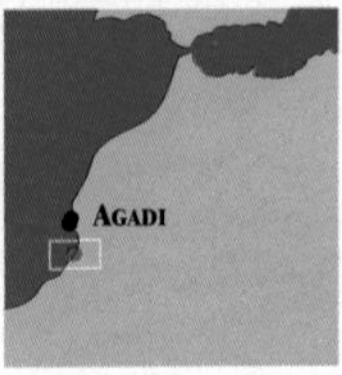

SIDI RBAT

MOUTH OF THE
OUED MASSA

SANDBANK

The fertile strip of the Sous-Massa National Park, lying in the arid region between Agadir and Tiznit, has one of the richest concentrations of Moroccan plant- and wildlife. The mouth of the Oued Massa is bordered by vast reed beds and its broad sandbanks attract migrating or overwintering birds. It crosses an area of traditional agricultural land (farmed both collectively and individually) and a nature reserve that extends to the shoreline, with its vast stretch of dunes, cliffs and forests.

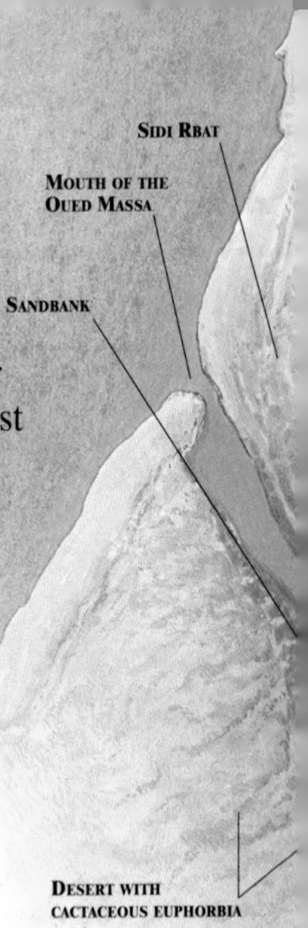

AGADI

DESERT WITH
CACTACEOUS EUPHORBIA

The vegetation of the desert regions bordering the mouth of the Oued Massa includes groundsel and cactaceous euphorbia.

REEDS (GRAMINACEAE)
The large reed beds along the banks of the Oued Massa provide protection for such migrating birds as reed warblers, herons and crakes.

EURASIAN WILD BOAR
In Morocco the wild boar's habitat ranges from the high-altitude forests to the fringes of the desert. It is often seen on the banks of the Oued Massa, where it comes to drink.

THORNY EUPHORBIA
This indigenous species is well established along the shoreline, on the desert plains and at the foot of the mountains in the southwest.

TAMARISK
A shrub with pliant branches and pink flowers. It provides shelter for migrating sparrows and plays a vital role in stabilizing sand dunes.

EGYPTIAN MONGOOSE (PHARAOH'S RAT)
This carnivore is usually seen at dusk as it sets off to hunt.

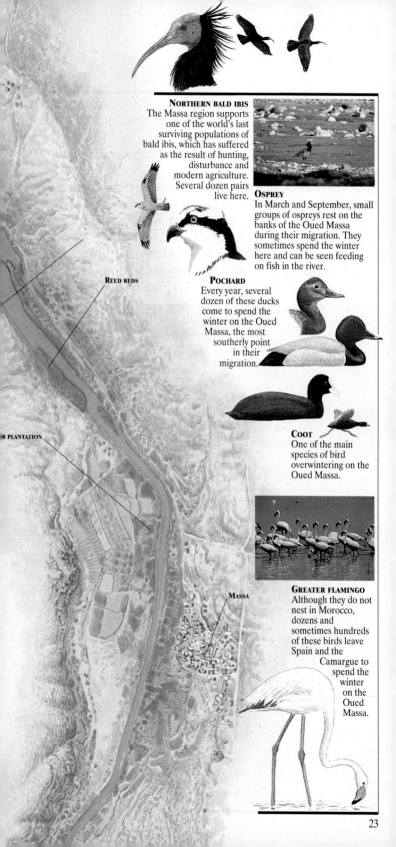

NORTHERN BALD IBIS
The Massa region supports one of the world's last surviving populations of bald ibis, which has suffered as the result of hunting, disturbance and modern agriculture. Several dozen pairs live here.

OSPREY
In March and September, small groups of ospreys rest on the banks of the Oued Massa during their migration. They sometimes spend the winter here and can be seen feeding on fish in the river.

POCHARD
Every year, several dozen of these ducks come to spend the winter on the Oued Massa, the most southerly point in their migration.

COOT
One of the main species of bird overwintering on the Oued Massa.

GREATER FLAMINGO
Although they do not nest in Morocco, dozens and sometimes hundreds of these birds leave Spain and the Camargue to spend the winter on the Oued Massa.

REED BEDS

PLANTATION

MASSA

23

Several high mountain ranges rise beyond the Atlantic plains and broad coastal plateaux of Morocco. The rugged Rif Mountains curve along the Mediterranean coast, while the Middle and High Atlas, enclosing high, arid plateaux to the east and a broad sloping valley and a series of low plains to the west, form the great "backbone" of Morocco and act as a natural divide between the Atlantic coastal region and the Sahara. The Anti Atlas, bordered by alluvial plains, bare rocky ridges and stony arid plateaux to the south, runs parallel to the High Atlas. The deep valley in these southern Atlas Mountains (between the High and Anti Atlas) is interrupted by the volcanic Jebel Siroua before it sweeps westward to the vast plain of the Oued Sous.

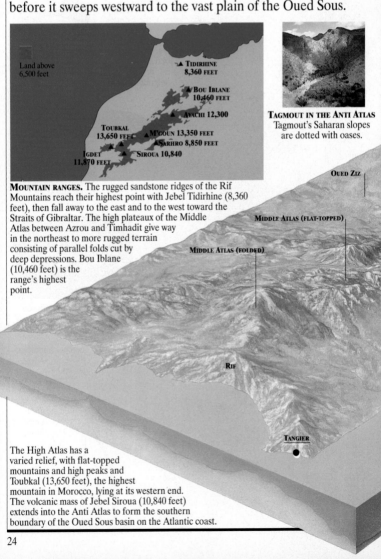

Land above 6,500 feet

▲ TIDIRHINE
8,360 FEET

▲ BOU IBLANE
10,460 FEET

▲ AVACHI 12,300

TOUBKAL
13,650 FEET

▲ M'GOUN 13,350 FEET

▲ SARHRO 8,850 FEET

IGDET
11,870 FEET

SIROUA 10,840

TAGMOUT IN THE ANTI ATLAS
Tagmout's Saharan slopes
are dotted with oases.

MOUNTAIN RANGES. The rugged sandstone ridges of the Rif Mountains reach their highest point with Jebel Tidirhine (8,360 feet), then fall away to the east and to the west toward the Straits of Gibraltar. The high plateaux of the Middle Atlas between Azrou and Timhadit give way in the northeast to more rugged terrain consisting of parallel folds cut by deep depressions. Bou Iblane (10,460 feet) is the range's highest point.

OUED ZIZ

MIDDLE ATLAS (FLAT-TOPPED)

MIDDLE ATLAS (FOLDED)

RIF

TANGIER

The High Atlas has a varied relief, with flat-topped mountains and high peaks and Toubkal (13,650 feet), the highest mountain in Morocco, lying at its western end. The volcanic mass of Jebel Siroua (10,840 feet) extends into the Anti Atlas to form the southern boundary of the Oued Sous basin on the Atlantic coast.

M'GOUN
The domed peak of M'goun (13,350 feet), in the central High Atlas, is traversed by narrow gorges and deep valleys.

TOUBKAL
At 13,650 feet Toubkal is the highest point in North Africa. This squat-looking range conceals deep, narrow valleys that are virtually inaccessible, particularly in winter, when they are shrouded in snow.

▲ **THE MIDDLE ATLAS PLATEAU**
The limestone plateau of the Middle Atlas consists of a series of arid plateaux that were partially covered in lava following recent volcanic activity. The terraces of these plateaux are covered with beautiful forests of cork oak, holm oak and Atlas cedar.

DAYET AFOURGAH
The lake has formed in one of the karstic depressions that litter the limestone plateau of the Middle Atlas.

JEBEL ANRHOMER
Rising to over 11,800 feet, Jebel Anrhomer dominates the vast, arid plain of Ouarzazate-Skoura and forms the mineral floor of the Tamda lake.

HAMADA DU GUIR
HAMADA DU DRAA
OUED DRAA
JEBEL BANI
OUGNAT
SARHRO
OUARZAZATE
EXTINCT VOLCANO OF SIROUA
ANTI ATLAS
M'GOUN
TOUBKAL
HIGH ATLAS
OUM ER RBIA
MARRAKESH
MOROCCAN MESETA
OUED BOU
OUED SÉBOU
RABAT

THE RIF
This is the lowest of the four great Moroccan ranges. Its wet Atlantic slopes are covered with oak, cedar and pine forests, while the wild and arid Mediterranean slopes are sparsely covered with junipers and thujas (see *matorral* ■ 27).

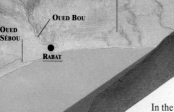

In the west, the Rif and the Atlas Mountains enclose the tableland of the Moroccan Meseta, which rises from the sea in a succession of terraces and meets a belt of low plains and coastal plateaus.

HIGH ATLAS

MOUNTAIN PASTURE IN THE TINGUERF
Many annual plants and flowers thrive in the wet pastureland of the Tinguerf.

The High Atlas, which forms a frontier between the palearctic and tropical regions of Morocco, is the highest mountain range in North Africa. These arid mountains consist of vast plateaux, deep valleys, almost bottomless canyons, craggy peaks and mountaintops eroded by wind and rain. The northern slopes are mainly forested with holm oaks, thujas, cedars and Aleppo pines growing at mid-altitude. Higher up, these are replaced by thuriferous juniper and then by plants growing in cushion-like formations. The southern slopes, being influenced by the Sahara, have a steppe-like vegetation, with a scattering of red cedar and thuriferous juniper dominating at altitudes of 6,400 to 9,800 feet.

LAMMERGEIER
This vulture haunts the high mountain ranges, feeding on the carcasses of sometimes quite large mammals.

The deep, narrow valleys of the High Atlas open up on to broad plains that are intensively cultivated with market gardens, cereals and orchards.

MEDIUM MOUNTAINS (4,900–8,200 FEET)

TERRACING
Terracing makes the most of the land around villages in the open valleys in the interior of the High Atlas.

HORNED LARK
One of the main inhabitants of the high mountain steppe.

DIPPER
Hunts for food on the beds of mountain streams and nests in banks and under waterfalls.

LOW MOUNTAINS (<4,900 FEET)

MOUNTAIN PEAKS (>11,500 FEET)

RED-BILLED CHOUGH
This noisy, aerial acrobat nests among high mountain crags.

HIGH MOUNTAINS 8,200–11,500 FEET)

BOOTED EAGLE
Nests on the edge of forests. Pairs give very acrobatic aerial displays.

GOLDEN EAGLE
A giant bird with a wingspan of over 6½ feet. It dominates the high mountains, nesting on inaccessible cliff faces.

THURIFEROUS JUNIPER
The trunk of this species, which can reach some 30 feet in circumference, is heavily exploited for its bark.

THORNY XEROPHYTE
High-altitude plants grow in cushion-like formations as a way of surviving the cold.

BARBARY SHEEP (AOUDAD)
The long chest hairs do not affect the speed and agility of this sure-footed mountain goat.

"MATORRAL"
A sparse and stunted vegetation resulting from damage inflicted by humans. It is found throughout the High Atlas.

27

CEDAR FORESTS

The great spotted or pied Numidian woodpecker has a characteristic red nape patch.

FEZ
AZROU
MIDELT

Cedar forests several thousand years old cover around 325,000 acres of the Rif, the High and the Middle Atlas (185,000 acres). Among the conifers in these forests are some extremely fine specimens, some of which grow to heights of around 200 feet and can be up to 400 years old.

Atlas cedars, which need moisture, grow at altitudes of 4,000 to 9,200 feet. Their wood is highly prized by cabinetmakers and makers of stringed instruments. These dark forests provide shelter for large numbers of macaques, which are hunted by the last surviving leopards. The large-leaved peony is just one of many flowers and plants that thrive in the forests' rich undergrowth.

At lower altitudes, holm oaks and pines grow among the cedars. Higher up, these are replaced by thuriferous junipers and maples.

PEONY
The large-leaved peony is the only type of peony found in Morocco. It has large, denticulate leaves and produces bright red flowers in April and May.

SCOPS OWL
From the end of March, the single, soft notes of the scops owl can be heard, usually in the sunniest parts of the forest.

SHORT-TOED EAGLE
Often hovering to search for its prey, this variably coloured bird feeds mainly on snakes and lizards.

BARBARY MACAQUE
This extremely social monkey, also known as the Barbary ape, is active during the day

COMMON GENET
This shy predator feeds mainly on rodents and birds. It hunts in the forest by night and always leaves its droppings in the same place.

and feeds mainly on plants, which it stores in its cheek pouches.

LEOPARD
This beautiful member of the big cat family is becoming very rare. The cedar forests are home to about a dozen individuals.

THE ATLAS CEDAR
The leaves of the Atlas cedar consist of rosettes of pine needles, while its smooth cones are a carefully arranged spiral of flowers.

RED CROSSBILL
A member of the finch family which feeds on the seeds of pine cones, using its remarkable crossed bill.

FIRECREST
The smallest bird to inhabit these forests. It feeds on the insects it finds among the leaves.

BLUE TIT
The blue tit, indigenous to the Atlas Mountains, has a distinctive dark blue skullcap.

R. Desbordes

◼ ARGAN FORESTS

ESSAOUIRA
AGADI
OUARZAZATE
TIZNIT

The argan tree, indigenous to Morocco, grows in arid, misty regions. It is most commonly seen, either cultivated or growing wild, in light forests in the Essaouira region, the eastern foothills of the High Atlas and the foothills of the Anti Atlas and, to a lesser extent, at the foot of the Hamada du Draa. Argan nuts have a hard stone containing two kernels from which a strongly scented, orange-colored oil is extracted. The evergreen foliage provides "treetop" grazing for herds of goats, which are extremely fond of argan leaves. These intrepid climbers can often be seen feeding high among the branches.

LEAVES AND FRUIT OF THE ARGAN TREE

MOUSSIER'S REDSTART
This close relative of the wheatear is indigenous to northwest Africa and tends to prefer open forests.

CRESTED LARK
This seed- and insect-eating bird nests on the ground, its plumage providing excellent camouflage.

DARK CHANTING GOSHAWK
An extremely rare bird of prey from tropical Africa.

BARBARY SQUIRREL
This squirrel, known to the Berbers as *anzet* or *anzid*, is very common in Morocco. It feeds on argan and pistachio nuts.

Atlas cedar

Thuriferous juniper

Holm oak

Phoenician juniper

Thuja

Cork oak

Pistachio tree

Argan tree

ARGAN TREE
A heavily fruiting tree found in arid regions up to altitudes of 4,900 feet. Morocco has over 1,600,000 acres of light argan forests.

CAROB
The seeds of the carob tree (*kharroub, karats*) were used as a measure of weight for jewelry (carats). They are also used in the preparation of medicine.

RED CEDAR
The *ar aâr el horr* is highly resistant to drought as well as to cold and wet. Vast cedar forests extend along the coast of Morocco up to altitudes of 6,500 feet.

MOUNT ATLAS PISTACHIO
Most of the light *betoum* ● *34* forests on the arid and semi-arid plains have been destroyed, since their wood is used to make cade oil.

BERBER THUJA
The thuja develops huge outgrowths known as burls. Its wood is much prized among cabinetmakers for its luster and mottled effect.

ARGAN OIL
Argan nuts look rather like olives. The rich oil extracted from the kernels in the stone is used in cooking.

It takes around 220 pounds of nuts and ten hours of grinding to produce 2 pints of oil.

MOUNT ATLAS PISTACHIO
The reason why this fine pistachio has been spared the axe is probably because it is growing near a shrine.

MAMORA FOREST

MAMORA WILD PEAR
This is the only other tree that grows among the cork oaks of the Mamora Forest. It can reach a height of 40 feet and from January to March is covered with white flowers.

As well as its eucalyptus, pine and acacia plantations, 138,000 acres of the Mamora Forest are covered almost entirely in cork oaks, which are grown for their cork but also produce edible acorns and are used as a source of firewood. The forest is also an important source of food for large numbers of sheep and cattle, and the consequences of this are clearly visible. The foliage is grazed from below by cattle, trees have been cut back and, more seriously, no young shoots can form. Although the forest itself is under threat, its rich undergrowth still provides shelter for several species of resident and migratory birds as well as the remarkable chameleon, while the shores of its *dayas* (temporary lakes) are a favorite haunt of the white stork.

SPOTTED FLYCATCHER
A summer visitor to the forest between April and September that swoops to catch flies and other winged insects in flight.

ROLLER
A migratory bird that feeds on large insects, spiders, scorpions and small lizards.

TURTLE-DOVE
This little dove, smaller than a pigeon, arrives from tropical Africa in April and nests in the bushes of the forest. Its numbers are declining as it is still hunted in Morocco.

The Mamora Forest ▲ *178* lies between Rabat, Kénitra and Meknès.

PEELING CORK FROM THE CORK OAK
This process, which involves removing the outer layers of bark, begins when the tree is twenty-seven years old and is repeated every

BLACK-SHOULDERED KITE
This rare bird of prey feeds on the ground and nests in foliage.

AFRICAN CHAMELEON
The chameleon comes down to the ground only during the autumn rains, to lay its eggs in the damp ground.

ASPHODEL
The flora of the Moroccan cork-oak forest is extraordinarily rich and varied, with over 800 species and subspecies. In early spring, the forest floor is carpeted with asphodels.

nine years until it is seventy to seventy-five years old. The first peeling removes the deeply furrowed "male" bark, while subsequent peelings remove the so-called "female" bark used in cork production. The tree also produces tannin for the leather industry.

STEPPE

GALEODE
A nocturnal, non-poisonous spider that inhabits dry, arid regions. It is a quick-moving, voracious hunter, capable of devouring a scorpion.

The vegetation of the Moroccan steppe is typical of that of all arid regions. Alfa-grass predominates on the higher ground and sagebrush in the low-lying, drier areas, while impressive *betoums* (Mount Atlas pistachios) grow in wadi and *daya* beds. In spite of its moribund appearance, the steppe is teeming with life. Below ground, termites form the basis of the food chain that explains this abundance of wildlife. There are various species of insect and spider (such as the nimble galeode, which is attracted to fires at night), lizards (including the agama and the mastigure) and snakes. The steppe also supports birds and various mammals such as small rodents, gazelles, foxes and jackals.

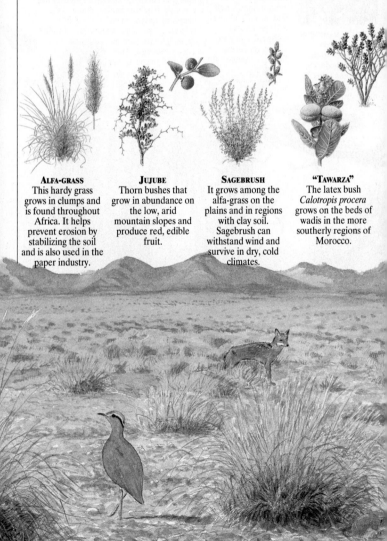

ALFA-GRASS
This hardy grass grows in clumps and is found throughout Africa. It helps prevent erosion by stabilizing the soil and is also used in the paper industry.

JUJUBE
Thorn bushes that grow in abundance on the low, arid mountain slopes and produce red, edible fruit.

SAGEBRUSH
It grows among the alfa-grass on the plains and in regions with clay soil. Sagebrush can withstand wind and survive in dry, cold climates.

"TAWARZA"
The latex bush *Calotropis procera* grows on the beds of wadis in the more southerly regions of Morocco.

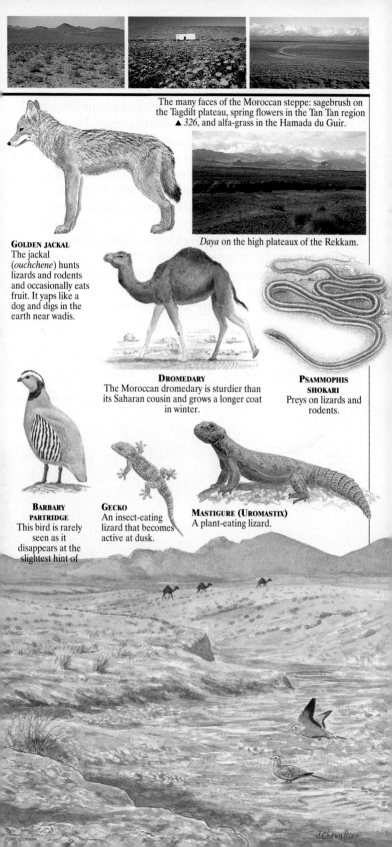

The many faces of the Moroccan steppe: sagebrush on the Tagdilt plateau, spring flowers in the Tan Tan region ▲ 326, and alfa-grass in the Hamada du Guir.

Daya on the high plateaux of the Rekkam.

GOLDEN JACKAL
The jackal (*ouchchene*) hunts lizards and rodents and occasionally eats fruit. It yaps like a dog and digs in the earth near wadis.

DROMEDARY
The Moroccan dromedary is sturdier than its Saharan cousin and grows a longer coat in winter.

PSAMMOPHIS SHOKARI
Preys on lizards and rodents.

BARBARY PARTRIDGE
This bird is rarely seen as it disappears at the slightest hint of

GECKO
An insect-eating lizard that becomes active at dusk.

MASTIGURE (UROMASTIX)
A plant-eating lizard.

DESERT

True desert has an annual rainfall of less than 4 inches. The Moroccan desert stretches from Jebel Siroua in the east to the foot of the Anti Atlas in the west. Its wide variety of vegetation ranges from the succulent plants that grow in the relatively damp oceanic belt to the desert flora of the drier, pre-Saharan region. The Moroccan desert is stony rather than sandy, having been formed from a vast rocky plateau. Sand carried by burning Saharan winds accumulates there and forms dunes. These are usually fairly low, except at the Erg Chebbi to the south of Erfoud.

HORNED VIPER
Hides in the sand and kills its prey with its poisonous, fast-acting venom.

THE DESERT BY DAY
Birds often seek refuge from the heat of the day in the shadow of plants, while mammals take to cool burrows. Reptiles bury themselves in the sand, contracting their eyes and nostrils. Insects keep cool by beating their wings.

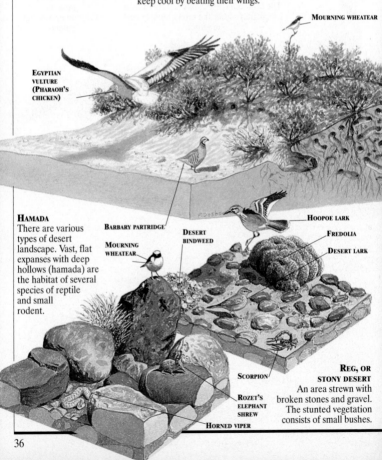

MOURNING WHEATEAR

EGYPTIAN VULTURE (PHARAOH'S CHICKEN)

HAMADA
There are various types of desert landscape. Vast, flat expanses with deep hollows (hamada) are the habitat of several species of reptile and small rodent.

BARBARY PARTRIDGE

MOURNING WHEATEAR

DESERT BINDWEED

HOOPOE LARK

FREDOLIA

DESERT LARK

SCORPION

ROZET'S ELEPHANT SHREW

HORNED VIPER

REG, OR STONY DESERT
An area strewn with broken stones and gravel. The stunted vegetation consists of small bushes.

DESERT MONITOR
This large lizard with powerful jaws retreats to its burrow during the hottest hours of the day.

BLACK SCORPION

LANGUEDOC SCORPION

Scorpions are easily recognized by their claws and the poisonous sting in their tail. They are nocturnal creatures that hide under stones or bury themselves in the sand in winter. Scorpion stings should be treated immediately.

REG
A stony, windswept landscape.

AGAMA LIZARD
During the mating season the male's body turns orange, and its legs and tail go a purplish-blue.

SKINK. This solitary, smooth-scaled lizard, popularly known as the medicinal skink, buries itself in the sand up to 15 inches deep.

THE DESERT BY NIGHT
Most desert animals have become nocturnal in order to survive. Mammals, for example, tend not to leave their dens or burrows until dusk. As an adaptation to this way of life their hearing has become particularly acute, as demonstrated by the size of the fennec fox's ears. Some species abandon their nocturnal habits in winter, when the nights become extremely cold.

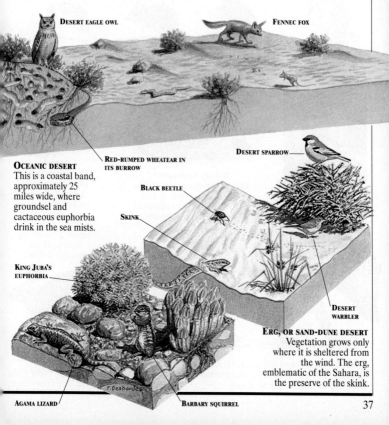

DESERT EAGLE OWL

FENNEC FOX

OCEANIC DESERT
This is a coastal band, approximately 25 miles wide, where groundsel and cactaceous euphorbia drink in the sea mists.

RED-RUMPED WHEATEAR IN ITS BURROW

DESERT SPARROW

BLACK BEETLE

SKINK

KING JUBA'S EUPHORBIA

DESERT WARBLER

ERG, OR SAND-DUNE DESERT
Vegetation grows only where it is sheltered from the wind. The erg, emblematic of the Sahara, is the preserve of the skink.

F. Desbordes

AGAMA LIZARD

BARBARY SQUIRREL

37

BLACK-BELLIED SAND GROUSE
In spring it drinks from the wadis and stores water in its neck feathers, to take back to its young.

CROWNED SAND GROUSE
This very rare desert bird is found in the extreme south of Morocco.

PIN-TAILED SAND GROUSE
Lives in large groups in the steppe regions of eastern Morocco.

FAT SAND RAT

RED-RUMPED WHEATEAR
Nests in a hole at ground level or among fallen rocks.

WHITE-CROWNED BLACK WHEATEAR
Lives farther east in rocky ravines. The young have black heads.

DESERT WHEATEAR
Found throughout the gravel desert regions.

FAT SAND RAT
A small rodent found near wadis.

ROZET'S ELEPHANT SHREW
Named after its trunklike snout.

LIBYAN JIRD
The Libyan jird is very partial to bitter-apples (desert melons).

GERBIL
A nocturnal rodent that digs its burrow in the sand, where it may spend the winter.

CAPE HARE

DESERT HEDGEHOG
This solitary creature becomes very active at dusk. It lives among vegetation and feeds on insects and frogs.

JERBOA
The solitary jerboa lives in the steppe, hamada, erg and rocky regions. It is entirely nocturnal and, after sealing the entrance to its long burrow, sleeps through the day.

STRIPED HYENA. Found in the extreme south of Morocco. It is a nocturnal hunter that can make long journeys in search of food.

FENNEC FOX
Lives in the sandy deserts of the south.

CAPE HARE
Takes cover in the wadis of the Moroccan steppe.

BLACK-BELLIED SAND GROUSE
As she sits on her nest, the female (right) is virtually invisible, her plumage merging with the surrounding steppe. The male is shown left.

SPOTTED SAND GROUSE
This sand grouse is quite often seen in the Tafilalet, on the edge of the desert.

TRUMPETER FINCH
Has a characteristic nasal call rather like a toy trumpet.

CREAM-COLORED COURSER
In flight, this bird reveals the black underside of its wings.

TEMMINCK'S HORNED LARK
Has long hornlike feathers on either side of its head.

DESERT LARK
Its unremarkable plumage enables it to blend easily with its surroundings. It is very common south of the Atlas Mountains.

DESERT SPARROW
Tends to haunt fairly inaccessible regions of southern Morocco, although it is also found between Merzouga and the south of the Tafilalet.

HOUBARA BUSTARD
Once a very common species in Morocco.

LANNER FALCON
Lives on the edge of the desert and feeds on rodents.

BIFASCIATED LARK
Characterized by its melancholy call and strange mating display.

HOUBARA BUSTARD
The bustard has been hunted to the point of extinction in eastern Morocco, as in many other parts of the world. Despite its size, it is well camouflaged against the sagebrush of the Moroccan steppe.

DORCAS GAZELLE
The dorcas has been hunted for centuries. It inhabits the dunes and regs of southern Morocco.

SAND CAT
This desert cat hunts by day in winter and by night in summer. It lives in the Tafilalet.

OASES

OLEANDER

COMMON BULBUL
The bubbling calls of the inquisitive bulbul are heard in parks, orchards and oases.

An oasis is a naturally occurring phenomenon that forms in the middle of the open desert or at the foot of a desert mountain. With their characteristic stands of date palms, oases are havens of peace and tranquillity; under the cool shade of trees, bright green vegetable and cereal plots are set out between irrigation channels dug in the earth. Originally, these crops were grown for local consumption but they are now being replaced by a systematic date-palm monoculture, which has raised annual yields to as much as 5 or even 7 tons per acre.

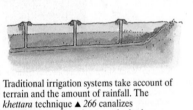

Traditional irrigation systems take account of terrain and the amount of rainfall. The *khettara* technique ▲ 266 canalizes underground water along gently sloping drainage channels.

SECONDARY CHANNEL, OR "MASRAF"

MAIN IRRIGATION CHANNEL, OR "SEGUIA"

CEREAL PLOTS
Cereals are planted in the autumn. They are not watered, and depend on rainfall for their growth and survival.

CORN   BARLEY   OATS

HOUSES
These are usually located outside the palm plantation so as not to spoil the agricultural land.

SPRING
The pure spring water is used for drinking and cooking.

UPPER POOL
The water in this pool is used to wash in and for washing clothes.

MAURITANIAN TOAD
Its deep-throated croaking can be heard throughout the night. It is silent during the dry season.

LOWER POOL
This provides drinking water for livestock and for watering crops.

POOL RESERVOIR
The bottom of the pool is lined with clay. It is used for irrigation and bathing.

BASIN RESERVOIR
The sluices in this shallow basin enable water to be channeled into one of the *seguias*.

PALM PLANTATION
Date palms follow the underground waterline of the wadi, and fields are laid out in the flood plains.

WELL.
A donkey-operated pulley system feeds water into the channels.

CORN FLAG GLADIOLUS

CORIANDER

The date palm originated in Arabia. It belongs to the most primitive group of palms, which first appeared 100 million years ago. The cylindrical trunk does not thicken with age and can grow up to around 100 feet high. The leaves, or palms, grow in tightly packed rosettes on the trunk and live for four to five years before dying off. Both the male and female trees flower in March or April and are naturally pollinated by the wind. The date is a berry with sugar-rich flesh and parchment-like skin. Palm plantations in Morocco currently cover 200,000 acres, with a total of approximately 4.7 million date palms.

Dates are sold either loose or "on the branch". The best varieties are the semi-soft "nutmeg" dates.

DOUM-PALM
The dwarf fan-palm, or palmetto, can grow to its full height if it is not grazed or cut.

Besides the doum and date palms, there are at least twenty-five different species of palm tree, which have been introduced into the parks and gardens of Morocco.

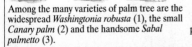

Among the many varieties of palm tree are the widespread *Washingtonia robusta* (1), the small *Canary palm* (2) and the handsome *Sabal palmetto* (3).

The terminal bud of the palm tree is covered in a fibrous floss (the *fibrilum*). This is where the palms and bunches of dates are formed.

Palms that are cut at the base have a scaly appearance and they are also much easier to climb during the date harvest.

DATES

There are over one hundred varieties of this extremely nutritious fruit, which comes in various colors, shapes and sizes.

Today, growers assist pollination by cutting off the male flowers and placing them among the bunches of female flowers.

Every part of the palm tree has a use. The palms are burnt as fuel or used to make windbreaks (1), mats (2), furniture and baskets (3). The trunks are hollowed out to make gutters (4) or used as roof supports (5).

1 **2** **3** **4** **5**

SHOOTS
Palm trees reproduce by throwing out shoots from the main trunk.

PALM ROOTS
Under ground, the bulb of the palm tree is surrounded by a vast root system. These fine, hair-like roots spread out in all directions in search of water.

43

Morocco is a major producer of fruit and vegetables. Since 1980 innovations such as greenhouses, and new techniques such as micro-irrigation, the use of high-yield hybrids and *in vitro* reproduction, have been

introduced. This has further increased production, which not only feeds the local population but also provides large amounts of fruit and vegetables both for export and for the Moroccan food industry, which produces canned foods, jams and fruit juices. Tomatoes are the most important crop, closely followed by citrus (oranges and clementines) and other types of fruit (apples, pears, apricots, nectarines, peaches, quinces and plums). Recently introduced exotic fruits such as kiwi, custard apple, kumquat, feijoa and guava are also grown.

SOUKS
In the country, weekly souks not only provide an opportunity to buy and sell livestock but are also an important source of fresh fruit and vegetables. They are usually well stocked with a wide variety of brightly colored and richly scented produce.

DRIED FRUIT
Dried fruit is extremely popular at the end of the fast of Ramadan ◆ *339*.

CANNED FOOD IN BRINE OR VINEGAR
Canned vegetables, olives, pimentos and lemons are widely used in cooking and eaten as appetizers.

FRESH VEGETABLES
Pimentos, eggplants, peppers, zucchini, fennel, carrots, tomatoes, cabbage, onions and other fresh vegetables are essential in Moroccan cooking and are used to vary the flavor and appearance of tajines ● *82*, couscous and stews.

ABSINTH **CORIANDER** **THYME**

MINT

BAY **PARSLEY**

Every Moroccan
garden has its own
bed of mint, which
varies according to
season. It is used to
make mint tea, the
sweet, thirst-
quenching national
drink. Although most
of Morocco's tea is
imported from the
East, it is also grown
in the wettest regions,
in the shelter of cork
oaks.

The flavor of mint is
enhanced by various
types of thyme or
fresh absinthe,
depending on the
region.

BAY
Bay is grown
in the Middle Atlas
for export.

PRICKLY PEAR
The prickly pear is a
fleshy plant
indigenous to the arid
regions of Morocco.
Its sweet fruit is
collected with long
sticks.

PERSIMMON

PRICKLY PEAR

POMEGRANATE

FRESH FRUIT
Clementines and Valencia
and navel oranges account
for more than 80 percent of the
fruit grown in Morocco, although
plums are now increasingly widely grown for
dried fruit in the Meknès region ▲ *232*.
Apple, cherry and nut trees, introduced by
Greek and Spanish settlers, are found in the
northern foothills of the Middle Atlas. More
recent introductions, such as avocados, kiwi
fruit, persimmons and pomegranates, are
exported or sent to the major Moroccan
cities. In the Gharb ▲ *212* and Sous Valleys
▲ *316*, bananas are now grown under glass.

■ SPICES

Moroccan cooking is
based on a sophisticated
blend of different spices. It
favors sweet-and-sour and
subtly seasoned flavors and skillfully
combines peppers, herbs, seeds and roots.
Although some of these spices, including cinnamon, ginger and
cloves, are imported from the East, most are grown in Morocco
and include such aromatic plants as coriander, cumin, fennel,
sesame and thyme. Many of these plants have medicinal
properties and traditional herbal medicine is a respected art.
Every souk has its sellers of medicinal herbs, offering the rural
population affordable herbal remedies.

CINNAMON
Bark of the Indian
cinnamon. Used as
powder for cakes and
pastry and in sticks
for tajines ● *82*.

CUMIN
Cumin and salt are
sprinkled on kebabs
and grilled meat.

PAPRIKA
Mildly spicy red
powder from a type of
pepper.

"RAS EL HANOUT"
Ras el hanout ("head
of the shop") is a
special blend of spices
(cloves, roses and
cinnamon) made up
by grocers.

SESAME
Soft, sweet-tasting
sesame is used in the
sweetmeat halva,
which can be brown,
pure white or black.

CLOVES
Clove trees take
twenty years to reach
maturity and continue
to bear fruit for the
next fifty years.

GREEN TEA
This forms the basis
of mint tea and is
grown on damp
ground in the shelter
of cork oaks.

VERBENA
The Moroccans are
great producers of
scented verbena
which, like thyme, is
used in infusions.

MUSK
Musk, secreted by the
abdominal glands of
animals, is used
mainly for its
fragrance.

YELLOW AMBER
This hard, translucent
fossilized resin is used
as a fragrance or
burnt as incense.

INCENSE
A special Berber
blend of aromatic
plants, musk and
yellow amber that is
used to perfume
the home.

LAVENDER
Used as an ingredient
in *ras el hanout* as
well as in infusions
and perfumes.

**MEDICINAL
HERB SELLER**
Herb sellers offer
perfumes as well as
medicinal herbs.

**CEREALS, GRAIN, VEGETABLES AND DRIED
FRUIT**

PIMENTO
Two hundred varieties
of pimento are grown
throughout the world.
It is a hot, tonic plant,
rich in vitamin C.

CORIANDER
Originally a
Mediterranean plant,
with a fresh, peppery
flavor that is much
stronger in Morocco.

FENNEL
A sun-loving plant
that is very similar to
anise, although not as
sweet. It is used to
flavor a number of
different dishes.

**BLACK AND WHITE
PEPPER**
Black pepper comes
from the seeds of the
unripe fruit, white
from the ripe fruit.

HARISSA
This searingly hot
paste, made with
pimentos, garlic, salt,
cumin, coriander and
olive oil, is used in
tajines and couscous.

CAPERS
These are the flower
buds of the prickly
caper bush that grows
in the arid, stony
deserts of Morocco.

"BOULGHOUR"
Crushed wheat. The
rounded grains of
corn or couscous are
used in a dish of the
same name and also
in some breads.

ALMONDS
Almonds are grown
over a total area of
more than 232,000
acres. The trees
flower in February.

ROSES
Cultivated in the
Dadès Valley and
used in various blends
of spices, in pastry
and in perfumes.

HENNA
Henna was once
cultivated along with
other dyes. It is still
used for dying the
hair, the palms of the
hands and the feet.

"GHASSOUL"
An absorbent clay
(smectite) that
dissolves in water. It
effectively removes
grease and is used for
washing the hair.

ANTIMONY SULFIDE
Lead- and sulfur-
based galena. This
mineral is ground into
powder to make kohl
● 66 for the eyes.

FISHING

Moroccan waters are extremely rich in fish, with around 240 species. The most famous of these is the sardine, which is exported all over the world. Morocco's deep-sea and mid-water fishing industry has a fleet of large boats backed up by an industrial infrastructure that enables it to catch and process 163,000 tons of fish per year. Deep-sea fishing concentrates mainly on octopus and squid (114,000 tons) and mid-water fishing on prawns and shrimps. Small-scale coastal fishing is conducted using drawnets, trawls, lines and nets, with vessels ranging from sardine boats, wooden trawlers and small trawlers to motorized dinghies. The Moroccan fishing industry is a mixture of modern methods and various traditional techniques used by small-scale local fishermen to supply hake, sea bream, bonito, mullet, red mullet, dorados, bass, lobsters, octopus, cuttlefish and squid for local consumption.

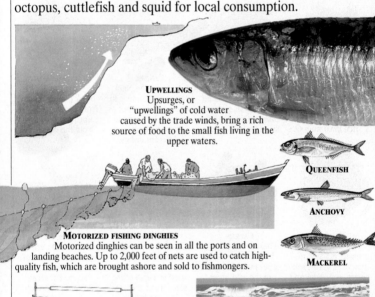

UPWELLINGS
Upsurges, or "upwellings" of cold water caused by the trade winds, bring a rich source of food to the small fish living in the upper waters.

QUEENFISH

ANCHOVY

MACKEREL

MOTORIZED FISHING DINGHIES
Motorized dinghies can be seen in all the ports and on landing beaches. Up to 2,000 feet of nets are used to catch high-quality fish, which are brought ashore and sold to fishmongers.

DRAGNETS
Dragnet fishing occurs all along the Moroccan coast, wooden trawlers catching around 88,000 tons of hake, prawns, sea bream, sole and skate. A sound knowledge of the coastal waters is essential if damage to the net is to be avoided.

FISHING FROM THE SHORE
On the beaches, fishermen set their nets at low tide to catch bass and sole.

TRAWL NET

Morocco's sardine industry is concentrated in Agadir (the country's major port) and Tan Tan. Essaouira, Safi, Casablanca and Tangier are secondary centers of the trade.

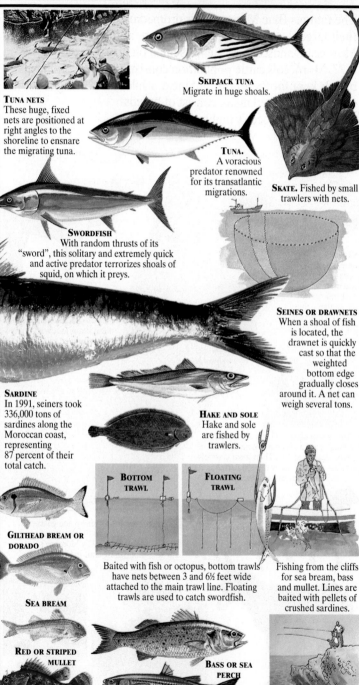

SKIPJACK TUNA
Migrate in huge shoals.

TUNA NETS
These huge, fixed nets are positioned at right angles to the shoreline to ensnare the migrating tuna.

TUNA.
A voracious predator renowned for its transatlantic migrations.

SKATE. Fished by small trawlers with nets.

SWORDFISH
With random thrusts of its "sword", this solitary and extremely quick and active predator terrorizes shoals of squid, on which it preys.

SEINES OR DRAWNETS
When a shoal of fish is located, the drawnet is quickly cast so that the weighted bottom edge gradually closes around it. A net can weigh several tons.

SARDINE
In 1991, seiners took 336,000 tons of sardines along the Moroccan coast, representing 87 percent of their total catch.

HAKE AND SOLE
Hake and sole are fished by trawlers.

GILTHEAD BREAM OR DORADO

SEA BREAM

RED OR STRIPED MULLET

LARGE-SCALED SCORPION

BOTTOM TRAWL

FLOATING TRAWL

Baited with fish or octopus, bottom trawls have nets between 3 and 6½ feet wide attached to the main trawl line. Floating trawls are used to catch swordfish.

Fishing from the cliffs for sea bream, bass and mullet. Lines are baited with pellets of crushed sardines.

BASS OR SEA PERCH

MULLET

49

■ LIVESTOCK

MIXED TEAM
Donkeys and dromedaries
are used as draft animals and
are often seen harnessed to
the same plow.

The famous Blue Men on their dromedaries and herdsmen with
their large flocks of sheep and goats are as much a part of the
Moroccan landscape as the horseman on his Arab thoroughbred
● 72. Morocco's cattle population consists largely of indigenous
breeds kept for their milk and meat, while sheep and goats, the
main source of red meat, consist of breeds
adapted to Morocco's highly diverse
environment.

MEHARI
The buff-colored,
Saharan dromedary
used by the
Camel Corps.

**SAHARAN
DROMEDARY**
Both ridden
and used as a
pack animal by
the Berbers, these
make up 6 percent of
the camel population.

DROMEDARY
The dromedary is used by the
Moroccans as a draft animal.
Plains dromedaries tend to be
leaner, while the mountain
dromedaries have thicker
coats.

SHEEP AND GOATS. Goats and over 15
million head of sheep make up the bulk of
Moroccan livestock. Their meat is widely
consumed, particularly mutton, which is eaten
at important feasts and celebrations.

The skins of sheep and goats,
together with 12,000 tons of wool a
year, are used by Morocco's
flourishing craft industry.

DONKEYS
Morocco's 800,000 donkeys are used
for transport and as draft animals.

TRANSHUMANCE
Common law tightly
regulates seasonal
transhumance ▲ 280.

HISTORY AND LANGUAGE

PREHISTORY

13,000 BC
Cave paintings at Lascaux (Dordogne, France).

1500 BC
Construction of the temples of Luxor and Karnak.

EARLY INHABITANTS. The earliest tools found in North Africa were discovered in Casablanca ▲ *136* and prove that the Atlantic coast of present-day Morocco was inhabited as early as 800,000 BC. By c. 5,000 BC the descendants of these early inhabitants had been joined by new populations from the Near East who became the ancestors of the Berbers, a group that was subsequently enlarged by new immigrants from the Mediterranean.

A PASTORAL COMMUNITY. During the Bronze Age (c. 1600 BC) Berber shepherds carved images of daggers, haldberds, hatchets and shields on rocks of the High Atlas ▲ *260*. These weapons were used by the Mauretanians for hunting and fishing, their two main activities.

ANTIQUITY

Rock carvings in the High Atlas.

The historical period in Morocco began c. 800–600 BC when the ancient Libyan script invented by the Berbers appeared in the Atlas Mountains and pottery (found on the island of Essaouira ▲ *156*) was decorated with Phoenician lettering. Around 500 BC the Ethiopians, a race "burnt by the sun", settled in Morocco. In the north, they were a sedentary people who lived in troglodyte settlements, while in the south they were nomadic horsemen who lived by hunting. The Atlantes, after whom the Atlantic Ocean is named, populated the central Atlas.

753 BC
Foundation of Rome.

447–32 BC
The Parthenon, in Athens, is built by order of Pericles.

359 BC
Philip II becomes King of Macedonia.

Bust of Juba II, praised by contemporary historians for his culture and style of government.

BIRTH OF MAURETANIA (4TH CENTURY BC). The region inhabited by the western Libyans was known to the Greeks as Maurusia (the land of the Mauri, or Moors). The modern inhabitants of Morocco and western Algeria still refer to themselves as Maurusians. Juba II was made King of Mauretania by the Roman emperor Augustus and, based at the city of Volubilis, he reigned from 25 BC to AD 23. Juba described the country in a book that was later used by Pliny. He set up dye works to make purple dye on the island of Mogador, off the coast of Essaouira ▲ *160*, and had his navy explore the Canary Islands.

12 BC
Augustus becomes religious head of the Roman Empire.

AD 70
The temple of Jerusalem is destroyed.

410
Rome falls to the Visigoths.

THE ROMAN CONQUEST (AD 42). The Roman armies occupied Mauretania and divided it into two provinces. New roads meant that agriculture and trade in the western province of Tingitana flourished, as did the cities of Tingis ▲ *180*, Lixus ▲ *209*, Volubilis ▲ *244* and Banasa ▲ *212*. Roman influence continued in the south until 285 and in the north until 429, when the Vandals reached this part of Mauretania. It appears that from 533 onward the Byzantine and then the Visigoth fleets occupied Ceuta and Essaouira, although very little evidence of their presence remains.

> "SOME TOWNS, VOLUBILIS FOR EXAMPLE, WERE BUILT ON THE ROMAN MODEL; BUT THE COLONIZATION, INDEED THE *ROMANIZATION*, OF MOROCCO WAS ALWAYS EXTREMELY TENUOUS AND DID NOT EXTEND BEYOND THE BOU REGREG."
>
> HENRIETTE CELARIÉ

THE MUSLIM CONQUEST

THE ARRIVAL OF ISLAM. In 682 the Arab chieftain Sidi Okba Ibn Nafie, the founder of Kairouan, the first Muslim city in Tunisia, set out on an expedition to the Atlantic coast. Although the Berbers and Byzantines rose up against this Arab invader, the Muslims succeeded in extending their influence and spreading the Islamic faith among the local populations. In 711, the Berber chieftain Tarik Ibn Zijad reached Gibraltar: the conquest of Spain had begun.

622
Beginning of the Hegira, or Muslim era.

732
Charles Martel defeats the army of Abd er Rahman at the Battle of Poitiers.

Route taken by Sidi Okba Ibn Nafie in the northern Maghreb.

THE CALIPHATE IN CRISIS. Muslim influence became increasingly firmly rooted in spite of the establishment of kingdoms based on other religions, such as the Kharijite kingdom of Sijilmassa in the Tafilalet ▲ *295* and the kingdom of Berghouata on the Atlantic coast ▲ *136*. In 740 there was an uprising against the authorities in Damascus, the seat of the Ommayad caliphate. Morocco broke free from their power and fragmented into various principalities.

THE IDRISSID DYNASTY (788–1055)

THE BIRTH OF A STATE. In 786 Idriss I, a descendant of the Prophet Mohammed through his daughter Fatima and son-in-law Ali, fled Arabia to escape the massacre of his family ordered by the Caliph of Baghdad. He sought refuge in Morocco, where in 788 he was proclaimed imam (religious leader) by the Berber tribes of central Morocco. He consolidated the power of Islam, founded Fez in 789 and unified northern Morocco as far as Tlemcen. In 792 Idriss I was poisoned by order of the Caliph of Baghdad, Haroun er-Rachid, who was alarmed by his rapid success. On his accession to the caliphate, Idriss II extended his authority to new regions, imposed on his kingdom an organized state system and developed and improved the city of Fez ▲ *214*.

762
Foundation of Madinet as-Salam (modern Baghdad).

785
The Great Mosque in Córdoba is built.

800
Charlemagne is crowned Emperor in Rome.

THE KINGDOM DISINTEGRATES. On the death of Idriss II in 828, control of the kingdom passed to his sons and then to his brothers. Commerce in Fez was flourishing and in 857 and 859 the Kairouyine ● *86*, ▲ *224* and Andalous ▲ *229* mosques were built. By the early 10th century the Idrissid court was attracting Andalous scholars. Caravans bringing gold from Guinea drew the attention of the armies of two rival caliphs, the Tunisian Fatimid and the Spanish Omayyede. In the early 11th century the Idrissids were proclaimed caliphs of Córdoba but the division of Spain led to their decline and ultimate withdrawal in 1055. This coincided with the arrival of the Almoravid tribes from a desert *ribat* (hermitage).

Tomb of Idriss I at Moulay Idriss.

859
The Andalous Mosque in Fez is consecrated.

1037
Ferdinand of Castile becomes King of León.

53

● History of Morocco

The Almoravid Dynasty (1073–1146)

1099
Jerusalem is taken by the Crusaders.

1114
Failure of the Almoravid expedition to Barcelona.

The Almoravids were nomadic Berber warriors who made their way rapidly northward on a mission to purify and strengthen the weakened Islamic faith. In 1055 they captured Sijilmassa ▲ 295 and Aoudaghost ▲ 260, gaining control over the trans-Saharan trade routes, and went on to conquer Fez in 1069. In c. 1070 they founded the city of Marrakesh ▲ 260, which became the capital and gave its name to the kingdom of Morocco. The Almoravids continued northward and occupied Spain as far as the River Ebro. Their leader, Youssef Ibn Tachfine, was succeeded in 1106 by his son Ali Ben Youssef, who reigned for the next thirty-seven years.

The Almohad Dynasty (1147–1269)

1147
Santarém and Lisbon are recaptured by Afonso I of Portugal.

The casbah of Tin-Mal where Ibn Toumert died in 1130.

RELIGIOUS RECOGNITION. In the city of Tin-Mal ▲ 303, south of Marrakesh, a would-be *Mahdi* (messenger of God) was preaching purity, austerity and the unity of God. In 1121 Mohammed Ibn Toumert (the Torch), whose followers became known as the Almohads (unitarians), rebelled against the Almoravids and preached a doctrine of radical religious reform. The Almohad conquest of Morocco culminated in the capture of Marrakesh in 1147. Ibn Toumert's disciple, Abd el Moumen ▲ 261, succeeded him as caliph, setting himself on a par with those of Baghdad and Córdoba, and founded a new dynasty.

Capital of the Mosque of Tin-Mal.

1187
Jerusalem is recaptured by Saladin.

1258
The end of the Abbassid caliphate.

The Hassan Mosque, Rabat.

THE ALMOHAD EMPIRE. Although Abd el Moumen succeeded in unifying North Africa before his death in Rabat in 1163, it was his successor, Yacoub el Mansour (the Victorious), who annexed Andalusia, defeating the Spanish and Portuguese in 1195 at the battle of Alarcos. After El Mansour's death, the empire in Spain disintegrated and the religious doctrine of Ibn Toumert was abandoned.

The Merinid Dynasty (1269–1465)

1375
Ibn Khaldoun writes the history of the Berbers.

Merinid tombs, Fez.

A NEW DYNASTY BEGINS. In 1248 the Beni Merin, Zenata people from the Moulouya basin ▲ 299, took advantage of the weakening Almohad dynasty to capture Fez, Rabat and Salé and the fertile plains of the Sais and the Gharb ▲ 212. Abou Youssef Yacoub seized Marrakesh in 1269 and ousted the Almohad dynasty.

A PRECARIOUS POSITION. The Merinids then tried to rebuild the empire and undertook some moderately successful expeditions to Spain. Although Abou el Hassan (the Black Sultan) lost Spain and Algeciras in 1340, he kept Gibraltar and went on to take Tlemcen and Tunis in 1347. A year later bubonic plague and the Tlemcen and Tunis uprisings marked the decline of the Merinid dynasty, which failed to drive back the Portuguese and Spanish armies.

THE SAADIAN DYNASTY (1525–1659)

FINDING A LEADER. In 1508 the Portuguese, who had colonized the Atlantic ports of Morocco, began to compete with trans-Saharan trade. The marabouts (holy men) advocated a Holy War and found their leader in the Arab tribe of the Beni Saad, descendants of the Prophet Mohammed, from the Draa Valley. In 1509 the Saadian Chérif El Kaim held out against the Portuguese army and established the power of the new dynasty with the capture of Marrakesh in 1525.

RECONQUERING LOST TERRITORY. After driving the Portuguese from Agadir in 1541 Mohammed Sheikh recaptured their enclaves with the exception of Mazagan. He went on to Fez and ousted the Beni Ouattas, who had been in power since 1471. In 1578 Ahmed el Mansour Eddahbi (the Victorious and the Golden), victor at the battle of the Three Kings ▲ *201*, finally defeated the Portuguese. The Saadians gained control of the gold route by capturing Timbuktu and the bend of the River Niger.

DECLINE OF THE DYNASTY. Following the death of Ahmed el Mansour in 1602, the Saadian dynasty disintegrated. Andalous Muslims driven out of Spain between 1609 and 1611 set up an independent republic at Salé ▲ *175*, which lasted from 1620 until 1639.

THE ALAOUITE DYNASTY

BIRTH OF THE MOROCCAN EMPIRE. The Alaouite dynasty was descended from the *chorfa* of the Tafilalet, descendants of Ali and the Prophet's daughter Fatima, who had acted as independent rulers since the middle of the 15th century. The dynasty was founded by Moulay Ali Chérif ▲ *295* in 1666. The objective of Moulay Chérif and his successors was to reunify Morocco and, to this end, they introduced rigid economic and military policies. Moulay Ismail ▲ *232*, who exerted absolute power between 1672 and 1727, continued the work of his predecessors. He recaptured Larache and Tangier, then abolished local political and religious systems and founded the Moroccan empire. He extended his rule to Senegal by constructing a network of fortresses in which he deployed a professional army, and, in a bid to strengthen foreign relations, dealt on an equal footing with Louis XIV of France and James II of England.

On the gold route, Timbuktu.

1492
Grenada is captured by the Catholic Kings.

1498
The first Andalous Muslims and Jews exiled.

Fourteenth-century Portuguese vessel.

1566
Philip II retaliates against the Mudéjars.

During the 17th century pirates from Salé threatened the great maritime powers.

1661
Death of Cardinal Mazarin and the accession of Louis XIV.

1715
Death of Louis XIV.

1771
Mohammed III recognizes the independence of the United States.

The Alaouite sultan Moulay Ismail.

1783
The Treaty of Versailles and end of the American War of Independence.

Moulay Slimane.

1801
The Treaty of Madrid ends the armed conflict known as the War of the Oranges between Spain and Portugal.

1869
The Suez Canal opens.

Economic crisis: Following the death of Moulay Ismail, his pretorian guard (the Abids or Black Guard) ran amok in the cities and countryside and Morocco was plunged into a state of civil war. The reign of Sidi Mohammed Ben Abdullah brought in a welcome period of respite. He built Essaouira ▲ 156, drove the Portuguese out of Mazagan ▲ 220 and declared the country open to foreign trade. However, drought, plague and the end of the *djihad* (piracy) imposed by the sultan Moulay Slimane (and the subsequent end of maritime trade), dealt a serious blow to the country's prosperity. Internal and external political tensions forced Moroccan rulers to operate a policy of withdrawal.

Political crisis. The support given by the Moroccan empire to the Algerian emir Abd el Kader provoked the military intervention of France in 1844 and Spain in 1859–60. Moulay Hassan (1873–94) tried to strengthen his power by calling on the tribes of the High Atlas ▲ 260 and to modernize the country while maintaining independence, but treaties were imposed on Morocco by Great Britain, Spain and France. The country ran up debts with foreign banks.

The Protectorate (1912–56)

Moulay Hafid.

The Moroccan delegation at the Conference of Algeciras (January 16 to April 7, 1906).

1922
Italian fascists march on Rome.

Roosevelt and Sidi Mohammed Ben Youssef (Anfa, 1943).

1933
Hitler becomes chancellor of the Reich.

Foreign intervention. At the conference of Algeciras ▲ 181 in 1906, which brought together twelve nations, France and Spain were appointed trustees of the new Banque Nationale du Maroc. Following the assassination of a number of Europeans, France occupied Casablanca in 1907. Moulay Hafid was proclaimed sultan in the same year. In 1909 Spain embarked upon the conquest of the Rif crescent ▲ 194 and in 1911 Moulay Hafid called upon French troops to liberate Fez, which was besieged by insurgent tribes.

Morocco becomes a protectorate. The French advance into the interior led the sultan to agree to sign a treaty on March 30, 1912, making Morocco a French protectorate and giving Spain a sphere of influence. Moulay Hafid abdicated and was succeeded by his brother, Moulay Youssef. In 1912 General Lyautey was installed as Morocco's resident French general ▲ 104, and made Rabat his headquarters. Working with the urban planning expert Léon Henri Prost, he began to modernize Morocco's cities.

A time of revolt. The mountain tribes rebelled against European domination. In 1921 Mohammed Ben Abdelkrim led a revolt in the Rif, which was put down in 1926 by a Franco-Spanish coalition. Following the departure of Lyautey in 1925 France reduced the power of the Moroccan central government while increasing its own involvement in direct administration. Resistance was organized mainly by young, elite groups from the cities but was interrupted by World War.

MOROCCO IN THE 20TH CENTURY

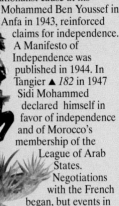

TOWARD INDEPENDENCE. The Allied landings in 1942 and President Roosevelt's open support of the Moroccan nationalist cause at his meeting with Sidi Mohammed Ben Youssef in Anfa in 1943, reinforced claims for independence. A Manifesto of Independence was published in 1944. In Tangier ▲ *182* in 1947 Sidi Mohammed declared himself in favor of independence and of Morocco's membership of the League of Arab States. Negotiations with the French began, but events in Casablanca on December 7 and 8, 1952, were just a foretaste of the bloodshed that was to follow. On August 20, 1953, the sultan was forced to abdicate, and went into exile. The Moroccan resistance movement gained support while Spain sided with the opposition. Setbacks in Indochina and the 1954 Algerian uprising forced the French government to seek a political solution.

INDEPENDENCE RESTORED. Mohammed V's return from exile on November 16, 1955, opened the way for independence and Morocco was recognized by France on April 7, 1956, and by Spain on October 29 of the same year. King Mohammed V was responsible for drawing up the major part of the constitution that was adopted after his death in 1962 by his son Hassan II. The first elections were held in 1963. Later that year Moroccan and Algerian forces clashed in the Western Sahara. From 1964 the government had to confront political and economic crises. In 1970 Hassan II published the draft of a second constitution which was adopted by referendum in July 1971. In June 1972 Hassan II presided at the conference of the OAU (Organization of African Unity) held in Rabat.

EXTERNAL POLICY. The de-colonization of the Western Sahara provoked a mass mobilization of the Moroccan people who, in November 1975, went on what became known as the Green March. The western Sahara was subsequently divided between Mauritania and Morocco. With Algerian support and Libyan weapons, the Popular Front for the Liberation of the *Saguia el-Hamra* and the Rio de Oro (also known as the Polisario Front) fought for the independence of the former Spanish colony for the next decade.

Sidi Mohammed Ben
Youssef, later
Mohammed V.

1945
The Yalta Conference.

1956
*Suez canal
nationalized and
Tunisia declared
independent.*

1962
*Algeria declared
independent.*

1973
*Morocco sends troops
to Suez and Syria
during the Israeli-
Egyptian war.*

1985
*Morocco applies to
join the European
Economic
Community. Pope
John Paul II visits
Casablanca.*

1989
*Creation of the
Maghreb Arab League.*

The Green March.

NOVEMBER 1989
*The Berlin wall
collapses.*

1990
Iraq invades Kuwait.

1991
Break-up of the USSR.

King Hassan II.

57

● ARABIC AND BERBER

**"DDUNIT TGA AS͟T͟TA GAN WUSSAN IFALAN
ASS NNA IRA RBBI BBINT UR AKK° IKMMIL"**

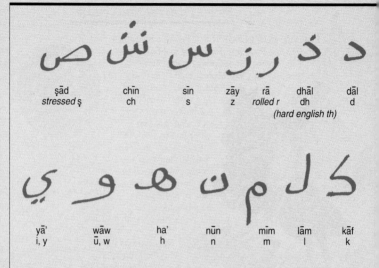

ص	ش	س	ز	ر	ذ	د
ṣād	chīn	sīn	zāy	rā	dhāl	dāl
stressed ṣ	ch	s	z	*rolled r*	dh	d
					(hard english th)	

ي	و	ه	ن	م	ل	ك
yā'	wāw	ha'	nūn	mīm	lām	kāf
i, y	ū, w	h	n	m	l	k

Phonetic guide to the Arabic alphabet.

MOROCCO'S ORIGINAL LANGUAGE

Before it came under Islamic influence in the late 7th and early 8th centuries, Morocco had its own language – Berber – which seems to have developed during the centuries immediately before the Christian era. Berber, like Arabic, belongs to the Hamito-Semitic group of languages, but the fact that it does not have a written form makes tracing its history extremely difficult. The first recorded instance of Berber proper nouns occurs in the *Periplus of Hanno*, the account of a voyage undertaken by a Carthaginian navigator in the mid-5th century BC. Various similarities between place names translated into Greek and the Berber form of these names appear to confirm that Berber was spoken at that time. The names of certain Roman towns and cities that sound similar to names in their Berber form seem to corroborate this theory. However, apart from this academic evidence, no written evidence exists of the Berber dialects that were spoken in ancient Morocco. Neither do writers in classical antiquity make any reference to the cultural life of Morocco's early inhabitants. However, although part of Morocco was Romanized and Christian, it is generally agreed that, immediately prior to the arrival of Islam, the majority of Moroccans were still Berbers. Roman influence brought

A legal document in Arabic

in an entire vocabulary, still used in modern everyday speech, usually related to newly introduced aspects of civilization such as the calendar, culture and houses. The arrival of Islam in Morocco prevented the Berber language from developing and acquiring written status. This was reserved for Arabic, which became the vehicle of propaganda as the new conquerors spread the Holy Word through the Koran. This campaign of Islamization and Arabization was not in fact led by the Arabian invaders but by dynasties of Berber origin, such as the Almoravids and Almohads. These dynasties imposed on

> "LIFE IS A LOOM, WHOSE THREADS ARE THE DAYS. GOD DECIDES WHEN TO CUT THE THREADS, EVEN THOUGH [THE WORK] IS UNFINISHED."

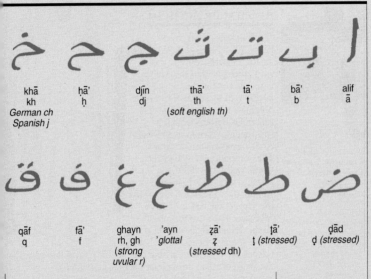

| khā / kh / German ch / Spanish j | ḥā' / ḥ | djin / dj | thā' / th / (soft english th) | tā' / t | bā' / b | alif / ā |

| qāf / q | fā' / f | ghayn / rh, gh / (strong uvular r) | 'ayn / 'glottal | ẓā' / ẓ / (stressed dh) | ṭā' / ṭ (stressed) | ḍād / ḍ (stressed) |

Morocco and Spain an orthodox form of Islam expressed exclusively in Arabic. Although the wide use of Arabic did not entirely wipe out Berber, it considerably supplanted it, reducing the areas in which it continued to be spoken to inaccessible mountain regions. A law dated January 26, 1965, stated that Arabic was to be the only language used in any form of legal proceedings, whether for the defense, deeds and titles or judgments.

BERBER DIALECTS

Forgotten or ignored by historians and Arab writers, Berber remained an exclusively spoken language. The many different dialects of which it consists are spoken throughout Morocco, though primarily in the mountainous regions of the Rif ▲ 194 and the Middle ▲ 225, High ▲ 260 and Anti Atlas ▲ 308. These dialects can be divided into two main groups: Zénatiya and Berbero-Chleuch. The first group comprises the Rif dialects spoken in the Mediterranean region of Morocco, and the dialects of the Beni Iznassen, Beni Bou Zeggou and Zkara tribes of eastern Morocco, as well as those of the southern tribes of the Aït Seghrouchen and Figuig. Berbero-Chleuch is divided into two distinct sub-groups: Tamazight, which comprises the Berber dialects of central and pre-Saharan Morocco, and Tashelhayt, which includes the Shluh (or Chleuch) dialects of the inhabitants of the Atlas, Anti Atlas and the Sous region (Agadir ▲ 310, Taroudant ▲ 316). Although Arabic is the official spoken and written language of Morocco and the language taught in schools, Berber dialects are still spoken in almost half the country, both in towns and cities and in rural areas.

BERBER DIALECTS
Although Berber dialects are spoken throughout half of Morocco, they are not taught in schools. However, Berber does have its own traditional literature, handed down orally, and some of this has now been transcribed and published. In recent years Berber has become a new vehicle for political and artistic expression.

Tangier
Fez
Rabat
Casablanca
Essaouira

Arabic
Bedouin
Berber (Tamazight)
Berber (Tashelhayt)
Berber (Zénatiya)

● ARABIC AND BERBER

Man from the
Aït Moussa tribe
wearing a
qchaba.

ARABIZATION AND ISLAM

The founding of the city of
Fez in 789 by Idriss I ▲ *213*,
an Arab Chérif from the East,
led to the spread of the Arabic
language throughout the
kingdom of Morocco. Fez rapidly
became a religious and cultural
center for Berbers from the
surrounding regions as well as for
Andalous and Tunisian Arabs.
The occupation of Spain by the
Ommayads (756–1030),
Almoravids (1073–1146) and
Almohads (1147–1269) also aided
the irreversible Arabization of
Morocco. The introduction of
Arabic relegated all other languages
to the status of dialects and, because it
was the the only written language, Arabic was used to spread
the Word of Islam throughout the newly conquered
kingdoms.

A COMPLEX WEB OF LANGUAGES

These historical and linguistic circumstances explain why
literary Arabic has for centuries been the official language of
the Arabic- and Berber-speaking nations. Unlike Berber,
whose many dialects are not comprehensible to all Berber
speakers, the Arabic dialect spoken in Morocco on an
everyday basis is uniform (with some variations in
pronunciation and vocabulary) and understood throughout the
country. This dialect is a regional development of classical
Arabic and is neither taught nor written. However, it is used
to transmit a rich literary tradition which is often transcribed
using Arabic script. This complex linguistic heritage, which is
not exclusive to Morocco, has produced a naturally bilingual
people who use different languages to suit different
situations. The Arabic dialect is used in everyday speech,
while Berber is used more colloquially. Literary (or
standard) Arabic, inherited from classical Arabic, is
automatically used for written forms of communication
such as teaching, the press and in literature. Although
literary Arabic is common to all Arab countries, it has
nevertheless been adapted to meet the demands of the
modern world, while the French presence in Morocco was
also responsible for the introduction of French in
education and administration. French is still used in areas
of modern terminology not covered by Arabic, in spite of
sustained efforts to promote the Arab culture and
language since Moroccan independence.

UNIVERSITY OF FEZ
Kairouyine University
▲ *224*, founded in the
10th century,
provided free
education, which
included law,
literature and science
as well as religious
studies. It declined
during the 15th
century. In 1912,
reforms were
introduced to
reorganize traditional
Muslim education.

Berber woman
wrapped
in her
hendira
● *78*.

Detail of the Arabic
inscription (right) at
the entrance to the
Moulay Ismail
Mausoleum ▲ *238*.

ARTS AND TRADITION

● ISLAM

Left: the word *Allah* written in Arabic.

Islam was the faith that the Prophet Mohammed, who lived from c. 570 or 580 to 632, professed in the Arabian city of Mecca during the 7th century AD. The citizens' hostility was such that Mohammed and his followers were forced to leave Mecca for the neighboring city of Medina on July 16, 622. This date marks the beginning of the Muslim era, or *Hegira* (exile). Islam preaches obedience to the only God, Allah, his messenger, Mohammed, and to the book revealed to him, the Koran. The five religious duties of all Muslims are the *shahada* (profession of faith, i.e. that Allah is the only God and that Mohammed is His prophet), *salat* (prayer), *zakat* (charity), *sawm* (the fast of Ramadan) and, at least once during their life, *hajj* (pilgrimage to Mecca).

From the top of a minaret ● *88*, the muezzin calls the faithful to prayer five times a day.

THE KORAN

The Koran consists of 114 *surah* (chapters) divided into *ayat* (verses) and constitutes the basis of Muslim legislation, covering morals and customs as well as law.

THE KAABA

A 7th-century cubical building (above) in the courtyard of the mosque in Mecca into which the black stone given to Abraham by the Archangel Gabriel has been built.

PRAYER

All Muslims, after performing ritual ablutions, must pray five times a day, facing Mecca (or the qibla).

FRIDAY PRAYER

Friday is a day of rest for Muslims, who gather at the mosque to hear the weekly sermon. In Morocco, Friday prayer is an occasion on which the ruler prays with his subjects. A sultan and his train leaving the mosque (above).

A detail (above) and page (below) from the Koran.

All prayers begin with: "In the Name of God the Merciful, the Compassionate" (written below).

THE "KOUBBA"

The word *koubba* (dome) has come to mean the white domed building containing the tomb of a saint or holy person, usually the head of a religious community or a warrior imam, revered by the people.

Implements used in calligraphy: a *calame* (reed pen), portable writing desk and inkwells.

Historically, the spread of written Arabic and the emergence of the art of calligraphy were linked to the teaching of Islam. The need to produce a written form of the Koran gave rise to a more elaborate style of writing to make it a worthy vehicle for the Holy Word. The fact that Islam forbids all forms of figurative representation also contributed to the development of calligraphy as an art form. Several regional variations of the original Arabic script developed their own particular characteristics in the countries converted to Islam. The traditional art of calligraphy still plays an important role in Moroccan society.

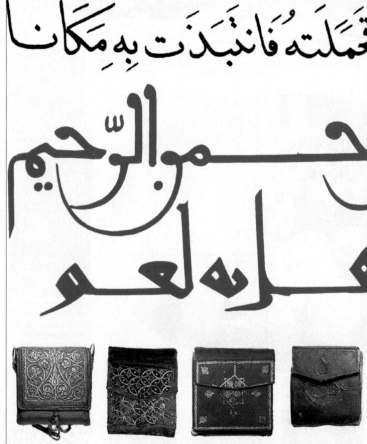

KORAN CASES
These small engraved and embroidered leather cases both protect the Koran during journeys and preserve its sacredness.

Certain decorative motifs, such as illuminated characters, have a very specific meaning for the reader of the Koran. They mark pauses, the beginning of verses and chapters and divisions of the text.

THE KORAN IN MAGHREBI SCRIPT

DIFFERENT SCRIPTS
During the 10th century Ibn Moqlah, an Islamic calligrapher, formalized the rules of calligraphy. Over the centuries many different styles of script were developed, each style having its own particular use. The first forms, angular and somewhat austere, were replaced by the Kufic script (bottom left), which was rapidly perfected and became the only script used to transcribe the Koran (a variant of this script is still used in the Maghreb). It was later replaced by more flowing, cursive forms. Six main styles of script are used today. One is the *naskhi* (top left), which is the most widely seen in Arabic books and newspapers. Morocco started to develop its own artistic forms of script in the 11th century. The delicate and gracefully formed Maghrebi script (centre left) is characterized by fine, elegant curves and more rounded loops.

KORANIC BOARD
These are used to teach reading and writing in Koranic schools. The master decorates the board with calligraphy when the Koran has been memorized.

Metal stamps used to decorate the covers of the Koran.

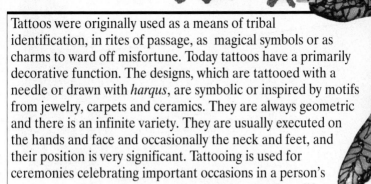

● TATTOOS
AND MAKEUP

Tattoos were originally used as a means of tribal identification, in rites of passage, as magical symbols or as charms to ward off misfortune. Today tattoos have a primarily decorative function. The designs, which are tattooed with a needle or drawn with *harqus*, are symbolic or inspired by motifs from jewelry, carpets and ceramics. They are always geometric and there is an infinite variety. They are usually executed on the hands and face and occasionally the neck and feet, and their position is very significant. Tattooing is used for ceremonies celebrating important occasions in a person's life.

KOHL
Kohl is a black powder made from antimony sulfide. According to the Koran its use was originally therapeutic (strengthening the eyesight and making the lashes grow), but it is now used as a makeup to highlight the eyes. It is kept in small, richly decorated flasks or containers (above and below) that take various shapes and may be made from a variety of materials. Kohl is applied using a small stick with a carved end that usually acts as a stopper.

Round pottery box decorated with fine concentric circles, containing *aker*, a vegetable- (safflower) or chemical-based rouge. Red is an extremely significant color in makeup because, like henna and saffron, it is thought to bring good fortune to the wearer.

KOHL BOXES
1. Bone box with pyrographic design from the Anti Atlas.
2 and **3**. Engraved and carved wooden boxes used in the oases of the Draa, Dadès and Tafilalet.
4, **5**, **8** and **9**. Silver boxes with engraved floral motifs and coral decoration, used in cities. The stick is an elaborately worked metal "needle".
6. Copper box.
7. Ebony and silver box from Fez.
Right: Modern flasks made of inlaid and painted wood.

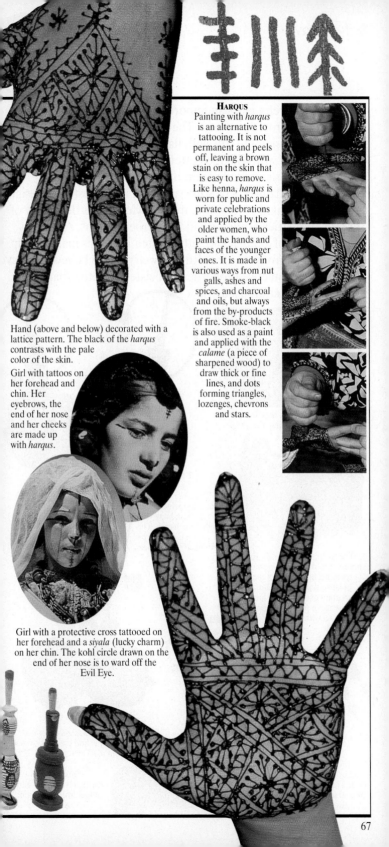

Hand (above and below) decorated with a lattice pattern. The black of the *harqus* contrasts with the pale color of the skin.

Girl with tattoos on her forehead and chin. Her eyebrows, the end of her nose and her cheeks are made up with *harqus*.

HARQUS

Painting with *harqus* is an alternative to tattooing. It is not permanent and peels off, leaving a brown stain on the skin that is easy to remove. Like henna, *harqus* is worn for public and private celebrations and applied by the older women, who paint the hands and faces of the younger ones. It is made in various ways from nut galls, ashes and spices, and charcoal and oils, but always from the by-products of fire. Smoke-black is also used as a paint and applied with the *calame* (a piece of sharpened wood) to draw thick or fine lines, and dots forming triangles, lozenges, chevrons and stars.

Girl with a protective cross tattooed on her forehead and a *siyala* (lucky charm) on her chin. The kohl circle drawn on the end of her nose is to ward off the Evil Eye.

Jewelry plays an important role in the social life of Moroccan women. The gold and silver gilt jewelry worn in the city, with its finely engraved, openwork and worn filigree patterns set with precious stones and pearls, is reminiscent of the jewelry of medieval Andalusia. The wide variety of more austerely designed silver jewelry found in the rural areas of Morocco is the legacy of Spanish and African influence in the Berber regions. As well as being a means of amassing wealth, it often indicates membership of a particular group or tribe. Rural jewelry is also believed to have magical and protective properties associated with the shape, symbol and materials used.

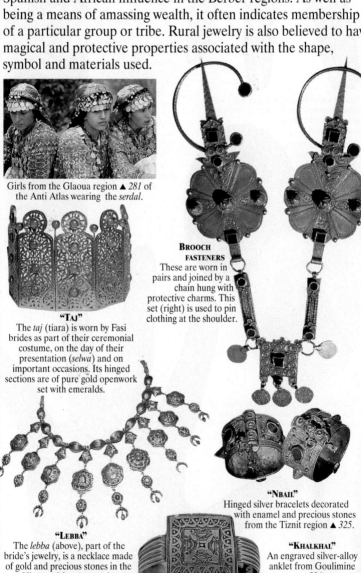

Girls from the Glaoua region ▲ *281* of the Anti Atlas wearing the *serdal*.

"TAJ"
The *taj* (tiara) is worn by Fasi brides as part of their ceremonial costume, on the day of their presentation (*selwa*) and on important occasions. Its hinged sections are of pure gold openwork set with emeralds.

BROOCH FASTENERS
These are worn in pairs and joined by a chain hung with protective charms. This set (right) is used to pin clothing at the shoulder.

"NBAIL"
Hinged silver bracelets decorated with enamel and precious stones from the Tiznit region ▲ *325*.

"LEBBA"
The *lebba* (above), part of the bride's jewelry, is a necklace made of gold and precious stones in the Hispano-Moresque style.

"KHALKHAL"
An engraved silver-alloy anklet from Goulimine ▲ *326*.

Wooden jewelry boxes in various styles: carved (Atlas and Rif Mountains), painted (Fez), inlaid (Essaouira), leather-covered (Sahara) and damascened (Meknès).

"SERDAL"

The *serdal*, widely worn in the Middle Atlas ▲ 225, is a headband made from coins and strips of coral sewn onto a silk or woollen band.

A small engraved silver and openwork Koran case (right) worn as a pendant by the women of the Atlas Mountains ▲ 260.

A cast, openwork brooch (center right) in the form of talismanic symbols: the hand of Fatima and the figure five.

Silver ring used to decorate the braids of Saharan women.

AROUSA COSTUME

Fasi Muslim brides, in all their finery, are presented during the ceremony known as the *selwa*. A bride (left) wears a *taj*, a *lebba*, a *madaij* (pearl necklaces with jade clasps), a *selta* (braided headband decorated with green stones) and a *zrair* (clusters of pearls).

Music is an integral part of everyday life in Morocco and an important aspect of every kind of celebration. In the traditional form of Arabic music, or *andalous*, which developed in Fez, Tetouan and Rabat, musicians skillfully play their instruments (lutes, mandolins and flutes) in unison. They are sometimes joined by a singer, and produce subtle and varied melodies. Popular Berber music, which accompanies dancing and singing with the sound of tambourins (long, narrow drums), combines the sensuality and sacredness of the *haidous* and *ahouach* of the Atlas with ancient ancestral rhythms.

TAMBOURINS

Tebilat (above left), a pair of drums consisting of two earthenware pots fastened together with leather thongs and covered with skin. These freestanding drums are played at popular celebrations and sometimes by Andalous musicians. *Taarija* or *derbouka* (above right), pottery tambourins held under the arm, figure in all kinds of celebrations.

Dolls representing (left to right) a *chikhate*, or professional dancer and musician, a *derbouka* player, a musician from the Sous Valley ▲ *316* complete with *guembri*, and a lute player from Khémisset ▲ *258*.

"GHAYTA" AND "NIRA"
The *ghayta* is a Berber oboe made of two cane tubes and a horn bell. The *nira* is a reeded cane flute with six, seven or eight holes, used by the tribes of the High Atlas ▲ *260*.

Qarqab, the heavy iron castanets used by the Gnaoua brotherhood ▲ *159* (above).

Xylophone of the African *sanza* type (right).

"REBAB"
The *rebab* (the rebec of medieval Europe) is often used by Andalous musicians to accompany the lute. It is played with a bow and the strings are not pressed against the fingerboard but plucked from the side.

"QUS"
The *qus*, the short, curved bow used to play the *rebab*, is made from horsehair.

"GUEMBRI"
The *guembri* is an early form of lute with two or three strings. It is still used for playing popular music.

Aissawa dance near Meknès ▲ *232*. They use *derboukas* to beat out the rhythm on their heads.

Acrobatic dance of the Gnaoua brotherhood, whose members are the distant descendants of African slaves. The music of these traveling performers is influenced by African rhythms. One of their favorite venues is the Djemaa el-Fna, a square in Marrakesh ▲ *277*.

71

The Barbary horse, or Barb, from which Moroccan horses are descended, originated in central Asia. It took its name from the Berbers, the early inhabitants of Morocco. The Arab thoroughbred was introduced during the 7th century as Arab horsemen spread the Word of Islam, and it is still considered the only true Moroccan thoroughbred. Morocco's tradition of horsemanship is preserved and perpetuated through fantasias, symbolic re-enactments of battles that celebrate the skill and prowess of mounted warriors. These displays are held during all the major festivals, especially the religious festivals, or *moussems*.

CANTLE
Made of lightweight wood, covered with skin.

HEADBAND

BREASTPLATE
Covered with embroidered satin.

BRAID COLLARS
Decorated with tassels and paillettes.

STIRRUPS
Broad and rectangular, to help the rider keep his balance.

SADDLECLOTH
There are usually seven of these.

BRIDLE
The circular ring in the bit enables the rider to pull up his horse in seconds, even from a gallop. The headpiece is decorated with embroidery, braid and, as here, tassels.

DECORATED SADDLES
The decoration on these saddles and their trappings is inspired by *zellige* (Moorish decorative tile) motifs ▲ *173* and enhanced by gold-thread embroidery ● *76*.

FANTASIAS. The fantasia (from the Latin *phantasia*, an entertainment) is based on early-19th-century displays in which traditional forms of military combat were re-enacted. Armed horsemen begin with their feet thrust firmly into their stirrups, their knees well forward and their heels dug into the girth, then take up a fighting position by standing up in their stirrups, pushing their feet forward and bringing their knees back. They fire a round of powder known as a *baroud* which, in the 17th century, replaced the crossbow.

THE ARAB SADDLE

The Arab saddle (left) is developed from the saddle used by Zenata tribesmen of the Algerian Aurès Mountains, the best horsemen in the Maghreb and among the first to use a saddle and stirrups. The saddle was deep, with sharp angles which, because they rode short (with their knees well forward and their heels drawn back), could be used as a spur. The Spanish were impressed and took to riding *a la gineta* (Zenata-style). The term has found its way into French in the expression *à la genette* (to ride with short stirrups).

STUDS

Above every loosebox at the Meknès stud are plates giving the name, pedigree and breed of each horse. From top to bottom: Arab thoroughbred, Barbary and Barbary-Arab. Breeders can use stallions from the Moroccan national studs and foals are issued with an "identity card" recording their pedigree.

THE BARBARY AND ARAB THOROUGHBRED

The Barbary is an even-tempered, sturdy saddle horse that existed in Morocco before the arrival of the Arabs. Byblos (far right), was the black Barbary stallion that played Black Beauty in the American television series. The Arab thoroughbred (right) was introduced into Morocco by Arab horsemen in the mid-8th century.

a   b   c

1
2
3

Morocco's Berber origins and superimposed
Islamic civilization have produced a doubly diverse culture that
is reflected in its handwoven carpets. The Moroccan carpet
industry developed in cities, which were open to Oriental
influence, during the 18th century. The carpets produced were
extremely sophisticated, with luminous colors and designs and
floral decorations that evoked Moroccan gardens. Berber
carpets from the Middle and High Atlas and from the Haouz
plain have much more distant, ethnic origins and are
characterized by rigorously geometric, linear
designs and muted tones. Today, they still
epitomize the inventive vitality
of the Berber people.

7

LOW-WARP LOOM
With several treadles
cotton and wool can be
woven much more
rapidly (left).

TOWN CARPETS
Rabat carpets (**1** and **7**) belong to a group
of Islamic carpets in the urban tradition.
These finely textured, short-pile carpets
have a characteristic diamond-shaped
or hexagonal central medallion, or
koubba, set against a red
background decorated with a
variety of motifs. The broad
border consists of between three
and seven bands filled with
floral, zoomorphic and
geometric motifs based on
Turkish designs.

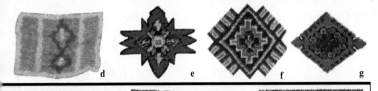

d   e   f   g

4

5

6

BERBER CARPETS

Berber carpets, woven with thick wool in a range of muted colors, are used as mattresses and blankets.

Carpets made by the Zémmour (**3**), Beni M'Guild (**6**) and Marmoucha (**4**) tribes of the Middle Atlas have a monochrome ocher or red background. Simple, geometric designs arranged vertically or horizontally create an impression of space and movement. The carpets from the Haouz plain, with their characteristic madder-red background covered with arcane symbols, are woven by the Ouled Bou Sbaa (**5**), Chiadma and Rhamna Arab tribes, who settled along the Tensift Valley

▲ 155 during the 16th century. Médiouna (**2**) and Casablanca carpets have a greater number of medallions, which are either octagonal or cruciform. Their motifs are reminiscent of those used on 16th-century Spanish and traditional Berber carpets.

Details (top) of carpets made by the Ouled Bou Sbaa (**a** and **d**) and the Beni M'Guild (**f**), and of carpets made in Rabat (**c**, **e** and **g**) and Zémmour (**b**).

HIGH-WARP LOOM

With this vertical, fixed loom, several people can work on a carpet at the same time. The (horizontal) weft yarn is passed through the (vertical) warp yarn, which determines the length, fineness and thickness of the carpet.

Brightly colored skeins of wool hung out to dry by dyers on the shading mats of the souk.

Embroidering clothes and household linen was for a long time one of the principal pastimes of wealthy women and a livelihood for professional embroiderers. In monochrome or a riot of different colors, the embroidered motifs evoke distant Mediterranean, Nordic or Oriental traditions. This fine art became particularly well developed in the towns and cities of northern Morocco, each one having its own particular style.

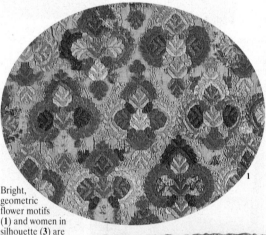

Bright, geometric flower motifs (**1**) and women in silhouette (**3**) are typical of Rabat embroidery. The *aleuj* embroidery (**2**) of Fez, which died out in the 19th century, contained gold and silver threads. *Aleuj* is named after the Levantine concubines who are said to have introduced the craft.

Azemmour ▲ *148* embroidery (**4**), evoking the fantastical Byzantine bestiary, incorporates chimeras, dragons and birds. The design is silhouetted against a red background.

Tétouan ▲ *190* embroidery favors stylized bouquets (**8**), while Chechaouen ▲ *196* combines geometric and floral motifs with a brilliance of color reminiscent of mosaics and illuminated manuscripts. Embroidered gold stars add to the vividness of the work (**9**).

In Fez, exquisite blue and red embroidery makes delicate geometric patterns out of birds, trees and other motifs taken from nature (**5**).

5

6

7

Salé
▲ *175*
embroidery
is executed in single
(**7**) or a blend of two
or three (**6**) colors.

8 **9**

● COSTUME

In rural areas the basic item of clothing for men is the *burnous* or *selham*, a circular cloak with a large square hood worn over a belted tunic. Women drape themselves in two pieces of material, a top and a bottom, which they cover with a piece of woollen cloth known as the *haik*. The richness of Moroccan ceremonial costumes, which vary from region to region and from tribe to tribe, has dazzled generations of travelers. In the cities, European clothing is gradually replacing traditional costume.

THE KAFTAN
The kaftan, originally a Persian garment introduced into Morocco via Andalusia, is a long, collarless robe with wide sleeves. The silk and lampas brocade from which it is made used to be woven in Fez.

Ways of draping the *haik* vary from region to region. The Ouaouzguit and Chaiouia methods are shown above.

A peasant from the Rif ▲ *195* (right) wearing a short *djellaba* over a tunic known as the *tchamir*.

A *mokhazni*, a soldier of the sultan's guard.

The *fez*, or tarbouche, is a conical hat made of red woollen cloth.

THE "FOUTA"
Northern Moroccan peasant girls wearing the *fouta*, a piece of white material with red (and sometimes blue or black) stripes worn as a skirt. Their wide-brimmed straw hats tied with ribbons and decorated with colored tassels are equally characteristic of the region.

Sandal from the Aka region.

Wooden shoe, known as a *qouaqeb*.

Leather sandal from the Middle Atlas ▲ 255.

Turkish slipper in embroidered velvet.

MAKHZEN COSTUME
The costume was named after the Makhzen (government) hairstyle that was popular among the women of the pasha's palace. This type of costume is not seen today, although the famous *hzam squelli*, the high, stiff belts made of Fez lamé, may still be found in the shops of some antique dealers.

Today the traditional art of embroidery is used on everyday items of clothing.

THE "HENDIRA"
The *hendira*, the rectangular woollen blanket worn as a cloak, is an essential piece of Berber clothing, shown here worn by women of the Aït Haddidou ▲ 293 tribe.

79

Moroccan ceramics range from the terracotta vessels produced in rural areas to earthenware manufactured in the cities. Lead-glazed pottery for domestic use is made by the women and baked under a fire of branches. Earthenware for commercial use, made by the men, is thrown on a wheel, fired in a kiln and decorated with enamels, which are glazed during a second firing. Strict rules govern shape and decoration, which include specific but very varied elements.

ANTIQUE FEZ POTTERY DISHES
During the 10th and 11th centuries Fez ▲ *220* was famous for its elaborately decorated earthenware, examples of which can be seen today in museums. Left to right: an 18th-century *ghotar* dish with scale motif; an 18th-century *mokfia* dish with turtle motif; a 19th-century *ghotar* dish with the distinctive blue design of Fez pottery; and an 18th-century *mokfia* dish with feather motif.

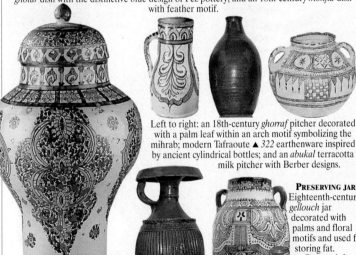

Left to right: an 18th-century *ghorraf* pitcher decorated with a palm leaf within an arch motif symbolizing the mihrab; modern Tafraoute ▲ *322* earthenware inspired by ancient cylindrical bottles; and an *abukal* terracotta milk pitcher with Berber designs.

PRESERVING JARS
Eighteenth-century *gellouch* jar decorated with palms and floral motifs and used for storing fat.
Bottom left: a *jobbana* (covered jar for storing cheese) with the typically 19th-century "centipede" motif.

Nineteenth-century *khabia* jar based on the Chinese ginger jar and decorated with Hispano-Moresque palms. It was used for storing preserved meats.

Glazed earthenware oil bottle, made in Fez, of the type used by the Jewish communities of the Tafilalet ▲ *294*.

A stall in the Fez pottery souk, where items on display include water coolers decorated with tar patterns.

According to Moroccan superstitious belief, the piece of ground on which a potter works is sacred. If it is taken over by another potter, the pots that the newcomer makes each day will crumble to pieces that night.

GHOTAR DISH, FEZ
Nineteenth-century *ghotar* dish on which the *boteh* design in blue, cobalt and gold is based on a Paisley design.

RAW MATERIALS
Red clay (above) is used for making bricks. A finer, bluish clay is used for terracotta and earthenware.

POTTER AT WORK
While his foot keeps the wheel rotating, the potter controls the curve of the jar with one hand and raises the neck of the vessel with the other.

There are endless ways of preparing a tajine, the traditional Moroccan dish named after the earthenware vessel with the cone-shaped lid in which meat, fish and vegetables are slowly cooked. The recipe for tajine of mutton with sesame and almonds is a subtle blend of sweet-and-sour flavors that is reserved for special occasions. It is served after salad and is usually followed by vegetable couscous, fruit and honey cakes.

1. Cut the meat into pieces and finely chop the garlic and one of the onions.

2. Place the meat in a large pan with the salt, oil, chopped onion, garlic and spices. Add enough water to cover. Cover and cook over a moderate heat, stirring occasionally.

5. Steep the almonds in boiling water for 1 minute.

6. Drain the almonds and remove the skins.

9. Brown the sesame seeds in a dry pan.

10. Cook the prunes separately in the reserved liquid. When they are cooked, add 3 rounded tablespoons of sugar and the ground cinnamon.

INGREDIENTS: 3½ lb shoulder of mutton, 2 onions, 3 cloves garlic, 1 lb prunes (soaked in water), ½ cup sesame seeds, 1 cup almonds, 1 rounded tablespoon ground cinnamon, 2 cinnamon sticks, a pinch of saffron, 5 rounded tablespoons granulated sugar, 2 tablespoons olive oil, salt, water.

3. When the meat is cooked and comes apart easily, remove the lid and bring to the boil. Reserve two ladles of the liquid.

4. Slice and add the remaining onion. Sprinkle with sugar and stir. Cook for 10 minutes, occasionally turning the meat.

7. Brown the almonds in a pan.

8. Drain them on paper towels.

11. Arrange the meat and prunes in the earthenware tajine. Add the liquid and sprinkle with sesame seeds and grilled almonds.

83

● TYPICAL MOROCCAN PRODUCTS

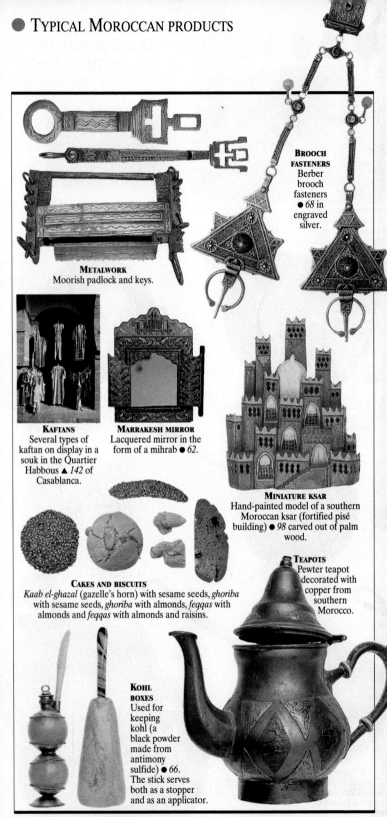

METALWORK
Moorish padlock and keys.

BROOCH FASTENERS
Berber brooch fasteners ● *68* in engraved silver.

KAFTANS
Several types of kaftan on display in a souk in the Quartier Habbous ▲ *142* of Casablanca.

MARRAKESH MIRROR
Lacquered mirror in the form of a mihrab ● *62*.

MINIATURE KSAR
Hand-painted model of a southern Moroccan ksar (fortified pisé building) ● *98* carved out of palm wood.

TEAPOTS
Pewter teapot decorated with copper from southern Morocco.

CAKES AND BISCUITS
Kaab el-ghazal (gazelle's horn) with sesame seeds, *ghoriba* with sesame seeds, *ghoriba* with almonds, *feqqas* with almonds and *feqqas* with almonds and raisins.

KOHL BOXES
Used for keeping kohl (a black powder made from antimony sulfide) ● *66*. The stick serves both as a stopper and as an applicator.

ARCHITECTURE

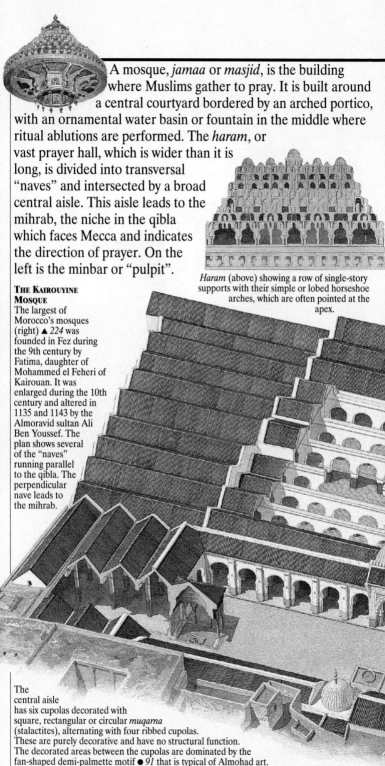

A mosque, *jamaa* or *masjid*, is the building where Muslims gather to pray. It is built around a central courtyard bordered by an arched portico, with an ornamental water basin or fountain in the middle where ritual ablutions are performed. The *haram*, or vast prayer hall, which is wider than it is long, is divided into transversal "naves" and intersected by a broad central aisle. This aisle leads to the mihrab, the niche in the qibla which faces Mecca and indicates the direction of prayer. On the left is the minbar or "pulpit".

Haram (above) showing a row of single-story supports with their simple or lobed horseshoe arches, which are often pointed at the apex.

THE KAIROUYINE MOSQUE
The largest of Morocco's mosques (right) ▲ *224* was founded in Fez during the 9th century by Fatima, daughter of Mohammed el Feheri of Kairouan. It was enlarged during the 10th century and altered in 1135 and 1143 by the Almoravid sultan Ali Ben Youssef. The plan shows several of the "naves" running parallel to the qibla. The perpendicular nave leads to the mihrab.

The central aisle has six cupolas decorated with square, rectangular or circular *muqarna* (stalactites), alternating with four ribbed cupolas. These are purely decorative and have no structural function. The decorated areas between the cupolas are dominated by the fan-shaped demi-palmette motif ● *91* that is typical of Almohad art.

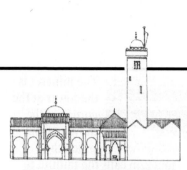

Elevation of the façade of the Kairouyine Mosque (above).

GATEWAY
The huge cedarwood gateway (right) is richly carved and painted and surmounted by a carved cedarwood canopy.

MINBAR
The minbar (pulpit) from which the imam delivers his Friday sermon. The minbar of the Kairouyine Mosque was built in 1144. Pine cones feature among its finely carved geometrical and floral motifs.

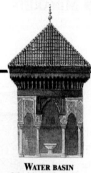

WATER BASIN
Marble basin dating from 1202 in a pavilion in the main courtyard, used for ritual ablutions before entering the *haram*.

MINARET
Like most Maghrebi minarets ● *88*, the minaret of the Kairouyine Mosque, built in 955–6, is square.

MINARETS

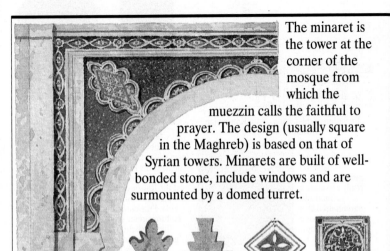

The minaret is the tower at the corner of the mosque from which the muezzin calls the faithful to prayer. The design (usually square in the Maghreb) is based on that of Syrian towers. Minarets are built of well-bonded stone, include windows and are surmounted by a domed turret.

Entrance to the Andalous Mosque, Fez ▲ 215, 229 (below).

Oriental and Berber motifs figure prominently in Almohad decorative art. Left to right: fleuron with vertical domed palmette, "step" or "toothed" merlon, *zellige* (Moorish tiles) ▲ 173, wood marquetry with carved and painted floral motifs.

HASSAN TOWER, RABAT
The unfinished 12th-century minaret ▲ 169 of the Hassan Mosque has a lozenge decoration with festoons and lambrequins bordering the arches of blind or gemel windows.

MINARET OF KOUTOUBIA
This is a classic example of Almohad art ▲ 268. Each of the four sides has a type of different decoration.

CHELLAH MINARET, RABAT ▲ 171
The marble, stone and earthenware decoration in the top story of this minaret is similar to that of the mihrab.

Minarets have several single or gemel windows and are often decorated with carved geometrical designs, polychrome terracotta or calligraphy.

MINARET OF THE MOULAY IDRISS MOSQUE
Built in 1939, this cylindrical structure is one of the most modern minarets in Islamic architecture. *Surah* from the Koran ▲ *250* are inscribed in Kufic script on the green-glazed terracotta.

ALMOHAD DECORATIVE MOTIFS

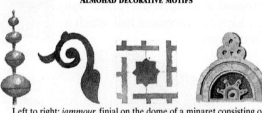

Left to right: *jammour,* finial on the dome of a minaret consisting of one, three or four copper spheres that decrease in size toward the top; fan-shaped palmette, Solomon's seal surrounded by Kufic calligraphy, semicircular arch surmounted by a trefoil motif.

MINARET OF THE KASBAH MOSQUE, MARRAKESH
Built in 1180, this was used as a model by architects in the 13th and 14th centuries.

MINARET OF THE KASBAH MOSQUE, TANGIER. An octagonal 17th-century minaret decorated with glazed terracotta, crowned with merlons, in the Mechouar ▲ *186*.

MINARET OF THE ANDALOUS MOSQUE, FEZ. The green and white *zellige*, the tiers of windows with multifoil horseshoe arches, the merlons and the turret of this mid-10th century minaret ▲ *229* betray Hispanic influence.

MINARET OF THE EL BERDAÏN MOSQUE, MEKNÈS. The sides of this 17th-century minaret are covered with tiers of blind arches ▲ *235*.

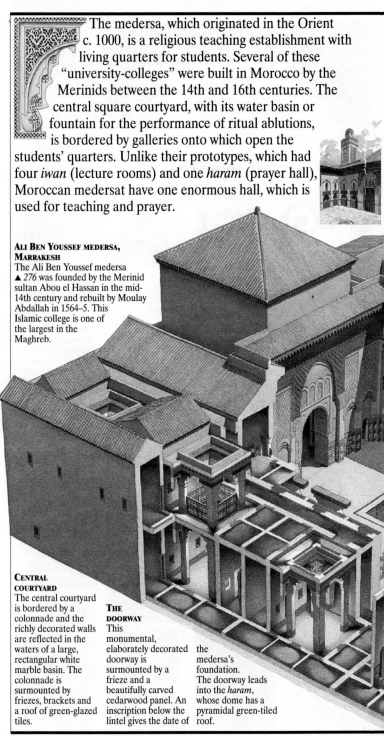

The medersa, which originated in the Orient c. 1000, is a religious teaching establishment with living quarters for students. Several of these "university-colleges" were built in Morocco by the Merinids between the 14th and 16th centuries. The central square courtyard, with its water basin or fountain for the performance of ritual ablutions, is bordered by galleries onto which open the students' quarters. Unlike their prototypes, which had four *iwan* (lecture rooms) and one *haram* (prayer hall), Moroccan medersat have one enormous hall, which is used for teaching and prayer.

ALI BEN YOUSSEF MEDERSA, MARRAKESH
The Ali Ben Youssef medersa ▲ 276 was founded by the Merinid sultan Abou el Hassan in the mid-14th century and rebuilt by Moulay Abdallah in 1564–5. This Islamic college is one of the largest in the Maghreb.

CENTRAL COURTYARD
The central courtyard is bordered by a colonnade and the richly decorated walls are reflected in the waters of a large, rectangular white marble basin. The colonnade is surmounted by friezes, brackets and a roof of green-glazed tiles.

THE DOORWAY
This monumental, elaborately decorated doorway is surmounted by a frieze and a beautifully carved cedarwood panel. An inscription below the lintel gives the date of the medersa's foundation. The doorway leads into the *haram*, whose dome has a pyramidal green-tiled roof.

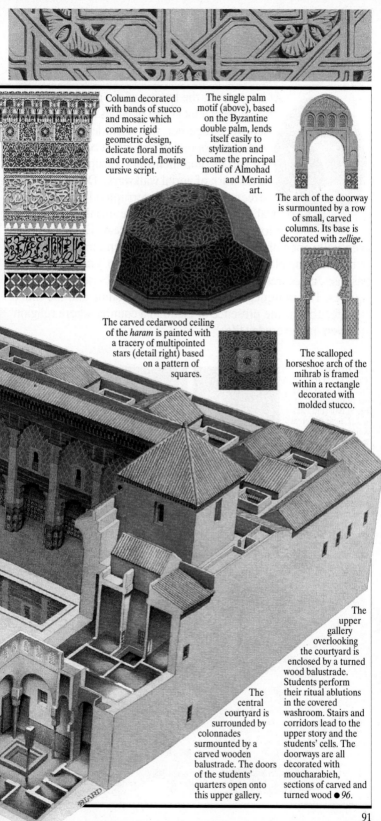

Column decorated with bands of stucco and mosaic which combine rigid geometric design, delicate floral motifs and rounded, flowing cursive script.

The single palm motif (above), based on the Byzantine double palm, lends itself easily to stylization and became the principal motif of Almohad and Merinid art.

The arch of the doorway is surmounted by a row of small, carved columns. Its base is decorated with *zellige*.

The carved cedarwood ceiling of the *haram* is painted with a tracery of multipointed stars (detail right) based on a pattern of squares.

The scalloped horseshoe arch of the mihrab is framed within a rectangle decorated with molded stucco.

The upper gallery overlooking the courtyard is enclosed by a turned wood balustrade. Students perform their ritual ablutions in the covered washroom. Stairs and corridors lead to the upper story and the students' cells. The doorways are all decorated with moucharabieh, sections of carved and turned wood ● 96.

The central courtyard is surrounded by colonnades surmounted by a carved wooden balustrade. The doors of the students' quarters open onto this upper gallery.

BIARD

At street level, the houses of the medina (old town) form a labyrinth of cubes and prisms. Crowded together, they exclude the outside world but open inward onto a central courtyard or garden, and their flat rooftop terraces form a network of aerial walkways. Down below, the streets run along uninterrupted lines of blank walls that give no hint of the social standing, high or low, of the homes they conceal. These corridors eventually open onto squares, markets and fountains and other public meeting places, all densely packed within a maze of passages, arcatures, overhanging upper stories, blind alleys and squares. The mosque, the very heart of the medina and the soul of city life, affirms the presence of Islam in a country where religion is woven into everyday life.

THE MEDINA, FEZ
The heart of the medina (above) is in the southern part of Fez el Bali (old Fez) ▲ *221*, near the great Kairouyine Mosque ● *86*, ▲ *224*, and the Moulay Idriss Shrine. It is a city within a city, where every aspect of public and private, religious and secular activity is an integral part of everyday life. Its labyrinth of alleyways reflects its social structure.

TRADITIONAL CRAFTS
Craftsmen in the medina bring a sense of timelessness to everyday life. Above, left to right: a knife-grinder sharpening his knives, a shopkeeper sieving flour for cakes and biscuits, and a snail seller.

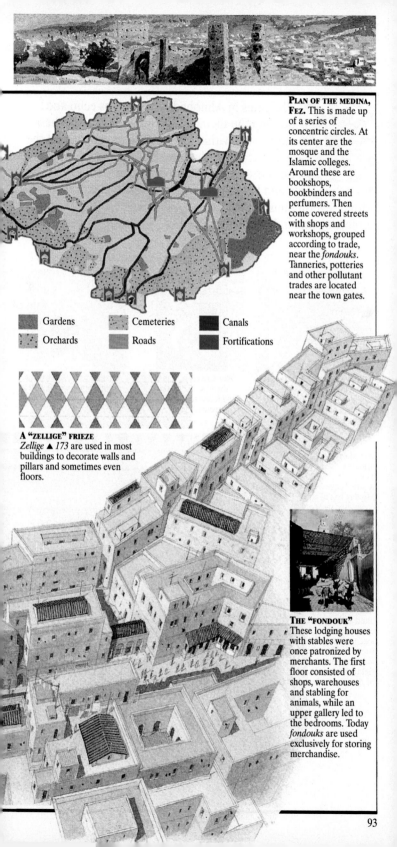

PLAN OF THE MEDINA, FEZ. This is made up of a series of concentric circles. At its center are the mosque and the Islamic colleges. Around these are bookshops, bookbinders and perfumers. Then come covered streets with shops and workshops, grouped according to trade, near the *fondouks*. Tanneries, potteries and other pollutant trades are located near the town gates.

Gardens	Cemeteries	Canals
Orchards	Roads	Fortifications

A "ZELLIGE" FRIEZE
Zellige ▲ 173 are used in most buildings to decorate walls and pillars and sometimes even floors.

THE "FONDOUK"
These lodging houses with stables were once patronized by merchants. The first floor consisted of shops, warehouses and stabling for animals, while an upper gallery led to the bedrooms. Today *fondouks* are used exclusively for storing merchandise.

The gates in Almohad fortifications echo and develop the theme of the mihrab. Their arches are framed within a horizontal rectangle, and the spandrels are either blank or decorated with flowers and foliage, geometric or shell motifs. The horseshoe arch, and less commonly the semicircular arch, is set within several multifoil curves or curves formed with alternately projecting and indented archstones.

BAB AGNAOU, MARRAKESH
In this 12th-century gate ▲ 270, a gadrooned semicircular arch encloses a horseshoe arch that in turn encloses a pointed arch.

BAB CHELLAH, RABAT
Shells ▲ 172 fill the spandrels of this 14th-century gate.

KASBAH GATE, AZEMMOUR
A 16th-century gate with a semicircular arch ▲ 148.

BAB MANSOUR, MEKNÈS
The Mansour gate ▲ 239, begun by Moulay Ismail and completed by Moulay Abdallah in 1732, has a monumental pointed horseshoe arch. It is flanked by two bastions whose arches, also horseshoes, are supported by marble pillars. The extremely rich decoration with blind arches, tracery of enameled lozenges, inscribed frieze and "toothed" merlons (detail top right), is reminiscent of Almohad minarets.

MERLON
A crenellated brick motif known as a "step" or "toothed" merlon.

CURSIVE SCRIPT
Elegant, flowing Arabic script makes an ideal decorative motif ● 65.

LINTEL
Lintels decorated with a pattern of obliquely set bricks are a feature of earth buildings.

LOZENGE TRACERY
Tracery relies for its effect on the relief of the sculpted lattice, which provides the basic framework, and the color of the lozenges. Islamic art frequently exploits this technique to emphasize light and shadow without breaking the monumental effect of the surface.

BAB EL KHEMIS, MEKNÈS
The design of this 18th-century gate, set between two high, crenellated towers, is typically Almohad ▲ 235.

RISSANI GATE
A remarkable frieze of green-glazed tiles ▲ 294 decorates the 13th-century Rissani Gate.

BAB MRISA, SALÉ
Two rectangular towers ▲ 176 flank the pointed 14th-century horseshoe arch, with carved decoration.

The double-palm motif of this capital (above) is inspired by Byzantine decorations.

The façade of the Bab el Khemis towers (below) consists of large pieces of rubble.

For five thousand years the Moroccan townhouse has remained unchanged. The walls facing the street are pierced only by small windows, but beyond the *skiffa*, the inset entrance closed by a heavy wooden door, the house opens onto a galleried patio often overlooking a garden. The *dar*, a single- or two-story house, consists of several rooms surrounding an interior patio. The whole building, from the central courtyard to the rooftop terrace, is completely enclosed and insulated from the outside world.

LANTERNS
These are mostly in bronze although some are in copper, brass (above) or tin, all set with colored glass.

DOORS
The main entrance to the house, which is very inconspicuous, is often decorated with studs and hooks and hinges. Decorative ironwork, once widely used, has been replaced by fittings in copper and bronze.

PALACES AND HOUSES
Moroccan houses have very little furniture and few permanent fixtures. Instead there are cushions, carpets, mats and low tables that can be moved, rolled up and put away to give the maximum amount of space. Interiors are often extremely luxurious, as in the Belghazi palace ▲ *228* (right), where walls are paneled with brightly colored tiles and marble pillars are decorated with *zellige*

▲ *173*, and topped by painted or molded stucco capitals (detail far right). There is sometimes even a wall fountain. The upper gallery is decorated with a moucharabieh balustrade. The colored glass roof diffuses natural light while a host of lanterns light up dark corners.

> "MASON, I WANT A HOUSE THAT,
> LIKE THE HEART,
> LOOKS INWARD."
>
> AHMED SEFRIOUI

METALWORK

Ironworkers are much in demand in cities such as Fez, Meknès and Marrakesh, where fine decorative ironwork is increasingly sought for windows and balconies, to replace moucharabieh (which is much more intricate and time-consuming). Today there is a special "guild" of craftsmen specializing in *chbayka*, or grilles. Freestanding and hanging lamps, charcoal pans,

cooking pots and other domestic or decorative objects are also made. This wrought-iron and brass star (left), the symbol of Morocco, set within a crescent, hangs on the first floor of the Belghazi palace.

ROOFS

Terraced or double-pitch roofs are the most widely used, both for town- and country houses. They are usually made from local materials: wood for the beams, plant products for the flooring, and lime or earth for filling in and sealing. The roofs of the houses in Chechaouen ▲ *196* (above) are covered with Roman tiles.

CAPITAL

Although the design of this marble capital is not typically Islamic, the carved rosette, the palms, palmettes and other foliage and the braiding in the upper section are traditional motifs.

ARCH

The painted wood and delicately molded stucco complements the colorful tiles, which feature arabesques and interlaced motifs and the multipointed star design so popular in Hispano-Moresque art.

97

Berber architecture is integral to the High Atlas, Draa and Dadès and the Ziz and Tafilalet Valleys, the regions in which it originates. The typical buildings of dry stone or earth are designed to function as powerful, massive and uncompromising strongholds. Villages, hamlets, farms and fortified collective granaries resembling Egyptian and Sumerian architecture are built with local materials and are ideally adapted to the Moroccan climate. As strongholds they were designed to protect people, animals and food stocks against attack but they also reflect the socio-political organization of their inhabitants.

Earth or pisé (mud and rubble) structures are reinforced by oak, thuja, pine or palm beams that also support the flat or terraced roof. The foundations are made of river shingle or rubble. The overhanging terrace is bordered by "step" merlons.

IRONWORK
The simple designs of the door knockers (**1** and **2**) and hook and hinge (**3**) made of imported or locally wrought iron are stamped with a steel die. The wooden lock (**4**) and key (**5**) have geometric designs.

IMILCHIL ▲ 293. This *agadir* (fortified granary), built of pisé, has four crenellated towers and is decorated with lozenges and chevrons against a whitewashed background.

AÏT BENHADDOU ▲ 286. This ksar (fortified pisé community) in the valley of the Assif Mellah consists almost entirely of *tighremt* (granaries) perched on the hillside.

"TIGHREMT". The *tighremt* or *agadir* (fortified granary) looks like a massive tower pierced by arrow slits. Structures like this existed in Roman times and were used to shelter and protect people and animals. The ksar or kasbah (fortified oasis village) is based on the *tighremt*. A narrow door opens onto the first floor, where the livestock is kept. A staircase or ladder leads to the second-floor granary and the third-floor living quarters.

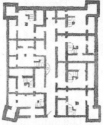

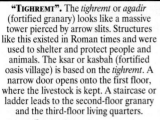

KSAR. In this basic layout, for eight families, there are four dwellings on either side of a central, covered alley, where the well is located. The blind outer walls form a rampart fortified by the four towers, which are also used as granaries. The single entrance is protected by a barbican.

THUJA CEILING
Ceiling (above) made of thuja branches laid at an angle across the main beams, and supported by a wooden pillar. The oblique lines create an impression of depth.

DOUBLE DOOR
Blind arches decorate the upper section of this walnut, cedar or oak door. The middle section has a grille motif and the lower section is plain.

PISÉ
Pisé, a mixture of clay and rubble packed between two planks, is one of the main construction materials in Morocco. It is also very effective as insulation against cold and heat.

KASBAH, TAOURIRT ▲ 282
The building is surrounded by high, blank earth walls, with setbacks and high bastions opening up on the upper stories.

KASBAH, TIN-MAL ▲ 303
The overhanging roofs, of dry stone and wood, give protection against the harsh climate.

The tent is the communal dwelling of the nomads and herdsmen of Morocco. The roof consists of an awning made of *flij* (narrow strips of woven wool and hair) sewn together along the edges. This is placed over a ridgepole supported by two uprights with braces secured to tent pegs by ropes. The sides are held by poles and a piece of cloth is used to close the tent at night. These tents are easily adapted to weather conditions, can quickly be put up and taken down again, and so are ideally suited to the nomadic life of Moroccan herdsmen.

THE MEN'S AREA
The area reserved for the men and their guests is closed off by *amèssu* vegetable-fiber matting decorated with threads of colored wool. The reception area is furnished with an *agertil* mat and cushions.

Corner for newborn lambs and kids.

STORAGE AREA
Corn, barley and wool are stored in sacks.

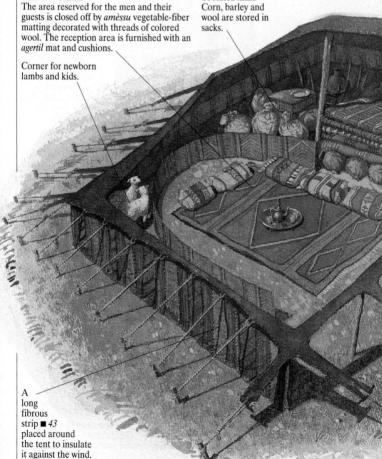

A long fibrous strip ■ *43* placed around the tent to insulate it against the wind.

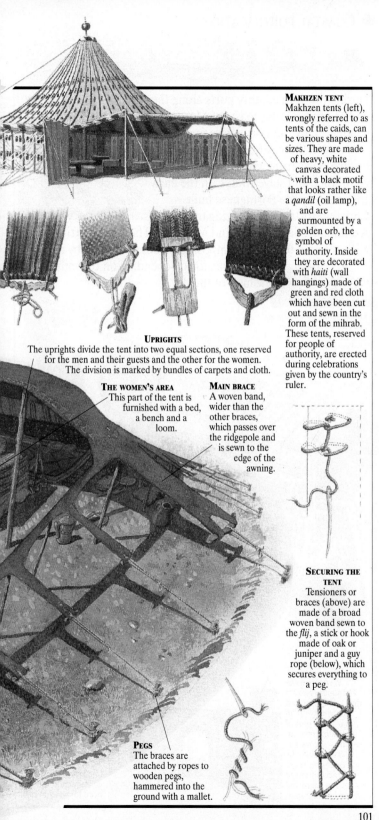

MAKHZEN TENT
Makhzen tents (left), wrongly referred to as tents of the caids, can be various shapes and sizes. They are made of heavy, white canvas decorated with a black motif that looks rather like a *qandil* (oil lamp), and are surmounted by a golden orb, the symbol of authority. Inside they are decorated with *haiti* (wall hangings) made of green and red cloth which have been cut out and sewn in the form of the mihrab. These tents, reserved for people of authority, are erected during celebrations given by the country's ruler.

UPRIGHTS
The uprights divide the tent into two equal sections, one reserved for the men and their guests and the other for the women. The division is marked by bundles of carpets and cloth.

THE WOMEN'S AREA
This part of the tent is furnished with a bed, a bench and a loom.

MAIN BRACE
A woven band, wider than the other braces, which passes over the ridgepole and is sewn to the edge of the awning.

SECURING THE TENT
Tensioners or braces (above) are made of a broad woven band sewn to the *flij*, a stick or hook made of oak or juniper and a guy rope (below), which secures everything to a peg.

PEGS
The braces are attached by ropes to wooden pegs, hammered into the ground with a mallet.

● COASTAL FORTIFICATIONS

During the 15th century ports along the Atlantic and Mediterranean coasts of Morocco were conquered by the Portuguese and Spanish, who saw in them safe, comfortable trading posts from which to control the gold, spice and slave routes. In the early 16th century the Portuguese built Christian fortresses in Mazagan, Azemmour, Safi, Agadir and Mogador. These had fortified walls set with towers and imposing gateways flanked by round or square bastions, depending on the military fashion of the day.

THE BASTION OF ESSAOUIRA
The bastion projects beyond the battlements of the *Skala* (fortification facing the sea) of the port of Essaouira ▲ *158*.

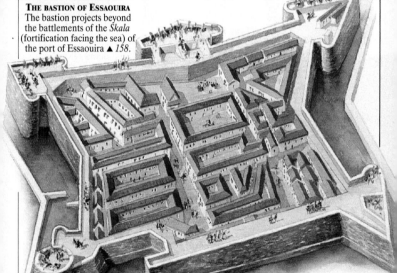

THE PORTUGUESE CITADEL OF MAZAGAN
The citadel was built on a rocky outcrop. Its thick walls, punctuated by broad embrasures designed to take the mouth of a cannon, are protected by five radially projecting bastions. This piece of military ingenuity, perfected by the Italians, was in fact used by the Portuguese in 1516 when they rebuilt the fortress of Mazagan (modern El Jadida) ▲ *150*. The bastions were designed in such a way as to eliminate blind spots and, consequently, the need for watchtowers.

WATCHTOWERS
The square bastion (right) that protected the battery of the *Skala* in the port of Mogador (modern Essaouira – see top), is surmounted by watchtowers. These projections were designed to guard and defend a blind spot.

Morocco
AS SEEN BY ARTISTS

Although Henri Matisse (1869–1954) spent some time in Algeria, it was not until he visited Tangier in 1912 (1) that he discovered the true spirit of the Orient. Abandoning traditional Oriental themes, he began to portray Tangier from a different angle using color and the effects of light, which he described as "so soft", in a new way.

In Tangier Matisse managed to combine the abstract and the figurative so as to express spirituality through the tangible. Later, he said that his visits to Morocco had enabled him to make this transition and that he had experienced nature in a way that he could never have done simply by following a style such as Fauvism – which, although it had a certain vitality, was somewhat limited.

In Morocco his drawing became purer, his perspectives foreshortened and his figures simplified as he tried to banish from his painting anything that might detract from its harmony. This is illustrated in *The Casbah Gate* (3) (1912-13) and *The Standing Riffian* (2) (1912), where only brush strokes break up the dense areas of

"WHAT A BLEND OF LIGHT, NOT AT ALL LIKE THE CÔTE D'AZUR
[...]. AND THERE IS A FRESHNESS ABOUT IT THAT MAKES IT
DIFFICULT TO REPRODUCE WITH BLUE, RED, YELLOW AND GREEN."

HENRI MATISSE

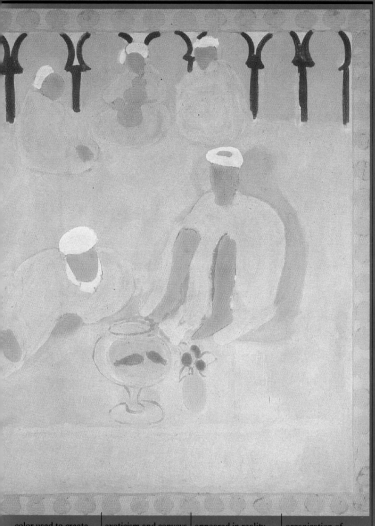

color used to create the impression of unlimited space. In *The Moroccan Café* (1912-13) (4), one of Matisse's major large-format works, six Moroccans are sitting on the floor of a small kasbah café, their faces and limbs patches of ocher picked out on the canvas like flowers scattered across a field. The artist has eschewed the tradition of anecdotal exoticism and conveys instead the contemplative mood of the figures by reducing them to impersonal patches of color. Their featureless faces are in keeping with his desire for visual homogeneity and pictorial harmony. So that nothing should interfere with the uninterrupted areas of pure color, he has also ignored the tones and outlines of the scene as it would have appeared in reality. The technique was succinctly summarized by Pierre Schneider in the phrase "less is more".

Matisse's visit to Tangier, during which he produced some sixty drawings and several paintings, marked a turning point in his career. His subsequent work reflects his newly found freedom: bursts of exuberance, a sculptural organization of densely warm space, a spiritual framework containing a wealth of human emotion. According to Matisse this was *intimisme*, the painterly style of the moment.

"On one side were the Jewish women […] dressed for the occasion […]. On the other were high-ranking Moorish women […] whose presence at the wedding was considered an honor."

Eugène Delacroix

During his stay in Morocco, Eugène Delacroix (1798–1863) ▲ *202* witnessed a ceremony during which Muslims and Jews listened to music from ancient Andalusia. This was the inspiration for *Jewish Wedding in Morocco* (2) (painted 1837–41). Whereas the Jewish women were prepared to sit for the painting, their Muslim counterparts were more reluctant. Delacroix therefore agreed to depict their features only superficially (in accordance with Muslim tradition), concentrating instead on the detail of their costumes. When the painting was exhibited at the Palais du Luxembourg in Paris, Delacroix's contemporaries were impressed by the rigor of its composition and new freedom of expression. The fragmented brush strokes and the close juxtaposition of primary and complementary colors foreshadowed the artistic revolution that was to come. Artists began to visit Morocco and some, like the Spanish artist Francisco Lameyer y Berenguer (1825–77), returned to the theme of the Jewish wedding (4). The French artists Emile Vernet-Lecomte (1821–1900) and Alfred Dehodencq (1822–82), who painted a number of scenes based on the Jewish community, also painted portraits of Jewish brides (3 and 1).

1	2	3
	4	

THE ORIENTAL DREAM

The 19th-century artistic imagination perceived the Orient as a land inhabited by people in turbans who spent their time reclining on luxurious couches in clouds of incense, surrounded by semi-naked slaves and languid odalisques. This was the mythical world of the Orient as depicted in Western art. The French artists Henri Regnault (1) and Georges Clairin, who discovered Hispano-Moresque art in Spain and were enchanted by the work of Mariano Fortuny (1838–74) and his account of travels in Morocco between 1860 and 1863, perpetuated this myth of the Oriental dream world. Henri Regnault (1843–71) moved to Tangier in 1868 and was joined several months later by his friend and colleague Georges Clairin (1843–1919). The two artists shared a studio. In 1870 Regnault completed his *Execution Without Trial Under the Moorish Kings of Grenada* (2), a theme supposedly taken from the history of Muslim Spain. Clairin painted *Entrance to the Harem* (4) the same year. The outbreak of the Franco-Prussian War forced the two artists to return to Paris.

"EVERY TIME WE GO OUT ONTO OUR TERRACE, WE ARE DAZZLED
BY THE GLARE OF THIS CITY OF SNOW… AT LAST I AM LOOKING AT
THE ORIENT!"

HENRI REGNAULT

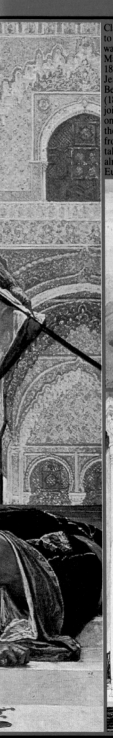

Clairin later returned to Tangier, where he was joined by Mariano Fortuny. In 1872 Clairin and Jean-Joseph Benjamin-Constant (1845–1902) ● *112* joined Charles Tissot on a trip to Fez where they recorded scenes from everyday life, taking up themes already explored by Eugène Delacroix in 1832 ▲ *202*. The relaxed nonchalance that captured the imagination of the Orientalists, as these European painters were known, also inspired the Russian artist Elie-Anatole Pavil (1873–1944). In 1892 he moved to Rabat, living up on the Kasbah of the Oudayas ▲ *166*. His many paintings of Moroccan women include *On the Terrace* (3) in which the semi-naked figures embody Oriental exoticism.

Moroccan streets and public squares provided artists with a constant source of invaluable inspiration. The interplay of light, space, movement and color at public events was meticulously recorded by the English artist Edmund Aubrey Hunt (1855–1922), whose *Caravan Entering Tangier* (1) is his major Moroccan work. The Spanish artist José Gallegos y Arnosa (1859–1917) was also fascinated by the exoticism of Tangier ▲ *184*, with its bustling streets and the animation of its crowded souks. His *Arab Vendor, Tangier* (2) was based on a sketch he made while in Morocco.

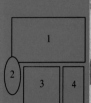

inspiration in the souks, craftsmen and storytellers of Morocco. Their respective paintings, *Storytellers in Tétouan* (3) and *Storyteller in Marrakech* (4), reflect the very different European perceptions of the Orientalists ● *108*.

The Belgian Jean-François Portaels (1818–95), and the Frenchman Adolphe Gumery (1861–1943) were among the many artists who found

1	
2	
	3	4

The Market at Bab el Khemis, which the Polish-born artist Adam Styka (1890–1959) painted while in Morocco, displays harsh contrasts of light. Benjamin-Constant ● *109* added a touch of exoticism to *The Tailor's Workshop* by exaggerating the amount of typically Moroccan paraphernalia depicted in the scene.

Morocco
AS SEEN BY WRITERS

MOROCCO BY MULE

Determination and curiosity drove William Lithgow (1582–1645?) on "nineteene Yeares Travayles, from Scotland to the most Famous Kingdoms in Europe, Asia and Africa". In this minutely observed account, the Scottish traveler describes his journey, in a caravan of mules and donkeys, from the west coast of Morocco and his entry into Fez. Lithgow, like most northern Europeans of the time, finds the appearance of Moroccans intimidating ("awfull") but he praises the country for its fruitfulness, which he pronounces to be "wondrous great".

❝It was my fortune here in Algier, to meete with a French Lapidator, who intending to visit Fez, joyned company with me. Whence advancing our way, some on Mules, and some on foote, with Asses carrying our baggage and provision; we left the marine Townes ... and facing the in-land wee marched for three dayes through a fruitfull and populous soyle: And although the peoples barbarous and disdainefull countenances were awfull, yet we two went still free of tributs, as not being a thing with them accustomary, to execute exaction on Francks as the Turkes and Moores do in Asia, neither understood they what wee were, being cled with company, and after their fashion. ... In this misculat journeying of paine & pleasure we found every where strong Wines, abundance of excellent bread, and thebest, and greatest Hens bred on the earth, with plenty of Figges, Fruits, Olives, and delicious oyle, yea, and innumerable Villages, the houses whereof are all builded with mudde, and platformed on their tops; and so are they in Asia, and all Affrick over. Upon the fourth day having past the Plaines, we entered in a hilly Countrey, yet pastorable; where I beheld here and there clouds of Tents, filled with maritine people, that were fled hither from the Sea coast for the fresh and cooling ayre. And upon these pleasant and umbragious heights, I saw the fields overcled with flocks of Sheepe and Goats: which Sheepe are wondrous great, having from their rumpes and hips, broad and thicke tayles growing, and hanging to the ground, some whereof when sold, will weigh 16, 18 or 20 pounds weight, and upwards. Here among the mountaines, our company knowing well the Countrey, tooke a great advantage of the way, and on the seventh day in the morning, wee arrived at the great Towne of Fez: where the French man and I were conducted by some of our company to a great Moorish Inne or Taverne: & there received, we were as kindly & respectively used, as ever I was in any part of the Turks Dominions, being now out of them, & in the Empire of Morocco. This City of Fez is situate upon the bodies and twice double devailling faces of two hills, like to Grenada in Andelosia in Spaine; the intervale, or low valley betweene both (through which the torride River of Marraheba runneth Southward) being the Center and chiefest place, is the most beautifull and populous part of the City; the situation of which, and of the whole, is just set under the Tropick of Cancer. Over which River, and in this bottome, there are three score and seaven Bridges of stone and Timber, each of them being a passage for open streetes on both sides. The intervayle consisteth of two miles in length, and halfe a mile broad; wherein, besides five Chereaffs or Market places, there are great Palaces, magnificke Mosquees, Colledges, Hospitals, and a hundred Palatiat Tavernes, the worst whereof, may lodge a Monarchicke trayne: Most part of all which buildings, are three and foure stories high, adorned with large and open Windowes, long Galleries, spacious Chambers, and flat tectures or square platformes. The streetes being covered above, twixt these plaine-set Fabrickes, have large Lights cut through the tectur'd tops every where; in whose lower shoppes or Roomes are infinite Merchandize, and Ware of all sorts to bee sold…. The two Hills on both sides the planur'd Citty, East, and West, are over-cled with streetes and Houses of two stories high, beeing beautified also with delicate Gardens, and on their extreame devalling parts, with numbers of Mosquees and Watch-towers: On which heights, and round about the Towne, there stand some three hundred Wind-mils; most part whereof pertayne to the Mosquees, and the two magnifick Colledges erected for education of Children, in the Mahometanicall Law. This City aboundeth in all manner of provision fit for man or beast, & is the goodliest place of all North Affrick, contayning a hundred and twenty thousand fire-houses, and in them a million of soules: Truely this is a world for a City, and may rather second Grand Caire, than subjoyne it selfe to Constantinople, being farre superior in greatnesse with Aleppo: For these are the foure greatest Cities, that ever I saw in the world, either at home or abroad.**

WILLIAM LITHGOW, *RARE ADVENTURES AND PAINFULL PEREGRINATIONS* 1614–32, GLASGOW, 1906.

MOROCCO ON FOOT

Ahmed Sefrioui, born in 1915 of Berber parentage, was educated in Fez and later he worked for the Moroccan tourist board in Rabat. He is an acclaimed writer in his own country.

**To my mind there is only one way of learning to know a country, and that is by going on foot. In our days few people practise this magnificent method, which is yet so economical. Sites and landscapes appear in their true scale, and you will draw nearer to men and learn to love them. Along the roads in the springtime, flowers will greet you. They will smile at you, rise and sway in bowing welcome. In addition to the perfume of the flowers you will encounter the grave looks of men…. Rest in the shade of the olive-tree and watch the

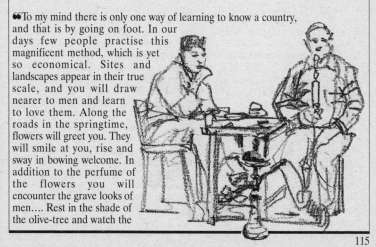

115

little caravan as it advances at the rate of the short steps of its asses on its way to some distant town. Or perhaps the little caravan is merely on its way home to the next village, to those rock-coloured houses that cling to the side of the hill and seem to be watching you, crouching behind their rampart of cactus. This path here leads to the spring. Women come away from it, bent under the weight of heavy jars of red earthenware. … The plain stretches into the far distance, dotted with stones and tufts of asphodel. It dies away at the foot of a mountain of amethyst hue. The road is long. … At last the weary traveller sees, outlining itself against the grey-mauve of the sky, the indistinct silhouette of a minaret. Behind the wall there is a town with a dream-name, Fez the well guarded, Meknes of the olives, Rabat of victory, or Marrakesh the red.**

AHMED SEFRIOUI, *MOROCCO*, PARIS, 1956.

FEZ

MAGIC AND MYSTERY
Nina Epton, writing in the 1940's, evokes the heady and exotic atmosphere of the medina in Fez.

I had already been in many *souks*, or Moorish markets. There was the *souk* of Tangier with its feasts of colour, there was the *medina* of Rabat with its Hassan Tower, but the *medina* of Fez was unique. For Fez is ancient and noble, a voluptuous and subtle charmer, overpowering the soul, lulling one's senses with its poison – for poison it must surely be that weakens all ties with the outside world and drugs you with forgetfulness of all previous life. Here there is no sense of time or space. Here magic carpets are woven, love philtres are brewed; magicians and sorcerers stalk through narrow, winding streets by daylight, to disappear suddenly as though by enchantment into the recesses of those white walls. No one can spend a night during Ramadan under the moonlit ramparts of Fez, submitted to the aphrodisiacal influence of Arab music, and still remain entirely European. Something has happened. Part of the soul of Fez has become imprinted on your soul. There are many voices in the *souks*: the chant of beggars crouching in the corners by the fountains; the sighs of veiled mothers; the shouts of weaving-masters as they direct the children who hold their threads; the prayers rising from mosques five times daily; the laughter of women gossiping at the tomb of St Moulay Idriss, where criminals still seek sanctuary; the voices of the Berber tribesmen from the hills as they order their long lines of patient donkeys to the right or to the left according to the intonation of their voices; there is the solemn voice of the Caid, erect on a tall mule, as he brushes past the dust-laden *djellabas* of the pedestrians, and of the whispering Nationalists who urge their countrymen to regain their pride and claim back their country from the foreigners; and, finally, there is the voice of the foreigner himself, separated by barriers of centuries, to whom the voices of the *souks* sound strange and unreal and remote, for he lives in a town apart where there are no visible walls or ramparts, but which is, nevertheless, much more difficult to besiege. Meanwhile, the imperial city, white and compact within its crenellated walls, rising gently on a hill fringed with olive trees and willows, and surrounded by mountains, glowed like a coronet of pearls on pale green velvet. Along the powdery roads leading into town through its vast horseshoe gateways, white-robed peasants marched majestically beside their donkeys. Between crumbling mounds of earth and tortured cactus plants covered with egg-shaped tumours rose the anonymous tombstones of the Muslim cemeteries; here, every Friday, the veiled women come to enjoy their weekly conversations in the presence of their dead. Lean camels graze on thick burned grass; they are kept for their meat, for the earth here is too hard on their tender feet and nobody uses them for transport. Once inside the immense gateways, you turn your back on the twentieth century; the streets are only wide enough for three or four people to walk abreast. In the box-shaped shops the owners sit cross-legged among their wares, or fan themselves in the shadows of a windowless recess. Here is a man hammering metal; here is another patiently tracing traditional designs on leather. Every trade has its own specific area. From the tanners' quarter rises an odour of stale cheese and rotting carcasses. A bloodstained goatskin is being dragged into a workshop. An old man stirs an immense basin of blue dye. The sun shines through a trellis of leaves where herbalists sit behind pyramids of fresh green mint. Outside the Quaraouine University, where scholars have pored over the Koran since the eleventh century, two students pass, immersed in gentle discussion. There was much to learn and admire in Fez: the mother washing her child's feet in the blue-

tiled fountain; the blind man being helped on his way by the crowd – in this country, every hand is outstretched to help the needy wanderer; the sick man on a donkey, whose arms cling to the two friends who walk beside him; the beggar child who looked up, with shaven head and pigtail tuft, to admire the coloured candles being taken into the sanctuary of Moulay Idriss.**99**

NINA EPTON, *A JOURNEY UNDER THE CRESCENT MOON*, LONDON, 1949.

FEZ BY MOONLIGHT

The prolific French writer Colette (1873–1954) went to Morocco in 1926 as a guest of the Pasha of Marrakesh, who also lent her his palace in Fez. She fell in love with North Africa. This evocation of Fez by night is typical of her lyrical powers of description.

66Full moon over Fez, a great bright moon of silver tinged with pink like the snow that gleams on the Atlas. Is it night already then? One had not thought so. With the night comes a deepening of the green on the slopes where Fez slides into the hollow of its valley; the deeper redness of a shawl and a burnous clinging to the steps of the old cemetery, while a long river of copper torn from the sunset stretches over the barley. It is night, come as a pageant and presided over by the rainbow. The full round moon, elsewhere dragging up the tide, absorbs what's left of pallor over Fez, takes suck from this hollowed breast where the last shrill mixed cries of children and swallows now submerge, now uncover the uneven beating of a distant drum. Our European curiosity has already deserted us. What point in leaving this belvedere? The secret streets of Fez – secret? Perhaps the secret of this city is that it has no secrets. Everything it seems to hide fascinates: high walls of pinkish clay, closed doors whose two rings – one at a horseman's height, the other for the passer-by – strike the nail-studded door; captive gardens, inaccessible, guessed at, which display their young leaves and flowers at the top of their prisons. … Between the closed doors, the too-high walls, along the stifling streets where my outstretched arms touch both walls, we return in imagination to those recent times when the blameless traveller who ventured into the half-roofed alleys below the Jamai Palace risked an encounter with a well-placed blade. From the height of the Jamai we can see it all – everything that matters: the hollow of Fez with its raised borders, its minarets, its conglomerated rectangles, its morning whiteness, its rust-coloured evenings, its blue-white sky like the sky that mirrors the sands, its confused murmur pierced by sudden cries – and the Atlas Mountains. From this height we experienced only the flower of such a fine estate. In the evening, at the call of the muezzins, a bouquet of women erupts spontaneously over the terraces and an an etherealized, insubstantial Fez climbs up to us.**99**

COLETTE, *PLACES*, LONDON, 1970

SLEEPLESS NIGHTS AT RAMADAN

Though overshadowed by his more famous sister Edith and brother Osbert, Sacherevell Sitwell (1897–1988) was nevertheless a prolific poet, travel writer, art historian and biographer. His extensive peregrinations in Europe produced many travel books.

❝The most exciting experience of Fez, emotionally and aesthetically, is the first walk in the town, but, before that, the night must be lived through. It is to be hoped that it is Ramadan; but Ramadan is so variable a festival, occurring in months as wide apart as November or April, that there can be no certainty. If it is Ramadan, sleep, to any person with imagination, will be out of question. Trumpets and conch shells are blown, all night long, from the minarets, and the voice of the muezzin is seldom silent. There are persons to whom a night of Ramadan, in Fez, would be unforgettable and of potent inspiration. Such a spirit, we cannot doubt, would have been Debussy, whom we may mourn here as nowhere else, thinking of the music that he would have written. But, even on an ordinary night, there is never silence. Singing and music are always to be heard, together with extraordinary sounds of voices that cannot be explained. If you go to the window and look out, the town lies in darkness. You have the knowledge, too, that nothing could ever guide your footsteps in the direction whence it came. But, also, at intervals, all through the night, there are the muezzins, and though, during my recent visit, it was ten years since I had been in Fez I distinctly recognized the voice of one muezzin who has the passion and skill of some great operatic singer but, as it were, in terms of music that we cannot understand. It is impossible not to lie awake listening. You can hear many other muezzins, too; for Fez is a holy town of Islam and there may, indeed, be but few other cities in the modern world where they pray with such fervour and where the muezzin has such ringing tones.❞

SACHEREVELL SITWELL, *MAURETANIA: WARRIOR, MAN AND WOMAN*, LONDON, 1940

MARRAKESH

The English traveler James Richardson (1806–51) paints this picture of Marrakesh in the 19th century.

❝Morocco, or strictly in Arabic, Maraksh, which signifies "adorned", is the capital of the South, and frequently denominates the capital of the empire, but it is only a *triste* shadow of its former greatness. It is sometimes honoured with the title of "the great city", or "country". Morocco occupies an immense area of ground, being seven miles in circumference, the interior of which is covered with heaps of ruins or more pleasantly converted into gardens. Morocco was built in 1072 or 1073 by the famous Yousef-Ben-Tashfin, King of Samtana, and of the dynasty of the Almoravedi or Marabouts. Its site is that of an ancient city, Martok, founded in the remotest periods of the primitive Africans, or aboriginal Berbers, in whose language it signifies a place where everything good and pleasant was to be found in abundance. ... The mosques are numerous and rich, the principal of which are El-Kittabeeah, of elegant architecture with an extremely lofty minaret, El-Moazin, which is three hundred years old and a magnificent building; and Benions, built nearly seven hundred years ago of singular construction uniting modern and ancient architecture. Nine gates open in the city wall; these are strong

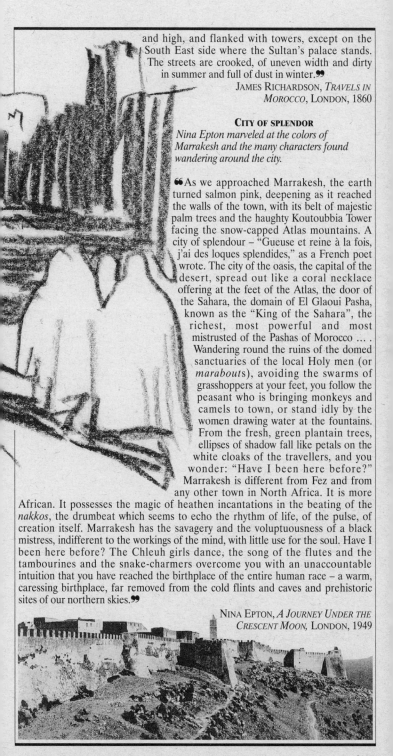

and high, and flanked with towers, except on the South East side where the Sultan's palace stands. The streets are crooked, of uneven width and dirty in summer and full of dust in winter."

JAMES RICHARDSON, *TRAVELS IN MOROCCO*, LONDON, 1860

CITY OF SPLENDOR

Nina Epton marveled at the colors of Marrakesh and the many characters found wandering around the city.

"As we approached Marrakesh, the earth turned salmon pink, deepening as it reached the walls of the town, with its belt of majestic palm trees and the haughty Koutoubbia Tower facing the snow-capped Atlas mountains. A city of splendour – "Gueuse et reine à la fois, j'ai des loques splendides," as a French poet wrote. The city of the oasis, the capital of the desert, spread out like a coral necklace offering at the feet of the Atlas, the door of the Sahara, the domain of El Glaoui Pasha, known as the "King of the Sahara", the richest, most powerful and most mistrusted of the Pashas of Morocco … . Wandering round the ruins of the domed sanctuaries of the local Holy men (or *marabouts*), avoiding the swarms of grasshoppers at your feet, you follow the peasant who is bringing monkeys and camels to town, or stand idly by the women drawing water at the fountains. From the fresh, green plantain trees, ellipses of shadow fall like petals on the white cloaks of the travellers, and you wonder: "Have I been here before?" Marrakesh is different from Fez and from any other town in North Africa. It is more African. It possesses the magic of heathen incantations in the beating of the *nakkos*, the drumbeat which seems to echo the rhythm of life, of the pulse, of creation itself. Marrakesh has the savagery and the voluptuousness of a black mistress, indifferent to the workings of the mind, with little use for the soul. Have I been here before? The Chleuh girls dance, the song of the flutes and the tambourines and the snake-charmers overcome you with an unaccountable intuition that you have reached the birthplace of the entire human race – a warm, caressing birthplace, far removed from the cold flints and caves and prehistoric sites of our northern skies."

NINA EPTON, *A JOURNEY UNDER THE CRESCENT MOON*, LONDON, 1949

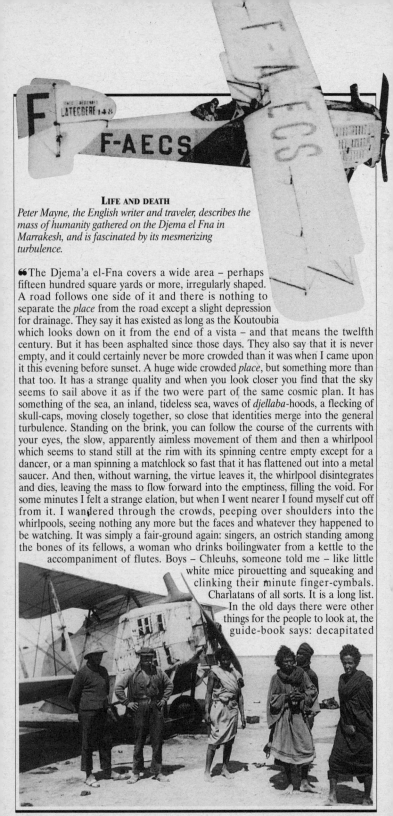

LIFE AND DEATH

*Peter Mayne, the English writer and traveler, describes the
mass of humanity gathered on the Djema el Fna in
Marrakesh, and is fascinated by its mesmerizing
turbulence.*

❝The Djema'a el-Fna covers a wide area – perhaps
fifteen hundred square yards or more, irregularly shaped.
A road follows one side of it and there is nothing to
separate the *place* from the road except a slight depression
for drainage. They say it has existed as long as the Koutoubia
which looks down on it from the end of a vista – and that means the twelfth
century. But it has been asphalted since those days. They also say that it is never
empty, and it could certainly never be more crowded than it was when I came upon
it this evening before sunset. A huge wide crowded *place*, but something more than
that too. It has a strange quality and when you look closer you find that the sky
seems to sail above it as if the two were part of the same cosmic plan. It has
something of the sea, an inland, tideless sea, waves of *djellaba*-hoods, a flecking of
skull-caps, moving closely together, so close that identities merge into the general
turbulence. Standing on the brink, you can follow the course of the currents with
your eyes, the slow, apparently aimless movement of them and then a whirlpool
which seems to stand still at the rim with its spinning centre empty except for a
dancer, or a man spinning a matchlock so fast that it has flattened out into a metal
saucer. And then, without warning, the virtue leaves it, the whirlpool disintegrates
and dies, leaving the mass to flow forward into the emptiness, filling the void. For
some minutes I felt a strange elation, but when I went nearer I found myself cut off
from it. I wandered through the crowds, peeping over shoulders into the
whirlpools, seeing nothing any more but the faces and whatever they happened to
be watching. It was simply a fair-ground again: singers, an ostrich standing among
the bones of its fellows, a woman who drinks boilingwater from a kettle to the
accompaniment of flutes. Boys – Chleuhs, someone told me – like little
white mice pirouetting and squeaking and
clinking their minute finger-cymbals.
Charlatans of all sorts. It is a long list.
In the old days there were other
things for the people to look at, the
guide-book says: decapitated

heads, specifically. It gives a translation of the name, Djema'a el-Fna: Congregation of the Departed. With the coming of the French Protectorate, the decapitations were stopped, but the people still crowd the *place* just the same, and I shall come too. There is something living here which I would like to share, a sort of animal force that we have forgotten about in the temperate zones.**"**

PETER MAYNE, *THE ALLEYS OF MARRAKESH*,
LONDON, 1953

NATIVE VIEW

Mohammed Mrabet (b.1940) was an illiterate house servant in Morocco at the time this impression of the Djemaa el Fna in Marrakesh was committed to paper. Mrabet's accounts of indigenous life were tape-recorded, transcribed and translated from the Maghribi by Peter Bowles, the American expatriate in Tangier. By the same method, Mrabet "wrote" his novel, "A Life Full of Holes", which was published in 1964.

"Reeves drove me out to my house and waited while I went in to tell them I was going to be travelling around Morocco for a while. I said good-bye to them all, and we started out. ...Early the next morning we were on the road. We bypassed Casablanca, and did not stop until we got to Marrakech. Reeves drove to the Hotel Tazi, near the Medina. It was run by an old French couple. He took two rooms, each with two beds. I washed and shaved and changed, and so did Reeves. Then we knocked on Maria's door, and all three of us went out and walked to the Djemaa el Fna. I had never seen anything like it before, anywhere, with so many people at once all doing different things. There was a group of Gnaoua pounding drums and spinning around, and there were Jilala, and some Aissaoua making their cobras dance for them. We watched trained monkeys and men riding bicycles standing up on the seat, and others in crazy costumes dancing by themselves. It was such a new thing to me that all I could do was laugh. I stood and laughed at everything. What do you think of all this? Maria asked me. I've never seen such a place! Do you have such places in America? She laughed. Americans have to spend a lot of money to get to see this, she said. That's why they take pictures all the time, once they get here.**"**

MOHAMMED MRABET,
LOOK AND MOVE ON,
LONDON, 1989.

TANGIER

AN ORIENTAL PICTURE

Before he wrote "The Adventures of Tom Sawyer" and "Huckleberry Finn", books that made him internationally famous, the American writer and journalist Mark Twain (1835–1910) had already traveled widely, both in the United States and in Europe. "Traveling with the Innocents Abroad" describes a naïve American tourist's travels around Europe and North Africa and this particular extract deals with a trip to Morocco.

66Tangier is a foreign land if ever there was one. And the true spirit of it can never be found in any book save the Arabian Nights. Here are no white men visible, yet swarms of humanity are all about me. Here is a packed and jammed city enclosed in a massive stone wall which is more than a thousand years old. All the houses nearly are one and two-story; made of thick walls of stone; plastered outside; square as a dry-goods box; flat as a floor on top; no cornices; whitewashed all over – a crowded city of snowy tombs! And the doors are arched with the peculiar arch we see in Moorish pictures; the floors are laid in vari-colored diamond-flags; in tasselated many-colored porcelain squares wrought in the furnaces of Fez; in red tiles and broad bricks that time cannot wear; there is no furniture in the rooms (of Jewish dwellings) save divans – what there is in Moorish ones no man may know; within their sacred walls no Christian dog can enter. And the streets are oriental – some of them three feet wide, some six, but only two that are over a dozen; a man can blockade the most of them by extending his body across them. Isn't it an oriental picture?99

MARK TWAIN, *TRAVELING WITH THE INNOCENTS ABROAD*,
OKLAHOMA, 1958

MEKNÈS

*The French traveler and writer Pierre Loti (1850–1923), otherwise known as
Louis Marie Julien Viaud, began his working life as a seaman. As a naval officer he
made trips to Turkey, Senegal, Japan and Tahiti, where the women of the South Seas
gave him the name Loti (Flower of the Pacific). He pursued a life of travel and writing,
the one being the inspiration for the other. He went to Morocco in 1889, as part of an
embassy sent by the French government. "Morocco", the account of his journey from
Tangier to Fez and Meknès, was first published as a serial in the French journal
"L'Illustration" in 1889.*

66Mekinez! On the limit of the desolate plain, seeming still very far away, Mekinez appears. One realises that one sees it only by virtue of the unbroken lines of the ground and the wonderful clearness of the air. It is a little blackish band – the walls, no doubt – above which bristle, scarcely visible, slender as reeds, the towers of the mosques. We ride on for some time yet, until we reach a point where the view is hidden from us by old, crumbling walls, which seem to enclose immense parks. We are at the outskirts of the town. Through a breach we enter these enclosures, to find ourselves in a region of olive-trees planted regularly in quincunxes, and on soil covered with very fine grass and moss, such as is only met with in places that have long been tranquil, untrodden by men. These olives, moreover, are exhausted, dying, covered with a kind of mouldiness, a malady of age, which turns their foliage black, as if it had been smoked. And the enclosures follow one another, always in ruins, confining these same phantoms of trees aligned in all directions as far as eye can see. They might be a series of parks abandoned for centuries, promenades for the dead. ... As we issue from these walls and these olives, Mekinez suddenly reappears, very close to us now and immense, crowning with its grey shadow a succession of hills behind which the sun is setting. We are separated from the town only by a ravine of verdure, a medley of poplars, mulberry-trees, orange-trees, any trees you will, all in their fresh tints of April. Very high against the yellow sky show the lines of the superposed ramparts, the innumerable terraces, the minarets, the towers of the mosques, the formidable embattled *kasbahs*, and, above a number of fortress walls, the green-tiled roof of the Sultan's palace. It is even more imposing than Fez, and more solemn. But it is only a phantom of a town, a mass of ruins and rubbish, inhabited by scarce more than five or six thousand souls, Arabs, Berbers and Jews.99

PIERRE LOTI, *MOROCCO*,
WERNER, 1900

RABAT

IN A SECRET GARDEN

In Rabat, Colette wandered through an Elysian garden replete with exotic perfumes and cadent birdsong.

❝Dazzle of stars and orange-trees. Throbbing of nightingales, twinkling of starlight. The perfume of the orange smothers everything. The grape-fruit in flower has a lingering sweetness that the orange lacks. The twittering birds before dawn, a great rushing of birds. After daybreak a cadence of the nightingale echoes still, a fragment of the night. At first light the swallow utters her piercing cry. Then the liquid throaty gurgling of the common oriole and the blackbird. The last songs rise from a damp shingle whose every pebble is the sound of a sparrow and the kisses, kisses, kisses of myriad tomtits. ...How long can one browse in the contemplation of a secret garden, a filigree of fine metalwork against a leafy background? How much time can one spend in waiting for the wind at last to stir the rigid, immense torch of a cypress that seems to buttress an angle of the house and create the illusion that the palace itself is swaying? For today, and the two previous days, the

illusion has lasted. It is simply that luxury beguiles one's sense of everyday life; and here, as elsewhere, luxury is stillness and silence.❞

COLETTE, *PLACES*, LONDON, 1970

WASHERWOMEN OF SEFROU

Sacheverell Sitwell writes here about the small town of Sefrou, twenty miles from Fez.

❝Here the Jews may form nearly one half of the population. The French colonists are few in number and hardly to be seen. Sefrou lies just under the hills, near to the rocky valley which is celebrated for its cascades. Plentiful water is assured, while advantage of those forces has been taken in the matter of electrical power. But Sefrou must always have been rich, within its own small environment. The modern quarters of the town show fine boulevards lined with orangetrees, and every villa appears to have a beautiful garden. But, in fact, the fruit trees of Sefrou surround the town as though with an oasis of almond and apricot. It is famous, moreover, for strawberries, which grow wild in the hedges and are cultivated for market in cleverly watered beds. No other town in Morocco gives this impression of fertile orchards and gardens. The pleasanter side of life is in the ascendant upon the picturesque. Inside the town, the eternal squalor of the Orient is tempered by the possibility that there is wealth behind the walls. The river flows through the town, dividing it into two parts. It runs in a rocky ravine strewn with boulders, the houses

123

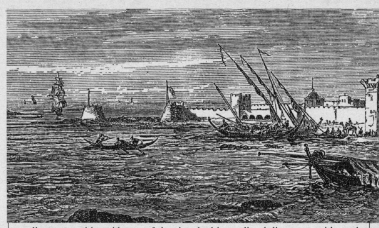

standing up on either side out of the river bed in medieval directness, without the dignity of an embankment. The air, in this curving valley or corridor of masonry, is charged with mist or smoke and dampened by spray. A bridge crosses the river, in midst of this, giving a near view of what we have come here to see. The first impression is one of overwhelming dampness, the sort of wet that would induce pneumonia or rheumatic fever, an association in the mind with damp sheets ending in grave illness. This is, in fact, an open-air laundry. And the laundry women are all Jewesses. It is a witch's Sabbath, on a day that is compound of August and November, in extreme of heat and of humidity. The washerwomen have little cauldrons smoking and boiling upon the rocks. In these they steep the linen, and, we may think, while casting spells and making divination, are brewing in the same moment some noisome concoction on which they make their midday meal. ...Their ragged clothes are of different colours, black predominant, but most of them, in coquetry, wear a little round, black hat, or tambour, we wonder for whose pleasure and into what dark mirror they must gaze, this round hat or cap being in spiteful parody, as it were, upon modern fashion. It is, indeed, inordinately smart or chic, bearing back to the little round hats of the crinolined 'sixties, as seen in the finest fashion plates of Compte Calix or Jules David, with echoes, again, of those Spanish fashions that designers of that time adapted from the seventeenth century in compliment to a Spanish Empress. While at their work they never, for a moment, stop quarrelling; they are as tenacious of what they conceive to be their rights as a string of cormorants fishing in the Yellow Seas. It would not appear possible that any individual laundress had a single friend among her sisters, or was vowed to anything but eternal war or intrigue towards them. ... This extraordinary scene, which has been often, and badly, sketched or painted by artists, deserves some more worthy memorial. ... To anyone who has noticed them, the washerwomen of Sefrou must remain one of the strangest and most peculiar of his Moroccan memories. Such a quantity of unveiled hags could be seen nowhere else in this land of Moslems. That fact, by itself, puts them as aliens in the veiled alleys, where no woman, from ten years old to a hundred, goes unmasked. It belongs to a different tradition. It is something of medieval Europe, of Cracow, of Strasbourg, in this temperate Africa of almond and orange-tree. For this reason, the typical Morocco of its surroundings is thrown into deeper emphasis. **99**

SACHEVERELL SITWELL, *MAURETANIA: WARRIOR, MAN AND WOMAN,*
LONDON, 1940

MONEY AND COMMERCE

MONEYCHANGERS OF TANGIER
Twain's Innocent here offers advice to travelers about dealing with the merchants and thieves of Tangier.

66The general size of a store in Tangier is about that of an ordinary shower-bath in a civilized land. The Mohammedan merchant, tinman, shoemaker, or vendor of trifles, sits cross-legged on the floor, and reaches after any article you may want to buy. You can rent a whole block of these pigeon-holes for fifty dollars a month. The market people crowd the market place with their baskets of figs, dates, melons,

apricots, etc., and among them file trains of laden jackasses, not much larger, if any, than a Newfoundland dog. The scene is lively, is picturesque, and smells like the San Francisco Police Court. The Jewish money-changers have their dens close at hand, and all day long are counting bronze coins and transferring them from one bushel basket to another. They don't coin much money nowadays, I think. I saw none but what was dated four or five hundred years back, and was badly worn and battered. These coins are not very valuable. Brown went out to get a Napoleon changed, so as to have money suited to the general cheapness of things, and came back and said he had "cleaned out the bank; had bought eleven gallons of coin, and the head of the firm had gone on the street to negotiate for the balance of the change." I bought nearly half a pint of their money for a shilling myself. The Moors have some small silver coins, and also some silver slugs worth a dollar eachl. … They have also a small gold coin worth two dollars. And that reminds me of something. When Morocco is in a state of war, Arab couriers carry letters through the country and charge a liberal postage. Every now and then they fall into the hands of marauding bands and get robbed. Therefore, warned by experience, as soon as they have collected two dollars' worth of money, they exchange it for one of those little gold pieces, and when robbers come upon them, swallow it.**99**

MARK TWAIN, *TRAVELING WITH THE INNOCENTS ABROAD*,
OKLAHOMA, 1952

THE SCIENCE OF COMMERCE

Paul Bowles (1910–86) began his career in New York as a composer and music critic, only taking up writing in the late 1940s. With his wife, the writer Jane Auer, he went to live in Europe and the couple settled permanently in Tangier in 1952. The theme that runs through Bowles's novels "The Sheltering Sky" (1949), "Let It Come Down" (1952) and "The Spider's House" (1955) is that of Westerners displaced in an Oriental world. "In Their Heads Are Green" Bowles chronicles his encounters with Hindu, Muslim, Buddhist and Central American culture.

66I do not claim that the Moslems of North Africa are a group of mystics, heedless of bodily comfort, interested only in the welfare of the spirit. If you have ever bought so much as an egg from one of them, you have learned that they are quite able to fend for themselves when it comes to money matters. The spoiled strawberries are at the bottom of the basket, the pebbles inextricably mixed with the lentils and the water with the milk, the same as in many other parts of the world, with the difference that if you ask the price of an object in a rural market, they will reply, all in one breath: "Fifty, how much will you give?" I should say that in the realm of *beah o chra* (selling and buying; note that in their minds selling comes first), which is what they call business, they are surpassed only by the Hindus, who are less emotional about it and therefore more successful, and by the Chinese, acknowledged masters of the Oriental branch of the science of commerce.

In Morocco you go into a bazaar to buy a wallet, somehow find yourself being propelled toward the back room to look at antique brass and rugs, are presently

125

seated with a glass of mint tea in your hand and a platter of pastries in your lap, while smiling gentlemen modelling ancient caftans and marriage robes parade in front of you, the salesman who greeted you at the door having completely vanished. Later on you may once again ask timidly to see the wallets, which you noticed on display near the entrance. Likely as not, you will be told that the man in charge of wallets is at the moment saying his prayers, but that he will soon be back, and in the meantime would you not be pleased to see some magnificent jewellery from the court of Moulay Ismail? Business is business and prayers are prayers, and both are a part of the day's work.**99**

PAUL BOWLES, *THEIR HEADS ARE GREEN AND THEIR HANDS ARE BLUE*,
JONATHAN CAPE, LONDON, 1963

SURVIVAL IN THE SOUK

Edith Wharton (1862–1937), lifelong friend of Henry James, was already established as a novelist and short-story writer in New York society when she moved to France in 1910. She traveled widely in Europe, recording her observations of France and Italy. She made a trip to North Africa in 1917; the result was "In Morocco", an evocative guidebook to the country.

66Dark, fierce and fanatical are these narrow *souks* of Marrakech. They are mere mud lanes roofed with rushes, as in South Tunisia and Timbuctoo, and the crowds swarming in them are so dense that it is hardly possible, at certain hours, to approach the tiny raised kennels where the merchants sit like idols among their wares. One feels at once that something more than the thought of bargaining – dear as this is to the African heart – animates these incessantly moving throngs. The *souks* of Marrakech seem, more than any others, the central organ of a native life that extends far beyond the city walls into secret clefts of the mountains and far-off oases where plots are hatched and holy wars fomented – farther still, to yellow deserts whence Negroes are secretly brought across the Atlas to that inmost recess of the bazaar where the ancient traffic in flesh and blood still surreptitiously goes on. All these many threads of the native life, woven of greed and lust, of fetishism and fear and blind hate of the stranger, form, in the *souks*, a thick network in which at times one's feet seem literally to stumble. Fanatics in sheepskins glowering from the guarded thresholds of the mosques, fierce tribesmen with inlaid arms in their belts and the fighters' tufts of wiry hair escaping from camel's-hair turbans, mad Negroes standing stark naked in niches of the walls and pouring down Soudanese incantations upon the fascinated crowd, consumptive Jews with pathos and cunning in their large eyes and smiling lips, lusty slave-girls with earthen oil-jars resting against swaying hips, almond-eyed boys leading fat merchants by the hand, and bare-legged Berber women, tattooed and insolently gay, trading their striped blankets, or bags of dried roses and irises, for sugar, tea, or Manchester cottons – from all these hundreds of unknown and unknowable people, bound together by secret affinities, or intriguing against each other with secret hate, there emanated an atmosphere of mystery and menace more stifling than the smell of camels and spices and black bodies and smoking fry which hangs like a fog under the close roofing of the *souks*.**99**

EDITH WHARTON, *IN MOROCCO*, LONDON, 1920

PEOPLE

William Lithgow explains 16th-century Moroccan customs in dress and manners.

66The women through all Barbary, weare abundance of Bracelets on their armes, and Rings in their eares, but not through the nose and lips as the Egyptians doe; and turne also the nayles of their hands and feete to red, accounting it a base thing to see a white naile: The men here for the most part, are the best Archers, and Horsemen that are in Affrick, and take great pleasure in breeding of their Barbes: So are they both active and couragious, and very desperate in all their attempts, being all of the Mahometanicall Religion, though more ignorant thereof than the Turkes: some whereof are subject to the Turke, some to the Emperour of Morocco, and some to their owne barbarous Princes. The people of both kindes are cloathed in long breeches and bare Ancles, with red or yellow shooes shod with Iron on the Heeles, and on the Toes with white Horne; and weare on their bodies long Robes of Linning or Dimmety, and silken Wast-coates of diverse Colours: The behaviour of the Vulgars being far more civill toward Strangers then at Constantinople; or else where in all Turkey. The Women here go unmasked abroad, wearing on their heads, broad, and round Capes, made of Straw or small Reedes, to shade their faces from the Sunne; and damnable Libidinous, beeing prepared both wayes to satisfie the lust of their Luxurious Villaines; neyther are they so strictly kept as the Turkish Women, marching where they please.**99**

WILLIAM LITHGOW, *RARE ADVENTURES AND PAINFULL PEREGRINATIONS 1614–32*, GLASGOW, 1906

A MOROCCAN HOUSE

James Curtis visited Morocco in the early 19th century in his capacity as Surgeon to the British Embassy. Here an experience of fulsome Muslim hospitality ends in exasperation for the British visitors.

66Our house consisted of four large apartments, with folding doors to each opening in front of an extensive garden filled with fruit trees; a square courtyard, in the centre of which was a cold bath of considerable dimensions, supplied at each extremity by a fountain. The house was furnished in the Moorish style, with fine carpets and cushions &c. but we desired them to be removed and substituted in their places our beds and camp furniture. The Emperor had sent ten large dishes of *cus-cus son*, made of fowls, mutton, and fruit, six huge baskets filled with apples, pears, plums and various kinds of fruit from his garden. Presently after, he sent an additional supply of six dishes of *cus-cus son*, some of which weighed an hundred pounds, for our supper, which enabled us to afford a glorious repast to our soldiers and muleteers. When we retired to rest, we flattered ourselves that after a fatiguing march of eleven days, we might enjoy the luxury of undisturbed repose. But the vast numbers of frogs and toads which infest the city and its vicinity with their hideous croaking from sun-set till sun-rise, and the quantity which were about our bath, absolutely deprived us of rest. When I rose on the morning of the 6th, and offered some money to the Moors if they would either destroy or remove them from the bath, they peremptorily refused, on the grounds that they were blessed by the Prophet, and if one were killed, the destroyer would inevitably be fixed with some malady.**99**

JAMES CURTIS, *A JOURNAL OF TRAVELS IN BARBARY IN THE YEAR 1801*, 1803

TEA, GOSSIP AND SMOKE

The Moroccan custom of drinking tea both fascinated and irritated Arthur Leared, who visited Morocco in the late 19th century. Describing the equipment used to prepare it and the variety of ways of serving it, he marvels at the time the "turbaned squatters" devoted to this sociable practice. Smoking, by contrast, was done in private.

MOROCCO AS SEEN BY WRITERS

❝There was nothing in Morocco we tried more to avoid than the customary tea-parties, both on account of their effects and the loss of time. Tea is the dissipation of the country, and is indulged in at all times of the day. By this habit many of the Moors impair their health. Unfortunately, it is contrary to etiquette to refuse tea, as it used to be in England to refuse wine when your host called upon you to refill your glass. Tea has been known to the Moors for a long period, and it is curious to find this exotic beverage in such universal use. They are great connoisseurs, and will only drink fine green tea, which makes the practice all the more injurious to the nerves of a stranger. It is imported from England, and sells in Morocco at from four to six shillings a pound. The equipage in which it is served is often elegant and costly – the teapot among the wealthy being of silver; and the cups, which are always shaped like those used in England for coffee, are sometimes fine specimens of Oriental or European porcelain. Usually, however, tea is taken in small footless glasses adorned with gilding, and of German manufacture. The tea is washed before it is infused, and a great quantity of sugar is put into the teapot. It is, in fact, a syrup; and it might be supposed that people so particular about flavours as are the Moors would find such excessive sweetness objectionable. Yet, what is more extraordinary still, they endeavour apparently to suppress the delicate tea flavour altogether. Tea has to be taken in regular course, impregnated with different flavours, which are all more or less disagreeable to the novice. The order may vary; but from the numerous opportunities we had of judging, the following seemed the rule in "the best circles". First there was a round of plain green tea with no addition but sugar. Milk or cream was never used. Then came a second course, in which spearmint was infused – a horrible compound. Third, an infusion of tea with wormwood, not quite so objectionable. Fourth, one flavoured with lemon verbena. Fifth, one with citron. Sixth, and more rarely, as being an expensive luxury and intended as a great compliment, tea with a little ambergris scraped into it, which could be seen floating like grease on the surface. Of this the flavour, if peculiar, was not disagreeable. Each course of tea was taken while very warm, and with a loud smacking noise of the lips; nothing, meanwhile, was eaten. As time is of no value to the Moors, many hours are consumed at a sitting. The tea-party is frequently held in the open air, often in a garden under the shade of lofty trees. Here carpets are spread by the servants, who also light a fire, and boil the water for tea. At these parties politics – as far as may be done with safety – are discussed, and the retail of gossip is an invariable and important business. Tea and gossip, proverbially associated, are supposed to belong exclusively to the fair sex, but in the country of the Moors the turbaned squatters seem equally masters of the situation.**❞**

ARTHUR LEARED, *MOROCCO AND THE MOORS*, LONDON, 1891

A MOORISH MEAL
Nina Epton provides some useful tips about the etiquette required at Moroccan meals.

❝We sat on leather cushions round the low table, while the servants brought silver bowls, towels and kettles of cold water, so that we could rinse our hands before eating. The food is eaten with fingers only: the first three fingers of the right hand may be used – or, rather, the thumb and first two fingers. After the meal, the silver bowl is passed round again, this time accompanied by soap. The fingers must be clean. You cannot tear into a plump pigeon carefully wrapped in boiling tomato pulp, and share it with your neighbours, unless they are scrupulously washed. Soup, served in blue bowls with long wooden spoons, was followed by *pastilla*, which is the *summum bonum* of all Moroccan culinary art. The Spanish *paella* is only a degenerate, far-removed relation of this wonder. The *pastilla* which was served to us that night was as large as the top of a table. Underneath the almost transparent, flaky layers of pastry were delicious surprises in the form of tasty morsels of chicken, vegetables, meat of all kinds. It was as complex in flavour as a Chinese dish, and the hall-mark of a civilized race.**❞**

NINA EPTON, *A JOURNEY UNDER THE CRESCENT MOON*, LONDON, 1949

Traveling around Morocco

"The entire universe is contained in the teapot. Or, to be
more precise, the *sinia* [round tray] represents the earth, the
teapot represents the sky and the glasses represent the rain;
the sky is united to the earth by rain.**"**
Abdallah Zrika

▲ The high dunes of Merzouga.

▲ The red, laterite-rich earth of the Dadès Valley.

The crenelated *pisé* (mud and rubble) towers of the *Ksour* and kasbahs. ▼

The effects of erosion: a goat track in the rock face of the Todra Gorges. ▼

▲ At the foot of the snow-covered peaks of M'Goun, the stony plateaux of Boulemane du Dadès.

▲ The foothills of the High Atlas.　　　　The valley of the Aït Bouguemez. ▼

IN AND AROUND CASABLANCA

MOULAY YOUSSEF PIER
MAHAKMA DU PACHA
BOULEVARD MOHAMMED V
KOUBBA OF SIDI BEYLIOUT
PLACE MOHAMMED V
WILAYA (PREFECTURE)

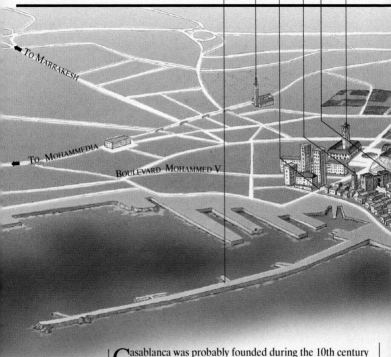

TO MARRAKESH

TO MOHAMMEDIA

BOULEVARD MOHAMMED V

✳ One day

A PROSPEROUS TOWN
In his *Geographical
History of Africa*
(1600) Leo Africanus
remarked that the
remains of Anfa
suggested that it had
been a town of many
temples, beautiful
shops and tall
palaces. The
engraving (right),
dating from 1572,
shows the tomb of
Sidi Beyliout, the wall
surrounding the
cemetery and the bay
of Sidi Beyliout.

Casablanca was probably founded during the 10th century
BC, when Berber fishermen settled on the hill to the
south of the modern city. During the 7th century BC the
Phoenicians used the inlets on that part of the coast as
stopping places during the long sea voyage to Essaouira
▲ *156*. The discovery of a Roman galley off the coast suggests
that the Romans were using the port around 15 BC. A hoard
of 169 silver denarii was found in the wreck and this is now in
the Banque Nationale du Maroc in Rabat ▲ *161*.
ANFA, A BERBER SETTLEMENT. During the 7th century, while
the Maghreb was being converted to Islam, an important
Berber tribe, the Barghawata, settled in the plain between the
Oum er Rbia and the Oued Bou Regreg ▲ *162*. The fertile
area surrounding the *anfa* (hill) to the north of the Oum er
Rbia was an ideal place for a settlement. Rejecting Islam, the
Berbers formed an independent kingdom, with Anfa as its
capital. For four centuries Anfa resisted the repeated attacks
of the Ommiads and Idrissids ● *53* but, after two sieges (one

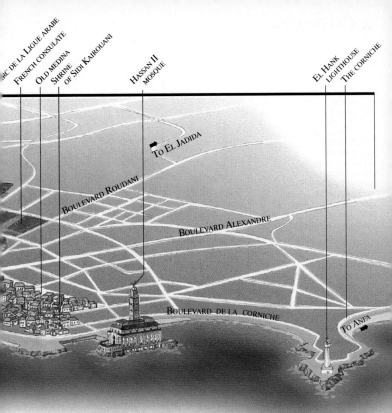

PARC DE LA LIGUE ARABE
FRENCH CONSULATE
OLD MEDINA
SHRINE OF SIDI KAIROUANI
HASSAN II MOSQUE
EL HANK LIGHTHOUSE
THE CORNICHE

TO EL JADIDA

BOULEVARD ROUDANI

BOULEVARD ALEXANDRE

BOULEVARD DE LA CORNICHE

TO ANFA

of which lasted six years), the settlement finally fell to the Almoravids in 1068.

TOWARD ISLAMIZATION. In the 14th century the Merinids ordered Anfa to be rebuilt on the lines of a Muslim town and installed their own governor. A medersa ● *90* built within the walls was the first stage in the process of the town's Islamization. During the first half of the 14th century Anfa became the trading center for locally produced corn, leather and wool, and the port was renowned from Genoa to Catalonia and the Balearic Islands. During the 15th century Anfa regained independence. Its pirate ships were menacing the Tagus estuary off the port of Lisbon and for this audacity the Portuguese retaliated with a raid in 1468 in which Anfa was sacked for the second time. The Portuguese rebuilt it a century later, using it as a military outpost to defend the important route to Mazagan (modern El Jadida ▲ *149*). They abandoned the area after the earthquake of 1755.

DAR EL BEIDA. In 1770 the sultan Moulay Ben Abdallah began to rebuild Anfa. He built a great mosque and *zaouia* (religious centers) ▲ *198* within the walls and, to mark Anfa's conversion to Islam, it was renamed Dar el Beida (House of the White Princess). According to legend, the name was chosen in memory of the patron of fishermen, Allal el Kairouani and his daughter Lalla Beida (White Princess). The town acquired its Spanish name, Casa Blanca (White House), in 1781 when Mohammed III granted a Spanish shipping

"When I returned to Morocco in 1920, the boat docked at Casablanca. The port, which had a reputation for being 'impossible', had been fairly extensively restored. Huge piers enclosed a sheltered harbor where steamers could dock safely and unload their cargo quickly and easily [. . .] The 'impossible' had been achieved."

Claude Farrère,
En Méditerranée

137

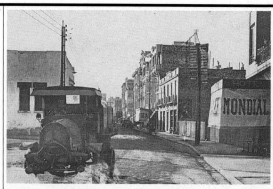

MUNICIPAL WATERCART
In 1912, under the French protectorate, the Moroccan government introduced a public health scheme to improve general living standards, particularly in major cities. In 1920 a highways department was created in Casablanca to organize the collection and treatment of garbage. A municipal watercart (right) cleans the city's main streets.

SUPPLYING THE CAPITAL
Before the introduction of road and rail transport, supplies were brought to Casablanca by camel. The first narrow-gauge railway was built in 1907 to transport goods for export from places such as Fez ▲ 213, Meknès ▲ 232, the Gharb ▲ 212 and Doukkala ▲ 148 to the port of Casablanca.

company permission to export corn. During the first half of the 19th century, the port regained its importance as a trading center for wool, cereals and tea. An increasing number of European steamships were now calling at Casablanca and, by the end of the century, trade had become international. An influx of European settlers increased the city's population, which rose from just six hundred inhabitants in 1830 to almost eight thousand in 1868.

CASABLANCA, ECONOMIC CAPITAL OF MOROCCO. In 1906, when Casablanca was a relatively small town, still contained within its city walls, the port area was extensively developed and modernized. In 1912, when Morocco became a French protectorate ● 56, General Lyautey ▲ 164 decided to turn Casablanca into the country's economic capital. At his request the architect Henri Prost drew up the first homogeneous urban development plans, imposing some order on the city's previously uncoordinated growth. He decided to build the modern districts around a central point, the present-day Place Mohammed V, where the 18th-century El Kebir souk was held. By 1920 Casablanca had become Morocco's leading port, hosting many international political, economic, commercial and cultural conferences and events. Two further phases of urban development, the first in 1946 and the second in 1984, were implemented to rationalize the city's growth.

Today Casablanca is the largest city in the Maghreb. In the space of three generations its population has increased one hundredfold, and the city is now home to over four million people. Despite its size, Casablanca retains a very real charm, thanks in large measure to its Art Deco architecture.

THE 1930'S

Casablanca's great building boom took place in the 1930's. From the time that Morocco acquired new status as a French protectorate in 1912, Casablanca, aspiring to be the most modern city in Morocco, was gripped by development fever. Architects arrived from France, Algeria and Tunisia. Although the residential blocks that they built during the 1930's betray an obvious French influence, these architects did allow for the Moroccan climate and take account of the country's architectural tradition.

Façades were richly decorated with cupolas, belvederes, pillars, cedarwood balconies, skylights, *zellige* ▲ *173*, stucco and wrought iron. Decorative detail in Art Nouveau and Art Deco style, as well as motifs taken from Renaissance, Neoclassical and Moorish traditions, were also incorporated. Visitors can see the façades of these buildings in the central districts of Casablanca, particularly in the Boulevard Mohammed V, the pedestrianized Rue Prince Moulay Abdallah and the former European district of Mers Sultan.

This well-known restaurant, which opened in 1957 and is famed for its fine cuisine, overlooks the bay south of Aïn Diab.

The walls of the *Hyatt Regency Hotel's* piano-bar are hung with memorabilia of *Casablanca*,

directed by Michael Curtiz in 1942. The film put Casablanca on the map, even though it was shot entirely in a studio!

A bar in the Mers Sultan district still bears the name of the Casablancan boxer, Marcel Cerdan, who won the 1948

world championship in the United States.

PLACE MOHAMMED V
The pedestrian subway beneath the Place Mohammed V is surmounted by a cupola designed by the architect Zevaco.

THE CITY CENTER

PLACE MOHAMMED V. The Place Mohammed V, around which run Casablanca's main streets, links the old town and the new. The square was built at the turn of the century and then redesigned and extended in the 1950's to accommodate the traffic flow between east and west sections of the city. The black and red bulk of the *Hyatt Regency Hotel* incongruously standing out from the white facades of the residential blocks is explained away as "a black beauty spot on the pale skin of a woman's face." To the right of the hotel and next to the Bab Jedid (the south gate of the medina) stand the TOUR DE L'HORLOGE (clocktower), a "secular minaret" built in 1910 by the French army officer Dessigny as a symbol of colonial time and order. It was demolished in 1940 and replaced by an exact replica in 1992. Opposite the clocktower is the 1920's *Excelsior Hotel.*

BOULEVARD MOHAMMED V. Residential blocks dating from the 1930's line this busy shopping street. Numbers 3, 40, 67, 73 and 97 are a charming combination of European and Oriental architectural styles. Halfway along the boulevard is the *Brasserie du Petit Poucet*, a fashionable gathering place in the 1920's. Illustrated letters from the French writer Antoine de Saint-Exupéry, congratulating the owner on the high standard of his establishment, still hang on the walls. The most eye-catching façade is that of no. 208. The colorful *zellige* ▲ *173* with which it is faced mark the contribution that Moroccan craftsmen made to the construction of buildings designed by French architects. Casablanca's main market, which takes place every morning along the boulevard, offers a wealth of the finest Moroccan produce from the agricultural regions of Fez ▲ *213*, Meknès ▲ *232*, the Gharb ▲ *212* and the Doukkala ▲ *148*.

The Rue Colbert, next to the market, leads into the AVENUE DES FORCES-ARMÉES-ROYALES, where Casablanca's banks, travel agents and luxury hotels are concentrated.

PLACE DES NATIONS-UNIES (United Nations Square). This square, designed in 1920 by the French architect Joseph Marrast, is the city's administrative center. The CONSULAT DE FRANCE (French consulate), with a statue of General Lyautey ● *164* in its main courtyard, stands between the WILAYA (prefecture) and the former Palais de Justice (lawcourts), built in 1925. The 1930's tower next to the prefecture has a siren that sounds every evening during Ramadan ▲ *339* to announce the end of the fast. This 200-foot tower commands a splendid view over the city and port. At weekends a *son et lumière* display takes place in the square, in which the cascades of the huge circular FOUNTAIN are illuminated to the sound of music.

PARC DE LA LIGUE ARABE (League of Arab States Park). The park, through which runs a long vista of palm trees, was opened in 1918. It is a huge expanse of greenery, with arcades, pergolas and shady terraces with cafés, that invite the visitor to stop and relax. Among gardens to the north of the park stands the former CATHEDRAL OF THE SACRÉ COEUR. It

Details of the Moresque-style friezes in the courtyard of the *wilaya* (prefecture).

François Cogné's equestrian statue of General Lyautey, Morocco's first resident French general, unveiled in 1933. It stands in the courtyard of the French consulate as a monument to Lyautey's influence on the history of modern Morocco.

COPPER AND BRASS
The copper and brass souk of the Quartier Habbous (the district of religious leaders) whose craftsmen produce hammered metalware. One of their specialties are round trays that can be mounted on three-legged stands and used as tables for celebration meals. Teapots, cooking pots, candlesticks, vases and hanging lamps are among the many household articles and cooking utensils that they make for sale both to local people and for the tourist trade.

was built in 1930, subsequently deconsecrated and converted first into a warehouse and then into a concert hall. Today it is a theater.

NOTRE-DAME-DE-LOURDES. The church Our Lady of Lourdes, built in concrete in the mid-1950's, stands at the entrance to the Quartier Habbous. Its stained-glass windows, covering a total area of 8,600 square feet, are the work of Gabriel Loire, a master glazier from Chartres. Scenes depicting the Immaculate Conception and the apparitions of the Virgin Mary, especially at Lourdes, are set against a background of blues and reds that evoke the colors of Moroccan carpets.

▲ CASABLANCA

All the major foreign-language newspapers are sold in Casablanca's many kiosks.

THE NEW MEDINA

The new medina ● *92*, still known as the Quartier Habbous, lies in the south of Casablanca behind the royal palace and the Boulevard Victor Hugo. It was built in 1923 by French town planners to accommodate the influx of people from rural areas who had settled in the southern outskirts of the city. With its small squares and narrow, arcaded streets it is a fine example of the successful adaptation of modern town planning to the traditional rôle of the medina.

MAHAKMA DU PACHA ★ (Pasha's courthouse). Building on this marble, stone and wooden edifice started in 1948 and ended in 1952. With no fewer than sixty rooms, it was simultaneously a Muslim lawcourt and the pasha (governor) of Casablanca's reception hall. Today it is used as an administrative building. In his book *Casablanca* (1985) Jean-Michel Zurfluh claims that the Pasha's courthouse embodies every conceivable architectural feature and decorative motif in Hispano-Moresque art.

THE OLD MEDINA

Little of the old Muslim town remains. It was partially destroyed in the earthquake of 1755 and in 1770 the sultan Sidi Mohammed Ben Abdullah began to rebuild it. The old medina was originally surrounded by ramparts stretching as far as the old El Kebir souk, and parts of these can still be seen near the Place Mohammed V. Arab-Islamic and western-style buildings were built in the old medina in the 19th century.

THE PORT. Centre 2000, a shopping area with restaurants and shops selling luxury goods, stands at the entrance to the port of Casablanca, the city's economic center, where the day's business starts early with a large auction. Built almost entirely by the French at the turn of the century, the port complex covers an area of 445 acres and is protected from the Atlantic by the 10,450-foot Moulay Youssef pier. It has several docks, shipyards, a marina, a rail terminal and a dock for cruise ships. The export of phosphates and import of metallurgical products, hydrocarbons and timber are two of its main activities. Between them Casablanca and the port of Mohammedia ▲ *145* handle around 70 percent of Morocco's maritime traffic.

THE "KOUBBA" OF SIDI BEYLIOUT. Overlooking a small cemetery to the north of the old medina is the late 19th-century *koubba* (shrine) ● *63* of the marabout Sidi Beyliout,

"AROUND THE DAR EL MAKHZEN, THE MEDINA, THE QUARTER OF THE MUSLIM BOURGEOISIE, EUROPEAN CONSULATES AND THEIR REPRESENTATIVES AND WEALTHY JEWISH FAMILIES."

WEISGERBER

patron saint of Casablanca. Reputedly disillusioned by the shortcomings of the human race, Sidi Beyliout is said to have put out his own eyes and gone to live among the wild beasts of the forest. When he died, so the story goes, the animals stood guard over his body until he was buried. He became known as Abou Louyout (Father of the Lions). Next to the shrine is a fountain said to have magical powers; anyone who drinks from it will one day return to Casablanca.

Shrine of Sidi Kairouani.

THE "SKALA". The old cannons of the *Skala*, an 18th-century fortification opposite the fishing port, still point out to sea. This is one of the few remains surviving from the reign of Sidi Mohammed Ben Abdullah. There is a splendid view of the Atlantic Ocean from the terrace.

INDUSTRY IN CASABLANCA
Sixty percent of Morocco's industry (including the most advanced) is concentrated in Casablanca.

THE SHRINE OF SIDI KAIROUANI. The mortal remains of Casablanca's first patron, Sidi Allal el Kairouani, and his daughter Lalla Beida are enshrined in tombs on the Rue de Tnaker. According to a 14th-century legend, Sidi Allal el Kairouani set sail from Kairouan for Senegal but his ship sank off the coast of

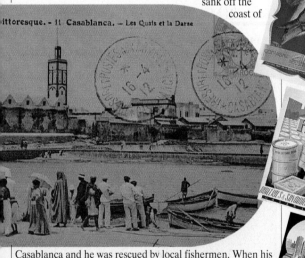

ittoresque. - 11 Casablanca. - Les Quais et la Darse

Casablanca and he was rescued by local fishermen. When his wife died he sent for his only daughter, Lalla Beida, but she was drowned when her ship sank on the journey to Casablanca. Sidi Allal buried her facing the sea and asked to be interred beside her. The shrine was called Dar el Beida (House of the White Princess) in memory of Lalla Beida, who was famous for her pale skin.

THE "KOUBBA" OF SIDI BOU SMARA. In the center of a quiet little square in the western district of the old medina, in the shade of an old banyan tree ■ *44* with a great tracery of aerial roots, stands the *koubba* of Sidi Bou Smara. In the 10th century Sidi Bou Smara (Man of the Nails) was passing through the town and asked for water to perform his ritual ablutions. There was a terrible drought at the time and the only reply he received was a hail of stones and insults. He struck the ground with his pilgrim's staff and a spring

143

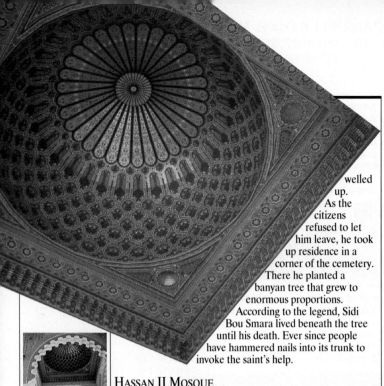

welled up. As the citizens refused to let him leave, he took up residence in a corner of the cemetery. There he planted a banyan tree that grew to enormous proportions. According to the legend, Sidi Bou Smara lived beneath the tree until his death. Ever since people have hammered nails into its trunk to invoke the saint's help.

HASSAN II MOSQUE

AN AMBITIOUS PROJECT. King Hassan II wanted to build a mosque at the most westerly point in the Muslim world. He was assured that this great building would, symbolically speaking, be the North African equivalent of the Statue of Liberty. In 1980 work began on the Hassan II Mosque, which was built right on the sea on the site of the former municipal swimming pool (1934) south of the city. The work was financed largely by national subscription. A laser beam visible up to 22 miles away shines from the top of the 650-foot minaret, indicating the direction of Mecca. The entire structure, which covers a total area of 24,000 square yards, is

The walls of the Hassan II Mosque, designed by the French architect Michel Pinseau, are covered with finely sculpted plasterwork and *zellige* ▲ *173*. The building has granite pillars supporting capitals and arches decorated with *muqarna* (stalactites) and also several carved cedarwood cupolas. Around five thousand women can be accommodated in an upper prayer hall, hidden from public view by moucharabieh work ● *96*, ▲ *165*.

designed on a gigantic scale. The prayer hall accommodates 25,000 worshippers, with space for a further 80,000 pilgrims to pray on the esplanade. A cultural center, with a library, museum and Koranic schools, adjoins the main building. The mosque was opened to the public in 1994, and is to be followed by an extensive program of urban development in which whole areas in the immediate vicinity of the mosque will be demolished and wide access roads constructed.

THE CORNICHE ★

From the El Hank lighthouse northward, the BOULEVARD DE LA CORNICHE is bordered by an uninterrupted sweep of beaches, swimming pools, cafés, hotels and restaurants. Casablancans come here to take an evening stroll, have a drink and breathe the sea air.

Overlooking the sea, THE FONDATION SAOUDIENNE IBN SEOUD (Ibn Saud Saudi Foundation), built in 1985, comprises a mosque, a center for higher education and an ultra-modern library. At the far end of the corniche near the resort of Aïn Diab are the Casablanca health clinic and the SINBAD AMUSEMENT PARK.

THE MARABOUT OF SIDI ABD ER RAHMAN. People suffering from psychological problems or nervous disorders often visit this shrine. It consists of a group of whitewashed tombs perched in a striking position on a rocky promontory that can only be reached at low tide. Every year a large number of pilgrims come to bathe and spend the night there.

ANFA. Some of the most luxurious villas in Casablanca are found behind the corniche, in the residential district of Anfa. It was in one of these hilltop houses in 1943, that Churchill and Roosevelt met to plan the Allied landings in Normandy and Sicily. Although the Spanish secret service had been informed of a possible meeting in "Casa Blanca", they were unable to prevent it taking place because they were under the impression that it was to be held in the White House in Washington, DC.

MOHAMMEDIA

The town of Mohammedia (formerly Fedala) lies between Rabat and Casablanca. It was renamed by Mohammed V on June 25, 1960. The port of this small commercial center was developed in the 18th century during the reign of the sultan Sidi Mohammed Ben Abdullah. It was not until the 1930's that it began to specialize in petroleum and became known as an oil port but today it is Morocco's second-largest industrial town. Tourists can enjoy Mohammedia's beaches, one of the most dynamic yacht clubs in the country, and its lively casino and well laid-out golf course.

EL HANK LIGHTHOUSE
Sea swell and a great sandbank once made access to the port of Casablanca extremely dangerous. To help ships negotiate these obstacles, the French built the El Hank lighthouse in 1905, on the rocky headland to the west of Casablanca.

SINBAD AMUSEMENT PARK
Carousels, dodgems, slides and pedalos are some of the park's many amusements.

JAMAA ERRADOUANE
Erradouane Mosque and its

minaret, in the Rue Changuitte, has stood as a central landmark in Mohammedia since it opened in 1991. A square with white marble paving leads up to a triple-arched entrance.

▲ CASABLANCA TO BENI MELLAL

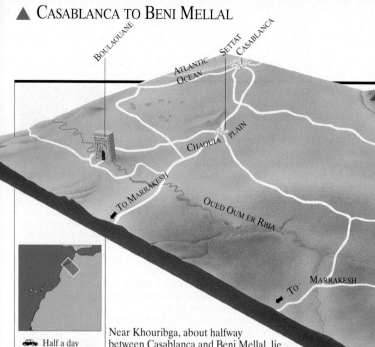

BOULAOUANE
SETTAT
CASABLANCA
ATLANTIC OCEAN
CHAOUIA PLAIN
TO MARRAKESH
OUED OUM ER RBIA
TO MARRAKESH

🚗 Half a day

"One of the most gifted examples of a successful blend of dual identity, inherited from his Berber mother and his Muslim Arab father [...] but also of Maghribi art and western painting.**"**

Cherkaoui drew on his dual heritage: his mother's body tattoos and the writing of his father's holy scriptures.**"**
Pierre Gaudibert,
La Nouvelle Critique

Near Khouribga, about halfway between Casablanca and Beni Mellal, lie the world's richest phosphate deposits, which yield 65 percent of Morocco's phosphate production. The road crosses the Tadla region, a fertile plain to the north of Beni Mellal ▲ *306*.

BOUJAD

Before Morocco became a French protectorate, this small town was a provincial capital. It is built around the holy city founded in the 16th century by Sidi Mohammed ech Chergui, patron of the Tadla region. One of the *zaouia* ▲ *199* destroyed during the 18th century was rebuilt during the 19th, and is today inhabited by the descendants of the saint. The *baraka* (good fortune) of their holy ancestor is said to have been passed down from one generation to the next. Brightly colored, striped woolen *bizaras* (blankets) are a specialty of the region. One of Morocco's best-known modern painters, Ahmed Cherkaoui, was born in Boujad.

SETTAT

Sultans traveling from Fez ▲ *213* to Marrakesh ▲ *259*, and wanting to avoid the reputedly dangerous Middle Atlas, used to break their journey in the town of Settat. At the entrance to the walled town stands the kasbah built by Moulay Ismaïl ▲ *233* in the 17th century. Settat is now the economic capital of the Chaouia plain, a rich, fertile region known as the "granary of Morocco", which accounts for 15 percent of the country's cereal harvest. Some farmers specialize in intensive cattle and sheep breeding ■ *50*. Textile, chemical and agricultural foodstuff industries have also grown up around Settat.

146

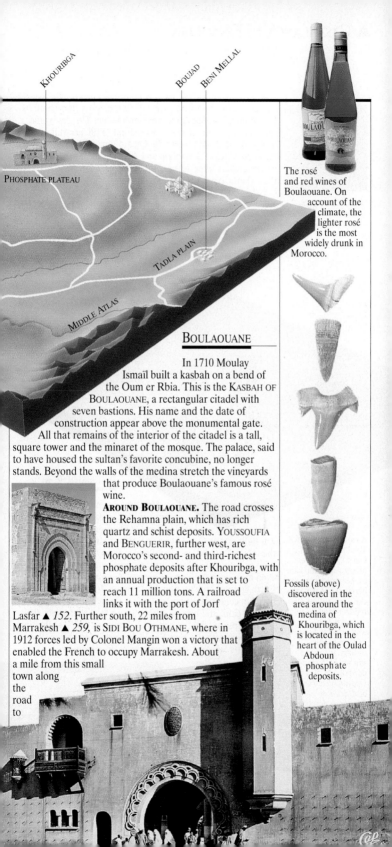

KHOURIBGA   BOUJAD   BENI MELLAL

PHOSPHATE PLATEAU

MIDDLE ATLAS

TADLA PLAIN

The rosé and red wines of Boulaouane. On account of the climate, the lighter rosé is the most widely drunk in Morocco.

BOULAOUANE

In 1710 Moulay Ismaïl built a kasbah on a bend of the Oum er Rbia. This is the KASBAH OF BOULAOUANE, a rectangular citadel with seven bastions. His name and the date of construction appear above the monumental gate. All that remains of the interior of the citadel is a tall, square tower and the minaret of the mosque. The palace, said to have housed the sultan's favorite concubine, no longer stands. Beyond the walls of the medina stretch the vineyards that produce Boulaouane's famous rosé wine.

AROUND BOULAOUANE. The road crosses the Rehamna plain, which has rich quartz and schist deposits. YOUSSOUFIA and BENGUERIR, further west, are Morocco's second- and third-richest phosphate deposits after Khouribga, with an annual production that is set to reach 11 million tons. A railroad links it with the port of Jorf Lasfar ▲ 152. Further south, 22 miles from Marrakesh ▲ 259, is SIDI BOU OTHMANE, where in 1912 forces led by Colonel Mangin won a victory that enabled the French to occupy Marrakesh. About a mile from this small town along the road to

Fossils (above) discovered in the area around the medina of Khouribga, which is located in the heart of the Oulad Abdoun phosphate deposits.

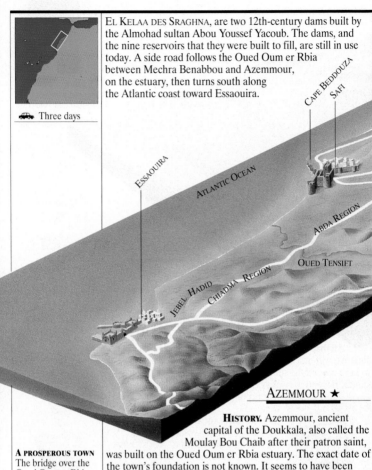

Three days

EL KELAA DES SRAGHNA, are two 12th-century dams built by the Almohad sultan Abou Youssef Yacoub. The dams, and the nine reservoirs that they were built to fill, are still in use today. A side road follows the Oued Oum er Rbia between Mechra Benabbou and Azemmour, on the estuary, then turns south along the Atlantic coast toward Essaouira.

CAPE BEDDOUZA
SAFI
ESSAOUIRA
ATLANTIC OCEAN
ABDA REGION
OUED TENSIFT
JEBEL HADID
CHIADMA REGION

AZEMMOUR ★

HISTORY. Azemmour, ancient capital of the Doukkala, also called the Moulay Bou Chaib after their patron saint, was built on the Oued Oum er Rbia estuary. The exact date of the town's foundation is not known. It seems to have been used as a port of call by Carthaginian navigators and may even have been the ancient town of Azama frequented by the Carthaginians and later by the Romans. Toward the end of the 15th century Portuguese traders flocked there to buy cereals, cloth and horses. After various failed attempts, they finally captured the town in 1513. The port, which at the time was trading with the New World, became even busier. Twenty-eight years later the Portuguese were driven out of

A PROSPEROUS TOWN
The bridge over the Oued Oum er Rbia offers a splendid view of Azemmour, a town perched in a striking clifftop position. Its reddish-brown ramparts and whitewashed houses look on to the estuary, whose waters run red with alluvial deposits. In his *Geographical History of Africa* Leo Africanus noted that shad fishing took place between October and the end of April and that Portuguese merchants came to Azemmour once a year to buy vast quantities of this abundant fish.

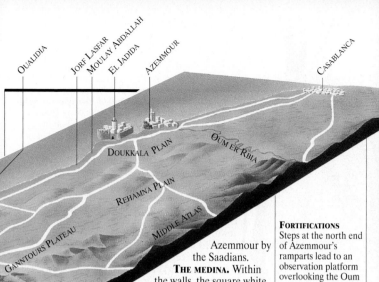

DOUKKALA PLAIN

OUM ER RBIA

REHAMNA PLAIN

MIDDLE ATLAS

GANNTOURS PLATEAU

Azemmour by the Saadians.

THE MEDINA. Within the walls, the square white houses covered with dark-red bougainvillea rise in terraces among olive ■ *44* and pomegranate trees. The carved keyhole arches of the doorways betray a strong Portuguese influence. The inner ramparts of the kasbah ● *94* and the bastions (complete with cannons) date from the 16th century.

SHAD. Shad fishing was once widespread, the spring floods of the Oum er Rbia making the fish easier to catch as they made their way upstream to spawn. Since a dam was built on the Oum er Rbia in 1920, their numbers have dwindled.

EL JADIDA

El Jadida, whose ramparts ● *102* follow the line of the famous Sidi Bouzid beach, was built on the shores of the Atlantic by the Portuguese. It was considered to be the most protected site along the entire western coast of Morocco and could have become the country's largest port had the development of nearby Casablanca ▲ *135* and Safi ▲ *153* not thwarted its expansion.

FORTIFICATIONS
Steps at the north end of Azemmour's ramparts lead to an observation platform overlooking the Oum er Rbia and the rampart walk.

"Standing overlooking the town of Azemmour, the mouth of the Oum er-Bia and the Atlantic, Hineb watched the shimmering waters of the river."

Driss Chraïbi,
The Mother of Spring

DAR EL BAROUD
A huge tower stands over the ruins of this powder magazine, built into the ramparts of Azemmour between the kasbah in the north and the medina in the south.

149

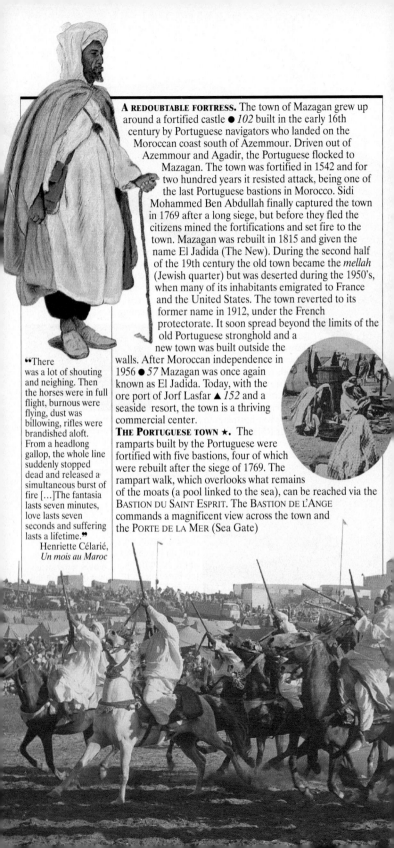

A REDOUBTABLE FORTRESS. The town of Mazagan grew up around a fortified castle ● *102* built in the early 16th century by Portuguese navigators who landed on the Moroccan coast south of Azemmour. Driven out of Azemmour and Agadir, the Portuguese flocked to Mazagan. The town was fortified in 1542 and for two hundred years it resisted attack, being one of the last Portuguese bastions in Morocco. Sidi Mohammed Ben Abdullah finally captured the town in 1769 after a long siege, but before they fled the citizens mined the fortifications and set fire to the town. Mazagan was rebuilt in 1815 and given the name El Jadida (The New). During the second half of the 19th century the old town became the *mellah* (Jewish quarter) but was deserted during the 1950's, when many of its inhabitants emigrated to France and the United States. The town reverted to its former name in 1912, under the French protectorate. It soon spread beyond the limits of the old Portuguese stronghold and a new town was built outside the walls. After Moroccan independence in 1956 ● *57* Mazagan was once again known as El Jadida. Today, with the ore port of Jorf Lasfar ▲ *152* and a seaside resort, the town is a thriving commercial center.

THE PORTUGUESE TOWN ★. The ramparts built by the Portuguese were fortified with five bastions, four of which were rebuilt after the siege of 1769. The rampart walk, which overlooks what remains of the moats (a pool linked to the sea), can be reached via the BASTION DU SAINT ESPRIT. The BASTION DE L'ANGE commands a magnificent view across the town and the PORTE DE LA MER (Sea Gate)

❝There was a lot of shouting and neighing. Then the horses were in full flight, burnous were flying, dust was billowing, rifles were brandished aloft. From a headlong gallop, the whole line suddenly stopped dead and released a simultaneous burst of fire […]The fantasia lasts seven minutes, love lasts seven seconds and suffering lasts a lifetime.❞

Henriette Célarié,
Un mois au Maroc

through which the Portuguese fled in 1769. The BASTIONS DE
SAINT ANTOINE and SAINT SÉBASTIEN defended the southern
part of the town. Within the walls are the former Portuguese
residences, with pilasters and wrought-iron balconies. The
minaret of the mosque standing next to the deconsecrated
Church of OUR LADY OF THE
ASSUMPTION was built on the ruins of a
pentagonal watchtower. It is probably the
only five-sided minaret in the Islamic
world.

PORTUGUESE CISTERN
It was used in the
filming of *Othello*
(1951), *A Black Stal-
lion Returns* (1983)
and *Harem* (1985).

THE PORTUGUESE RESERVOIR ● *102* ★.
This crypt-like structure, in unexpectedly
Gothic style, was built by the Portuguese
in 1514 at the same time as the castle. It
was originally used as a magazine before
being converted into a reservoir in 1542.
Lying beneath the ruins of the old town, it was forgotten for
150 years until it was rediscovered, by chance, in 1916 during
extension work on a local grocer's shop. Workmen discovered
the great 1,315-square-yard underground reservoir half-full of
water and lit by a central well shaft.

MOULAY ABDALLAH

Near the fishing village of Moulay Abdallah are the remains
of the 12th-century *ribat* (fortified monastery) that formed
part of the ancient town of Tit. With the arrival of the
Portuguese in the 15th century, the site was abandoned and
remained uninhabited until the fishing village was founded.
In August, up to 200,000 people come to the *moussem*
(religious festival) ▲ *339* in Moulay Abdallah. Around
15,000 horses take part in parades and fantasias ● *73* and
the best horsemen in Morocco come together in a
magnificent display of harness, trapping and costumes.

THE MINARET OF TIT
The minaret inside
the walls of the
ancient town of Tit
was built at the same
period as the
Koutoubia minaret ▲
268. On one of its
façades a square
architrave is pierced
by two gemel
windows decorated
with multifoil arches.

Jorf Lasfar

Once a tiny lobster port, Jorf Lasfar (Yellow Rock) is now Africa's main exporter of phosphates. It has a direct rail link with the phosphate mines lying 87 miles to the south on the Ganntours Plateau and handles 17½ million tons of raw phosphates per year. Morocco has 75 percent of the planet's phosphate reserves and is the world's leading exporter of phosphates. Since 1975 manufacturers have moved into the artificial fertilizer industry. The port's administration center is based in the industrial zone that has developed around the docks.

JORF LASFAR Raw materials for the petrochemical industries that have grown up around the port of Jorf Lasfar are delivered by sea. An industrial complex specializing in the processing of phosphates has been built near the quays where ore carriers dock. Artificial fertilizer is produced for export at Jorf Lasfar.

Oualidia ★

The coast road between Jorf Lasfar and Oualidia runs along salt marshes, oyster beds and agricultural land on which acres of early fruit and vegetables are grown each year. Oualidia, which overlooks a roadway, was founded by the Saadian sultan El Oualid, who gave the town its name. In 1634 he built a kasbah to defend the entrance to the harbor. As well as being a popular seaside resort, modern Oualidia is famous for its oyster farms, which were developed during the 1950's.

Cape Beddouza

Cape Beddouza is thought to be the ancient Cape Soloeis where the Carthaginian scholar and navigator Hanno erected a shrine to Poseidon in the 5th century BC. Carthaginian ships are said to have sailed around this rocky headland and run aground on neighboring beaches under the cliffs. Stones found here that were carved with the symbol of Tanit bear witness to the presence of Carthaginian sailors.

Sidi Bouzid

OYSTER FARMING Portuguese and, more recently, Japanese oysters are farmed in the sheltered oyster beds of Oualidia.

The 500-foot cliff of Sidi Bouzid offers a magnificent view across the town of Safi and the area of the surrounding coast. The salt marshes stretch away in a northerly direction, their eye-catching pools varying in color from yellow to orange and light brown. On November 8, 1942, part of the Allied fleet under the command of General Patton made a successful landing at Sidi Bouzid. The former French position, which offered very little resistance when attacked by Patton's forces, is today inhabited by shepherds.

SAFI

A THRIVING PORT. The first recorded reference
to Asfi, the modern town of Safi, was made by the
11th-century geographer El Bekri. In 1481 the Portuguese
established a trading center at the entrance to the harbor,
where they acted as brokers ● 55. In 1508 they took
advantage of internal conflict to seize the town, which
they subsequently fortified. Later they built a
fortress in a position nearby on the Atlantic
coast. The Portuguese were driven out of
Safi by the Saadians in 1541. Toward the
end of the 16th century and throughout
the 17th, trade with Europe continued
to expand and Safi became Morocco's
leading port. The thriving port's
activity was further boosted in the
20th century by the development
of a sardine fishing industry and
the construction of a
phosphate-processing
plant.

DAR EL BAHR (Castle of the
Sea)**.** The fortress was built
by the Portuguese during
the 16th century to defend
the north entrance to the old
port. The platform of this square
fortress, measuring 65 yards a side, still has its old
17th-century cannons, some of which were cast in Spain and
others imported from Rotterdam, The Hague, France and
Portugal.

The Dar el
Bahr (Castle
of the Sea) was the
official residence of
governors and sultans.

THE MEDINA. Running from the Place de l'Indépendance
(occupied by street traders in the morning and public
entertainers in the evening) to the BAB CHABA (Valley Gate)
the Rue du Souk passes through the heart of the medina ● 92.
The entire length of this street, the busiest in this former
Portuguese town, is lined with the stalls and workshops of
local traders and craftsmen displaying all kinds of goods made
using traditional skills. To the south of the medina, behind the
Great Mosque, is the Portuguese chapel, built in 1519 in the
choir of the cathedral. To the east of the ramparts the
KECHLA, a 16th-century Portuguese stronghold, overlooks the
roofs of the medina. Its monumental gate opens onto a
mechouar (assembly area), a palace and a private chapel.
During the 18th century a mosque and a garden were added
to the Kechla. The Muslim cemetery, with its immaculately
kept tombs, is situated on the coast road and extends along
the Atlantic coast above the Dar el Bahr.

**THE PORTUGUESE
CHAPEL**
The chapel bears the
carved insignia of the
Holy See and various
royal coats of arms,
including those of
Portuguese
sovereigns.

SAFI, MOROCCO'S LEADING SARDINE PORT
Sardine fishing led to the development of a local canning industry that, during the 1920's, created many seasonal jobs. Today a freezer chain regulates supplies to factories and helps provide continuous employment for the (mainly female) local workforce.

SARDINE FISHING. The Moroccan sardine fleet comprises some five hundred vessels, which ply the Atlantic coast. These 50- to 60-foot wooden boats and trawlers are made in the shipyards of Safi, Essaouira ▲ *156* and Agadir ▲ *309* and are based mainly in the port of Safi. The sardine shoals tend to be distributed in three main areas. The first, known as the Saharan stock, accounting for around 716,000 tons, is located to the south of CAPE BOUJDOUR ▲ *328*. The second and largest stock, estimated at around 882,000 tons, occurs between Safi and Larache. The third, near Tangier, further

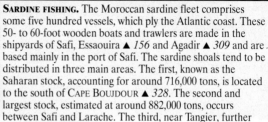

north, is estimated at around 13,000 tons. In spring the sardines belonging to the Saharan stock migrate northward toward Tan Tan ▲ *327*, Agadir and Safi. The largest summer catches are therefore made along the coast between Boujdour and Safi. Morocco's coastal fishing fleet catches an estimated 330,000 tons of sardines every year.

THE CANNING INDUSTRY. Almost half of Morocco's sixty-odd food-canning plants are in Safi and 75 percent of their production is given over to sardines. Around 90 percent of Morocco's canned food production is exported, 50 percent going to EC countries. There are also around twenty plants in Safi, Essaouira and Agadir that process the by-products of the fishing industry to extract such commodities as flour and fish oil.

THE POTTERS' QUARTER. Because they are a fire hazard, the potters' workshops ● *80* are located outside the old town, crowding together close to the north walls. The pottery trade, which has the advantage of an exceptionally high-quality local clay, was revitalized in 1875 when a Fasi potter, Mohammed Langassi, set up the first earthenware workshop. In 1923 he reintroduced polychrome decoration, which had been abandoned during the 19th

century in favor of the characteristic blue and white of Fez pottery. Today Safi pottery has an international reputation and produces a wide range of items thrown on the wheel as well as traditional tiles, which are very much in demand on

SAFI POTTERY
There are various theories about the origins of Safi pottery, which is essentially a skillfully executed variant of Fasi pottery. It was the nature of the local clay, which is very chalky and rich in iron oxide, that led Safi potters to use polychrome decoration.

the home market. The potters of Safi have formed a cooperative that has set up a teaching center and opened a gallery where the potters' work is exhibited for sale.

The "Ra". In the 1960's Thor Heyerdahl and his crew set sail from Safi aboard the *Ra* in their bid to prove that African navigators could have sailed across the Atlantic to America 4,500 years ago. The raft was built of reeds, papyrus and bamboo in the style of the *madias*, the traditional craft still used in Morocco at the turn of the century. The *Ra*, driven by strong Canary currents, took fifty-seven days to reach Barbados, in the West Indies.

The Chiadma region

A minor coast road runs southward from Safi for about 20 miles to Souira Kèdima (Old Walled Place), where the restored ruins of a *ribat*, built by the Portuguese in 1525, are open to the public. Some six miles further south, after fording the Oued Tensift, the road passes the ruins of the Kasbah of Hamidouch, built by Moulay Ismaïl in the 18th century. This former fortress, surrounded by a wall measuring 500 feet each side and set with towers, had the function of controlling the regions of Abda to the north and the Chiadma to the south.

The Regraga. The road crosses the Chiadma region in which Jebel Hadid (Iron Mountain) is the central landmark. In spring the Regraga, Berber inhabitants of the region, hold major celebrations to commemorate the arrival of Islam ● *62* in Morocco. According to popular legend, when Mohammed began to preach the doctrine of Islam, seven of the Regraga tribe traveled to Mecca and, entering a prayer hall where the Prophet happened to be, asked a group of worshippers in Berber which one of them was the messenger of God. Miraculously, Mohammed is said to have answered them in their own language, telling them who he was and inviting them to follow him. They adopted the new religion and returned to Morocco to convert their fellow tribesmen. They are believed to be the first to bring the new teaching of Islam to the Maghreb. Today these "disciples" are known as the *Sebaatou Rijal* (The Seven Men). Their *moussem* ▲ *339* centers around their seven marabouts and is marked in villages throughout the region by celebrations lasting forty-four days.

> ❝'Since I, a Berber, am to baptize the boat, I think goat's milk would be most suitable,' she said, showing my wife, Yvonne, the white contents of the pitcher. 'Goat's milk is Morocco's ancient symbol of hospitality and good wishes!' The harbour was packed with colourful throngs of people. Our golden boat was decked out festively, with the flags of all the participant countries fluttering in the wind. Aïcha smashed the fine pitcher into a thousand fragments against the wooden cradle, so that goat's milk and potsherds sprayed over papyrus and distinguished guests alike. 'I name you Ra in honour of the sun-god!'❞
>
> Thor Heyerdahl, *The Ra Expeditions*

A second defensive wall was built inside the ramparts of the Kasbah of Hamidouch.

▲ ESSAOUIRA

In Essaouira's shipyards, trawlers are built by traditional methods, using teak and eucalyptus.

Murex, the mollusk that secretes a purple dye.

❝I know of only one castle in which I would care to be locked up. Better to die than surrender the keys. And that is Mogador in Africa.❞
Paul Claudel,
Le Soulier de satin

THE 1844 BOMBARDMENT
On August 15, 1844, while the Battle of the Oued Isli was being fought on Morocco's border with Algeria, a unit of soldiers five hundred strong led by the Prince de Joinville attacked Essaouira. Many of the citizens fled the violence of the bombardment and the Moroccan forces surrendered. According to Abd el Kader Mana, author of *Essaouira*, the sultan was so enraged that he ordered the beards of a group of *kaids* serving in the army to be shaved off by way of reprisal.

The town of Essaouira stands on a peninsula that is permanently swept by the trade winds. Its year-round temperate climate made it popular with navigators in classical antiquity, who would pause there on their journey up and down the Moroccan coast. The Phoenicians also called there in the 8th century BC. A piece of pottery signed with the name of the Carthaginian general Mago and found on the island of Essaouira proves the presence of the Carthaginians in c. 630 BC.

PURPLE DYE AND SUGAR. During the 1st century AD the islands of Essaouira were renowned throughout the Roman Empire for the manufacture of purple dye. In the 10th century Essaouira was named AMOGDOUL (The Well-Guarded) after its Berber patron Sidi Mogdoul, who is buried about two miles outside the town. All merchandise from the Sous region and southern Morocco once passed through Amogdoul. In the 15th century it became a Portuguese trading center ● *54*

and assumed the name Mogdoura, which was subsequently changed to Mogadour by the Spanish and finally to Mogador by the French. In 1506 King Manuel of Portugal built a fort ● *102* at the entrance to the port to defend the town, and some of the ruins can still be seen today. During the 16th century a major influx of Portuguese immigrants settled in Essaouira and were responsible for the intensive cultivation of sugar-cane in the region.

FROM MOGADOR TO ESSAOUIRA. In 1764 the Alouite sultan Sidi Mohammed Ben Abdullah decided to use the port of Mogador as a naval base. He wanted to punish the citizens of Agadir ▲ *309*, who had openly revolted against the authorities and were also monopolizing European trade. To ensure the success of his plan he had Théodore Cornut, a captive French engineer, produce a plan for a new town. It was built on a grid system of broad streets and was

Sardine and anchovy trawlers unloading their catch in the port of Essaouira.

surrounded by ramparts similar to those designed for Saint-Malo by Vauban ● *94*. Mogador was given the new Arabic name ESSAOUIRA (Image) or Es Saouira (Fortified Place), which was more in keeping with Cornut's plan, and which it has kept to the present day.

A COSMOPOLITAN TOWN. To populate his town Sidi Mohammed ordered the European consuls of Salé ▲ *175* and Agadir ▲ *309* to move to Essaouira. He also sent for the wealthiest families in the kingdom, the *tujjar el sultan* (royal merchants), and for a long time the town had a large Jewish population. Many of the sultans are said to have been spellbound by the beauty and intelligence of the women of Essaouira and several were kidnapped, "converted" to Islam and taken to the harems of Fez ▲ *213*. Through the centuries tribes from the various groups that make up the modern population of Morocco have been drawn together in Essaouira. The Haha, a Berber-speaking tribe from the south, lived alongside the Arabic-speaking Chiadma ▲ *155* from the north and the Gnaoua, the descendants of African slaves from the Sudan, Senegal and Guinea, who worked on the sugar-cane plantations and in the sugar factories of the Oued Ksob.

TRADE. In 1780 around a dozen businesses employed about a thousand Europeans and Essaouira handled 40 percent of Morocco's maritime trade. A century later, the ports of Casablanca ▲ *135* and Agadir ▲ *309* were developed under the French protectorate and trade in Essaouira suffered as a result, even though the modern town was built outside the ramparts at about this time.

ESSAOUIRA ON FOOT

The best way to see Essaouira, the blue and white town, is on foot. Inside the 18th-century ramparts interesting architectural features include gates ● *94* and windows with intricately carved decoration.

THE PORT AND RAMPARTS ★. The port of Essaouira is situated at the foot of the town's ramparts and at the end of a beautiful long sandy beach. With its gaily painted fishing boats and brightly colored nets piled up on the quayside, it is a bustling and attractive place. Trawlers are built there following the traditional style of sturdy, ancient dhows. Fish and shellfish are auctioned every

In 1949 Orson Welles chose the imposing battlements of Essaouira as the setting for the outside shots of *Othello*, the film of the Shakespearean tragedy. In his book *Orson Welles* André Bazin says that the battlements of Mogador provided the framework for an imaginary dramatic architecture that Welles endowed with all the grandeur and beauty of real, natural stone, worn by centuries of wind and sun.

❝When you walk along the ramparts of the *Skala* and look out over the town, and the unique union of town and Ocean, do not try to understand the mystery.❞
Edmond Amram el-Maaleh, *Essaouira l'oubliée*

157

▲ ESSAOUIRA

A FORTIFIED TOWN
As part of Essaouira's defenses Sidi Mohammed Ben Abdullah placed batteries of cannons at strategic points around the bay and built a circular fort, the Borj el Bermil, at the entrance to the port. During the same period the Borj el Assa (Surveillance Fort) was built on the island of Mogador and the Borj el Baroud (Powder Fort) at the south end of the bay of Essaouira, on the Oued Ksob estuary. It was thus possible to drive an enemy back with carefully aimed crossfire. These fortifications also defended the town from attack by insurgent tribes on the landward side.

morning. The PORTE DE LA MARINE was built in the reign of Sidi Mohammed Ben Abdullah to give access between the port and the town. The date of its construction, 1184 of the *Hegira* (1769 in the Gregorian calendar) is carved on the pediment. A little bridge links the Porte de la Marine with the SKALA ● *102* and the ramparts that divide the town into several districts: two kasbahs, a *mellah* and a medina ● *92*.

THE MEDINA ★

From the PLACE MOULAY EL HASSAN, in which Moroccan and Portuguese architectural styles are combined, narrow shopping streets run past the CLOCKTOWER and the GREAT MOSQUE and into the square of the BAB EL SEBAA. This small, shaded square crowded with Moorish cafés invites the visitor to pause. The RUELLE SIAGHINE, near the Rue Mohammed el Gorry, houses the town's jewelry workshops. The Jewish gold- and silversmiths of Essaouira were once renowned for their skillful filigree work ● *68*. Today the

Place Moulay el Hassan (below).

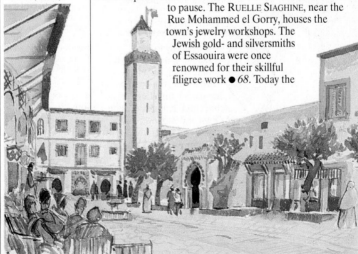

> ## "A WHITE CITY BUILT OVER THE WAVES [...]
> ## AND PERMEATED BY THE BREATH OF THE OPEN SEA."
> ### J. BERQUE AND J. COULEAU

jewelers of Essaouira work only in silver, while jewelry made in other materials is produced in Casablanca. Near the Great Mosque, the Avenue de l'Istiqal crosses an arcade that opens on to the Avenue Oqba Ben Nafia, forming a long, narrow square.

MARQUETRY. The 650-foot artillery platform of the BASTION NORD (North Bastion) is surrounded by crenellated walls that once served as Essaouira's defence against maritime attacks. Today the platform offers a superb view over the town and SKALA ● *102*. A vaulted passageway leads to the first floor, where the casemates house the workshops of around one hundred and fifty of the best marquetry craftsmen in Morocco. Essaouira's craftsmen have been renowned for their fine marquetry work since classical antiquity. According to Cicero the magnificent marquetry tables of Essaouira were highly prized in Rome, some fetching as much as one million sesterces.

Essaouira's marquetry craftsmen use the burls of the thuja ■ *30*, a tree found throughout the region, which they inlay with citron wood, walnut, ebony, mother-of-pearl and copper and silver wire.

SIDI MOHAMMED BEN ABDULLAH MUSEUM. The RUE DERB LAALOUJ runs from the fortification of the *Skala*, past the former FRENCH CONSULATE where Charles de Foucauld stayed in 1884, to the Sidi Mohammed Ben Abdullah Museum. The museum, in the former pasha's residence, houses collections reflecting regional arts and traditions. On the lower floor is a display of local and Andalous musical instruments ● *70* and documents relating to Berber Imazhigen songs. The upper floor is devoted to jewelry ● *68*, weaponry, costumes ● *78*, carpets ● *74* and reproductions of designs originally painted on the body ● *60* with henna for special celebrations as well as a collection of Koran boards decorated by the pupils of Koranic schools.

THE "MELLAH"

The RUE MOHAMMED ZERKTOUNI runs through Essaouira's Jewish quarter, which is situated at the northern end of the town. It is the *mellah*'s most picturesque street and is bordered by a market extending as far as BAB DOUKKALA. Outside the gate the EUROPEAN CEMETERY is a reminder of the town's cosmopolitan character.

"GUEMBRI"
The Gnaoua musicians of Essaouira play *guembri*, stringed musical instruments decorated with marquetry, to accompany dancing ● *71*.

159

FOLKLORE. During the *moussems* held in Essaouira one of Morocco's finest folk troupes, members of the Haha from the Tamanar region, perform a ceremonial *ahouach* (war dance) ● *70*. The troupe of male dancers line up shoulder to shoulder, stamping their feet and clapping their hands to the sound of *bendir* and *nira*. Two members of the group dressed in a *gandoura* then leave the ranks of the dancers and perform a mime representing a duel.

AN ARTISTS' MEETING PLACE.
Essaouira has long been known as a place of innovation and, in recent years, it has emerged as a major center for Moroccan artists. From its beginnings in the mid-18th century Essaouira attracted poets, scholars and craftsmen from all over Morocco. Today residents of the town include such established Moroccan artists as the sculptor Mustapha Boumazzoughi, the painter Houcine Miloudi and the glassmaker Boujemaa

GALERIE DAMGAARD
The Galerie d'Art Frédéric Damgaard in the Avenue Oqba Ben Nafia exhibits the work of artists and sculptors from Essaouira. Paintings by Nourredine Alioua (top left) and Mohammed Tabal (above) and stone sculptures by Mohammed Bouada (top right) are shown there.

Boufous, as well as a number of younger sculptors (Abdessamad Sedram and Mohammed Bouada) and painters (Hamza Fakir, Regragula Benhila and Fatima Ettabli).

THE ISLANDS OF ESSAOUIRA

The ISLES PURPURAIRES, half an hour's journey by motorboat from the port of Essaouira, are the setting for a delightful bird sanctuary stocked with gulls and Eleonora's falcons. The ruins of the huge 19th-century PRISON built by the sultan Moulay Hassan can be seen on the

DAR SOLTANE
The Tangaro by-road leads to Diabat, the tiny Berber village where hippies gathered in the 1970's and where Jimi Hendrix spent five years. On the beach to the south of Essaouira, near the Oued Ksob estuary, the half-buried ruins of the 18th-century palace of Dar Soltane (right) inspired the Jimi Hendrix song *Castles in the Sand*.

ISLAND OF MOGADOR where, in the 1st century BC, Juba II ● *52* of Mauretania built the purple-dye factory after which the islands were named. Juba's son, Ptolemy, is said to have been murdered by Caligula because he attended an important celebration wearing a purple toga, the color reserved for Roman emperors. Today the island of Mogador lies empty. It has been uninhabited since the end of Moulay Abdallah's reign.

IN AND AROUND RABAT

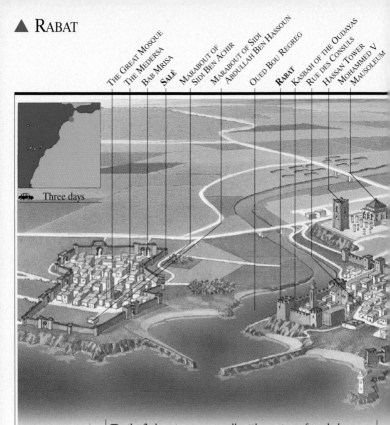

THE GREAT MOSQUE
THE MEDERSA
BAB MRISA
SALÉ
MARABOUT OF SIDI BEN ACHIR
MARABOUT OF SIDI ABDULLAH BEN HASSOUN
OUED BOU REGREG
RABAT
KASBAH OF THE OUDAYAS
RUE DES CONSULS
HASSAN TOWER
MOHAMMED V MAUSOLEUM

Three days

Terracotta pottery dating from the first half of the 1st century AD, from Rabat

Archeological Museum. The pottery was discovered in the Chellah Necropolis in 1917. The finely potted two-handled cup from Mauretania (left) is decorated with a latticework pattern. The mortar-like bowl (center) comes from Italy, and the squat *tazza* (right) is from Spain or Portugal.

In the 3rd century BC a small settlement was founded on Chellah territory on the Oued Bou Regreg estuary. The Phoenicians and later the Carthaginians used it as a port of call on long sea voyages. During the Roman occupation Chellah became known as Sala Colonia, and the region was called the province of Mauretania Tingitania (modern Morocco). In the 10th century loyalist Muslim warriors fighting heretics built a site for a *ribat* (fortified monastery) there. This first fortification, after which the town is named, was built on high ground on the south bank of the estuary. Today the Kasbah of the Oudayas stands on the site.

RIBAT EL FATH, THE ALMOHAD CAPITAL. In c. 1146 the Almohad caliph Abd el Moumen converted the *ribat* into a fortress and set up a camp to serve as a base for *moudjahidin* (Islamic soldiers engaged in a holy war) on the banks of the Bou Regreg. From this major military encampment preparations were made for a *djihad* (holy war) against Spain. In the late 12th century Ribat el Fath (Fortress of Faith) became the capital of the Almohad conqueror Yacoub el Mansour. After his victory over the Spanish kings of Castile and León at Alarcos, Yacoub el Mansour (the Victorious) built over three miles of fortifications. Two of the five gates built in these walls, the OUDAYA GATE and the BAB ER

ROUAH, still stand today. Yacoub el Mansour's
ambition was to make Rabat one of the most
prestigious towns in Morocco. In 1196 he started to
build a huge mosque ● 86 but he did not live to see its
completion and after his death work slowed down then
stopped altogether. All that remains of the initial project is
the minaret, the Hassan Tower ● 88. Following his death,
Yacoub el Mansour's vast empire, which stretched as far as
Tunisia and Moorish Spain, disintegrated. The collapse of
the Almohad dynasty brought about the decline of Rabat.
In an attempt to restore the town to its former glory and
prestige the Merinids built the Great Mosque and the
Chellah Necropolis, but in 1250 they abandoned Rabat and
made Fez the new capital of the kingdom of Morocco ▲ 54.
During the 16th century Rabat was a community of around
one hundred houses.

A CORSAIR REPUBLIC. Between 1609 and 1611 the arrival of
Muslim refugees from Andalusia revitalized Rabat. The
Andalous Muslims settled in NEW SALÉ, the present-day
medina. The Republic of
the Bou Regreg, a
corsair republic, was set
up in 1627 and lasted for
the next twelve years.
The pirates, who
operated on their own
account, organized a
djihad and brought
terror to the waters of
the Mediterranean and
the North Atlantic. In
an attempt to stop their

YACOUB EL MANSOUR
Following the
Almohad victory over
the Christians at
Alarcos ● 54 on
July 18, 1195, Abou
Youssef Yacoub took
the title *el Mansour*
(the Victorious).

In the 17th century
the first Andalous
refugees settled in the
Kasbah of the
Oudayas (below) and
set about restoring
the ramparts.

When Henry Kissinger visited Rabat in 1973 the treaty of friendship signed by Sidi Mohammed Ben Abdullah and George Washington on June 28, 1786, was printed in the Moroccan press. The aim of that agreement had been to formalize trade relations between the two countries at a time when Moroccan corsairs were attacking and sinking foreign vessels.

"This is the record of the conditions of the peace treaty agreed with the Americans and written down in this document to which we have affixed our seal in the hope that, God willing, the conditions will remain permanent.**"**

FONDOUK BEN AÏSSA
The commercial growth of Rabat and the development of industrial zones in the city are partly to blame for the disappearance of *fondouks* (lodging houses with stables) in the early 20th century. The *fondouk* at 109 Rue des Consuls was the largest in Rabat. Today it is a leather craftsmen's workshop.

piracy, foreign powers were forced to negotiate with the new republic, a process from which Rabat emerged much wealthier. In 1666 a governor was dispatched by the Alaouite sultan, Moulay Rachid, to cut short the corsairs' activities. On his accession in 1672 Moulay Ismail decided that one way of stifling piracy was to impose increasingly high taxes on the corsairs in order to make their way of life less attractive. In 1768 these various powers drew up treaties to protect themselves against possible attack by Morocco. By the 18th century only about thirty pirates remained and the republic finally came to an end in 1818, during the reign of Moulay Slimane.

CAPITAL OF MOROCCO. In 1912, when Morocco was made a French protectorate, Rabat once again became the capital of Morocco. It was General Lyautey, first resident general in Morocco, who decided to transfer the capital from Fez to Rabat, making it the administrative center of the protectorate and the seat of his official residence. Sultan Moulay Youssef followed suit by taking up residence in Rabat in a palace built on the site of the palace of his ancestor Sidi Mohammed Ben Abdullah. This decision was not reversed when Morocco declared independence in March 1956. In 1912, working with the French urban planning expert Léon Henri Prost, Lyautey set about developing the city. He was in favor of maintaining a distinction between the new European enclaves and the old districts. An entirely new town was built in the area between the medina and the Royal Palace, and the Hassan Tower and the Kasbah of the Oudayas.

A ROYAL CITY. Although Rabat remained the administrative and commercial capital of Morocco, it was never the country's economic capital. The shallowness of the Oued Bou Regreg estuary restricted shipping access, and this combined with the extension of the port of Casablanca in 1907 tended to prevent Rabat from playing an active role in the development of the country's heavy industry. Today Rabat is the second largest city in Morocco after Casablanca.

Lyautey, one of the founding fathers of modern Morocco, made a major contribution to the country's economic and social development. He was buried in Rabat but his body was repatriated and laid to rest in the Invalides in Paris in 1961.

THE MEDINA

The medina is situated between the Oued Bou Regreg and the Atlantic Ocean. It covers an area of around 150 acres and is built around three main thoroughfares, the Rue Sidi Fatah, the Rue Souika and Rue des Consuls. The southern end of the medina is separated from the city center by the MORISCOS (Andalous wall) built in the 17th century by Andalous Muslims. The western wall of the old town, with its six gates, was built by the Almohads in the 12th century. Today the BAB EL HAD (gate of the Sunday market), to the south of the medina, is the preserve of Rabat's public letter-writers. The gate opens onto an array of colorful souks that lead to the Marché Central. Incongruously sitting among the stalls of this covered food market is a French *charcuterie*, selling the kind of delicacies that one would expect to find in large French cities like Paris or Marseilles.

RUE SOUIKA. The Rue Souika, lined with stalls and restaurants for its entire length, is almost certainly the busiest shopping street in the medina. The MOULAY SLIMANE MOSQUE, standing at the corner of the Rue Sidi Fatah and the Rue Souika, was constructed in 1812 by the sultan Moulay Slimane. The Rue Souika leads to the GREAT MOSQUE, which was completely restored in 1882. Opposite the mosque are three ruined arches, vestiges of an old fountain, probably built in the 14th century by the Merinids. The Rue Souika ends in the SOUK ES SEBAT, which sells mainly cloth and jewelry.

THE "MAISON MAURE" (MOORISH HOUSE)
Behind rampart-like walls a repertoire of Moorish ornament decorates the *maison maure*. The courtyard is tiled with *zellige* ▲ *173* and the arches of the painted pillars decorated with *muqarna* (stalactites). One of the wrought-iron grilles beneath the gallery bears the date of the construction of the house, built in the medina in the year 1352 of the *Hegira* (1934).

WOODTURNERS
Craftsman carving a moucharabieh upright. He turns the wood as he carves, holding it firmly between his first and second toes.

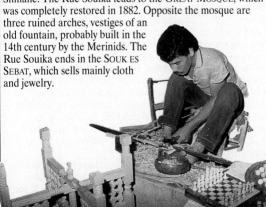

Bold floral motifs picked out in various colors (below) are typical of Rabat embroidery.

Unlike Muslim houses, the European-style houses on the Rue des Consuls face on to the street.

"Today the Kasbah of the Oudayas is a district of artists, people reminiscing about the past, rich foreigners in search of exoticism, people of modest means, poor, peaceable people. It is a place for people with time on their hands and for the idle rich."
Kamal Lakhdar, *Rabat*

A wall fountain in the Kasbah of the Oudayas.

SALÉ BOATMEN Turkish-style costume (right) brought to Rabat by the corsairs. It was worn by the boatmen who operated a rowing-boat ferry service between Rabat and Salé.

RUE DES CONSULS ★. Until 1912 ambassadors, consuls and other representatives of foreign governments were obliged to live on this street. Architecturally it is the most interesting street in the medina, with a number of old houses tucked away behind wooden gateways or nestling at the end of culs-de-sac. Today it is the center for tailors, carpet dealers and cloth merchants whose shops and workshops are gathered there. The narrow Ruelle du Consulat-de-France is a cul-de-sac that leads to the former French consulate, no. 62, where Louis Chénier, French consul and father of the poet André Chénier, lived between 1767 and 1782. The Rue des Consuls leads to the SOUK EL GHEZEL (wool market). Today carpets ● *74* are auctioned in a square where, in the 16th and 17th centuries, captive Christians were sold. From the Boulevard el Alou, which runs alongside the great Muslim cemetery, the RUE HADJ DAOUI and RUE SQAÏA EL MEKKI lead back to the center of the medina. In the Rue Taht el Hammam is the HAMMAM EL JEDID, a steam bath constructed by the Merinids in the 14th century. The Rue Sidi Fatah leads to the MOULAY MEKKI MOSQUE.

THE "MELLAH". The Rue des Consuls runs into the Rue Oukasa, which in turn leads to the old Jewish quarter built in 1808 by Moulay Slimane. Although some of its seventeen synagogues still stand, they have been converted into living quarters and warehouses.

KASBAH OF THE OUDAYAS ★

The Kasbah of the Oudayas stands on the south bank of the Bou Regreg estuary. It was named after a garrison of mercenaries from the Oudaya tribe that was set up in Rabat. The Oudayas, originally from Arabia, arrived in Morocco in the 13th century. The sultan Moulay Ismail ▲ *233* sent them to Rabat with orders to defend the town following a number of acts of violence carried out in the neighboring countryside by the Zaër tribe.

THE KASBAH FORTIFICATIONS. The wall surrounding the Kasbah of the Oudayas, built during the Almohad dynasty ● *54*, was reinforced during the 17th and 18th centuries. Moulay Rachid built the first bastion to defend the southern part of the town between 1666 and 1672 and some of its cannons can still be seen today. The wall, 8 feet wide and 26 to 32 feet high, is built of quarry stone and bordered by a sloping esplanade.

THE OUDAYA GATE. On the north side of the square stands the Oudaya Gate, a monumental archway in red-ocher ashlar with two tall wooden doors and flanked by two towers. It was built in the 12th century and appears to have been more ornamental than functional. The façade is decorated with partially erased Kufic lettering ● *64–5* and, unusually in Morocco, with depictions of animals. One of the towers has

> "IT IS THE FORMER CAPITAL OF MOROCCO, A PEACEFUL CITY OF DISTINCTION, A ZAOUIA, A GARDEN."
>
> IBN EL-KHATIB

been converted to incorporate three art galleries. The OUDAYA PALACE was built by Yacoub el Mansour ▲ *163*, who probably used it both as a court and as a reception hall. To the left of the palace lies the EL ALOU CEMETERY and further to the west the 17th-century fortress of MOULAY RACHID.

WITHIN THE KASBAH OF THE OUDAYAS. On the main thoroughfare of the Kasbah of the Oudayas and set back from the Rue Jamaa stands the JAMAA EL ATIQ, the oldest mosque in Rabat, built c. 1150 in the reign of Abd el Moumen. The minaret ● *88*, with its decorative arches, was restored in the 18th century by the renegade English architect Ahmed el Inglis. The DAR BARAKA (House of Good Fortune), which also stands on the main thoroughfare, has one of the most beautifully decorated doorways in Rabat. At the end of the Rue Jamaa, on a platform in an imposing position overlooking the Bou Regreg estuary and the town of Salé ▲ *175*, is a 17th-century signal station and an 18th-century warehouse now used as a school and carpet ● *74* workshop. At the north end of the platform a narrow street leads down to a small ROUND TOWER built as a defensive position, and then eventually to a beach. The TOUR DES CORSAIRES, a 17th-century bastion overlooking the Bou Regreg, stands in the cul-de-sac of the Rue Laalami, while the Rue Bazzo leads to the JARDIN ANDALOU (Andalou Garden), laid out between 1915 and 1918. At the end of the narrow streets that run to the southern end of the kasbah, a flight of steps leads up to two crenellated towers, complete with old cannons, and on to a rampart walk commanding a magnificent view of Rabat and, beyond the Bou Regreg and Hassan Tower, of the medina of Salé. Finally there is a PERSIAN WHEEL and a lucky FOUNTAIN, both of which have featured in the illustration on the old ten-dirham note ▲ *336*.

THE OUDAYA MUSEUM. Rabat's Museum of Moroccan Arts is housed in the

OUDAYA GATE
Serpentine motif (below) decorating the bases of the circular- and pointed-foil arch of the Oudaya Gate.

DAR BARAKA
During a siege the owners of this house are said to have taken in a cat, which could have been a welcome form of food in the starving town. Shortly afterward the creature is supposed to have led them to hidden treasure.

GARDEN OF THE OUDAYAS
Laid out in the early 20th century in the style of an Andalusian garden, it consists of terraced flower beds, straight pathways and fountains.

royal residence built by Moulay Ismail in the late 17th century. The building was converted into a medersa, or theological college ● *90,* and then shortly afterward became a museum. In one of the three rooms open to the general public a traditional Moroccan interior has been re-created, furnished with divans covered with gold and silk Fasi brocade ● *77.* A second, marble-tiled room houses exhibits of Fez ▲ *213* pottery ● *80,* Berber musical instruments, Berber and Hispano-Arabic jewelry, and a collection of beautifully illuminated manuscripts of the Koran ● *64.* The oldest of these date from the 13th century and one is said to have been produced by Omar el Mourtada, the brother of the Almohad caliph Es Saïd, while he was governor of Ribat el Fath. The residence's former mosque houses a collection of carpets ● *74* from various regions of Morocco, with the oldest Rabat

and Médiouna carpets dating from the 18th century. The museum's third room contains an exhibition of Moroccan costumes ● *78* as worn by inhabitants of the area situated just between the Rif and the Sahara. The *Café Maure* (right), a stone's throw from the Andalusian gardens, has a terrace laid out in a beautiful position on the ramparts, offering a magnificent view over the Oued Bou Regreg estuary. The Rue Tarik el Marsa runs from the Kasbah of the Oudayas to the craft center overlooking the old port area. Opposite the center the MUSÉE NATIONAL DE L'ARTISANAT (National Craft Museum), which has its home in a group of former shipbuilding warehouses, displays an extensive collection of Moroccan crafts (carpets ● *74*, jewelry ● *68*, embroidery ● *76* and ceramics ● *80*) produced in workshops that stand along the banks of the Oued Bou Regreg.

View of the Hassan Tower and the tiled esplanade of the mosque.

Detail of the multifoil arch in one of the sides of the Hassan Tower.

HASSAN TOWER

The center of Rabat is concentrated between the Hassan Tower, the Royal Palace and the BAB ER ROUAH (Gate of the Winds) and is bounded to the west and southwest by the Almohad fortifications. Beyond the Bab er Rouah lies the Agdal district.

HASSAN TOWER ● *88* ★. A minaret known as the Hassan Tower is all that remains of the mosque ● *86* begun in 1196. The name *Hassan* (goodness) was bestowed on the tower in the 14th century but the reason this was done remains a mystery. The sultan Yacoub el Mansour ▲ *163* had ambitions to build the second-biggest mosque in the Muslim world (the largest being the Samarra mosque in Iraq) but after his death in 1199 the project was never completed. The original plans indicate that the minaret was intended to reach a height of 260 feet but the Hassan Tower, which dominates the ruins of two hundred columns, is only 140 feet high. A flight of stairs leads to its various rooms. The minaret of this unfinished mosque, the second largest in Islam, is remarkable not so much for its rather heavy proportions as for its imposing grandeur, and the beauty and simplicity of its latticework decoration. The twenty-one aisles of the enormous prayer hall can accommodate forty thousand worshippers. It was here that Mohammed V presided over the first Friday prayer meeting ● *63* on his return from exile after the declaration of independence ● *57* in 1956.

"Outside the south gate, he [Yacoub el Mansour] had a tower built like the one in Marrakesh."
Leo Africanus, *Geographical History of Africa*

BAB ER ROUAH
The inner face of the Bab er Rouah (Gate of the Winds) is decorated with arabesques bordered by a verse from the Koran in Kufic script. Today it houses an art gallery.

THE "SKALA"
During the second half of the 18th century, the sultan Sidi Mohammed built the *Skala* to strengthen the defenses of the Kasbah of the Oudayas. The battery of Spanish cannons is still in place on the ramparts.

**MOHAMMED V
MAUSOLEUM**
The Vietnamese
architect Vo Toan
employed around
four hundred
Moroccan craftsmen
to build the
mausoleum. The
decorative elements
are found mainly
inside the building.
The entrance (above)
leads into the burial
chamber whose walls
are decorated with
zellige ▲ 173 and
stucco. The white
onyx tomb is the work
of the Fasi *maalem*
(master
craftsman)
Abdelkrim.
The cupola
to the right is
covered in
gold leaf.

**THE ROYAL
GUARD**
Members of the
royal guard wear
a flowing red and
white *burnous*
● 78 and carry a
mokhla
(ceremonial rifle)
inlaid with silver
and ivory. They
stand guard at the
entrance to the
esplanade of the
Hassan Tower and
the Mohammed V
Mausoleum.

THE UNFINISHED MOSQUE. In its finished state, the mosque
would have covered an area of over 30,000 square yards, and
would have had 19 naves and 424 columns and pillars. The
wood for the roof is said to have been used by the Almohad
caliph Es Saïd to build ships, and many of the columns and
other architectural features have been pillaged over the
centuries. The earthquake that destroyed Lisbon in 1755 also
damaged the mosque in Rabat. Today all that remains of the
walls, naves and columns of the original grand design are
foundations surrounded by modern paving.

MOHAMMED V MAUSOLEUM. Opposite the Hassan Tower the
Mohammed V Mausoleum commemorates the sultan who
enabled Morocco to achieve independence ● 56. It was built
between 1961 and 1969 by the Vietnamese architect VO TOAN
along the lines of traditional royal necropolises. The
mausoleum stands on an 11½-foot plinth and is surmounted
by a pyramidal roof of green tiles. Flights of steps lead up to
the *koubba* ● 63, where a gallery-cum-balcony looks on to the
impressive burial chamber containing the tomb of
Mohammed V. The granite block is so highly polished that the
tomb appears to be floating in a pool of turquoise (opposite
top, second from right). After construction of the mausoleum
was completed the sultan's body was transferred there on
October 30, 1971, ten years after his death.
It is watched over by theologians who work
in shifts around the clock, reading aloud
from the Koran ● 64. The tomb of
Mohammed's son Moulay Abdallah,
who died in December 1983, lies
close by, in one corner of the
chamber. The burial room
culminates in a magnificent
twelve-sided cupola of carved
mahogany and stained-glass
windows from which hangs a
huge bronze chandelier,
measuring 7½ feet in diameter
and weighing 1½ tons. Below the
paved esplanade of the Hassan
Tower ▲ 169 is a small mosque
with a special women's area.
Opposite the tower and the
ruins of the former Almohad
mosque is the Mohammed V
museum, whose exhibits trace
the history of the Alaouite
dynasty ● 55 from the
17th century to the present day.

"ITS COLOR HAS BEEN WIDELY PRAISED:
IT IS A WHITE CITY. EVERYTHING IS PAINTED WHITE,
A COLOR IDEALLY SUITED TO THE PLAY OF LIGHT."

HENRI BOSCO

CHELLAH NECROPOLIS

From the esplanade of the Hassan Tower ▲ 169, the streets
running through Rabat's foreign embassy district lead to the
BAB ZAËR, the town's south gate. The gate, which in turn
leads to the Chellah Necropolis, was built by the Almohads
in the 12th century and restored during the 18th. The
Chellah Necropolis stands outside the walls on the ancient
site of Sala, which lies about 1¼ miles from the city center.
Although it is only half an hour's walk from the Hassan
Tower, it is advisable to travel there by car. Several centuries
ago, Sala Colonia could be reached by river. It was once a
prosperous Roman town, but was abandoned during the 9th
century and, by the 10th, had declined to little more than a
ruin. It was transformed into a large cemetery by the
Merinids during the 14th century. The Chellah Necropolis
was destroyed by the earthquake of 1755 and is today
covered with a luxuriant vegetation of palm trees ■ 42,
hibiscus, banana and fig trees ■ 44.

THE SALA EXCAVATIONS. Excavations begun in 1931 in the
western section of the necropolis have uncovered the
remains of the ancient Roman town. The site consists of a
series of terraces on which were discovered the vestiges of a
fountain, the market, the baths, the *nymphaeum* and some
shops. At the top of the Roman site is a residential district.
Steps lead to the CURIA (senate house) built between 98 and
117 during the reign of the emperor Trajan. Next to
it are the remains of a
peristyle, a triumphal arch
and a small shrine.

BAB ZAËR
The gate contains
vaulted chambers and
offset corridors.

Behind the pink and
gray marble columns
of the unfinished
mosque stands the
Mohammed V
Mausoleum. The
esplanade of the
Hassan Tower is
paved with modern
marble slabs ▲ 169.

The exterior façade
of the monumental gate
of the Chellah Necropolis.

SALA COLONIA
Archeological
excavations have
unearthed the
*Decumanus
Maximumus* (main
street) of Sala
Colonia. It ran
between the forum
and the capitol and
led to the port, built
in the 1st century BC
and now silted up.

A MERINID NECROPOLIS ★. In front of the
Merinid shrine in the Muslim section of the
Chellah Necropolis stand the minarets ● 88
of the *zaouia* ▲ 199 and of the 13th-century
mosque (now in ruins) of ABOU YOUSSEF
YACOUB. He was the first sultan to be buried
in the Necropolis. To the south, beneath a
canopy decorated with *muqarna*, is the TOMB
OF ABOU EL HASSAN, who was responsible for
completing (in 1399) the stone and brick wall
begun during the reign of Abou Saïd and is the most famous
of the Merinid sultans buried in the Chellah Necropolis. He

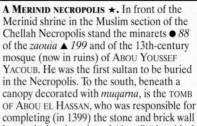

was known as the Black Sultan because
of his Abyssinian mother, who is also
buried in the Necropolis. In the tomb
next to her lies Shems Ed Duna
(Morning Sun), the European wife of
Abou el Hassan who was converted
to Islam.

THE "ZAOUIA". The ruins to the left of the
mosque are all that remains of the
zaouia, the seat of the Muslim fraternity.
The font in the courtyard is surrounded
by the base of what was once an arcade. Leading off the
courtyard were prayer cells and an oratory in which the
Prophet Mohammed is said to have prayed. A devotee who
completed seven circuits of the ambulatory surrounding the
mihrab ● 86 was once considered to have achieved the
equivalent of the *hajj* ● 62, the pilgrimage to Mecca. The
crumbling minaret that can be seen above the ocher-colored
walls of the *zaouia* was built by Abou el Hassan. Its skylight
is still decorated with multicolored *zellige* ▲ 173 and
sculpted marble.

SPRING OF THE CANNONS. A colony of eels believed to have
the power to cure sterility lives in the sacred *Aïn Mdafa*
(Spring of the Cannons). Votive
candles are ranged on its
banks beneath the trees
where, according to
legend, djinns guard
the hidden
treasure
belonging to
the sultan
Abou Youssef
Yacoub.

**"If you speak to the
workmen who have
taken over the
Chellah Necropolis,
they will tell you that
precious and
enchanted objects lie
hidden beneath its
great gateway. For
example, the famous
ring of King Solomon
to which the fate of
the Jewish empire
was linked. They will
tell you that the
people of the Sous
[Valley], who are
expert treasure
seekers, have dug in
the earth, searched
the walls, and climbed
to the very top of the
gateway where,
deceived by their
brilliance, they tried
to tear off pieces of
faïence."**

Henriette Célarié,
Un mois au Maroc

The art of making *zellige* (elaborate tile mosaics) first appeared in Morocco in the 10th century and reached its highest expression in the 14th century. The distinctively shaped and colored tiles are pieced together to create designs drawn up by the *maalem* (master craftsman) according to a rigid set of rules. Each type of design has its own particular name and colors in line with tradition. In the 10th century a wide range of whites and browns were used, with blue, green and yellow introduced in the 14th century. The use of red did not appear until the 17th century. There is a wide variety of designs. The patterning of some *zellige* was influenced by the Italian *maiolica* and Andalusian *azulejos*. The endlessly repeating geometric designs of other *zellige* echo that of decorated Kufic inscriptions. The *zellige* cutter sits with his arms on his knees, holding a sharp, heavy double-headed hammer. With precisely aimed blows, he chips away at the shape drawn on the glazed tile.

173

The Royal Palace houses the offices of the Moroccan Prime Minister and the *Habbous* (Minister of Religions).

DAR EL MAKHZEN. The present Dar el Makhzen (Royal Palace) dates from 1864. It was built on the ruins of the old royal palace constructed toward the end of the 18th century by Sidi Mohammed Ben Abdullah. Today, over two thousand people live in the complex. It comprises the supreme court, the imperial college, the Ahl Fas mosque and the former slave district as well as a small racecourse and the barracks of the Black Guard. Opposite the Royal Palace is the Mohammed V University, Morocco's largest, attended by almost 25,000 students.

ARCHEOLOGICAL MUSEUM. The museum contains the most important finds from Morocco's prehistoric and pre-Roman sites, Volubilis ▲ *243*,

MAURETANIAN COINS Coins (right) struck in Morocco at the beginning of the 1st century AD, now on display in the Archeological Museum.

Banasa ▲ *212* and Lixus ▲ *209*. It also houses a collection of objects from the Islamic and pre-Islamic archeological sites in the Chellah, Belyounesh and Sijilmassa regions. Among major antique bronzes exhibited in the museum's first room, the Salle des Bronzes are: the BUST OF JUBA II, King of Mauretania ● *52*; the IVY-CROWNED YOUTH; an EPHEBUS; the bust of a Berber youth; the HEAD OF CATO THE YOUNGER (or Cato of Utica); and the GUARD-DOG OF VOLUBILIS, which dates from the early 2nd century AD. A second room traces the history of Morocco ● *51* from pre-history to Roman and early Christian times. A display in the galleries on the upper floor contains items found at Banasa, Volubilis and Sala Colonia ▲ *171-2*, the three major Roman sites of Mauretania Tingitana. These objects provide a fascinating glimpse of the daily existence of Mauretanians in Roman times ● *52*. In the courtyards and gardens are collections of amphorae, marble statues, engraved boundary stones and stelae excavated at these ancient sites.

THE GREAT MOSQUE The Great Mosque, also known as the Jamaa el Sounna, was built in the 18th century by Sidi Mohammed Ben Abdullah and restored several times. It is an early example of the neo-Moresque style, to which Lyautey's architects returned in the 20th century.

CATHÉDRALE DE SAINT PIERRE. The Cathédrale de Saint Pierre, which stands next to the Great Mosque, was designed by the French architect Laforgue. Construction began in 1919 and the cathedral was inaugurated two years later. The mosaic *Stations of the Cross* dates from 1924, the organ was installed in 1929 and the facade restored in 1937. The nave is lit by stained-glass windows, some of Islamic inspiration, and a glass roof. The cathedral is the diocesan church of the Archbishop of Rabat.

"Our ship making
her course towards
the Canary Islands, or
rather between those
Islands and the
African shore, was
surprised in the grey
of the morning by a
Turkish rover of
Sallee...**"**
Daniel
Defoe,
*Robinson
Crusoe*

A cross the Oued Bou Regreg from Rabat, opposite the
Kasbah of the Oudayas, lies Salé's beautiful white
medina. The towns, once rivals, are today linked by a wide
modern bridge.

A THRIVING PORT. The exact date of the foundation of Salé is
unknown, although by the 10th century it was definitely the
capital of the Beni Ifren, a tribe of Berber Zenata.
By the end of the 12th century trade in Salé was
thriving and as a wealthy port it became a pawn
in the struggle between the Almohads and
Merinids. In 1260 the forces of Alfonso X of
Castile and León, spurred on by greed,
took advantage of these disputes to
sack the town. Abou Youssef Yacoub
Ben Abd el Haq recaptured it after
a campaign lasting only a few days
and began to build a fortified wall
around the city. Inside the walls
overlooking the river, he made a
number of important improvements,
building a medersa ● *90*, a *zaouia*
▲ *172, 199*, a medical school and the
Sour el Kouass aqueduct, beneath
which the main Tangier road now
passes. Salé became a flourishing trading
center, specializing in hides, wool, honey and ivory
and attracting merchants from all corners of the Christian
world. It became the main port in the kingdom of Fez.

A PIRATE STRONGHOLD. In 1609 large numbers of Andalous
Muslims, driven out of Spain by Philip III, settled on the
riverbanks. Soon after their arrival the newcomers turned to
the lucrative business of *djihad* (piracy). The corsairs' republic
of Salé, founded in 1627 and relatively short-lived, was
headed by an elected governor with a one-year term of office.
Between 1620 and 1630, the corsairs captured one thousand
ships. Provided that the town prospered and paid its taxes, the
central government of Morocco turned a blind eye to its
activities. In the early 18th century Moulay Ismail installed a
militia of black slaves (the Abids) to exercise a measure of
control in the vicinity. As Rabat expanded, Salé's
prosperity gradually declined and the inhabitants of the
city abandoned piracy and turned to craftsmanship,
religion and other more conventional activities.

THE SALÉ CORSAIRS
The geographical
location of Salé, the
development of
Atlantic trade and the
arrival of the
Andalous Muslims
from Spain were all
contributory factors
in the 17th century
djihad. Crews
consisted initially of
Moriscos (exiled
Andalous Muslims),
since the Moroccans
did not become
involved in the *djihad*
until the second half
of the 17th century.
The heroes of this
period included the
redoubtable
Moroccan captain
Sidi Abdullah Ben
Aïcha, who won a
great reputation for
himself in the 1690's.
The Salé Rovers
ventured as far afield
as the English
Channel, the coast of
Ireland and even
Newfoundland.

BAB MRISA
The Bab Mrisa once opened onto the inner harbor (now silted up) dug by the Merinids in 1260 to enable ships to drop anchor in the safety of the ramparts.

THE MEDERSA
The main entrance has a characteristically Merinid pointed stone archway with

trefoil arches and is surmounted by a wooden canopy covered in Roman tiles. In the inner courtyard leading to the prayer hall is the small marble font containing water for ritual ablutions.

THE MEDINA

The BAB MRISA (Port Gate) ● *95*, the oldest gate in the medina, stands at the southern end of Salé's whitewashed ramparts. The narrow streets of the old town are populated by carpet weavers, stone sculptors, cabinetmakers and

coppersmiths. Ironworkers are found in the Rue Haddadine, which passes through most of the many covered markets in the medina. In the SOUK EL KEBIR (the old slave market) and the SOUK SIDI MERZOUK, jewelers, embroiderers and silk-spinners predominate. The Rue Kechachine, filled with carpenters' workshops, leads into a square with an 18th-century fountain. Opposite are the Great Mosque and the medersa ● *90*.

THE MEDERSA ★. Constructed in 1333 by Abou el Hassan (the Black Sultan), the medersa provided accommodation for students who came to Salé for Koranic instruction. It is small but perfectly proportioned. One of the inscriptions on the façade extols the virtues of the architects who designed it, saying that the building is the equal of a royal palace and that its appearance is as resplendent as the pearls on a bride's necklace. The entrance, surmounted by a cedarwood canopy, opens onto a courtyard containing pillars decorated with *zellige* and honeycombed stucco. The prayer hall has an elaborately decorated mihrab ● *91* and the easily accessible roof of the medersa provides a magnificent view across the town, which looks like a sea of white rooftop terraces interspersed with minarets.

THE GREAT MOSQUE. Opposite the medersa is the Great Mosque, which dates from the second half of the 12th century. The original building was subsequently converted and partially restored by the sultan Abou el Hassan during the 14th century. Through side doors opening onto the street, a colonnaded prayer hall with hundreds of prayer rugs on the floor can occasionally be glimpsed. The entrance of the SIDI AHMED EL TIJANI ZAOUIA opposite the mosque is decorated with a number of mosaics and a frieze of arches embellished with stalactites.

"WERE THE SAND OF SALÉ TO CHANGE INTO RAISIN WINE, THE RBATI WILL NEVER BEFRIEND THE SLAOUI."

THE MARABOUT OF SIDI ABDULLAH BEN HASSOUN. The remains of the patron saint of Salé lie in a 19th-century marabout (shrine) below the medina. Every year, during the *Achoura*, which falls ten days after the Muslim New Year ▲ *339*, large lanterns made entirely of wax are carried to the marabout by Salé boatmen, dressed in traditional costume, to the sound of flutes and drums. The lanterns are amazing contraptions made from thousands of intricately carved pieces of brightly colored wax. The ceremony is said to date back to the days of the Barbary pirates when the corsairs of Salé used to bring offerings to the saint to ask for protection before setting off on a long and difficult expedition. According to another tradition, corsairs setting off on one of these voyages would, on the eve of their departure, lay colored sticks in a very specific order before the tomb of Sidi Ahmed Hadji. It was considered a favorable omen if the order of the sticks had changed by the following day.

THE MARABOUT OF SIDI BEN ACHIR. The vast Muslim cemetery extends from the old town to the shores of the Atlantic. The marabout of Sidi Ben Achir, a 16th-century grammarian, poet and reputed miracle-worker, stands next to the boundary wall. People still come to his tomb to pray for cures for nervous disorders and mental illnesses. The cemetery and *msala* (prayer wall) extend beyond the boundary wall, which is fortified by two 18th-century *borj* (small high-lying forts). The people of Salé gather at the tomb of Sidi Ben Achir for the Aïd es Seghir and Aïd el Kebir ▲ *339*.

CRAFTSMANSHIP AND INDUSTRY

Salé has become Rabat's dormitory town. While preserving its reputation for high-quality craftsmanship, it has developed several successful industries. The quarry of DAS EL HAMRA to the north of the town supplies a soft, easily carved stone widely used in the construction of arches and doorways, and the reed mats woven in Salé, used to cover the walls and floors of mosques, are considered to be the finest in Morocco. The local clay soil is ideal for making pottery and Salé, with Safi ▲ *153* and Fez ▲ *213*, has become one of Morocco's leading pottery ● *80* centers. There is a POTTERS' COOPERATIVE on the banks of the Oued Bou Regreg outside the town, where around twenty workshops are active, producing high-quality pottery. Salé is also home to a number of basket weavers who produce a range of wicker goods. Every Thursday a large market, the SOUK EL KHAMISS, is held in a collection of tents pitched near the main road. This is an opportunity for craftsmen from Rabat and Salé to get together to exchange products and regale each other with the latest news. The

THE FESTIVAL OF CANDLES
On the eve of the Muslim New Year the citizens of Salé parade through the streets, holding aloft the huge wax lanterns from the tomb of Sidi Abdullah Ben Hassoun.

THE BRIDES OF SALÉ
During the *selwa* ● *69* brides dressed in traditional Salé costume appear in public every afternoon for a week. Their hair, covered with artificial braids, is tied up in a *cherbyia* (silk scarf). To ward off misfortune no part of their clothing should be knotted.

177

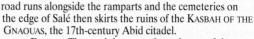

road runs alongside the ramparts and the cemeteries on the edge of Salé then skirts the ruins of the KASBAH OF THE GNAOUAS, the 17th-century Abid citadel.

MAMORA FOREST. The road then cuts through part of the Mamora Forest with its thin scattering of cork oaks and eucalyptus ■ *32*. Trees treated by the Sidi Yahia factory in the Gharb region have been replanted in areas of the forest that have been devastated by overgrazing.

The Mamora cork-oak forest ■ *32* covers 247,000 acres and accounts for half of Morocco's cork-oak plantations. Today the forest represents half the surface area covered at the beginning of the quaternary period.

EXOTIC GARDENS OF SIDI BOUKNADEL. These gardens, 7½ miles north of Rabat, were planted in 1951 by a French conservationist and horticultural engineer who wanted to introduce different types of plants to Morocco. The gardens, laid out over 10 acres, recreate various ecosystems from all over the world. About 12 miles further on is a nature reserve and the LAKE OF SIDI BOURHABA.

BORJ EL KEBIR
This monumental gate leads to the Borj el Kebir, a 19th-century circular fort built in the reign of Sidi Abd er Rahman. It is also known as the Borj Errokni (Angle Fort) because it forms a right-angled projection against the line of the ramparts.

MEHDIYA. The town of Mehdiya, originally called *El Mamora* (The Populous) by the Berbers, was built in the 5th century on the Oued Sébou estuary. It was fortified by Abd el Moumen in the 12th century. In the 17th century the fishing port was a safe haven for English pirates for a short while, but three years later the Spanish made it one of their ports of call and built a fortress to block access to the estuary. When Moulay Ismail captured the town in 1681 he named it *Mehdiya* (Gift) and installed the Abids. In 1795 the port was closed to maritime traffic but it was nevertheless used as one of the Allied landing points in 1942.

KENITRA. Kenitra, a new town, was built by the French in 1913 around an old fort that once defended the crossing of the Oued Sébou. Today Kenitra, which has undergone extensive industrial development and now has a large airdrome, occupies an important position as the capital of the Gharb's agricultural region. It is the sixth-largest port in Morocco and can accommodate ships with a draft of up to 13 feet. It is a thriving center for the export of wine, fruit and vegetables and timber from the Mamora Forest.

View of Mehdiya and the Oued Sébou at the turn of the century.

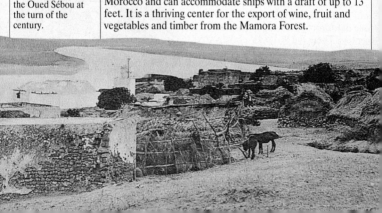

In and Around
Tangier

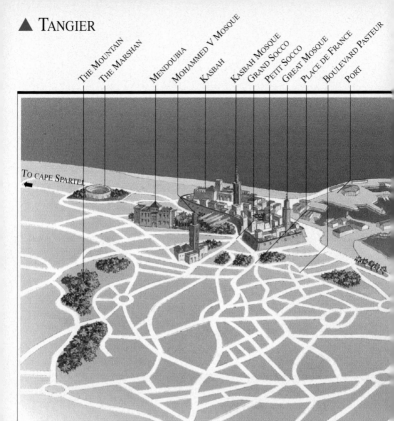

THE MOUNTAIN
THE MARSHAN
MENDOUBIA
MOHAMMED V MOSQUE
KASBAH
KASBAH MOSQUE
GRAND SOCCO
PETIT SOCCO
GREAT MOSQUE
PLACE DE FRANCE
BOULEVARD PASTEUR
PORT

TO CAPE SPARTEL

According to classical mythology, Tangier was founded by Antaeus, son of Poseidon, who named the town after his wife Tingis (Tanjah in Arabic and Tanger in French). The earliest evidence of human habitation on the site dates from the Paleolithic period, while the town itself probably dates from the protohistoric period somewhere between 3000 and 1000 BC. Tinga (Lagoon Town) was founded by the Berbers and, under the influence of the Phoenicians, it became an important trading center. For a century after the fall of Carthage in 146 BC the town remained the capital of the independent kingdom of Mauretania. The Romans then made it the capital of Mauretania Tingitania, present-day North Morocco.

MAURETANIAN AS
This bronze coin was struck in Tangier in the second half of the 1st century BC. The ears of corn on the reverse (above) symbolize Tangier's prosperity, while the Phoenician deity Baal Melkart on the obverse (below) proves Phoenician contact with Tangier. The coin is on display in the Banque Nationale du Maroc in Casablanca.

ARAB DOMINATION. During the 8th century the Arabs used the recently converted Berber troops ● *53* to capture Tangier, which was strategically placed at the point of convergence of the Atlantic and the Mediterranean and also within easy reach of Spain. The town subsequently fell into the hands of the Idrissids ● *53*, the Ommayads of Córdoba and then the great Moroccan dynasties. In the 15th century, Tangier became a prosperous town that maintained trading links with Genoa, Venice and Marseilles.

EUROPEAN DOMINATION. Between the 15th and 16th centuries the town was captured alternately by the Portuguese and Spanish. In 1661 Tangier, part of Catherine of Braganza's

MEDITERRANEAN SEA

TO CAPE MALABATA

🚗 Two days

IBN BATOUTA (1304–69)
Ibn Batouta traveled widely from his home town of Tangier to Samarkand and Timbuktu. He dictated an account of his travels, the *Rihla*, to the writer Ibn Juzayy.

dowry, changed hands yet again on her marriage to Charles II of England. The English continually fortified the town against the attacks of Moulay Ismail's troops. They were finally defeated in 1684 and withdrew, leaving the Muslims in control of Tangier. For two hundred years Tangier, known as "the gateway to Africa", continued to be the envy of Europe. In 1905, in response to the *entente cordiale* of April 8, 1904 ● 56, Kaiser Wilhelm II visited Tangier, where he made a startling declaration denouncing the motives of French and Spanish interest in Morocco. His speech had many repercussions in Europe and eventually resulted in the conference of Algeciras on January 16, 1906.

INTERNATIONAL ZONE. When Morocco became a French protectorate ● 56 in 1912, the future of Tangier was still a matter of controversy. France, England and Spain decided to look for an acceptable compromise. On December 18, 1923, Tangier was declared an international zone, controlled by eight countries and monitored by a *mendoub* (sultan's representative), where political and military neutrality was compulsory and where there was complete economic freedom. Two major initiatives were responsible for putting

THE CONFERENCE OF ALGECIRAS
The twelve signatories of the treaty of Algeciras recognized Moroccan independence and confirmed their support for the principle of free trade and the economic equality of the foreign powers in Morocco. They also approved the involvement of French and Spanish legations in the country's affairs. The Moroccan delegation (left) was led by Sidi Hadj Mohammed Torres, Moulay Abd el Aziz's Minister for Foreign Affairs.

181

The poster (below) gives a realistic impression of Tangier in the first half of the 20th century. It was painted by the French artist Jacques Majorelle who was living in Morocco in 1917 and whose work was widely used to promote tourism.

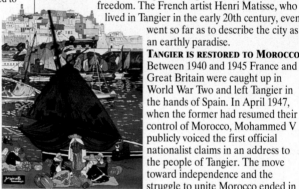

Tangier on the road to prosperity: first the introduction of free trade and, second, the abolition of taxes. New companies were established and foreign capital flooded into the city, which now attracted not only businessmen but also smugglers and spies. Jacques Majorelle, Kees Van Dongen, Tennessee Williams, Paul Bowles ● *125*, Jean Genet ▲ *211* and Paul Morand were among the many foreign artists and writers who were drawn to Tangier during the 1940's, and their work helped establish a new image for Tangier as a city of artistic freedom. The French artist Henri Matisse, who lived in Tangier in the early 20th century, even went so far as to describe the city as an earthly paradise.

TANGIER IS RESTORED TO MOROCCO. Between 1940 and 1945 France and Great Britain were caught up in World War Two and left Tangier in the hands of Spain. In April 1947, when the former had resumed their control of Morocco, Mohammed V publicly voiced the first official nationalist claims in an address to the people of Tangier. The move toward independence and the struggle to unite Morocco ended in 1956 ● *56*, when the country's independence was declared. This, and the simultaneous return of Tangier to Morocco, provoked the sudden departure of most of Tangier's foreign investors, which in turn caused a drastic decline in industrial and commercial activity.

A TOURIST TOWN. Since the 1970's Tangier (which today has a population of 300,000) has relied on tourism and related industries, particularly that of crafts, for its prosperity. It attracts around one million visitors every year and although this figure includes many thousands of Spanish, French and British tourists, large numbers of Moroccan holiday-makers also make the journey to Tangier. In summer it is one of the few Moroccan towns that offers a degree of respite from the heat, with temperatures rarely exceeding 75 degrees Fahrenheit (provided the *chergui*, a searingly hot easterly wind, is not sweeping relentlessly along the Moroccan coast). Tangier is also the crossing point for Moroccans working in European countries and wanting to return home by car. Standing at a cultural and commercial crossroads, and a stepping stone between Europe and Africa, Tangier is the gateway to Morocco.

THE FUTURE OF TANGIER. Tourism has helped channel foreign capital into foods and textiles but Tanjaoui industry and commerce are looking for new sources of capital. On June 7, 1991, an international financial market was

❝R'mel qala. The sand has spoken. That is the name of a small bay of sandstone and legends, where sirens meet to exchange tales and dream of the future. R'mel qala. Here the *chergui* becomes a swirling spiral of dust, spitting fire, tearing at the faces of city dwellers and bruising the bodies of children before dying out in this sinister corner of the earth, the birthplace of the imaginary shared by the city. The Tanjaouis can express words born of this sand.❞
Mohammed Choukri,
Autrement

> "I SKETCHED HASTILY AND WITH GREAT DIFFICULTY BECAUSE OF THE MUSLIM ATTITUDE TOWARDS IMAGES."
>
> EUGÈNE DELACROIX

Eugène Delacroix, *Moorish Interior* (1832).

KEES VAN DONGEN
The Dutch-born French artist was one of the precursors of Fauvism. He was first noticed in Paris in 1904 at Ambroise Vollard's well-known shop and visited Morocco in 1910 where he painted *Moroccan Woman at Cap Spartel* (left). After World War One he became a fashionable portrait painter.

created to encourage foreign investment in Morocco and prevent Moroccan capital leaving the country. The government re-established Tangier as a free trade zone, and also considered the exciting possibility of a fixed link between Tangier and Spain, in other words between Africa and Europe. Plans are currently afoot for the construction of a nineteen-mile bridge spanning the Straits of Gibraltar between Cape Malabata ▲ *189*, near Tangier, and the Cabo Enseneda de Bolonia, in Spain. This gigantic piece of engineering would enable ten million people, two million vehicles and five million tons of merchandise to cross between Spain and Africa every year. It would also encourage tourism and automatically boost Tangier's economy.

OLD TANGIER
This 18th-century engraving (below) shows old Tangier's extensive fortifications before they were destroyed in various attacks, the most serious of which were the bombardments inflicted by the Spanish navy in 1791 and the French in 1844.

THE GRAND SOCCO
The peasant women in the Grand Socco are easily recognized by their straw hats decorated with tassels and their *fouta* ● 79, the piece of red and white material worn as a skirt.

❝Seen from the sea, it looks almost cheerful, with its outlying villas built in gardens *à l'européenne*; and yet it still has an air of mystery about it, with its snow-white walls, its high, crenelated kasbah and its minarets tiled with old faïence.**❞**

Pierre Loti,
Au Maroc

THE MEDINA

THE GRAND SOCCO. At the entrance to the medina is the Grand Socco, a huge permanent market where merchants and peasant women sell locally produced fruit, vegetables and poultry. The Place du Grand Socco was renamed the PLACE DU 9 AVRIL 1947 to commemorate the historic address calling for Moroccan independence, given by the sultan Mohammed V ● 56. Its location and the various economic activities carried on there make the Place du Grand Socco the busiest public square in Tangier. However, nothing remains of the *joutia* (flea market) or the cafés that were once the favorite haunts of the town's French, Spanish and English residents. At one end of the square stands the SIDI BOUABID MOSQUE whose minaret (built in 1917) is completely covered in colored tiles. Below the mosque is the "MENDOUBIA", the residence of the *mendoub*, a representative of the sultan who was responsible for monitoring the activities of foreign powers when Tangier was an international zone. Today the building is used as a courthouse. A long staircase leads to a commemorative monument engraved with the text of Mohammed V's address of April 9, 1947. The gardens of the *mendoubia* contain a giant banyan tree ■ 44, a dragon tree said to be eight hundred years old and bronze cannons salvaged from fleets sent by European powers in the 17th and 18th centuries.

THE PETIT SOCCO ★. From the BAB FAHS, the south gate of the old town, the Rue es Siaghin widens and opens on to the Petit Socco, a small square bordered by cafés and old residences. In the center is the *Fuentes* hotel, where the French composer Camille Saint-Saëns lived. The GREAT MOSQUE (right) stands in the next street on the site once occupied by a Portuguese cathedral. The mosque was built by the sultan Moulay Ismail to commemorate the withdrawal of English forces at the end of the 17th century. Opposite the mosque is a 19th-century Spanish church with a copy of the

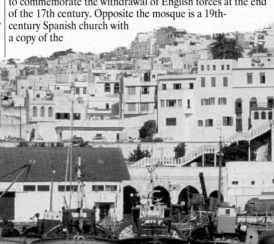

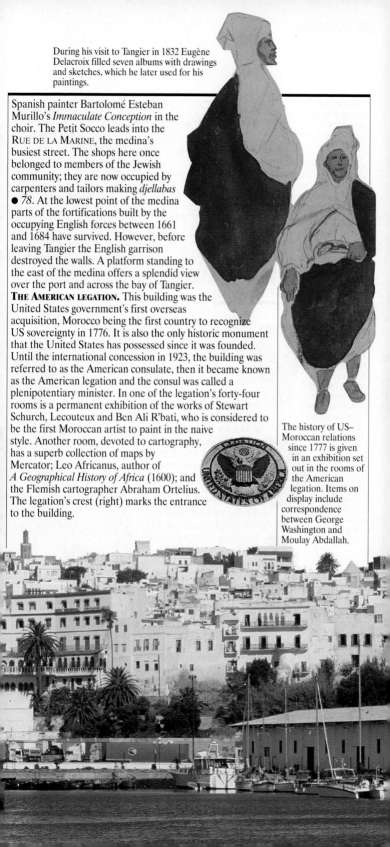

During his visit to Tangier in 1832 Eugène Delacroix filled seven albums with drawings and sketches, which he later used for his paintings.

Spanish painter Bartolomé Esteban Murillo's *Immaculate Conception* in the choir. The Petit Socco leads into the RUE DE LA MARINE, the medina's busiest street. The shops here once belonged to members of the Jewish community; they are now occupied by carpenters and tailors making *djellabas* ● 78. At the lowest point of the medina parts of the fortifications built by the occupying English forces between 1661 and 1684 have survived. However, before leaving Tangier the English garrison destroyed the walls. A platform standing to the east of the medina offers a splendid view over the port and across the bay of Tangier.

THE AMERICAN LEGATION. This building was the United States government's first overseas acquisition, Morocco being the first country to recognize US sovereignty in 1776. It is also the only historic monument that the United States has possessed since it was founded. Until the international concession in 1923, the building was referred to as the American consulate, then it became known as the American legation and the consul was called a plenipotentiary minister. In one of the legation's forty-four rooms is a permanent exhibition of the works of Stewart Schurch, Lecouteux and Ben Ali R'bati, who is considered to be the first Moroccan artist to paint in the naïve style. Another room, devoted to cartography, has a superb collection of maps by Mercator; Leo Africanus, author of *A Geographical History of Africa* (1600); and the Flemish cartographer Abraham Ortelius. The legation's crest (right) marks the entrance to the building.

The history of US–Moroccan relations since 1777 is given in an exhibition set out in the rooms of the American legation. Items on display include correspondence between George Washington and Moulay Abdallah.

The Kasbah

Tangier Pottery
Although most potters tend to copy ancient forms, some are more innovative. From top: a vase with polygonal star motifs in the style of *zellige*; a dish decorated with Berber geometric motifs; and a vase and dish with contemporary designs.

The Dar el Makhzen ★, the former governor's palace, was built during the reign of sultan Moulay Ismail, after the withdrawal of the English, in the 17th century. It was extended and converted several times during the 18th and 19th centuries. Today the palace houses Tangier's Museum of Moroccan Arts. Rooms opening onto a tiled courtyard contain exhibits from all parts of Morocco: carpets ● 74 from Rabat ▲ 161, jewelry ● 68, silks and ceramics ● 80 from Fez ▲ 213. In the adjoining palace, the Dar ech Chorfa (Museum of Antiquities) a collection of the archeological treasures found on the site of Volubilis ▲ 243, including a Roman mosaic on the theme of Venus, is displayed. In the *mechouar*, the main square of the kasbah, stand the octagonal minaret of the mosque and the Bit el Mal, the former treasury, constructed in 1684. The Dar ech Chera, with three imposing white marble columns standing at the entrance, is a former courthouse. The Place de la Kasbah, situated on a promontory and offering an unrestricted view across the bay and port of Tangier, opens onto a narrow street bordered with houses that are elaborately decorated with cherubs, ornate windows and colorful balconies.

The sultan's "Mokhazni"
The sultan's servants were distinguished by their red wool fez (pointed hats) ● 78 and their immaculate kaftan worn with a *farajiya* (a sort of lightweight tunic).

> "JUST AS OTHERS BELIEVED IN THE EXISTENCE OF ATLANTIS, I BELIEVED IN THE EXISTENCE OF TANGIER. IN THIS CITY THE FAIRY HAD A WAND WHICH WAS CALLED DARE."
>
> MOHAMMED CHOUKRI

THE MARSHAN

THE FORBES MUSEUM. The museum is housed in the former residence of the American millionaire, Malcolm Forbes, which lies in the Marshan to the west of the kasbah. Starting in 1978 Forbes built up a collection of 115,000 military miniatures which he bequeathed to Tangier shortly before his death in 1990. In two of the rooms on the first floor, some of the lead soldiers have been perfectly positioned in reconstructions of the world's greatest battles. Those represented include Waterloo (1815), the Somme (1916) and Dien Bien Phu (1954), as well as the Battle of the Three Kings ● 55. The museum's gardens, planted with palm trees, orange trees and eucalyptus, offer an exceptional view of the Straits of Gibraltar and the Spanish coast.

THE CAFÉ HAFA OR CAFÉ DES TILLEULS At the Café Hafa, just a short stroll from the Forbes Museum, most of the tables are set out on small terraces that descend steeply to the sea. Perched on the hillside among the flowers and shrubs, the Café Hafa is a haven of peace and tranquillity amid the bustle of the city. The expatriate American writer Paul Bowles ● 125 sometimes came here to drink mint tea.

THE NEW TOWN

BOULEVARD PASTEUR. The Boulevard Pasteur is modern Tangier's main thoroughfare. It starts at the PLACE DE FRANCE, where the FRENCH CONSULATE was built. At the entrance to the boulevard an esplanade overlooks the port, medina and the Straits of Gibraltar. On the boulevard itself are a number of European-style residential blocks, the oldest of which date from the turn of the century, and the majority of Tangier's banks and luxury shops. The Boulevard Pasteur runs into the BOULEVARD MOHAMMED V, which continues out of the center into the western suburbs of Tangier, where new blocks of flats have gone up at an amazing pace.

"EL MINZAH" HOTEL ★. The *El Minzah* hotel, opened in 1933, stands on the street linking the Place de France and the Place du Grand Socco. It was built by French architects and is the former residence of the 18th-century British prime minister, Lord Bute. With an Andalusian patio, a Moorish interior and exquisite fountains and gardens, this splendid building is incontestably Tangier's most beautiful hotel. It also boasts an unrivaled Moroccan cuisine. Today *El Minzah* has become part of Tanjaoui legend. Winston Churchill and Rita Hayworth were just two of its distinguished regular guests, and several film directors on location in Tangier have chosen to film here. In 1990 Bernardo Bertolucci shot scenes for *The Sheltering Sky* (adapted from the novel by Paul Bowles) in the *El Minzah* hotel, the Café de Paris as well as in the cafés of the Petit Socco in the medina and a number of hotels there with an "Arabian nights"-style décor.

THE BATTLE OF THE THREE KINGS
Part of the re-creation of the famous Battle of the Three Kings that forms the centerpiece of the Forbes Museum's toy soldier collection. In 1578 the armies of the sultan Abd el Malik fought the combined forces of Sebastian I of Portugal and the sultan Moulay Mohammed, and the battle ended with the death of the three kings. The model consists of over six hundred handmade figures, which were designed, modeled and painted by Edward Suren, one of the world's leading designers and makers of lead soldiers.

"He [Paul Bowles] described his idyllic life at the Hôtel el Minzah which had

just opened. 'Three dollars a day for full board!' The journalist made a mental note to cross out 'full board' as he didn't want to tarnish the idyll."

Robert Briatte,
Tanger s'il y a lieu

187

THE CAPE SPARTEL LIGHTHOUSE
The lighthouse, which was built by order of Sidi Abd er Rahman, was lit for the first time on October 15, 1864. Inside there are framed photographs of lighthouses from all over the world.

PHARE DU CAP SPARTEL
FARO DE CABO ESPARTEL
ENTREE INTERDITE
ENTRADA PROHIBIDA

"One Sunday we went to the Grottoes of Hercules, those mythical caves where you can look out onto the Atlantic from between rocky pillars and where precariously balanced Arab workmen hew millstones from the soft rock. The stones are used to grind grain in the time-honored manner of their ancestors."
Joseph Kessel,
Le Grand Socco

The rocky Atlantic coastline near Cape Spartel.

The round trip from Tangier to Cape Spartel, to the west of the city, can be made in a day. The most convenient route is the road that runs from modern Tangier across the city's residential district, known as the Mountain, or Jebel el Kebir. In the 17th century this wooded hill provided cover for the Moors in their battles against the Portuguese and later against the English when they occupied Tangier.

THE MOUNTAIN. The Rue de Belgique, with the modern MOHAMMED V MOSQUE, runs between the Place de France and Tangier's residential district. Palaces and Hispano-Moresque villas, built mainly by wealthy foreigners attracted to the city when Tangier was an international zone, are laid out among the eucalyptus ■ 32 and umbrella pines. A DOG'S CEMETERY under the eucalyptus trees is an incongruous reminder of this cosmopolitan period. Beyond the residential district lies the DONABO PARK, with a vantage point, the MIRADOR DE PERDICARIS, shaded by umbrella pines. The coast road to Cape Spartel follows a picturesque route beside sheer rockfaces and wide ocher-colored beaches. The scenery is well worth a stop on one of the bends overlooking the sea. Cape Spartel, known to the Romans as Caput Ampelusium (Cape of Vines), is a promontory on the northwest tip of Africa about 9 miles from Tangier. It is covered by varied scrub vegetation consisting of cork oaks ■ 32, holm oaks, heather, broom, rockroses and mastic trees, interspersed with palms ■ 42. A lighthouse marks the strait where the Atlantic meets the Mediterranean.

GROTTOES OF HERCULES ★. These natural limestone caves, which are flooded at high tide, lie about 6 miles from Tangier. They are dark and dank, since the only source of light is an opening onto the sea, which is shaped according to some like a human head and according to others like an inverted map of

"THE LIGHT AT THE [NORTHERN] TIP OF AFRICA STANDS AT THE
ENTRANCE TO THE STRAITS OF GIBRALTAR."

PHILIPPE PONS

Africa. In classical mythology, Hercules rested in these caves
after completing his labors. Legend has it that it was Hercules
himself who created the Straits of Gibraltar by pushing aside
the mountains to form Jebel Tarik (Gibraltar) on the north
side and Jebel Musa, in Africa, on the south. These headlands
are sometimes called "The Pillars of Hercules". Prehistoric
remains have been discovered on the site and the cave walls
are marked with hundreds of circular engravings thought to
have been made with flints by the early Atlanteans. The
pieces of limestone found in the caves were used as
millstones.

THE RUINS OF COTTA. These Roman ruins are about 550 yards
from the Grottoes of Hercules. A program of excavations has
revealed several wall sections and the layout of a Roman
town, probably dating from the 2nd and 3rd centuries. There
are the remains of a temple, a bathhouse, farms and huge
cemented vats, which has led historians to suggest that there
were oil mills and factories where *garum* (fish extract) was
made in Cotta. Also found on the site were several grooved
stones used in olive presses and two columns that stood as a
landmark for fishermen working the waters along the coast. A
few dozen yards away from the ruins, a concrete esplanade
runs along the edge of the shore and the Hassan II private
beach.

CAPE MALABATA

Cap Malabata, windswept and exposed, lies about 6 miles
east of Tangier on the Mediterranean coast. Like Cape
Spartel, it is topped by a
lighthouse, and the site offers
wide views across the town and
bay of Tangier. On the right,
before reaching the lighthouse,
can be seen a striking medieval-
style castle which dates from the
beginning of the 20th century. A
major coastal resort is being built
near the cape, with hotels,
holiday villages, villas and
apartments, together with a
conference center, casinos and a
marina with space for six hundred
boats. Sports facilities to be
added will include a 64-acre man-
made lake ideal for windsurfing
enthusiasts. Following plans for
the construction of a massive
bridge between Africa and
Europe, which would
automatically bring more visitors
to Tangier, the Moroccan
government has created a
nationalized company, in which it
has a 50 percent stake, to be in
charge of developing Tangier and
promoting tourism. Its aim is to
restore the ancient city to its
former glory.

*"Below Cape Spartel
are the ruins of Cotta,
the remains of a
Roman town by the
sea. It was here that
the Romans used to
make garum from the
intestines of
marinated fish. This
salty extract was
much sought after
throughout the
Empire. Pots of
garum were sent from
Tangier to be sold by
the finest grocers in
Rome."*
Daniel Rondeau,
Tanger

Kees Van Dongen,
The Young Arab, 1911.

189

▲ TANGIER TO FEZ

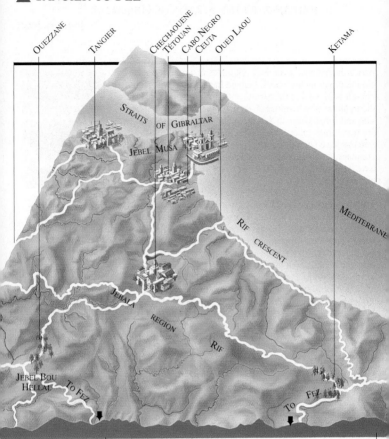

OUEZZANE · TANGIER · CHECHAOUENE · TÉTOUAN · CABO NEGRO · CEUTA · OUED LAOU · KETAMA

STRAITS OF GIBRALTAR

JEBEL MUSA

MEDITERRANEAN

RIF CRESCENT

JEBALA REGION

RIF

JEBEL BOU HELLAL

TO FEZ

TO FEZ

MULETEERS
The two figures
(below and opposite)
are details from
Eugène Delacroix's
▲ *202* painting
Muleteers of Tétouan,
now in the Museum
of Laon, France.

TÉTOUAN

In 1307, as part of the armed struggle against the Portuguese, who had occupied Sebta (Ceuta) ▲ *194*, the Merinid sultan Abou Thabit built a fort in the Rif Mountains ■ *24* on the borders of the Jebala region. Tétouan rapidly became a military base and the corsairs who plundered the ships sailing along the Mediterranean coast found it to be a convenient base for their activities. This earned the town some powerful enemies, and in 1399 Henry III of Castile decided that the best way to solve the problem of the Tétouan corsairs, who were terrorizing Spanish coastal waters, was to attack their base. His forces destroyed the town and dispersed its population.

FROM THE "RECONQUISTA" TO MOULAY ISMAIL. Normal life did not return to Tétouan until the end of the 15th century. The Christian Reconquest of Spain came to its conclusion when Grenada fell in 1492. Large numbers of Muslims and Jews who were driven out of the city and made homeless crossed the straits into Africa, settled in Tétouan and rebuilt the town. However, following in the tradition of the former corsairs, some of these exiles took to piracy, once again incurring the wrath of the Spanish sovereign. In 1565 Philip II of Spain imposed a blockade on the port, which naturally led to a decline in Tétouan's commercial activities. In the 17th century, however, the town's fortunes began to revive under the rule of the sultan Moulay Ismail, who encouraged the development of trade with the Europe.

In 1859 the Spanish navy crossed the Straits of Gibraltar with an army of fifty thousand men.

The installation of European consuls provided a further boost for the town's economy, and a French consulate remained in Tétouan until 1712. Still within its 17th-century ramparts, the now-prosperous town began to develop. Nevertheless, Spain continued to covet Tétouan and, encouraged in its ambition by the capture of Ceuta in 1859, launched a military campaign to conquer territory further south, recapturing Tétouan in 1860. The negotiations for a peace treaty to bring the Spanish occupation to an end lasted two years.

FROM THE SPANISH PROTECTORATE TO THE PRESENT DAY.
Following the Treaty of Madrid (1912) ● *56*, which gave Spain official control of the Rif, the Spaniards returned to Tétouan and in 1913 decided to make the town the capital of the Spanish protectorate. This was an important development in the history of the region but even so it was not until Morocco gained independence in 1956 that the Rif emerged from its isolation, mainly as a result of a program of road-building along the Mediterranean coast. From 1970, however, several years of sustained commercial development in and around Tétouan have turned it into a major city. Today it has a population of almost 365,000 and is the provincial capital of the Rif.

A HISPANO-MORESQUE TOWN. Architecture in Tétouan is a harmonious and fascinating blend of Arabic and Spanish styles reflecting the town's bicultural ancestry. Although Spanish is now rarely heard in Tétouan, Spanish culture still plays a significant part in the life of the city. Andalusian music has remained dominant and trade with Ceuta ▲ *194*, the Spanish enclave that is only about 25 miles away, keeps alive the historic links between the Arabic and Spanish cultures. Tétouan has benefited from the commercial activity of the port of Ceuta since early times. In 1068 El Bekri described Tétouan as dominating the lower reaches of the Ouadi Ras, which the writer Mohammed Ibn Youssouf (961–75) of Córdoba called the Medjekessa, because the river was wide enough at that point to allow small ships to sail upstream as far as Tétouan. Since 1982 the creation of an industrial belt around the town has helped Tétouan develop a range of industries, including tobacco, textiles, plastics, agricultural foodstuffs and stock-breeding ■ *50*. Today the city also has a thriving tourist industry.

🚗 Three days

THE CAPTURE OF TÉTOUAN. On the pretext of quelling an uprising of the Anjra tribe against Ceuta, the Spaniards attacked and captured Tétouan on February 6, 1860. In exchange for agreeing to leave the town they demanded a war indemnity amounting to a colossal twenty million duros. In 1862 the Moroccan government had to borrow from Britain to pay off the debt.

Uniforms of the engineers of the Spanish expeditionary force (left).

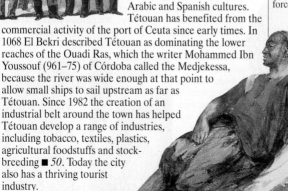

Silver Alaouite *mithqal* dated 1780.

Planispherical, bronze and silver astrolabe (below) made in Tétouan in the 18th century.

A tour of the city of Tétouan traditionally starts in the PLACE EL JALA with a visit to the Archeological Museum, which stands beyond the ruins of the town's former ramparts.

ARCHEOLOGICAL MUSEUM. The museum houses a large collection of mosaics and other items that have been discovered in the course of excavations at the many ancient sites of northern Morocco. In the first-floor gallery are mosaics depicting the *Three Graces* and the *Young Bacchus*. One room contains a delightful series of Roman mosaics with such themes as *Venus and Adonis* and *Mars and Rhea*, which were uncovered during excavations at Lixus ▲ *209*. Another is devoted to a collection of coins, bronzes and pottery dating from the 1st century AD and various sculpted figures, among them a statue of Hercules lifting Antaeus. Upstairs, pottery and coins found at the ancient site of TAMUDA, discovered a few miles from Tétouan, are displayed in a row of showcases. Tamuda (or Thamusida) is thought by historians to have been occupied in the 2nd century BC and razed by the Romans in AD 40. The museum library, built up under the Spanish protectorate, contains a superb collection of around 600,000 volumes relating to the history of the Maghreb and Islam ● *62*.

THE MEDINA ★. The old and new towns of Tétouan are linked by the Place Hassan II. THE PALACE OF THE KHALIFA, in the square, the former residence of the sultan's representative under the Spanish protectorate ● *56*, is the present royal palace. Built in the 17th century during the reign of Moulay Ismail and restored in 1948, it is a fine example of Hispano-Moresque architecture. The medina ● *92* lies inside a fortified wall with no fewer than seven decorated gates. Facing toward the medina, BAB EL OQLA, the old town's eastern gate, looks onto the MUSEUM OF MOROCCAN ARTS, whose well-maintained collections of regional costumes ● *78* and musical instruments ● *70* are a further reminder of Tétouan's Andalusian origins. The museum, which is housed in a 19th-century bastion, was opened in 1948. Facing toward the new town, Bab el Oqla opens onto the SCHOOL OF TRADITIONAL ARTS AND CRAFTS (right).

Exhibit (above) on display in the School of Traditional Arts and Crafts south of the Great Mosque (right).

THE MEDINA
"Many of the streets
are covered and are
like underground
tunnels . . . These
dark passages have
doors or grilles which
are closed at night.
Other streets are
covered with vines
and this unexpected
vegetation harbors a
precious coolness."
François Hoefer,
Empire du Maroc

For more than fifty years teachers at the school have been
instructing young artisans in such crafts as weaving ● *75*,
leatherwork and mosaics ▲ *173*, engraving, sculpture and
painting. Examples of the best work by teachers and pupils
have been collected and put on display in the school's great
hall. The building occupies a prime site, overlooking a
beautiful landscaped garden planted with a diverse and
pleasing selection of trees and other plants. There are several
mosques ● *86* situated in the medina, including those of SIDI
ES SAÏD, with its impressive minaret ● *88* attractively
decorated with *zellige* ▲ *173*, and SIDI BEN MESSAOUD, which
has an ornate carved entrance.

THE CRAFTSMEN OF TÉTOUAN. The RUE TERRAFIN, one
of the main thoroughfares in the medina, is lined
with an interesting variety of workshops and opens
onto an intricate maze of narrow streets and
souks. In the old town craftsmen are grouped
together according to their trade, with tanners
▲ *225*, carpenters, leather-workers, and
tailors making *djellabas*, each occupying
shops situated in clearly defined areas.
Until 1982 craft trades represented
Tétouan's greatest source of income, and the
town is especially renowned for its
embroidery ● *76* and pottery ● *80*. Although
their work is usually decorated with simple,
geometric designs, the potters and
embroiderers of Tétouan also use a range of
stylized motifs in traditional colors such as
yellow, red, blue and green.

TÉTOUAN KAFTANS
The women of
Tétouan used to wear
the kaftan ● *78*, a
robe with broad,
flared sleeves, made
in dark red or purple
velvet by the town's
tailors. The kaftan
was traditionally
fastened with a broad
embroidered belt
● *77*. In this costume
(left) the belt is
narrow, with
elaborate
braided
decoration.
Kaftans are
increasingly
rarely worn
today.

193

EL IDRISI
El Idrisi, an Arab geographer born in Ceuta in 1099, left a number of writings, including a *Description of Africa and Spain.* His map (right), drawn in 1154, does not respect modern cartographic conventions since the North is at the bottom.

PHILIP II OF SPAIN
After the sultan Abd el Malik, his Moroccan ally, trounced the Portuguese army, Philip II occupied Portugal and seized Ceuta in 1580.

According to Tahar Ben Jelloun, after the Battle of Serrallo (below) the city remained "under Spanish sovereignty and was a jealously guarded prisoner whose body was exhausted by trafficking of all kinds [...]. Ugly apartment blocks were built to erase the Arab presence, to eradicate the ashes of the past."

CEUTA

The name of the town of Ceuta (in Spanish), or Sebta (in Arabic), is derived from the Latin name *Septem Fratres* (Seven Brothers) referring to the seven hills that lie to the west of Monte Hacho, near Jebel Musa. Ceuta, built on the Monte Hacho promontory, expanded during the 8th century when the Berbers turned the peninsula into a military base and rallying point for the *djihad*. By the 13th century, the port was thriving, as it traded with Pisa, Venice, Genoa, Alexandria, Marseilles and Barcelona, importing carpets and cloth and exporting coral jewelry and copperware made in Tétouan. Strategically placed at the entrance to the Straits of Gibraltar, Ceuta was also able to control commercial shipping. This made the town a prize greatly coveted by foreign powers and led to its being besieged by the Portuguese in 1415 and placed under Spanish control in 1580. Today the enclave of Ceuta is separated from the rest of Morocco by a frontier and has been declared a free trade zone. The port is still Ceuta's main source of prosperity.
A SPANISH TOWN. After more than five centuries of Christian occupation Ceuta has lost all trace of its Muslim culture. Mosques have been gradually replaced by churches and in the CATHEDRAL that stands in the Plaza de Africa, the flagstones in the central nave bear the coats of arms of Spanish bishops. Near the cathedral stands the 18th-century Baroque CHURCH OF OUR LADY OF AFRICA. It is dedicated to the patron saint of the town, who is said to have rid Ceuta of a plague epidemic in the 16th century.

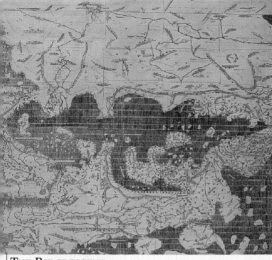

A seaside resort on the Rif crescent.

PENON DE VELEZ DE LA GOMERA
(Ghomara Isles)
Together with Ceuta, Mellila and the Islas Chafarinas, these islands are one of the Spanish *presidios* (fortified posts) that are still a matter of dispute between Morocco and Spain.

THE RIF CRESCENT ★

CABO NEGRO. From Ceuta the road runs along the Mediterranean coast and through the seaside resorts of SMIR RESTINGA, MDIQ, CABO NEGRO and MARTIL, on the bay of Tétouan. Cabo Negro is the largest of these resorts and, since 1960, has received a number of government subsidies to enable it to develop its tourist amenities. A holiday resort with beach clubs, hotels and family boardinghouses has now grown up centered around the little fishing port.

OUED LAOU. Further south, near Tétouan, the village of Oued Laou has preserved the simple charms of a fishing port while simultaneously developing its tourist industry. The best way to approach Oued Laou is along the minor road that turns off the main Tétouan-Chechaouene (Chaouen) road. The road, paved almost all the way, winds across a wild and semi-desert landscape of mountains and canyons before descending to the fertile plain of Oued Laou. In July a *moussem* ▲ *339* is held in the valley in which the local *tagarrabout* (small black boats decorated with ancient designs) take part.

GUEZENAÏA POTTERY Named after a Rif tribe from the Jebel Berkane region.

AL HOCEIMA. Further east along the Mediterranean coast stands the early 9th-century town of Al Hoceima. The French tried to establish a trading center there in the 17th century but were dissuaded by the presence of the British and Spanish. In 1926 the bay of Al Hoceima, birthplace of the Rif rebellion ▲ *196*, ● *56*, ■ *24*, underwent extensive development as a tourist resort.

MOHAMMED BEN ABDELKRIM
Mohammed Ben Abdelkrim, leader of the Rif rebellion and president of the confederate republic of the Rif, whose motto advocated death before retreat. Between 1920 and 1926 he lived in the village of Ajdir, three miles south of Al Hoceima.

"Under its rounded, red tiles Chaouen plays a thousand tricks in the sunlight. The bright splashes of its freshly painted blue and white walls are engaged in a game of hide-and-seek which lasts throughout the day; fine grilles and hidden vents cast delightful shadows, while cool, vaulted passages echo with the sound of trickling water and sing the praises of Sidi Ali Ben Rachid, who founded the town."

François Garrigues,
Le Maroc enchanté

CHECHAOUENE

Chechaouene, more commonly called Chaouen, nestles between two mountains known together as JEBEL ECH CHAOUEN (Horned Mountain).

A FORTRESS. The town was founded in 1471 by the chérif Moulay Ali Ben Rachid in a bid to prevent the Portuguese and Spanish from moving inland from Ceuta ▲ *194* and Ksar es Seghir ▲ *211*, where they had established themselves on the Moroccan side of the Straits of Gibraltar. The sultan built

a FORTIFIED CASTLE, parts of which can still be seen today. In the 15th century the town was populated by a first wave of Andalous Muslims who had been driven out of Spain. A second wave of refugees followed in the 17th century. For many years Christians were forbidden to enter Chaouen, but in the 19th century three Europeans managed to slip in despite the interdiction. In 1883, Charles de Foucauld spent the night there disguised as a Jew, William Harris went there in 1889 and William Summers was poisoned by the inhabitants in 1892.

THE RIF REBELLION. Chaouen was a focal point for resistance to the Spanish protectorate ● *56* and in 1924 became the battlefield in the confrontation between the forces of Mohammed Ben Abdelkrim ▲ *195* and the Spanish troops. With the help of French soldiers, who between 1912 and 1934 conducted a campaign of "pacification" to put down any localized rebellions (particularly in the Rif), Spain managed to impose its authority on the town in 1926. On the declaration of independence in 1956 Chaouen became part of Morocco.

A HOLY TOWN. To commemorate the goodness of Allah, who had caused a number of springs to rise in the Jebel ech Chaouen, the Arabs made Chaouen an important political and religious center and proclaimed it a holy town. Today Chechaouene has around twenty mosques and sanctuaries, the largest of which bears the name of its founder and patron, Moulay Ali Ben Rachid.The livelihood of Chechaouene's 300,000 inhabitants comes from agriculture, traditional crafts and tourism.

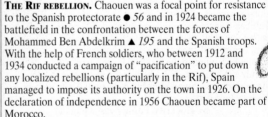

> "THE TOWN COMES INTO VIEW, BUILT AGAINST SHEER MOUNTAINS ON THE ONE HAND AND BORDERED BY GREEN GARDENS ON THE OTHER."
>
> CHARLES DE FOUCAULD

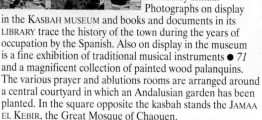

PLAZA UTA EL HAMMAM. The remains of the impressive 15th-century fortifications built by Moulay Ali Ben Rachid can still be seen in this charming tree-lined square, which is bordered by several small cafés and restaurants. A former prison lies within the red crenellated walls of the KASBAH, constructed in 1672 during the reign of Moulay Ismail. Photographs on display in the KASBAH MUSEUM and books and documents in its LIBRARY trace the history of the town during the years of occupation by the Spanish. Also on display in the museum is a fine exhibition of traditional musical instruments ● *71* and a magnificent collection of painted wood palanquins. The various prayer and ablutions rooms are arranged around a central courtyard in which an Andalusian garden has been planted. In the square opposite the kasbah stands the JAMAA EL KEBIR, the Great Mosque of Chaouen.

THE MEDINA ★. The houses that crowd together in the maze of alleyways at the top of the medina ● *92*, overlooking the town and valley, have typically Moroccan studded doors, carved cornices, porches and wrought-iron balconies. The lower part of each of these whitewashed houses is painted a blueish-mauve. This type of paintwork, originally used by the Andalusians, has been found to keep the houses cool even during the hottest periods, and also to ward off insects. From BAB EL KHADEM, the south gate of the medina, the road to Ouezzane passes a working WATERMILL and then, further south, an OIL MILL, once worked by mules, before climbing to the town's largest spring, the RAS EL MA.

JAMAA EL KEBIR
The Great Mosque, founded in the 15th century, is reminiscent of Andalusian architecture. The octagonal minaret is said to have been inspired by the Torre de Oro in Seville.

Legend has it that the route of the road that winds up to Tétouan was decided by allowing a donkey to make its own way up the mountain.

Landscape between
Chechaouene and Fez.

**"ENTRY OF THE
CHÉRIF OF OUEZZANE
TO THE MOSQUE"**
In 1869 Georges
Clairin traveled
widely in northern
Morocco and stayed
in Ouezzane. He was
fascinated by the
sights and sounds of
this country, which
for him epitomized
the mystery and
grandeur of
the Orient.

OUEZZANE

Ouezzane, formerly Dechra Jebel er Rihan (Village of the
Hill of Myrtles), stands on the slopes of the JEBEL BOU
HELLAL, which today are planted with varieties of olive and
fruit trees. The town grew up around the *zaouia* (religious
center) founded in 1727 by the Idrissid chérif Moulay
Abdallah, a descendant of Idriss II and founder member of
the Taïbia brotherhood, one of the most famous religious
fraternities in Morocco. Ouezzane continued to be extremely
influential in matters of religion until the 19th century. The
town's influence persisted up until the end of the 19th century
due to the fact that the chérif Si Abd es Salam ignored the
sultan's ban on trade with European countries and
encouraged the French to move into the Rif.

OUEZZANE AND THE SULTANS. The power of Ouezzane's
zaouia resulted from the relationship between the
Taïbia brotherhood and the sultans. Thus, in the
19th century, when the brotherhood was at the
height of its power, the newly invested sultan of
Morocco paid a symbolic visit to Ouezzane to
seek the support of the *zaouia*. The chérif of
Ouezzane paid homage to the sultan on behalf
of the mountain tribes and, in a gesture of
allegiance, helped him to mount his horse
when he left.

A RELIGIOUS TOWN
Ouezzane is to this day an
important religious center, with many of
its *chorfa* considered to be descendants of
the Prophet Mohammed. It is also a
place of pilgrimage for Moroccan Jews.
Every year they come in the thousands to
pay homage at the tomb of the Rabbi Ba
Amrane, an 18th-century miracle-worker
and the religious leader of Ouezzane's
Jewish community. He is buried at Aajèn,
five miles northeast of the town.

On the winding road
to Ouezzane.

THE MEDINA. The narrow, winding steps of the Rue de la
Zaouia lead from the PLACE DE L'INDÉPENDANCE to the
MOSQUE OF MOULAY ABDALLAH CHÉRIF and the ZAOUIA OF
THE TAÏBIA, with its octagonal minaret decorated with *zellige*
▲ *173*. The craftsmen's quarter, where the workshops are
grouped according to trade, is centered around these two
buildings. The top of the medina is occupied by carpenters,
tailors and weavers. The weavers of Ouezzane are renowned
throughout Morocco. Opening their workshops to visitors,
they demonstrate the traditional methods still used to weave
the *djellabas* and carpets ● *74* which are sold in the town's
souks. Ouezzane's main sources of income have long been
crafts and the production of olive oil. However, these
industries alone cannot sustain a population of almost sixty
thousand and today its economy appears to be slowing down.
These difficulties arise partly because Ouezzane is not a
prime tourist attraction and partly because the goods
produced in the town are mainly sold locally. At the bottom of
the medina are the old workshops of the IRONSMITHS' SOUK.
Their steep, double-pitch roofs, thatched rather than tiled
or corrugated, are typical of the towns of the Rif.
The narrow streets of the medina are lined with
beautiful old houses decorated with tiles,
which belong to the families of the former
chorfa of Ouezzane.

TO JEBEL BOU HELLAL. The road to Jebel
Bou Hellal is difficult and not always
negotiable by car. It follows the road to
Moulay Idriss and Meknès for a short
distance then skirts around a public garden
before climbing towards Jebel Bou Hellal (2,000
feet). A track beginning about halfway up this climb
leads to a vantage point offering a magnificent view over the
valley, the olive groves and the town.

TO FEZ. The best way to get from Ouezzane to Fez ▲ *213* is
to take the road to Fez el Bali (not to be confused with the
old town of Fez ▲ *221*) rather than to follow the more direct
route via Moulay Idriss ▲ *250*. The route to Fez el Bali offers
a number of attractions. About 19 miles south of Ouezzane
the road passes through MJARA and the VILLAGE OF FEZ EL
BALI before coming to the valley of the OUED OUERRHA and
the territory of the Beni Zeroual tribe. This southern Riffian
tribe was one of the first to give their support to Mohammed
Ben Abdelkrim ▲ *195*. In the heart of the valley, about
4 miles from Fez el Bali, stands the 12th-century fortress of
Jebel Amergou, built by the Almoravids as a means of
controlling the lands inhabited by the Ghomara Berbers.
From here one road runs eastward to the village of
OURTZARH, situated at the confluence of the Oued Ouerrha
and the Oued Aoulaï, and the FORT DES COULIS of El
Kelaa des Slès. A track leads northward to the
BELVEDERE OF LALLA OUTKA (5,230 feet). A second
road leads southward to MOULAY BOUCHTA and the
zaouia of Moulay Bouchta, patron saint of music and
dance, also known as El Khammar (The Drunk). According
to one local legend his prayers for rain during a drought were
answered with a much-needed downpour. The *koubba* ● *83*
of Sidi Ahmed el Bernoussi, patron saint of the imperial city,
stands just outside Fez.

THE JEBALA REGION
The isolated
mountain dwellers of
the Jebala region,
lying between
Chaouen and
Ouezzane, gather at
weekly souks and
moussem ▲ *339*. On
these occasions the
women wear their
red, blue or black and
white *fouta* and tuck
their hair under wide-
brimmed straw hats
● *79*.

THE "DJELLABA"
The *djellaba*,
traditional costume
● *78* for the
inhabitants of the
Rif, inspired French
painter Gabriel
Rousseau, the
president and
founder of *The
Kasbah*, an
association of
Moroccan artists, in
1923.

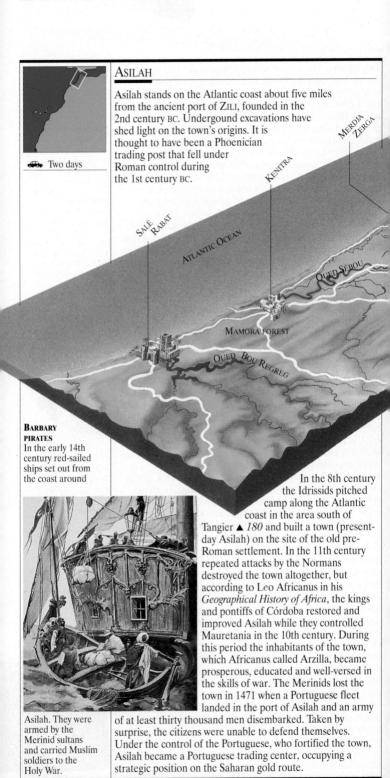

Two days

ASILAH

Asilah stands on the Atlantic coast about five miles from the ancient port of ZILI, founded in the 2nd century BC. Undergound excavations have shed light on the town's origins. It is thought to have been a Phoenician trading post that fell under Roman control during the 1st century BC.

MERDJA ZERGA

KENTRA

SALÉ RABAT

ATLANTIC OCEAN

OUED SEBOU

MAMORA FOREST

OUED BOU REGREG

BARBARY PIRATES
In the early 14th century red-sailed ships set out from the coast around Asilah. They were armed by the Merinid sultans and carried Muslim soldiers to the Holy War.

In the 8th century the Idrissids pitched camp along the Atlantic coast in the area south of Tangier ▲ *180* and built a town (present-day Asilah) on the site of the old pre-Roman settlement. In the 11th century repeated attacks by the Normans destroyed the town altogether, but according to Leo Africanus in his *Geographical History of Africa*, the kings and pontiffs of Córdoba restored and improved Asilah while they controlled Mauretania in the 10th century. During this period the inhabitants of the town, which Africanus called Arzilla, became prosperous, educated and well-versed in the skills of war. The Merinids lost the town in 1471 when a Portuguese fleet landed in the port of Asilah and an army of at least thirty thousand men disembarked. Taken by surprise, the citizens were unable to defend themselves. Under the control of the Portuguese, who fortified the town, Asilah became a Portuguese trading center, occupying a strategic position on the Saharan gold route.

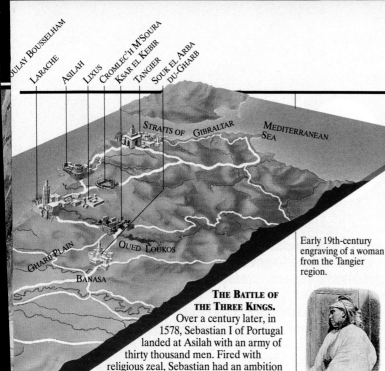

MOULAY BOUSSELHAM
LARACHE
ASILAH
LIXUS
CROMLEC'H M'SOURA
KSAR EL KEBIR
TANGIER
SOUK EL ARBA DU-GHARB

STRAITS OF GIBRALTAR
MEDITERRANEAN SEA

OUED LOUKOS

GHARB PLAIN

BANASA

Early 19th-century engraving of a woman from the Tangier region.

ARZILLA.

THE BATTLE OF THE THREE KINGS.

Over a century later, in 1578, Sebastian I of Portugal landed at Asilah with an army of thirty thousand men. Fired with religious zeal, Sebastian had an ambition to conquer Morocco. However, on April 4, 1578, his troops were trapped between the Oued Makhzen and the Oued Loukos in the region of Larache ▲ *210* and Ksar el Kebir ▲ *211*. There followed the famous Battle of the Three Kings ▲ *187* during which Sebastian was abandoned by his retreating army and died on the battlefield. The two sultans, Abd el Malik and Moulay Mohammed, also died in the battle, which some historians have described as the "Poitiers of the Maghreb". The defeated Portuguese were imprisoned and forced to relinquish all their trading centers on the Atlantic coast. Asilah was under Spanish control until 1691, when it fell to Moulay Ismaïl.

SULTAN OF THE MOUNTAINS. Asilah's history is closely linked to that of Moulay Ahmed el Raisouli (the Brigand), who for thirty years was the scourge of the countryside around Tangier ▲ *180* and Tétouan ▲ *190*. He made his fortune by holding the mountain tribes for ransom and acquired an international reputation when he kidnapped the English journalist Walter Harris. In return for Harris' release, Moulay Ahmed received $20,000 and the title of *Kaïd* for the region of Tangier. He unceremoniously expelled the existing pasha and captured Asilah in 1906. When World War One broke out Moulay Ahmed Raisouli, disregarding previous Spanish support, threw in his lot with the Germans. It was the defeat of his allies that brought about his downfall. Raisouli was driven out of Asilah by Spain and was captured by Mohammed Ben Abdelkrim in 1925. Asilah remained a Spanish enclave until Moroccan independence in 1956 ● *56*.

ASILAH IN 1575
Trade was Asilah's livelihood. The town exported cereals, wax, horses and cattle and imported textiles. It had trading links with Spain and Portugal, Genoa, Venice and Marseilles.

THE MARABOUT OF ASILAH
"Morocco is a country of drums, *djennouns*, sinuous snakes, parades, cavalcades and vague dreams of sleeping saints."

Paul Fort

201

207

The cemetery at Asilah (foreground), perched on the ramparts.

MURALS
During Asilah's cultural festival, the Zelachis (inhabitants of Asilah) help artists decorate the walls of the town.

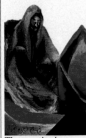

The practice is related to Asilah's history and the annual tradition of repainting the whitewashed houses.

A HISPANO-MORESQUE TOWN. The 15th-century ramparts ★, built by the Portuguese architect Botacca, overlook the Atlantic on one side and the town on the other. Three monumental gates and a concealed passageway lead into the medina ● 92 ★. The BAB EL BAHAR (Sea Gate) opens directly onto the Place Sidi Ali Ben Hamdouch, where a square tower houses a number of art galleries. In the next street is the former residence of EL RAISOULI, an early 20th-century building in Hispano-Moresque style that today hosts a variety of cultural events held over the summer. The promenade runs along the edge of the beach to a small FORT commanding an impressive view of the Atlantic coast, the old town and, further west, a cemetery whose tombs are decorated with ceramic tiles. The new town, which was built outside the fortifications during the period of the Spanish protectorate, has retained its Andalusian character.

A CULTURAL VENUE. Today Asilah is a small town of twenty thousand inhabitants. It is famous for its long, soft sandy beaches and as a venue for international cultural events such as concerts, dance performances, plays, conferences and debates. The varied crowd attending these events brings the medina's narrow streets to life in summer. Many Moroccan artists also come to Asilah at this time, leaving their mark in the form of murals and various geometric and abstract designs painted on walls around the town. Asilah's beaches were used as the setting for the film *La plage des enfants perdus* (*The Beach of Lost Children*), by the Moroccan director Jilali Ferhati, one of the official selections at the Venice film festival in 1991.

Eug. Delacroix.

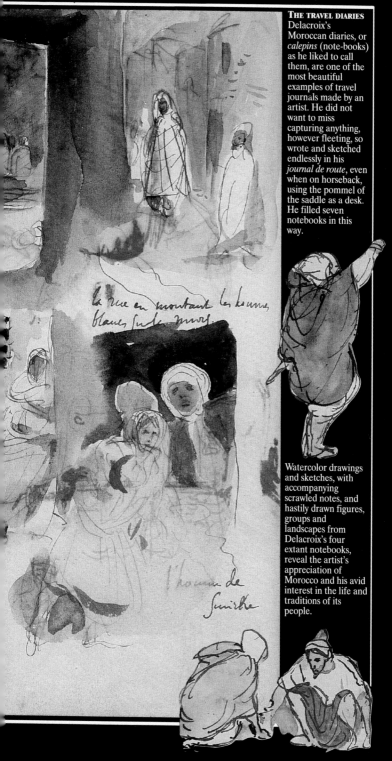

la rue en montant les hommes, blancs sur les murs.

l'homme de Suivikta

NOBLE HORSEMEN AND FIERY BEAUTY

In Morocco Delacroix encountered a nation of horsemen for whom the Arab thoroughbred ● 72 was most prized. It was a country where the sultan received visitors on horseback and where even the gentlest of these highly strung steeds were "demons". On arriving in Tangier Delacroix had noted the great attachment of Moroccan horsemen to their mounts, a relationship evident in such paintings as *Arab Saddling his Horse* (1855) (2). Traveling between Tangier and Meknès he had every opportunity to admire the nobility of these horsemen and the fiery beauty of the fantasias ● 73, held in honor of Morocco's official guests as they journeyed to the capital. These great equestrian displays, with their ritual headlong gallops and the terrifying explosion of the *baroud*, became one of Delacroix's favorite themes.

Arab Fantasia (1) (1832) was painted in his Paris studio using the life sketches (3) from his travel journals.

LIXUS ★

The ancient site of Lixus lies four miles outside Larache. According to classical mythology, it was in the region of Lixus that Hercules accomplished the eleventh of his twelve labors. The task involved gathering the golden apples which grew in the GARDEN OF THE HESPERIDES on Mount Atlas. Acting on the advice of Prometheus, Hercules asked Atlas to gather the fruit on his behalf while he supported the sky on his shoulders.

PHOENICIANS, CARTHAGINIANS AND ROMANS. The exact date of the foundation of Lixus is unknown and is still the subject of debate. However, historians do agree that it was probably established at some point in the 7th century BC by the Phoenicians, who made the town a fishing port and a trading center. In the 5th century BC, as he sailed southward along the Moroccan coast, the Carthaginian navigator Hanno dropped anchor at Lixus and established a colony that became a staging post on the Saharan gold route. Coins discovered on the site carry an engraving of a tuna, thought to be a symbol of the town's thriving fish-salting industry. After the fall of Carthage Lixus retained the right to strike its own coins. Around AD 40–5 the Romans took over the town and further developed the locally based industries for which Lixus was already renowned. It remained an important town until the late 3rd century AD, when it began to decline. With the fall of the Roman Empire, Lixus finally fell into obscurity.

THE ARCHEOLOGICAL SITE. The largest SALTING WORKS in Morocco was discovered during exploration of the ancient site of Lixus. Excavators unearthed a collection of around ten workshops and about 150 water tanks that the Romans used for salting fish and making *garum* (fish extract) until the end of the 3rd century AD. The ROMAN THEATER uncovered at Lixus in 1964 is thought to date from the 1st century AD. Consisting of a tiered semicircle and also containing an arena, it combines the typical features of a theater and an amphitheater. In the baths, discovered nearby, the *tepidarium* is paved with a fine mosaic of the head of the sea god Neptune. The site has several temples, the most famous of which (temple F) was built at the top of the acropolis in the period between the 1st century BC and the 1st century AD. Further north, between Larache and Asilah, is a burial mound on the ancient site of Cromlech de M'Soura.

NEPTUNE
The *tepidarium* at Lixus (above), the tepid bathing room that preceded the *caldarium* (hot baths), is paved with a mosaic depicting the face of Neptune in all its fierce majesty. The sea god's thick hair is entangled in the claws of crustaceans. The marble, earthenware and pottery mosaic, measuring 34 by 20 feet, incorporates medallions representing floral and geometric motifs.

"GARUM" POT
Pot used for making *garum*, a salty extract made from the intestines of fish, discovered among the ruins of the salting works at Lixus.

LARACHE

Larache was founded in the 7th century when a group of Muslim soldiers from Arabia extended their camp at Lixus onto the south bank of the OUED LOUKOS. In 1471 the Portuguese settlers from Asilah and Tangier drove the inhabitants out of Larache again, and it remained uninhabited until the sultan of Fez, Mohammed es Saïd ech Sheikh, decided to repopulate it and build a stronghold on the plateau above the Oued Loukos estuary. He constructed a fortress at the entrance to the port as a means of controlling access to the river. In the late 15th century the Portuguese spoke of Larache as the largest Berber port and possession of the town was soon greatly coveted although, for a long time, attempts on the part of the Portuguese, Spanish and French to take it met with little success. The kasbah, which was built in 1491 by Moulay en Nasser, subsequently became a pirate stronghold. In 1610 the town passed into Spanish hands only to be recaptured by the sultan Moulay Ismaïl in 1689. Attacks on Larache continued until, in 1911, it was once again taken by the Spanish, who remained there until the establishment of Moroccan independence forty-five years later ● 56.

A SUCCESSION OF CULTURES. Today Larache has a population of seventy thousand. The successive Spanish and Arabic invasions have left their mark on the town and architectural styles vary widely from district to district.

JAMAA EL KEBIR
Located in the Souk Sghir district, the Jamaa el Kebir (above left) was one of the first mosques built in Larache.

THE CLOCKTOWER
The former palace (above right) was built during the reign of Moulay Ismaïl as a residence for one of his sons. The Spanish added the tower in 1912.

The mosque of Larache (right).

The layout of the old town is typically Arabic, while houses in the new town tend to be Andalusian in style.

The *Escort of the Province of Larache* (left) is one of around a hundred drawings that the Italian artist Cesare Biseo made during a visit to Morocco in 1875.

JEAN GENET
The French writer lived in Larache's Rue Oudoua.

LARACHE ON FOOT. The bougainvillea-lined Boulevard Mohammed V runs across the new town to the PLACE DE LA LIBÉRATION, where the arcaded houses serve as a reminder of Larache's Andalusian past. The BAB EL KHEMIS, lying between the new town and the medina, leads into a busy little market with an ANCIENT FOUNTAIN surmounted by two cannons. To the right of this is the KASBAH gate. On the esplanade overlooking the valley and the Oued Loukos is a Hispano-Moresque-style palace, constructed by the Spanish in 1915, which is now used as a music school. Opposite the palace, a square-towered fort bearing the arms of Charles V of Spain houses the archeological museum, where coins and other finds from the archeological excavations at Lixus are displayed. The most famous building in Larache is the STORK'S CASTLE, built by Portuguese prisoners taken at the celebrated Battle of the Three Kings ▲ *201*, which was fought near Ksar el Kebir in 1578. Outside the town, the white stone tomb of the French writer Jean Genet can be seen in the Spanish cemetery, situated on a clifftop overlooking the sea.

KSAR EL KEBIR

Ksar el Kebir (Great Fortress) was probably founded in the 11th century, although it would not have assumed this name until a century later, when the Almohad sultan Yacoub el Mansour surrounded it with fortified walls. It was near Ksar el Kebir, at the confluence of the Oued Makhzen and the Oued Loukos, that the Battle of the Three Kings ▲ *201* was fought in 1578; during that battle the Arabs drove back the Portuguese, who had landed at Asilah ▲ *200*. In the 17th century the town became a pawn in power struggles between the sultans. In the 19th century, during the reigns of Moulay Slimane and Sidi Abd er Rahman, a civil war broke out ● *56* that hastened the decline of Ksar el Kebir.

❝Near the walls of Casar runs the river Luccus which is sometimes so swollen with rain that its waters enter the gates of the city. Casar has many craftsmen and merchants. It has several churches, a college and a hospice. It has neither spring

nor well but uses [a system of] cisterns.❞
Leo Africanus,
A Geographical History of Africa

MOULAY BOUSSELHAM

Moulay Bousselham, situated halfway between Tangier and Rabat, is bordered by the Atlantic on one side and the MERDJA ZERGA LAGOON on the other. The town's patron saint, Moulay Bousselham (Man with the Burnous), was buried here in 951 between the coastline and the lake. In the summer months Moroccans come to Moulay Bousselham in large numbers. Many make the journey to visit the saint's tomb but many are also drawn by the area's natural beauty and come to see the lagoon and beaches. It is now a nature reserve that attracts thousands of birds and has large colonies of herons and flamingos.

ARBAOUA

MERDJA ZERGA ★
The Merdja Zerga lagoon has the highest concentration of migratory birds wintering in Morocco. They include the shelduck, widgeon, graylag goose and flamingo.

The *Little Hermes of the West* (below) is one of the most beautiful of the mosaics discovered at Banasa.

About seven miles south of Moulay Bousselham the road forks towards the Oued Makhzen dam and passes through the village of Arbaoua. The village is set in an 86,500-acre game reserve, one of the finest in Morocco, with woodcock, ducks, teal, Barbary partridge, pheasant, quail and wild boar ■ *22*. The road then

runs for a short distance along the edge of the eucalyptus forests ■ *32* and the Doura and Foukroun canals, passes through SOUK EL ARBA DU GHARB, the administrative center of the Gharb region, and leads to the ancient site of Banasa.

BANASA ★

The remains of the forum, the capitol, a basilica and various temples can still be seen at the ancient site of Banasa, founded in the 3rd century BC and then rediscovered in 1871. The most interesting building on the site is the BATHS OF THE FRESCOES, with mosaics on the walls and floor depicting nymphs and bacchantes and a scene (left) representing Psyche being spirited away by Cupid.

In and around Fez and Meknès

▲ FEZ

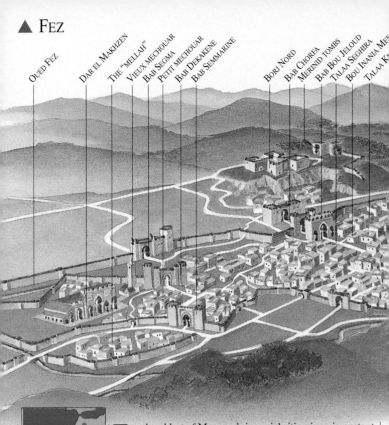

OUED FEZ • DAR EL MAKHZEN • THE "MELLAH" • VIEUX MECHOUAR • BAB SEGMA • PETIT MECHOUAR • BAB DEKAKENE • BAB SEMMARINE • BORJ NORD • BAB CHORFA • MERINID TOMBS • BAB BOU JELOUD • TALAA SEGHIRA • BOU INANIA ME... • TALAA K...

🦶 Three days

F ez, the oldest of Morocco's imperial cities, is an important religious, intellectual and cultural center. It is also renowned for its traditional crafts, and because of the particularly high reputation of its university it is known by many as the "Athens of Africa".

IDRISS I, FOUNDER OF FEZ. In the late 8th century AD Idriss ● *53*, persecuted by

IDRISSID DIRHAM
In 814, to proclaim his allegiance to the cause of the Prophet's son-in-law Ali, Idriss II had around a dozen different silver coins struck bearing the inscription "El Aliya" (City of Ali). After his death the coins remained in circulation until 856.

the Abbassids of Baghdad, sought refuge among the Berber tribes of central Morocco. His capital, founded on the right bank of the OUED FEZ in 789, was the first Islamic town to be built in Morocco. His son, Idriss II, welcomed several hundred Arabs from the central Maghreb and Spain and forced out the local Berber population. Almost 1,400 Andalusian families from Córdoba settled in the El Adoua (Andalusian) district, founded in 818 by a group of Spanish Muslim refugees. Seven years later the families of rich, educated craftsmen and merchants who had grown accustomed to city life were driven out of Kairouan (modern Tunisia). There were around three hundred of them, and they settled on the west bank of the river in what became known as the Kairouani district.

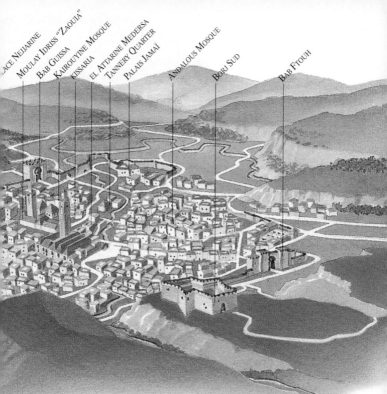

ACE NEJARINE
MOULAY IDRISS "ZAOUIA"
BAB GUISSA
KAIROUYINE MOSQUE
KISSARIA
EL ATTARINE MEDERSA
TANNERY QUARTER
PALAIS JAMAI
ANDALOUS MOSQUE
BORJ SUD
BAB FTOUH

FEZ, A POLITICAL AND CULTURAL PAWN. By the mid-9th century, the KAIROUYINE UNIVERSITY and the ANDALOUS MOSQUE had been built, and the library and court of Yahya IV, the most powerful of the Idrissids and ruler of Fez in the early 10th century, was attracting scholars from Spain. Fez became a political pawn, fought over by the Tunisian Fatimid ● 53 and Spanish (Cordoban) Omayyades ● 53 caliphs. In c. 917 Yahya IV was forced to recognize the authority of the Fatimid ruler, whose governors remained in Fez until 953. The Idrissid sultans, who had withdrawn to a stronghold in the Rif Mountains, were fighting to defend the country's national identity. Fez passed into Idrissid hands and was subsequently recaptured by the Fatimids in 960. In 985, the Omayyades, conquerors of Morocco, took the city and prevented the Fatimids from extending their power westward, thus depriving them of the African gold brought to Fez along the Saharan gold routes. In the early 11th century the fall of the Omayyade caliphate freed Fez from its Cordoban overlords. The city then expanded and became a prosperous trading center for a while, but later plunged into economic crisis.

FEZ UNDER THE ALMORAVIDS. After a six-year siege the veiled Almoravid sultan, Youssef Ibn Tachfine, took possession of Fez in 1069. The writer Abou Obeid el Bekri described Fez as two cities, each surrounded by a wall, separated only by a fast-flowing river with watermills and bridges. The two cities had a large population with a strong Jewish minority. Youssef Ibn Tachfine immediately replaced the two walls with a single defensive wall and built a fortress outside the city. Although this new

MINBAR ▲ 86
The minbar or pulpit of the Andalous Mosque, dating from 980, was made by the forerunners of the 9th- and 10th-century Fasi cabinetmakers. The technique of wood turning (see panel below) was used later in Merinid moucharabieh. The frieze consists of a border, a groove decorated with pearl and saw-tooth motifs and acanthus leaves.

The minbar, from which the imam (prayer leader) ends his sermon by extolling the glory of

the reigning dynasty, is the symbol of political and religious power. These two panels, from the Fatimid reign (above) and the Omayyades reign (right), reflect the bitter power struggle between the Fatimid and Omayyades caliphs. In 985 the Omayyades caliph sealed his victory by fitting this new back panel (right) to the minbar.

ROYAL PROCESSION Each week the sultan would go the the Great Mosque to join the faithful at Friday prayer ● *63*. He was escorted by his Black Guard in ceremonial dress and preceded by mounted soldiers and foot soldiers who cleared a way through the enthusiastic crowd.

216

ruler made not Fez but Marrakesh the Almohad capital, the town nevertheless became a thriving cultural and intellectual center. A medersa ● *90* with a library was built in 1096 and the Saharan gold route reopened.

FEZ UNDER THE ALMOHADS. In the mid-12th century the Almohad sultan Abd el Moumen captured the city, which by then had become a center for foreign travelers. It was also a growing center for trade. The Fasis were dealing with Spain, the central Maghreb, the Sahara and the Orient and also with several Christian countries. The Andalous refugees who had settled in Fez introduced a range of new silk-weaving, leatherwork and metalworking techniques. By the late 12th century Fez was a thriving city with 120,000 houses and, by the beginning of the 13th century, 3,500 workshops.

THE "GOLDEN AGE" OF FEZ. During the first half of the 13th century the Merinids took advantage of the Almohads' weakened situation to capture Fez, which in 1250 once again became the capital of the Merinid empire. Over the next two hundred years the Merinid rulers undertook a series of great building projects and Fez, a splendid city by the beginning of the 14th century, experienced a "Golden Age". The Merinids' strategy was both to extend their power in North Africa and to re-establish the traditional north-south territorial axis that linked the country with Spain. Fez, in a crucial position at the hub of these operations, was given a new administrative center, Fez el Jdid (New Fez). Palaces, mosques, fortresses and barracks and, notably, medersa ● *90* were built inside the walls. These were religious teaching establishments which also functioned as training centers for the political branch of Islam, whose members would be responsible for the Islamization of the imperial Maghreb and the unification of North Africa from the west. International trade flourished in the early 15th century, with merchants traveling to China, India, East Africa

> "SEVEN ANCIENT BUILDINGS ... KNOWN AS MEDERSA, AND WHICH ARE THE MOST BEAUTIFUL SIGHT THAT FEZ HAS TO OFFER."
> JÉRÔME AND JEAN THARAUD

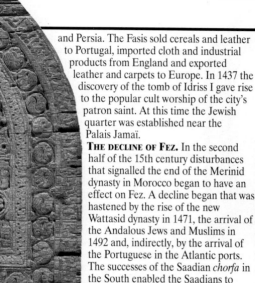

and Persia. The Fasis sold cereals and leather to Portugal, imported cloth and industrial products from England and exported leather and carpets to Europe. In 1437 the discovery of the tomb of Idriss I gave rise to the popular cult worship of the city's patron saint. At this time the Jewish quarter was established near the Palais Jamaï.

THE DECLINE OF FEZ. In the second half of the 15th century disturbances that signalled the end of the Merinid dynasty in Morocco began to have an effect on Fez. A decline began that was hastened by the rise of the new Wattasid dynasty in 1471, the arrival of the Andalous Jews and Muslims in 1492 and, indirectly, by the arrival of the Portuguese in the Atlantic ports. The successes of the Saadian *chorfa* in the South enabled the Saadians to establish themselves successfully in Marrakesh ▲ 259 in 1524 and capture Fez in 1549, when the capital was transferred to Marrakesh. In the early 17th century the population of Fez was decimated by plague, famine, poverty and civil war.

A POLITICAL POWER. In 1666 Moulay Rachid re-established order, revived trade and made Fez once again the capital of Morocco. The city experienced a long period of unrest during the first half of the 18th century. In the 19th century, a close alliance developed between the army and the leaders of the old Kairouyine university, which was the seat of an influential political force, and this restored order and prestige. Although it was beginning to be overshadowed by Casablanca, whose economic importance was increasing, Fez maintained its religious, intellectual and commercial influence.

THE FRENCH PROTECTORATE. In 1911 Moulay Hafid, faced with the prospect of an uprising, turned to the French army for help. A few months later, in March 1912, he signed the Treaty of Fez, which made Morocco a French protectorate ● 56. It was after this that work on the new, European-style city began, built following a tightly controlled urban development plan. The ancient city of Fez manages to coexist happily with its modern counterpart, losing none of its ancient charm and character.

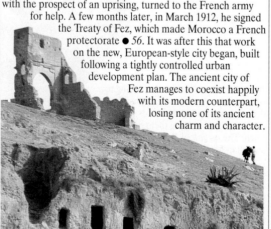

TOWARD INDEPENDENCE
On August 9, 1943, on an official visit to Morocco, and during a cease-fire between Moroccan nationalists and French troops, General de Gaulle visited Fez. When the

African army entered the war Fez sided with the resistance. The Kairouyine Mosque, stronghold of Islam, was also the seat of nationalism where the political agenda and the Declaration of Independence were prepared. The early governments after Independence (1956) included a number of prominent Fasis.

THE MERINID TOMBS
The Merinid necropolis honors the rulers largely responsible for the cultural and religious importance of Fez. Merinid art finds its full expression in the mosques and especially the medersat, where its principles were taught and perpetuated.

217

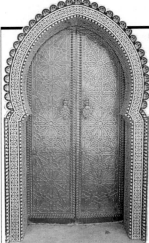

The new city of Fez, founded by the Merinid sultan Abou Youssef in 1276, was originally called El Medinet el Beida (White City) but later became known as Fez el Jdid (New Fez) to distinguish it from Fez el Bali (Old Fez). Today Fez el Jdid hums with the activities of Berber carpet sellers, snake charmers and street performers.

DAR EL MAKHZEN

The wide esplanade of the Place des Alaouites leads to Dar el Makhzen (Royal Palace), which was the sultan's residence and also served as barracks for his troops. It is not open to the public. The royal quarters consist of several palaces, *mechouars* (assembly areas), gardens (including the walled garden of Lalla Mina) and a mosque. It also has a medersa, founded in 1320 by the Merinid sultan Abou Saïd Othmane, a *koubba* ● *63* and a menagerie. Notable among many splendors is the magnificent ceiling of the DAR EL QIMMA (one of the palaces), which is impressive for its size alone and was exquisitely carved and painted by Fasi craftsmen. The bronze knockers (right) on one of the palace doors were also made by master craftsmen from Fez el Bali. The Place des Alaouites leads into the Rue Bou Khsissat, lined with houses decorated with wood and wrought iron, and the GRAND-RUE DES MÉRINIDES. This busy thoroughfare crosses the Jewish quarter and is crowded with a variety of shops, particularly jewelers' stalls.

DAR EL MAKHZEN
The royal palace with its "tightly closed doors, eggshell façade and pine-green Saracen tiles, the color that Mohammed said was as restful on the eye as a woman's face".
Slimane Zeghidour

PALAIS JAMAÏ
The palace was built in 1879 and converted into a luxury hotel, the Palais Jamaï Hotel, in 1930. The design of its letterheads (below) is based on the finely decorated inner courtyard and façades.

THE "MELLAH". The term *mellah*, referring to the Jewish quarter of a Moroccan town, comes from the Arabic word *melh* (salt). According to one story the Jews were responsible for draining and salting the heads of decapitated rebels before impaling them on the gates of the town. The *mellah* of Fez, considered to be the largest in Morocco, was once located near what is now the PALAIS JAMAÏ in the El Yahoudi district, the Jewish quarter at the northern end of the city. In the 15th century the Merinid sultan Abou Saïd moved it nearer the Royal Palace when he promised to protect the Jews in return for an additional tax. Until the 19th century the *mellah* was closed at night by an iron gate and various rules, for example forbidding the wearing shoes or riding outside the *mellah*, were imposed upon the Jews. These rules applied until the

> ## "At sunset, the gates of Fez closed in the long, crenelated ramparts."
>
> ### Pierre Loti

time of the French protectorate. Today, while many Jews have left Fez for Casablanca, France and Israel, Muslims now live in the overcrowded *mellah*. The buildings there include charming old houses with elaborately carved wooden balconies and Neoclassical colonnades, and a number of residential blocks with colored façades, constructed at the turn of the century. The white sweep of gravestones in the immaculately maintained Hebrew cemetery provides a striking contrast.

TOWARD DAR BATHA

The Grand-Rue crosses Fez el Jdid from the Bab Semmarine to the 16th-century BAB DEKAKENE, formerly the Bab es Siba. This bustling thoroughfare gives on to various souks and is bordered by two mosques, the JAMAA EL HAMRA (the red mosque with a 14th-century minaret) and the JAMAA EL BEIDA (the white mosque). In a nearby street is the JAMAA EL AZHAR, with its Andalusian entrance and minaret, built in 1357 by the Merinid sultan Abou Inan.

PETIT MECHOUAR. This small assembly area above the Oued Fez, surrounded by high walls, leads into the once-forbidden district of Moulay Abdallah and, beyond the souks, to the mosque named after the Alaouite sultan. The 82-foot minaret is decorated with vertical bands of green tiles and surmounted by four spheres. The sultan's remains lie in the *koubba*. The great Abou el Hak Mosque, named after the Merinid sultan who built it in 1276, is a much more impressive building. The former Bab es Siba (Gate of the Seven), named after Moulay Abdallah's seven brothers who succeeded each other to the throne in the 18th century, stands between the Petit Mechouar and the Vieux Mechouar. In 1443 the naked body of Ferdinand, brother of the King of Portugal, was hung from the gate for four days, and his coffin remained on view for twenty-nine years. There is a story that a drop of blood from the coffin fell on the forehead of a blind man and restored his sight.

THE "MELLAH"
The wealthiest houses in the Jewish quarter of Fez had windows painted in yellow or blue and wooden balconies decorated with wrought iron.

219

VIEUX MECHOUAR. The monumental gateway of the MAKINA, surmounted by two ornamental spires dating from the 1930's, opens on to the old assembly area where royal parades were once held. This former arms factory was built by an Italian mission in 1886 during the reign of Moulay Hassan. It has also served as a stable and today houses a factory producing traditional Moroccan carpets for export. It is open to the public. A few yards away the Merinid BAB SEGMA, flanked by two ancient water reservoirs, stands between Fez el Jdid and the former Kasbah of the Cherarda, and marks the boundary of the old *mechouar*. From the Bab Dekakene the Avenue des Français opens on to the BOU JELOUD GARDENS, designed and laid out in 1917 on the site of the old Moroccan gardens. During the French protectorate the gardens, which contained every variety of tree, were very popular both with the European residents of Fez and with Moroccan nationalists, who often held secret meetings there.

Fez pottery, tin-glazed earthenware decorated with predominantly cobalt-blue designs.

DAR BATHA

From the Bou Jeloud Gardens the Avenue des Français leads directly to the walled square of PLACE BAGHDADI, which links Fez el Jdid and Fez el Bali. Nearby the Dar Batha Palace, built in the Hispano-Moresque style by Moulay Hassan at the end of the 19th century, is surrounded by Andalusian gardens. Today it houses the MUSEUM OF MOROCCAN ARTS where collections of ancient pottery ● *80*, 11th- to 18th-century astrolabes, exquisitely executed *aleuj* (Fez gold-thread) embroidery ● *76*, illuminated Korans and carpets ● *74* are displayed. For a long time the museum's prize exhibit was the jujube and ebony minbar of the Andalous Mosque, which, dating from 980, is the second-oldest pulpit in the western Muslim world after the minbar of Kairouan. It was shown at Expo 92 in Seville and is currently on display in the Oudaya Museum ▲ *168* in Rabat.

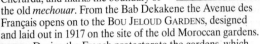

"Here, sky and earth merge in a single embrace. And in every house in this old quarter, the walls of the courtyard are pillars, pillars that support the roof: the sky."

Tahar Ben Jelloun,
Oublier Fez

To the west of the Dar Batha Palace the BAB BOU JELOUD leads into Fez el Bali across a square bordered by Almohad houses. This (below) is the city's most notable rampart gate, built by the Almohads in the 13th century and restored in 1913 in traditional style. It is decorated with a pattern of blue terracotta arabesques (symbolizing Fez) on one side and a layer of green terracotta tiles (symbolizing Islam) on the other. To the northwest the BAB CHORFA, flanked by two bastions surmounted by pointed crenellations, overlooks a kind of flea market.

THE MEDINA ★. Beyond the Bab Bou Jeloud lies the largest medina ● *92* in the Maghreb, so big that it was once subdivided into some twenty smaller medinas. Water

was channeled along a complex system of conduits which, according to the writer Abou Obeid el Bekri, was installed in 1068. The character of the medina has been preserved partly thanks to General Lyautey, France's first resident general, who prohibited the construction of new buildings within the old town and city centers ▲ *164*. Inside the medina even Fasi guides sometimes get lost in the maze of narrow streets, so the visitor is advised not to stray too far from the two main ones, the TALAA KEBIRA (Upper Ascent) and the TALAA SEGHIRA (Lower Ascent). The endless labyrinth of Fez el Bali's dark, narrow streets, which are less inviting but more authentic than the two main thoroughfares, conceal as many as a thousand *derbs* (blind alleys). In 1976 UNESCO declared the medina one of the world's cultural treasures and a rescue program is currently under way to combat problems caused by overcrowding and pollution. The layout of the old city does

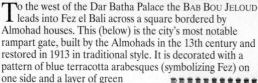

not lend itself to the installation of modern workshops, although the conttstruction of these is vital if the medina's many traditional craft industries are to be maintained. The palaces, mosques, medersat, *zaouias* and fountains of Fez el Bali are among the most beautiful in Morocco.

WALL FOUNTAIN
Fountains and baths are a common sight inside the ramparts and in the potters' quarter. The network of conduits supplying the city with water was designed in the early 11th century. It was reorganized during the reign of Youssef Ibn Tachfine in the 12th century, by the end of which the mosques, medersa and many of the houses had running water. The various branches of the network are virtual rivers which flow above and below ground. Today pollution makes it difficult to use this water supply.

TOWARD THE MOULAY IDRISS "ZAOUIA"

MEDERSA BOU INANIA. Constructed by the sultan Abou Inan
between 1350 and 1357, this was the last of the Merinid
medersat to be built except for the little El Habbadine
Medersa. It was also the largest medersa in Fez and one of
the most costly. The splendid stucco work, the cedarwood
paneling (now faded), the bronze, marble and onyx
decorations, and the windows with *muqarna* are all classic
Merinid architectural features. Under a green-tiled roof, the
walls of the inner courtyard are decorated with *zellige* ▲ *173*,
with stucco above. The prayer hall has some superb stained
glass windows and a magnificent minbar ● *86*. The DAR EL
MAGANA, opposite the medersa, houses the remains of an
extraordinary water clock dating from 1375 whose function it
was to sound the hour of prayer. It consists of seven small
cymbals placed on cedarwood blocks (of which there were
originally thirteen) and thirteen windows from which
clockwork falcons emerge. The clock was restored in 1990 by
a Moroccan horologist who figured out how the mechanism
worked. Farther on stand the mosque and *zaouia* ▲ *199* of
Sidi Ahmed Tijani, which are open exclusively to pilgrims
from Black Africa, for whom he is the patron saint. The Talaa
Kebira becomes the RUE ECH CHERABLIYINE where
babouches, the famous Moroccan leather slippers ● *79*, are
sold. The grayish-blue babouches are particularly prized.
PLACE NEJJARINE. The Place Nejjarine, with its splendid and
unusual fountain ★, takes its name from the Souk Nejjarine
(Carpenters' Souk), which is set out behind a wooden door in
a narrow street below the square. The extravagantly
decorated façade of the NEJJARINE "FONDOUK", probably
built in the 18th century, overlooks the square at the far end.

> "THOSE WHO PRAY TO MOULAY IDRISS ARE AS BLESSED AS IF THEY HAD VISITED ALL THE KOUBBAS IN MOROCCO, AND THEIR NUMBER IS INCALCULABLE."
>
> HENRIETTE CÉLARIÉ

This former lodging house was recently converted into a mosque. In the Rue el Attarine is the Souk Attarine (grocery market and spice-sellers' souk), the most colorful market in Fez. Nearby, in a quiet square planted with strawberry trees, the HENNA SOUK sells antimony sulfide (which is crushed into a powder to make kohl ● 66), blue eyeshadow, ghassoul (a kind of soapy clay used to perfume bath water), henna and all kinds of other ointments and salves, often with supposedly magical powers.

THE KISSARIA. The Kissaria stands on the site of a lunatic asylum built by the sultan Abou Youssef Yacoub in the 13th century. Today the market is renowned for its embroidery, silks and brocades even though the modern concrete buildings do not have the charm of the old souk, which was destroyed by a great fire in 1954. The Kissaria operates along the lines of the Turkish system whereby craftsmen are grouped within corporations and pool their profits into a communal fund.

MOULAY IDRISS "ZAOUIA". The Kissaria leads directly to the *horm*, the sacred wall surrounding the Moulay Idriss II ● 53 *zaouia* ▲ 199, constructed in the 9th century and rebuilt in 1437. Pilgrims are permitted to touch the tomb of Moulay Idriss II through a hole in a small copper plaque. The tomb is covered with a *ksaoua* (piece of material), a gift from the silk-weavers' corporation, which is replaced each year. A decree issued by General Lyautey in 1921 ▲ 165 prohibits non-Muslims from entering the shrine. Donkeys and mules are kept out of the streets leading to the *zaouia* by horizontal bars positioned about five feet off the ground. The population used to be protected by a right of asylum according to which Muslims could not be arrested inside the walls of the *zaouia*. It consequently became known as a sanctuary for criminals. Today Muslims visit the Moulay Idriss *zaouia* in search of *baraka* (good fortune).

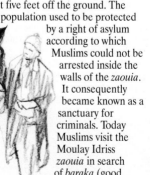

In *Le Chapelet d'ambre* the writer Ahmed Séfrioui compared the souk to the entrance of an anthill, with people scurrying in all directions without appearing to be going anywhere in particular.

NEJJARINE "FONDOUK"
The Nejjarine *fondouk* once accommodated travelers passing through Fez. On the lower floor the galleries, decorated with moucharabieh, were divided into stalls for animals, and the guest rooms were on the upper floor. Today *fondouks* are no longer used as lodging houses but are occupied by tradesmen and craftsmen or used as warehouses where retailers from the souks come to buy their stock.

In the 14th century stucco work decorated both the inside and outside of civil and religious buildings. This

AROUND THE KAIROUYINE MOSQUE

ATTARINE MEDERSA ★. Although it is relatively small, this is by far the most beautiful medersa in Fez. It was built between 1323 and 1325, during the reign of the Merinid sultan Abou Saïd and it is a beautifully crafted work of art. Especially notable are the bronze door, the inner courtyard with fine marble and alabaster pillars (left), the cedarwood canopy and the white marble font decorated with a rosette and *zellige*. Its timber framework is part palm-wood beams, which are pliant yet have proved strong enough to withstand the test of time and the tremors of earthquakes. The prayer hall has some very old stained glass windows and a bronze chandelier decorated with *surah*.

THE KAIROUYINE MOSQUE

The Kairouyine Mosque ● *86* was founded in 857 in a district occupied by Kairouani refugees● *214* , after whom it was named. In 933 the existing modest oratory was converted into a Friday mosque, so that the Friday prayer meeting could be held there. In 1135 it was extended and embellished by the Almoravid sultan Ali Ben Youssef and through

decorative technique is also seen on the walls of the Attarine Medersa, which have stucco *surah*.

these improvements became one of the largest mosques in the Maghreb. It is also one of the oldest religious teaching centers, with a university tradition dating from the 10th century, when the first *halaqat* (study groups) were being established in Morocco. Like most of Morocco's religious buildings, neither the mosque nor the university admit non-Muslims. Fourteen doors lead to the prayer room, which contains 16 naves and 270 pillars. The great inner courtyard and its two marble-pillared pavilions, reminiscent of the Court of Lions in the Alhambra Palace in Granada, can be glimpsed from the entrance. One of the pavilions was built by the Saadian Abdallah ech Sheikh in the 16th century. Among the many treasures within the mosque are the Almohad chandelier, dating from 1203, and the minbar, which was made in Córdoba. The KAIROUYINE LIBRARY was established in the 10th century and reorganized in the 14th by Abou Inan, who transformed it into a large hall housing manuscripts moved from the library in the sultan's palace. With a collection of 30,000 volumes, including 10,000 manuscripts, the library is one of the largest in the Arab world and its

ANDALOUS AND KAIROUANI REFUGEES
According to legend a rich Kairouani refugee living in Fez died, leaving his daughters a large fortune. Driven by religious rivalry, the two sisters each had a mosque built, Meriem the Andalous Mosque and Fatima the Kairouyine Mosque.

The central font (right) of the Kairouyine Mosque, built by the Saadians in the 16th century.

The inner courtyard and marble-columned pavilions (left) of the Kairouyine Mosque.

THE MINARET OF THE KAIROUYINE MOSQUE
The Kairouyine Mosque, with roof of emerald-green tiles (below), contains the most beautiful surviving examples of Idrissid art. A popular legend states that the sword of Idriss II will be found embedded in the top of the minaret (bottom) long after his death.

reputation attracts eminent specialists in Islamic culture. Some manuscripts, such as the copy of a 9th-century Koran made by the historian Ibn Khaldun in the 14th century, are extremely rare.

The Arabic inscription on the plaque (left) at the entrance to the Kairouyine Mosque reads: "This mosque was built in the year 245 of the Hegira (AD 859) by Fatima."

TOWARD THE TANNERY QUARTER

Near the Kairouyine Mosque stands the SEFFARINE (also known as the Halfaouin) MEDERSA, the first medersa to be built by the Merinids, in 1280. Abdelkrim, leader of the Rif rebellion against the French in 1925, was one of the many famous alumni of this Koranic school. The Place Seffarine leads into the Rue des Teinturiers, which was originally populated by dyers but is now mainly occupied by metalworkers. Similarly in the Rue Ras Cherratin shops selling traditional Moroccan clothing have mainly replaced the copper and brass workshops once found there.

THE TANNERIES. The Chouara, the colorful tanners' quarter, spreads out along the banks of the Oued Fez. The view from the rooftops is a memorable one: clusters of stone vats filled with red, yellow and brown dyes, and skins hanging everywhere, drying in the sun. In his book *Reconnaissance du Maroc* Charles de Foucauld noted that large quantities of wool, skins and wax were exported to Europe while the finest skins remained in Fez, where they were worked by craftsmen and used to make the *belras*, cushions, belts and other luxury items for sale throughout northern Morocco. The Rue Mechatin is occupied by copper- and brass-workers and craftsmen making horn combs.

Tanning is the process by which animal skins are rendered supple and rot-proof. First the skins are washed and soaked to make them ready for tanning. Currying is the process by which the tanned leather, known as "crust-tanned" leather, is impregnated with grease to turn it into the finished product. Tanning is carried out in huge stone or wooden vats known as fulling mills filled with tanning liquors, treatments which were originally vegetable-based (oak and chestnut bark) but are now synthetic (chrome-alum). The *takaout* (a tamarisk gall) is used for tanning white leather.

RAW MATERIALS
The skins of sheep, goats, cattle and dromedaries are the raw materials of the Moroccan tanning industry.

SUPPLIES
A donkey carrying sheepskins arriving at the gates of the tanners' souk in the medina in Fez.

DYING MILLS
Before being impregnated with a colored dye, the skins undergo five preparatory processes.

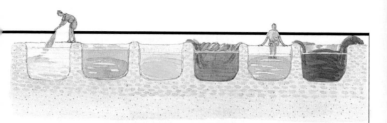

1. GRAINING AND FLESHING
The hair, flesh and fat are removed from the skin in lime baths. The skin is then delimed.

2. BATING AND PICKLING
The skins are bated to make them supple and pickled by plunging into a vat of water to which sulfuric acid and sea salt have been added.

3. TANNING
The skins are immersed for several days in vats containing a mixture of oils and natural or artificial tanning liquors, and then dried.

4. DRESSING
The leather is fed with emulsions of oil and water to lubricate it and make it supple. It is then ready for skiving.

5. SKIVING
The skins are scraped and stoned on the flesh side, smoothed out and fined down before being polished to make them shiny.

6. THE DYING MILLS
The skins are steeped in vats of dye in which vegetable pigments – indigo (blue), madder or cochineal (red), yellow weed (also known as dyer's weed) or safflower (yellow) – are mixed with mordants to fix the color.

7. DRYING
The dyed leather is laid out on the ground outside the medina to dry in the sun. It is later worked by master craftsmen and made into babouches, embroidered bags, embossed bindings, cushions, saddles and clothes for sale in the souks of Fez.

VATS IN THE TANNER'S MARKET IN FEZ
Because of the risk of pollution, the chemicals used for dressing and currying the leather, and for dyeing skins, are stored some distance away from Fez el Bali.

PLACE SEFFARINE
The marble fountain
is decorated with
fleurs de lis carved by
the French convicts
who built it in the
16th century.

ER RSIF MOSQUE
The Er Rsif Mosque,
beyond the Rue des
Teinturiers, was built
in the late 18th
century by Sidi
Mohammed Ben
Abdullah. The height
of its minaret, like
that of all the
mosques in Fez, was
calculated in relation
to the minaret of the
Kairouyine Mosque.
This was so that all
the muezzins ● *88*
could see the black
banner flown from
the top of the
Kairouyine minaret
on Fridays, indicating
the hours of prayer.

**THE BELGHAZI
PALACE**
The Palace is situated
on the right bank of
the Oued Fez.

> "THESE ROOF-TOP TERRACES, WHICH ARE SO IMPORTANT IN THE DAILY LIFE OF FASI WOMEN ... WHERE MEETINGS ARE ORGANIZED, AND INTRIGUES PLOTTED."
>
> MOHAMED SIJELMASSI

On the way back to the Place Nejjarine, it is well worth pausing to visit the GUERNIZ TANNERIES. Built by Moulay Ismaïl in the 17th century, they are the oldest tanneries in the city. Halfway along the Talaa Seghira, which leads back to the Bab Bou Jeloud, stands the perfectly preserved DAR MNEBHI, a 19th-century vizier's palace which was the residence of General Lyautey in 1912.

DAR MNEBHI
This former vizier's palace is today a restaurant offering a splendid view across the medina.

THE PALACES OF FEZ EL BALI

Dozens of palaces, either in a perfectly preserved condition or undergoing restoration work, are hidden away in the narrow streets and obscure culs-de-sac of Fez. Their entrances have the typical Moroccan carved and studded wooden doors, usually with two brass knockers, one for pedestrians and another, higher up, for the use of horsemen. Built over the centuries, these palaces are like milestones in the city's history. The finest are those of the Merinid dynasty (13th to 15th centuries). The 14th-century DAR CAÏD BEL HASSAN, near the Bou Inania Medersa, consists of a *dar kebira* (masters' residence) and *dar dwiria* (servants' quarters), and is richly decorated, with carved wood, engraved bronzes, multicolored *zellige*, stucco, marble pillars and moucharabieh. The DAR ZOUITEN, in the Guerniz district, is notable for its stables and particularly for the *massid* (religious school) that has been housed there for several generations. During the Alaouite dynasty (17th century to the present day) palaces were constructed all over the city. Although decoration in Alaouite palaces is often less elaborate than that of Merinid palaces, its style is just as impressive, with highly decorated balustrades and wrought iron grilles. The walls and porticos of the DAR ADIYEL in the Zqaq el Bgal district, one of the finest examples of classical 17th- and 18th-century architecture, still have their original stucco work in place. The early 20th-century DAR SLAOUI is decorated with blue and white *zellige* ▲ 173.

THE ES SAHRIJ MEDERSA
The Es Sahrij Medersa, named after the fine font in its courtyard, was built by Abou el Hassan Ali between 1321 and 1323. A second medersa, the Es Sebaïyin Medersa (of the Seven), was built nearby, next to the Andalous Mosque. Its name is derived from the fact that it taught the seven ways of reading the Koran. Only non-Fasi students were able to lodge there.

THE ANDALOUS QUARTER

The Andalous Quarter can be reached via the CHOUARA TANNERIES on the left bank of the Oued Fez, or alternatively via the BAB FTOUH.
THE ANDALOUS MOSQUE ▲ 86. This simple place of prayer was built in the 9th century by Meriem, one of El Kairouani's daughters. In 956 the caliph of Córdoba, Abd er Rahman III, paid for a minaret, identical to that of the rival Kairouyine Mosque, to be added. The mosque was then entirely rebuilt in the 13th century by the Almohad sultan En Nasser. A fountain and library were added shortly afterward and, in the 16th century, a Saadian sultan provided it with a font. Finally, it was restored in the 17th century by Moulay Ismaïl ▲ 233. The most remarkable feature of this mosque is the north entrance door ★, with carved wooden canopy.

RIVER OF PEARLS
The Oued Fez, also known as the Oued el Jawahir (River of Pearls), enters Fez el Bali through a gateway in the north ramparts (below). The river divides into several branches

which were redirected by the Almoravid sultan Youssef Ibn Tachfine. He named the town after the river.

THE FEZ TOUR

The Fez tour should be made by car, preferably in the morning or the late afternoon when the light over the medina and the surrounding hills is at its best. Leaving the modern city, the road follows the high walls of the medina ▲ *92* of Fez el Bali as far as an olive grove, where it climbs to the BORJ SUD ★. The fort, built by Christian prisoners in the early 17th century, offers an almost aerial view of the old city, which the scholar and traveler El Marrakchi described as "the Baghdad of the Maghreb". The route follows the road to Sidi Harazem and Taza for a short distance. Craftsmen in a potters' village about 1¼ miles outside Fez are happy to open their workshops to the public and demonstrate the traditional potting skills ▲ *80*. After the Bab Ftouh, ignore the route that skirts the medina and take the Rues Fekkarine and Sidi Boujida, which cross the Andalous quarter, rejoining the Fez tour at the BAB SIDI BOUJIDA. The route returns to the medina of Fez el Bali through a secondary gate leading directly to the Palais Jamaï. From the Bab Guissa the Fez tour continues via the MERINID TOMBS (above) where the El Kollatull ★, the highest point in Fez, offers a magnificent panorama of the city and its 785 mosques. A few upright sections are all that remains of the tombs whose marble and epitaphs were extolled by ancient chroniclers. However, the ruins, interspersed with olive trees, still possess a spellbinding atmosphere. During the few weeks of the year when Hassan II is in residence in Fez, the necropolis where the last of the Merinids lie buried is guarded by soldiers and is temporarily closed to the general public. The Saadian fortress of the BORJ NORD, immediately below the *Merinides* Hotel, stands in an impressive position

> "ETERNAL FEZ ... KEPT ALIVE BY
> THE INVISIBLE BRANCHES OF THE RIVER."
>
> JOSEPH PEYRÉ

above the troglodyte caves.

The fort, originally intended to defend the city, is now home to the MUSÉE D'ARMES (Museum of Weapons), which has fine collections of prehistoric arms, swords from all ages and displays of weapons such as arquebuses, flintlock rifles, percussion rifles and muskets from all over the world. The CASBAH OF THE CHERARDA near the BAB SEGMA, today houses an annex of the Kairouyine University and a hospital. The route ends in the modern city.

A Bedouin (left), at the gates of Fez, bringing supplies by mule to the medina, which is totally impassable for vehicles.

THE MODERN CITY

As with most modern Moroccan cities, the construction of the modern city of Fez began under the French protectorate. Unfortunately, it was developed according to a very regular plan and it has turned out to be totally devoid of charm. Was the poet Mohammed Bennis thinking of the modern city when he described Fez as "purity silenced in the carillon of dreams"? Its roads and avenues are broad and spacious. The main thoroughfare, the tree-lined AVENUE HASSAN II, with an artificial lake running along its length, was built during the protectorate with the help of French legionnaires. It stretches from the Place des Alaouites in Fez el Jdid to the north exit of the town, and passes the famous *Fez* Hotel.

600,000 FASIS
The population of Fez, which was 150,000 in 1940, currently stands at 600,000. It is particularly dense in the medina of Fez el Bali (below, left) and in the new districts of Fez el Jdid (above). The migration of the rural population into the city, combined with a rapid growth in population, has made Fez the third-largest city in Morocco.

231

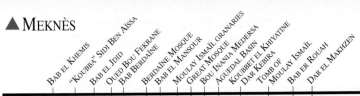

BAB EL KHEMIS
"KOUBBA" SIDI BEN AÏSSA
BAB EL JDID
OUED BOU FEKRANE
BAB BERDAÏNE
BERDAÏNE MOSQUE
BAB EL MANSOUR
MOULAY ISMAÏL GRANARIES
GREAT MOSQUE
BOU INANIA MEDERSA
AGUEDAL BASIN
KOUBBET EL KHIYATINE
DAR KEBIRA
TOMB OF MOULAY ISMAÏL
BAB ER ROUAH
DAR EL MAKHZEN

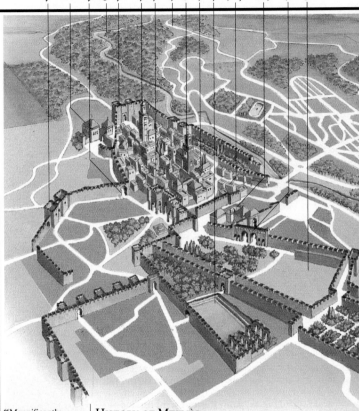

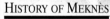

**"Magnificently
positioned on a hill
above the Oued Bou
Fekrane, Meknès'**

dozen or so minarets
can be seen from all
directions rising
above the white mass
of houses. At the foot
of the hill runs an
ocher band of high,
crenelated ramparts
with bastions
clustered around the
most vulnerable
points.**

Prosper Ricard,
*Les Merveilles de
l'autre France*

HISTORY OF MEKNÈS

Meknassa ez Zitoun (Meknès of the Olive Trees) was founded
in the 9th century when Zenata Berbers from the
Meknassa tribe settled in the fertile Saïs plain and a
series of small villages sprang up along the banks of
the OUED BOU FEKRANE.

THE EARLY ARCHITECTS. The Almoravids captured
the town in 1069 and built a fort and a kasbah where
the Touta district stands today. Meknès grew
prosperous and by 1120 had attracted the attention
of the Almohads. In 1145, after a siege lasting almost seven
years, the Almohad sultan, Abd el Moumen, entered the town
and ordered the execution of the rebels. Meknès was
abandoned. In the early 12th century the Merinids invaded
the region and took advantage of the Almohads' weakened
state to capture Meknès. They set to work and built a kasbah,
a mosque ● 86, a medersa ● 90, and several *fondouks* ▲ 223,
and the city became the official residence of the sultan's
viziers. But the fall of the Merinid dynasty led to the decline
of Meknès. In the early 15th century Berbers from the town
and the surrounding plain were driven out by the Arab
population and withdrew into the mountains. Meknès passed
into the hands of the Wattasids and then the Saadians ● 55
and enjoyed a "Golden Age" of growth and prosperity during
the reign of Moulay Ismaïl.

> "SUPERPOSED RAMPARTS, A SEA OF TERRACED ROOFS, MINARETS, THE TOWERS OF MOSQUES AND FORMIDABLE CRENELATED KASBAHS ARE OUTLINED HIGH AGAINST THE YELLOW TINGE OF THE SKY."
>
> PIERRE LOTI

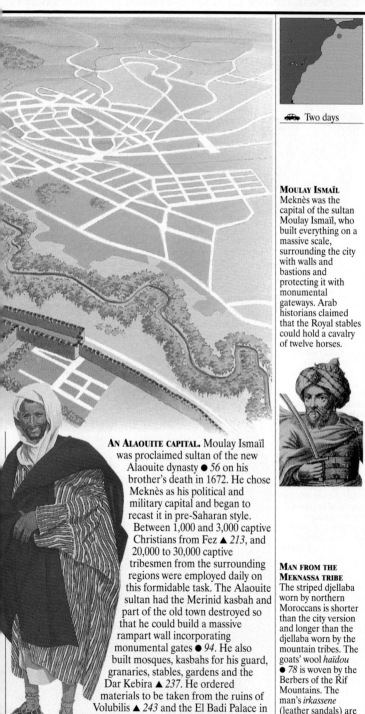

Two days

MOULAY ISMAÏL
Meknès was the capital of the sultan Moulay Ismaïl, who built everything on a massive scale, surrounding the city with walls and bastions and protecting it with monumental gateways. Arab historians claimed that the Royal stables could hold a cavalry of twelve horses.

AN ALAOUITE CAPITAL. Moulay Ismaïl was proclaimed sultan of the new Alaouite dynasty ● 56 on his brother's death in 1672. He chose Meknès as his political and military capital and began to recast it in pre-Saharan style. Between 1,000 and 3,000 captive Christians from Fez ▲ 213, and 20,000 to 30,000 captive tribesmen from the surrounding regions were employed daily on this formidable task. The Alaouite sultan had the Merinid kasbah and part of the old town destroyed so that he could build a massive rampart wall incorporating monumental gates ● 94. He also built mosques, kasbahs for his guard, granaries, stables, gardens and the Dar Kebira ▲ 237. He ordered materials to be taken from the ruins of Volubilis ▲ 243 and the El Badi Palace in Marrakesh ▲ 259 to build the Dar el

MAN FROM THE MEKNASSA TRIBE
The striped djellaba worn by northern Moroccans is shorter than the city version and longer than the djellaba worn by the mountain tribes. The goats' wool *haïdou* ● 78 is woven by the Berbers of the Rif Mountains. The man's *irkassene* (leather sandals) are tied with alfa-grass.

233

On February 21, 1909, the sultan Moulay Hafid received the French embassy in

Meknès and began negotiations with the foreign legations that led to the signing of the Treaty of Fez on March 30, 1912 ● 56.

PRINCESSE DE CONTI
On his return to Meknès from France Ben Aïcha told the sultan about his amazing travels and his meeting with Anne-Marie de Bourbon, the future Princesse de Conti and daughter of Louis XIV. His descriptions so aroused Moulay Ismaïl's interest that the latter asked Louis XIV for his daughter's hand. After this she was the source of inspiration for many court novelists and poets and Jean-Baptiste Rousseau dedicated a poem to her:
"O, great princess, your beauty inspires Admiration and arouses desires In distant lands under foreign skies; You have brought proud Africa to its knees, Achieving conquests by dint of your eyes Much greater than the exploits of Hercules..."
Moulay Ismaïl's suit was rejected.

Makhzen to the south of the city. This vast imperial city was intended to house his personal administrators and his harem, whose five hundred concubines were said to come from all corners of the world.

A MILITARY ENCAMPMENT AND FORTRESS NETWORK. The 150,000 men in Moulay Ismaïl's army included black African slaves, Arab immigrants, Sudanese, Andalous Muslims and Christians. To maintain and perpetuate this army he established a huge military encampment near the royal palace in Meknès. He provided women for his soldiers and any children born in the camp were trained to serve their country from an early age, joining the army at the age of fifteen. Moulay Ismaïl also created a network of seventy-six fortresses in strategic positions throughout his empire. These are still used as garrisons today.

AN UNFINISHED DREAM. Moulay Ismaïl wanted to strengthen trading links with France and in 1698 sent a mission charged with the task of securing a political alliance with France and negotiating the sale of prisoners. On February 16, 1699, Louis XIV received Moulay Ismaïl's envoy, Ben Aïcha, at Versailles but the two men were unable to reach an agreement. The wars of succession that broke out after the death of Moulay Ismaïl in 1727 and the Lisbon earthquake in 1755 marked the decline of Meknès. However, the city is still one of Morocco's most important military bases. Separated by the Oued Bou Fekrane, the old city and the new (built in the 1920's during the French protectorate ● 56) have a combined population of almost 300,000.

Details of the spandrels decorated with carved
zellige ▲ *173* (right) and colored ceramic tiles
(left) on the Bab Berdaïne.

THE RAMPARTS

The old city is surrounded by about 25 miles of triple
ramparts. The first, low wall was designed to stop horsemen.
The second, higher wall was to prevent foot soldiers entering
the city. The third, even higher, stopped anyone who had
managed to surmount the first two obstacles. This impressive
fortification, built during the reign of Moulay Ismaïl to defend
the entrance to the city, incorporated monumental gates,
towers and bastions.

BAB BERDAÏNE. The Bab Berdaïne, built in the 17th century
on the orders of Moulay Ismaïl, opens on to the pack-saddle
makers' district in the north of the medina from which the
gate takes its name. It is flanked by two square bastions
decorated with green terracotta, while the minaret of the
Berdaïne Mosque, constructed at the same time, can be seen
through the triumphal arch.

BAB EL KHEMIS ▲ *95.* This was the main entrance to the
"garden city" and the former *mellah*, built during the 17th
century on a site that Moulay Ismaïl gave to a Jewish doctor
who had cured one of the royal princesses. The gate, flanked
by two bastions whose spandrels feature a series of green
cartouches, is richly decorated with brightly colored
curvilinear motifs and Kufic script ● *64.* An inscription
engraved on the pediment of the gate conveys the ambition of
the sultan who ordered its construction: "I am a gate which is
open to all races, whether from the West or the East." The
"garden city" laid out to the west of the DAR KEBIRA was
completely destroyed in 1729 during the reign of Moulay
Abdallah. Modern blocks of flats have been built on the site
of the old Jewish quarter
and a new 20th-century
mellah lies to the right
of the Bab el Khemis.

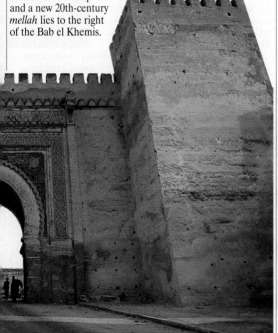

BAB EL KHEMIS
"Large Kufic
lettering is picked out
like black embroidery
on the frieze above
the deep horseshoe
arch. The majestically
formed strokes
compose a verse, a

beautifully written
phrase: 'I am the
fortunate gate which,
to my glory, is like the
full moon in the sky. I
was built by Moulay
Ismaïl. Success and
prosperity are
engraved on my
portals. I am
surrounded by good
fortune.'"
   Henriette Célarié,
   Un Mois au Maroc

BAB BERDAÏNE
The Bab Berdaïne
(Gate of the Pack-
saddles) is an
example of late-
17th-century
Alaouite
architecture,
inspired by the
military
architectural
tradition of the
Saadians. Its
massive bulk is
offset by the
predominately green
ornamental
ceramics and
decorative Kufic
script in carved
zellige ▲ *173*.

Eugène Delacroix, *Panorama of Meknès* (1832).

The royal stables of Moulay Ismaïl and the Dar el Ma (above).

"THE MARKET AT BAB EL HDIM", CAMILLE BOIRY, 1920
The rubble from the buildings that Moulay Ismaïl had ordered to be destroyed was piled up in this square. During his reign he was constantly building and demolishing. His theory was that it kept his subjects occupied.

AN IMPERIAL CITY

AGUOUDAL BASIN. Behind the three walls, each of which is closed by a gate, are the SULTANAS' GARDENS where Moulay Ismaïl installed an ostrich park. The 10-acre reservoir of the Aguoudal Basin (right) was dug near the imperial palace on the orders of Moulay Ismaïl. It was fed by a 15½-mile conduit system which ended near El Hajeb and was used to water the royal gardens and for the amusement of the sultan's favorite concubines. In times of war it provided the city's water supply.

MOULAY ISMAÏL GRANARIES ★. Farther south is the DAR EL MA (House of the Water), built during the 17th and 18th centuries. The Heri es Souani granaries adjoining the Dar el Ma were used as warehouses for the town's food stocks as well as stores for the hay and grain needed to feed the sultan's twelve thousand horses. A system of underground conduits, together with the thickness of the walls (23 feet) served to maintain a constantly low temperature inside the granaries. The conduits were fed by Persian wheels, operated by mules and horses, which drew water from cisterns 130 feet underground.

According to contemporary historians, Moulay Ismaïl's obsessive fear of being besieged explained the vast scale of the granaries which, if full, could have fed the population of Meknès for twenty years!

"Inside the kasbah there were fifty or so palaces, each with its own mosque, bath and ablutions room, which made it independent of its neighbor. This had never before been seen under any Arab or foreign government. It is said that 1,200 black eunuchs were charged with the task of guarding the gates of these palaces."

Az Zaïani,
Le Maroc de 1631 à 1812

In fact during his reign the longest siege lasted one week. In one of the storage chambers a huge carved wooden door from the royal palace has a central sun motif, formerly known as a rosette. It was the symbol of the Merinid dynasty and predates the emblem of Louis XIV (the Sun King) who has been wrongly credited as the source of Moulay Ismaïl's inspiration. The geometric symbols surrounding the rosette represent the cosmos and the forbidden, in other words what one cannot and should not seek to understand. Behind the first, perfectly preserved body of buildings is a huge trapezium-shaped edifice, now open to the sky, consisting of twenty-three naves and pisé pillars. The ceiling was originally almost 40 feet high and the length of the building at that period was two and a half times greater than it is today. The wall that truncates it was built by Moulay Abdallah in the 18th century. He installed an arsenal, which was later converted into a carpet factory. The roof collapsed in 1755 as a result of shock waves from the Lisbon earthquake, which were felt as far afield as Fez and Rabat. The kasbah consisted of over fifty palaces, each with its own mosque and baths. It was surrounded by a spacious garden planted with fruit trees and set with a huge artificial lake. A paved walkway led to the sultanas' perfume distillery.

DAR EL MAKHZEN. The Heri es Souani granaries are linked to the imperial palace by the *mechouar*. This large assembly area is closed by four great gates, including the gate of the Dar el Makhzen (Royal Palace), in which all the decorative elements of Moroccan architecture (friezes, tracery, rosettes and multi-colored *zellige* ▲ *173*) are combined. All that remains of what was once the most luxurious palace in Meknès are two walls enclosing a maze of corridors, now open to the sky, where marble pillars lie abandoned by builders and those who, after the death of Moulay Ismaïl, exploited the ruins for building materials.

DAR KEBIRA. The Bab er Rouah (Gate of the Winds), enclosed by marble-columned arches, looks onto the Place Lalla Aouda and the Dar Kebira, built in 1697. The Dar Kebira was the first palace built by Moulay Ismaïl. The three surrounding walls enclosed about twenty pavilions and two mosques, one of which was the Lalla Aouda Mosque.

DAR EL MAKHZEN
The recently restored main entrance of the Dar el Makhzen is richly decorated with glazed earthenware mosaics in the form of stars and rosettes, carved *zellige* and inscriptions in Kufic script.

MOULAY ISMAÏL MAUSOLEUM
The ceiling of the room leading into the funeral chamber

is decorated with carved and painted cedarwood. The ablutions room (below) has a marble fountain and a bronze chandelier.

THE MOULAY ISMAÏL MAUSOLEUM. The sultan Mohammed V authorized non-Muslims to enter the Moulay Ismaïl Mausoleum, despite the law ▲ 222 which prohibits them from setting foot in mosques. The Moroccans apparently appreciated the gesture made by General Lyautey when he refused an invitation from the distinguished citizens of Fez to attend a ceremony in the Great Mosque. As well as the mosque and the tomb of Moulay Ismaïl, the shrine also has several open courtyards, one of which, decorated with mosaics and glazed terracotta, leads into the square room containing the mihrab ● 86. The room has stuccowork galleries and the interior cupola is supported by twelve pillars from the ruins of Volubilis ▲ 243. The funeral chamber, decorated with stucco and mosaics, contains the tombs of Moulay Ismaïl and his wife, Lalla Khnouata, and those of his successors. On one of the walls is a plaque inscribed with a poem written by Mohammed V in honor of the Alaouite sultan, while the clocks (right) given to Moulay Ismaïl by Louis XIV are prominently placed on the richly carpeted floor.

"KOUBBA" EL KHAYATINE. In the nearby square stands the *Koubba* ● 63 el Khayatine (tailors' *koubba*), named after the corporation that occupies the square. The pavilion was used by Moulay Ismaïl to receive foreign ambassadors. A member of the French embassy present on one of these occasions described the sultan as a man of average build, with a long, thin face, a forked beard and an almost black complexion, a volatile expression and a loud voice. Vast underground chambers, known as the CHRISTIANS' PRISON and probably used as grain silos, are reached by a flight of steps adjoining the *koubba*. The prison is said to have been built by Cara, a Portuguese captive whom Moulay Ismaïl promised to free if he could build a prison that would hold 40,000 captives.

The triple-arched gateway (above) dominates the square in front of the Moulay Ismaïl Mausoleum.

BAB EL MANSOUR ● *94* ★. At the far end of the Place Lalla Aouda stands the Bab el Mansour el Aleuj (Gate of the Victorious Renegade), named after the Christian converted to Islam who built it. The gate, one of the most beautiful in Morocco, was the last architectural project undertaken on the orders of Moulay Ismaïl. Seeing it as the expression of the most refined and original taste, the French writer Pierre Loti ● *122* described the gate's rosettes, stars, endlessly intertwined broken lines and intricate geometric patterns as a vast, dazzling puzzle made of thousands of tiny pieces of raised and indented glazed pottery. He added that, from a distance, this gives the impression of a priceless piece of shimmering brocade hung over the battlements to break up the uniformity of the stone ramparts. Flanked by two bastions, whose arcades are supported by marble pillars, the gate is decorated with horseshoe designs, spandrels and networks of tracery against a background of green ceramic tiles and mosaics. The great Corinthian columns are said to have been transported from the El Badi Palace in Marrakesh ▲ *259*, which was destroyed by Moulay Ismaïl in an attempt to remove all traces of the Saadians. If the gate came under attack and the first set of doors was broken down with a battering ram, its offset entrance was designed to prevent the same from being done to the second by depriving the attackers

of room to maneuver. After inspecting the edifice, Moulay Ismaïl, so a story goes, asked the architect El Mansour if he could build an even more beautiful gate. When he said that he could El Mansour was executed on the spot. In spite of this, the work completed in 1732 appears to have been supervised by the same architect.

Bronze openwork door knocker.

"ALHAMBRA" VASE
This glazed vase, called an "Alhambra" vase because of its Hispano-Moresque style, is on display in the entrance hall of the 19th-century

palace ★ built by the vizier Jamaï. The Dar Jamaï was used as a hospital during the First World War and then converted into the Museum of Moroccan Arts in 1926.

"Inside, the town is well kept and well ordered, with some very fine churches. There are three colleges and about a dozen very large bath-houses. The market is held outside the town, near the walls, every Monday. Large numbers of Arabs from the region bring cattle, sheep and other animals as well as butter and wool. Everything is sold for next to nothing.**"**

Leo Africanus,
A Geographical History of Africa

THE MEDINA

In the various districts of the old town, which are arranged around the Great Mosque, craftsmen are grouped in areas according to their trade. The souks begin at the Bab el Khemis with the dyers' souk. Next is the SOUK SEKKARINE (cutlers and ironmongers), which runs along the edge of the former *mellah* and into the SOUK BEZZAZINE (baskets and materials) and reaches the Bab el Jdid, one of the town's oldest gates, built during the reign of the Almohads. Today its vaulted, offset chambers house sellers of musical instruments. The RUE SERAIRIA, the preserve of ironmongers and charcoal burners, runs parallel to the Souk Bezzazine and into the Rue des Armuriers, with its rock-salt souk, sawmills, millers and ironsmiths' workshops. The SOUK NEJJARINE (carpenters) is located in a street running at right angles to the Rue des Armuriers, near a 12h-century Almohad mosque with a minaret dating from 1756. Beyond the SOUK ES SEBBAT (cobblers) stands the BOU INANIA ★ MEDERSA ● *90,* whose construction was begun in the reign of the Merinid sultan Abou el Hassan and completed under Abou Inan in the 14th century. It is in a good position, overlooking the medina and the GREAT MOSQUE, the most important religious building in the city. In a nearby street a porchway marks the entrance to the 14th-century Kissaria, which houses the EL HERIR SOUK (silk). Beyond the SOUK EL GHEZARA, the butchers' souk once renowned for its dromedary meat, the workshops of the master craftsmen who make *zellige* ▲ *173* are clustered around a six-hundred-year-old mulberry tree on the site of the old grain market. To the south of the medina is the DAR EL BEIDA, the fortress built by Sidi Mohammed

THE IRONMONGERS' SOUK
Kitchen utensils, lamps and other items of tinware (a fine, soft metal covered in pewter) were once sold in the ironmongers' souk.

> **"THIS PRINCESS OF THE OLIVE TREES IS A STRANGER TO DECEIT, A PEASANT DEVOID OF ARTFULNESS, AN ARTIST BY APPLICATION; ONLY HER LOVERS UNDERSTAND HER, AND THAT IS ALL SHE CARES FOR."**
>
> MICHEL JOBERT

BOU INANIA MEDERSA
The Bou Inania Medersa presents a perfect visual balance between wood and plaster. The four arcades of this Merinid medersa rest on the neighboring houses An open brick cupola protects the entrance, which is decorated with *zellige* ▲ *173* and cedarwood carvings. The doors are covered with engraved bronze plaques.

Ben Abdullah at the end of the 18th century, which today houses a military academy. Barbary Arabs and Arab thoroughbreds ● *72*, ridden by members of the mounted section of the academy, are bred in the nearby NATIONAL STUD.

THE GREAT MOSQUE
The Great Mosque of Meknès was built in the 12th century by the Almoravids and

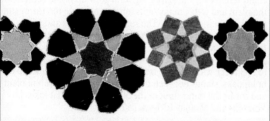

"KOUBBA" OF SIDI MOHAMMED BEN AÏSSA

Outside the medina, between the Bab Berdaïne and the Bab es Siba, lies the oldest MUSLIM CEMETERY in Meknès. It contains the *koubba* ● *63* of Sidi Mohammed Ben Aïssa, founder of the Aïssawa brotherhood. According to one story Sidi Mohammed Ben Aïssa, who was venerated in Meknès during his lifetime, possessed the power to turn leaves into gold and silver pieces. Another tells that the worshippers of the saint once made a pact with wild animals. Every year during celebration of the *Mouloud* (the Prophet's birthday) ▲ *339* the processions and ecstatic dances of the snake charmers and faith healers attract large numbers of pilgrims. The followers of Sidi Mohammed Ben Aïssa re-enact scenes during which a variety of animal species are represented.

altered in the 14th century. The entrance comprises a main doorway with a carved canopy and eleven secondary doorways. The builders of pillared mosques are said to have drawn their inspiration from the Prophet's house of exile in Medina. The domes supported on columns are based on the idea of a piece of canvas draped over a palm tree and filled by the wind.

241

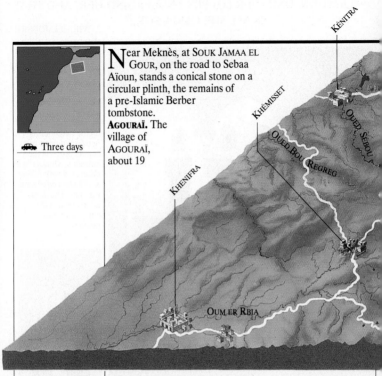

Near Meknès, at SOUK JAMAA EL GOUR, on the road to Sebaa Aïoun, stands a conical stone on a circular plinth, the remains of a pre-Islamic Berber tombstone.

AGOURAÏ. The village of AGOURAÏ, about 19

🚗 Three days

KÉNITRA

KHÉMISSET

OUED SÉBOU

KHÉMISSET

OUED BOU REGREG

KHENIFRA

OUM ER RBIA

"We are in a region of olive trees, regularly planted in alternate rows, where the ground is covered by that fine grass and moss which is only found in places that men have left undisturbed and untrodden for a long time."

Pierre Loti,
Au Maroc

miles south of Meknès, is reached by minor roads. Moulay Ismaïl is said to have given the village to the Christian prisoners in his empire in return for the favors of a particular Christian captive. During the reign of Moulay Ismaïl ▲ 232, the great Berber tribes occupied the KASBAH, from where they could watch over the slaves. Agouraï grew up in the center of the plain and today many of its inhabitants have the European names of their ancestors. The region's vineyards and wine cellars, including those of AÏT SOUALA, are renowned throughout Morocco.

JEBEL ZERHOUN. To the north of Meknès Jebel Zerhoun (3,368 feet), with its olive trees, orchards, vines and a scrub of holm oaks, stands between the Saïs valley and the Sébou plain and forms the outer limit of the 50-mile circuit that takes in Volubilis and Moulay Idriss ▲ 250.

"Jebel Zerhoun, which rises above Moulay Idriss and Volubilis, is a picturesque Mediterranean mountain with some magnificent olive groves reminiscent of an Ancient Greek landscape."

Encyclopédie par l'Image

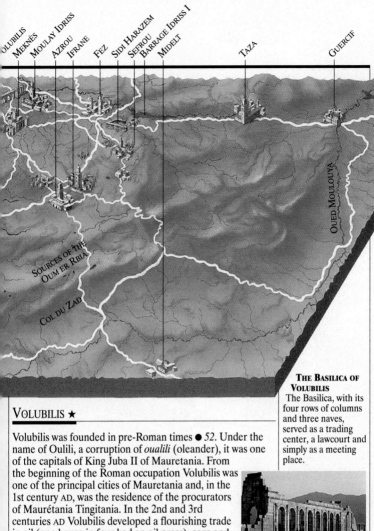

OULUBILIS MEKNÈS MOULAY IDRISS AZROU IFRANE FEZ SIDI HARAZEM SEFROU BARRAGE IDRISS I MIDELT TAZA GUERCIF

OUED MOULOUYA

SOURCES OF THE OUM ER RBIA

COL DU ZAD

VOLUBILIS ★

Volubilis was founded in pre-Roman times ● 52. Under the name of Oulili, a corruption of *oualili* (oleander), it was one of the capitals of King Juba II of Mauretania. From the beginning of the Roman occupation Volubilis was one of the principal cities of Mauretania and, in the 1st century AD, was the residence of the procurators of Maurétania Tingitania. In the 2nd and 3rd centuries AD Volubilis developed a flourishing trade in oil (one house in four had an oil press), corn and wild animals such as lions, panthers and elephants. Major building works, including the construction of the outer wall, the northwest district of the city, the triumphal arch and the Capitol, also took place at this period. But pressure exerted by the Berber tribes on the Romans led to the city's decline toward the end of the 3rd century. Descendants of the Baquates, Berbers who had been converted to Christianity occupied Volubilis until the 8th century. In 789 Idriss I was proclaimed imam of the city, which at the same time reverted to its former name of Oulili. The establishment of Fez ▲ *213* initiated the decline of the city, and it was finally destroyed by shock waves from the Lisbon earthquake in 1755. The ruins were identified in the 19th century by Tissot, the French minister plenipotentiary in Morocco. The first excavations were carried out in 1887 and continue to this day. A visit to the ruins begins with a tour of the ramparts (5¼ feet wide and 1½ miles long), which incorporate no fewer than forty bastions and eight 2nd-century gates.

THE BASILICA OF VOLUBILIS
The Basilica, with its four rows of columns and three naves, served as a trading center, a lawcourt and simply as a meeting place.

MOSAICS FROM THE HOUSE OF DIONYSUS
All the houses in Volubilis were built to the same plan. They had reception halls, private apartments and courtyards richly decorated with mosaics.

243

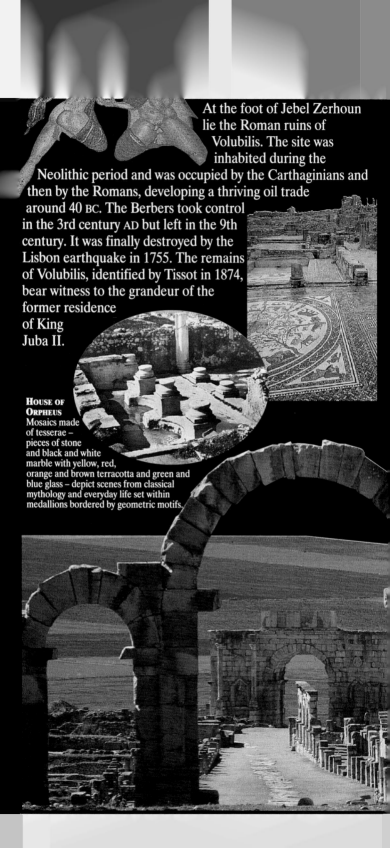

At the foot of Jebel Zerhoun lie the Roman ruins of Volubilis. The site was inhabited during the Neolithic period and was occupied by the Carthaginians and then by the Romans, developing a thriving oil trade around 40 BC. The Berbers took control in the 3rd century AD but left in the 9th century. It was finally destroyed by the Lisbon earthquake in 1755. The remains of Volubilis, identified by Tissot in 1874, bear witness to the grandeur of the former residence of King Juba II.

HOUSE OF ORPHEUS
Mosaics made of tesserae – pieces of stone and black and white marble with yellow, red, orange and brown terracotta and green and blue glass – depict scenes from classical mythology and everyday life set within medallions bordered by geometric motifs.

HOUSE OF DIONYSUS

The mosaic of the *Four Seasons* in the reception hall (below) depicts scenes of everyday work.

HOUSE OF THE EPHEBUS

The triclinium, or dining room (left) of the House of the Ephebus, named after the statue of an Ephebus crowned with ivy ▲ *249* that was found here, is paved with a splendid mosaic on the theme of Bacchus. The subject of the central medallion is a nymph riding a sea monster.

Forum

Triumphal Arch

DECUMANUS MAXIMUS AND TRIUMPHAL ARCH

Decumanus Maximus, the main paved street of Volubilis (below) crossed the town from east to west and was bordered by spacious and richly decorated houses. The marble Triumphal Arch which straddles it was built in AD 217 by the imperial procurator, Marcus Aurelius Sebastenus, in honor of the emperor Caracalla.

House of Orpheus

Capitol

Basilica

House of the Ephebus

Decumanus Maximus

House of Dionysus and the "Four Seasons"

House of the Cortège of Vénus

A forum, a basilica, wealthy houses paved with mosaics bordering the Decumanus Maximus, a triumphal arch and oil mills are all that remain of the ancient town of Volubilis. An open-air museum houses an on-site collection of fragments of sculptures and buildings, but the most important pieces are today housed in the Rabat Archeological Museum ▲ *174*. However, most of the mosaics, of which there are about thirty, remain at the site and are in very good condition.

BACCHUS DISCOVERS THE SLEEPING ARIADNE
The theme from Greek mythology, set in a hexagon (left) with a guilloche border, decorated dining rooms and reception halls.

HOUSE OF ORPHEUS
Wild and domesticated animals, very realistically depicted, wander in a natural setting (left) within a circle bordered by a Greek key pattern.

HOUSE OF THE LABORS OF HERCULES
The elaborate composition of the mosaic known as the Labors of Hercules (right) is based around the figure four. Ovoid and triangular medallions with a stylized floral decoration surround the portrait of Hercules in the central square.

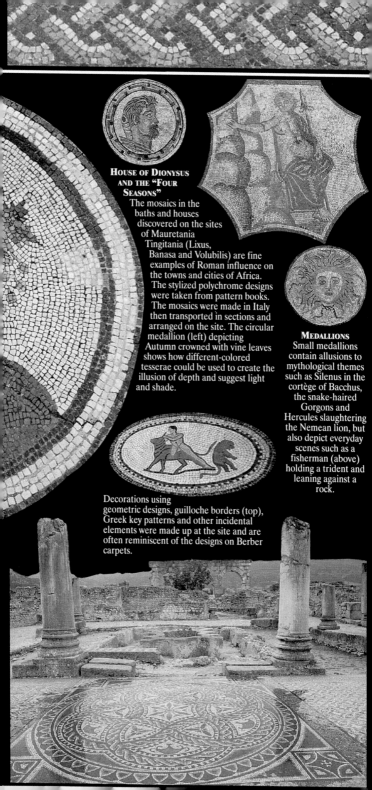

HOUSE OF DIONYSUS AND THE "FOUR SEASONS"

The mosaics in the baths and houses discovered on the sites of Mauretania Tingitania (Lixus, Banasa and Volubilis) are fine examples of Roman influence on the towns and cities of Africa. The stylized polychrome designs were taken from pattern books. The mosaics were made in Italy then transported in sections and arranged on the site. The circular medallion (left) depicting Autumn crowned with vine leaves shows how different-colored tesserae could be used to create the illusion of depth and suggest light and shade.

MEDALLIONS

Small medallions contain allusions to mythological themes such as Silenus in the cortège of Bacchus, the snake-haired Gorgons and Hercules slaughtering the Nemean lion, but also depict everyday scenes such as a fisherman (above) holding a trident and leaning against a rock.

Decorations using geometric designs, guilloche borders (top), Greek key patterns and other incidental elements were made up at the site and are often reminiscent of the designs on Berber carpets.

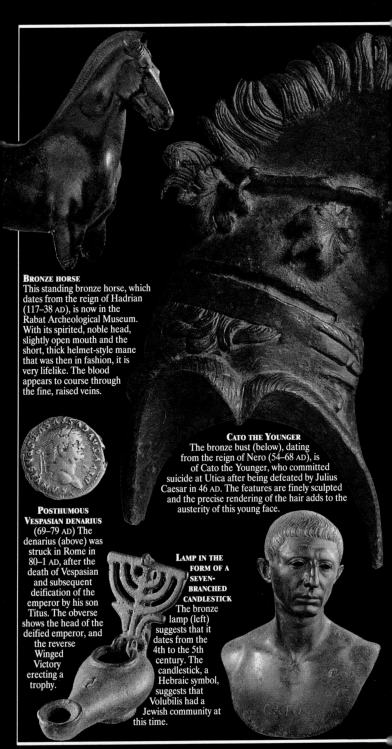

BRONZE HORSE
This standing bronze horse, which dates from the reign of Hadrian (117–38 AD), is now in the Rabat Archeological Museum. With its spirited, noble head, slightly open mouth and the short, thick helmet-style mane that was then in fashion, it is very lifelike. The blood appears to course through the fine, raised veins.

CATO THE YOUNGER
The bronze bust (below), dating from the reign of Nero (54–68 AD), is of Cato the Younger, who committed suicide at Utica after being defeated by Julius Caesar in 46 AD. The features are finely sculpted and the precise rendering of the hair adds to the austerity of this young face.

POSTHUMOUS VESPASIAN DENARIUS
(69–79 AD) The denarius (above) was struck in Rome in 80–1 AD, after the death of Vespasian and subsequent deification of the emperor by his son Titus. The obverse shows the head of the deified emperor, and the reverse Winged Victory erecting a trophy.

LAMP IN THE FORM OF A SEVEN-BRANCHED CANDLESTICK
The bronze lamp (left) suggests that it dates from the 4th to the 5th century. The candlestick, a Hebraic symbol, suggests that Volubilis had a Jewish community at this time.

MULE CROWNED WITH VINE LEAVES

This drunken mule, a bronze armrest bracket (left), is one of the masterpieces of the reign of Augustus. The strikingly realistic violence of its expression is emphasized by the flaring nostrils, the set of the jaw (which looks as if it is about to bite), and the tufted delineation of the mane. It can be seen in the Rabat Archeological Museum ▲ 174.

HORSEMAN

The bronze Ephebus (left), either original or a copy of a statue by Polyclitus, illustrates the archaic style that was fashionable during the reign of Hadrian (117–38 AD). The figure has the torso and narrow waist of an athlete, while the carriage of the head gives an air of assurance.

BUST OF JUBA II

This bust (below), in Greek sculptural style, probably dates from the period when the young prince was given the kingdom of Mauretania by Augustus in 25 BC. The young face, with the rounded, cleft chin, has a sad and disdainful expression.

HEAD OF A BERBER YOUTH

The detailed modeling of this expressive, vigorous head in fine-grained, white marble is typically Greek and exemplifies the classicism that predominated during the reign of Augustus.

IVY-CROWNED YOUTH

This bronze statue of a naked, ivy-crowned youth, now in the Rabat Archeological Museum, dates from the Roman period. The boy's left leg supports the weight of his body, and the right leg is bent slightly backward, toes barely resting on the ground. The hair is encircled by a crown of ivy with delicate tendrils, and the face has an arresting beauty.

249

Idriss Medersa was
built with materials
taken from the site of
Volubilis. Its modern
cylindrical minaret is
decorated with green
mosaics in the form
of a *surah* from the
Koran.

This view of the
mausoleum and town
of Moulay Idriss is
one of the hundred or
so etchings
illustrating scenes
from Moroccan life
by Edmond Valès, an
art teacher at the
Poeymirau Lycée in
Meknès.

MOULAY IDRISS ★

The holy town of Moulay Idriss was built to the east of
Volubilis on two rocky spurs, the Khiber and the Tasga, which
naturally divide the town into two distinct districts. The city
houses the shrine of Idriss I, the most venerated saint in the
whole of Morocco, a descendant of the Prophet's son-in-law
Ali ● *53* and Fatima, and founder of the Idrissid dynasty in
the 8th century.

THE HOLY FOUNDER. After his defeat at the Battle of Fekh in
786, fought between the followers of Ali and the forces of the
Abbassid caliph El Mansour, Idriss fled Damascus and sought
refuge at Oulili ▲ *243,* where he began to convert the Berbers
to Islam ● *62.* In his *Garden of Leaves* the historian Ibn
Azigar recounts that Idriss then undertook the conversion of
all the remaining Christian Berbers, Jews and idolaters in the
Maghreb. He preached with such energy and commitment
that the Berbers were moved to praise his virtue and his

descent from the Prophet, and
made him their religious,
military and temporal leader.
But his growing popularity
angered Haroun er Rachid, the
Abbassid Caliph of Baghdad
(on whom the villainous caliph
of the *Arabian Nights* is based);
in 791 the caliph had him
poisoned.

THE "ZAOUIA". The Moulay
Idriss Zaouia was built in the
center of the *horm*, the sanctuary
area delimited by horizontal
wooden bars that non-Muslims
are not permitted to enter. The
area appears to have been
extended to incorporate the
entire town, which has no Jewish
or Christian inhabitants. The

Watercolor of the holy town of Moulay Idriss and Jebel Zerhoun by the modern French artist and Orientalist Charles Kérivel.

koubba containing the tomb of Moulay Idriss was destroyed by Moulay Ismaïl in the 18th century. In the 19th century Sidi Abd er Rahman replaced it with a mausoleum decorated with a mass of colorful stained glass windows and beautifully crafted *zellige* ▲ *173*. The black and white marble pillars of the courtyard are in a variety of styles: plain, ribbed or carved with floral motifs. The lower section of the walls of the funeral chamber is covered with a display of rosettes made of glazed terracotta tiles. The tomb of Idriss I rests on a catafalque embroidered in gold, silver and silk, which was a gift from Hassan II in 1978.

THE "MOUSSEM". In August and September each year thousands of pilgrims flock to Moulay Idriss for the *moussem*. Then, the slopes of Jebel Zerhoun are covered in tents and the town is completely taken over by dancers, acrobats, story-tellers, a variety of other types of performers and an endless procession of the faithful.

SIDI ALI BEN HAMDOUCH. The road that skirts Jebel Zerhoun passes through the NESRANI KASBAH and the village of the Beni Rachid. The tomb of SIDI ALI BEN HAMDOUCH, who founded the Hamadcha brotherhood in the 18th century, is in the village. There is a story that one of his followers, Sidi Ahmed Dghoughi, used to strike his head against rocks to keep himself awake so as not to interrupt his meditation. On the death of his master he is said to have struck his head with anything that came to hand.

IFRANE★

The health resort of Ifrane (5,400 feet) was built in 1929 on what was then the main route between Fez and Meknès. Its huddle of identical chalets with their pink-tiled roofs and tiny gardens gives the place a distinctly European appearance. In 1936 Ifrane received government subsidies which enabled it to establish winter sports facilities. In summer hikers use Ifrane as a base or a stopping place and local trout and crayfish make it popular with fishing enthusiasts. A track to the south of Ifrane leads to the VALLÉE DES ROCHES and a curious outcrop of limestone that looks uncannily like ruined buildings. To the north a mountain track leads to the

The steep, narrow streets of the holy town are like the streets of Fez, except that these are empty and silent.

CASCADE DES VIERGES and the picturesque village of ZAOUIA D'IFRANE, which is still inhabited by a number of *chorfa* families. This tiny village is also a favored meeting place for craftsmen of the region.

IFRANE
The resort, built in an old volcanic crater, is covered in snow from December to March.

251

The first place of interest on the road between Fez
▲ *213* and Taza and Oujda is SIDI HARAZEM ★, named
after a 12th-century saint. In 1526 the geographer
and writer Leo Africanus ● *125* described how
the fourth Merinid sultan, Abou el
Hassan, built a fine residence on the
site of this thermal spring, where
the gentry of Fez used to stay for
three or four days every April.
Each year at *moussem* ▲ *339* the
local population proceeds to the
tomb of Sidi Ali Ben Harazem,
a great scholar from the Orient.
He is commemorated by a
cenotaph in Fez where he is said to
have taught the *djinns.* Further
south the BIRTAM TAM road
crosses the gorges of the OUED
SÉBOU, which flows between the Rif and the
Mamora Forest ▲ *178*, ■ *32.* Farther east, after the
great lake and *Barrage d'Idriss I,* is the village of SIDI
ABDALLAH DE RHIATA, where the JEBEL TAZZEKA tourist
route starts. The route passes through the gorges of the OUED
ZIREG and through cork-oak forests before crossing the
NATIONAL PARK OF JEBEL TAZZEKA. At the GOUFFRE DU

SIDI HARAZEM
The oasis of Sidi
Harazem is irrigated
by the waters of a hot
spring. The mineral

water, which is
beneficial for liver
and kidney
complaints, is sold
throughout Morocco.

FRIOUATO, natural underground galleries
running 590 feet deep, with stalactites
and stalagmites, are open to the public.
After passing old mining works, the road
runs on to the GROTTES DU CHIKER.

TAZA

In the foothills of the Rif and the Middle
Atlas ■ *24*, off the main tourist routes,
lies Taza, one of Morocco's oldest
towns. It was founded by the Meknassa
Berbers ▲ *233* in the 10th century at the
entrance to the TAZA CORRIDOR, which,
in linking the barren regions of the north
to the agricultural basins of western
Morocco, is one of the most frequented
routes in the Maghreb.

HISTORY. The town grew up around the fortified monastery
built by the Berbers in the 10th century. Its strategic position
on the road to Fez meant that it became a military stronghold
that was greatly coveted by invaders from the East who
wanted to conquer the kingdom of Morocco. Taza changed
hands with each new ruling dynasty. In 1074 the Almoravid
sultan Youssef Ibn Tachfine captured the town, and it
remained under his control until the end of the 11th century.
In 1132 it was seized by the Almohad sultan Abd el Moumen,
who made it the temporary capital of Morocco. As part of his
campaign against the Beni Merin, Zenata Berbers from the
pre-Saharan regions who were to found the Merinid dynasty
fifty years later, Abd el Moumen constructed a wall around
the medina ● *92.* These hefty ramparts were subsequently
strengthened in the 14th century by the Merinids and by the
Saadians in the 16th. In the 17th century Moulay Rachid

"In the distance a
mass of walls crowds
together on a rocky
hillside, square
buildings packed
tightly inside high
ramparts. Deep in a
gorge, a light gray
village is only just
distinguishable against
the dark gray
background of the
surrounding
mountains."

Pierre Dumas,
Le Maroc

seized Taza, and this brought him a step nearer to capturing Fez. He became the first sultan of the Alaouite dynasty, which has continued down to the present day. In 1902 Bou Hamara el Roghi (Man with the She-ass), a prominent member of the court of the sultan Abd el Aziz, returned to Morocco under a false identity after being exiled to Algeria. He suceded in being elected chérif of Taza and, on a religious pretext, persuaded the local Berbers to rebel against the sultan. Bou Hamara el Roghi remained in control of the town for seven years but finally, after selling mining concessions to Spain, lost the support of the mountain tribes. He met with a gruesome end. After being arrested in 1909, he was thrown to wild animals, shot and then burnt at the stake in Fez on the order of the sultan Moulay Hafid. In accordance with the treaty signed on March 30, 1912 ● 56, Taza became part of the French protectorate on May 10, 1914, and remained under French control until Moroccan independence was established in 1956.

VISITING TAZA. In the medina, next to the Great Mosque, stands the ABOU EL HASSAN MEDERSA, built in 1323. Its courtyard is tiled with mosaics and has an onyx water basin and two onyx capitals. On the town's main street are the GRAIN MARKET and the SOUKS wheres mats, carpets ● 74, jewelry ● 68 and a range of other traditional Berber items made in the mountains are displayed for sale. The street leads into an assembly area at the far end of which is the MOSQUE OF EL ANDALOUS, with a 12th-century minaret that is wider at the top than the bottom. The Rue Bab el Gebbour crosses the KISSARIA and continues to the MARKET MOSQUE where it rejoins the Bab Jamaa, Taza's main gateway. Farther south, opposite the BAB EL ROUAH (Gate of the Winds), the kasbah is closed by a 16th-century bastion.

THE GREAT MOSQUE, TAZA
The minaret of the Great Mosque, built in the reign of Abd el Moumen, rises above the roofs of Taza's medina. The 12th-century Almohad mosque has a carved wood and marquetry minbar ● 86 and a beautifully engraved openwork bronze chandelier. It has six hundred cups and weighs over 7,000 pounds and is one of the oldest bronze chandeliers in Morocco. The openwork cupola is one of the most beautiful in Morocco.

The ramparts of Taza were built in the 12th century and strengthened several times. In the 16th century the Saadian sultan Ahmed el Mansour added a square *borj*, 85 feet a side, with a portcullis and casemates below the terraces that show strong European influence.

253

The mosque of Bhalil (below).

BHALIL

There are several theories as to the origin of this village, which lies at the foot of JEBEL KANDAR, about 19 miles from Fez and before Sefrou. According to one, the inhabitants of Bhalil, to avoid being forced to convert to Islam by Idriss I, claimed Christian ancestry and denied any Arabic connections. The village appears to have been occupied by the Romans in the 1st century AD. There are troglodyte dwellings in the foothills of Jebel Kandar, beneath which the village nestles.

SEFROU ★

Sefrou (2,790 feet) lies in the foothills of the Middle Atlas, on a fertile plain irrigated by the OUED AGGAÏ, a river notorious for its devastating spring floods. Since the 12th century Sefrou has been a commercial center, and a meeting place for farmers from the agricultural regions of northern Morocco and the Tafilalet ▲ *294*. The region's Ahel Sefrou were Berbers who were converted to Judaism and subsequently to Islam by Moulay Idriss in the 8th century. In the 13th century the town also had a large Jewish community made up of Jews from the Tafilalet and southern Algeria, some of whose descendants still inhabit the town today. In the *mellah* of Sefrou, situated in the old town, to the south of the medina and separated from it by the Oued Aggaï, is the "ZAOUIA" OF SIDI LAHCEN BEN AHMED, a 17th-century saint. From here the old stone bridges over the river lead to the EL KEBIR MOSQUE and the souks of the medina. The old town is a maze of narrow, winding streets where houses rise in tiers against the rock. It is surrounded by 18th- and 19th-century crenelated ramparts. On the outskirts of Sefrou water mills and wash-houses border the Oued Aggaï, whose falls, situated to the northwest, were partly destroyed by the spring floods of 1977.

Every year during the cherry harvest, the local inhabitants make their way in procession to the grotto of Kef el Moumen, which contains the tomb of the Prophet Daniel. Here, according to the local legend of the Seven Sleepers,

seven faithful men and their dog fell asleep and remained so for the course of several centuries. Fantasias, singing and dancing are important parts of this agricultural festival. The miraculous spring of Lalla Rekia, west of the village, is said to cure madness. In a ceremony during the *moussem* the blood of sacrificed animals is mixed with the waters of the spring.

ROUTE DES LACS ★

From Sefrou the road crosses the fertile plains of the agricultural region of Fez ▲ 213 and then leads up into the mountains of the Middle Atlas ■ 24. Here the slopes are

covered in vegetation and the barriers at the roadside close off the road when the winter snows make it impassable.
ANNOCEUR. On the left, on the top of a hill, are the barely visible remains of the site of Annoceur (pronounced a-nass-air), which was once a lookout post on the *Trik es Soltan*, the Fez-Tafilalet trade route ▲ 294. A few sections of wall are all that remain of the original building. Roman inscriptions found here on pieces of quarry stone were once taken to suggest that this had been a Roman encampment, but it is now known that these were fragments from the site of Volubilis ▲ 243, and probably formed part of a consignment of stone being transported to the Tafilalet, where Moulay Ismaïl was having the Dar el Beida ▲ 240 built. Immediately after Annoceur the route forks right toward a series of *dayet* (lakes), the largest of which is the DAYET IFRAH, then winds its way up to the Abekhnanès pass (5,800 feet), leaving behind forest and pasture and entering an arid steppe landscape, the full beauty of which can be appreciated around the village of AÏT AMERU OUABID. The Midelt road passes through Boulemane and continues to the GORGES DE ROIFA before rejoining the *Trik es Soltan*. The mountains and high stony plateaux with thorny scrub stretch as far as Aït Kermouss.

Between here and Midelt the road crosses the pre-Saharan plateau of M'Guild, the peaks of JEBEL AYACHI rising in the distance, and passes through Taouerda, Boulôjoul and Zeida to reach the nature reserve of Midelt.

JEBEL AYACHI
Jebel Ayachi (12,260 feet) rises above Midelt.

BOULEMANE
Boulemane is the first town after Sefrou where drivers can fill up with gas or have tires repaired, and the last before Zeida.

AÏT KERMOUSS
The minaret of the recently built mosque of Aït Kermouss, to the south of Boulemane, overlooks the holm-oak-covered slopes of the Aït Youssi region.

DAYET IFRAH
The oueds of the Middle Atlas form a number of natural and artificial lakes. A road leads from Ifrane to the Dayet Aoua, which lies in the heart of a wildfowl reserve, and then on to Dayet Ifra (left), one of the largest lakes in the region, frequented by common herons, tufted herons and cranes.

"Then you begin the long climb into the Middle Atlas, through an old cedar forest and holm oaks lashed by the wind. ... Beyond Timhadite lies another, completely barren plateau which is reminiscent of certain lunar landscapes. ... The ground is pitted with small volcanic craters, some filled with rainwater, known here as aguelmane. The largest of these craters, Sidi Ali [is] an immense lake bordered by steep cliffs. The dampness of the air and the almost permanent clouds at these altitudes mean that the slopes are covered with beautiful trees which are reflected in the vast mirror of the lake. Solitude weighs heavily on

this prehistoric landscape."
A. t'Serstevens,
L'Itinéraire
Marocain

Before climbing to the Col du Zad, it is worth making a detour via the village of ITZER, situated on the main timber route of the area. In the village square, now lined with cafés, foresters once met to negotiate the price of timber. The oued on the edge of the village is crowded with women washing clothes. The road to the COL DU ZAD (7,150 feet) passes through one of the most beautiful natural sites in the Middle Atlas. Hundred-year-old cedar forests cover the watershed between the Atlantic and the Mediterranean, separating the Sebou and Moulouya basins. The AGUELMANE DE SIDI ALI (6,600 feet), beyond Azrou, is a 2-mile-long lake lying at an altitude of 6,000 feet. It is well stocked with trout, carp and perch, and is a major attraction for fishermen. The Aguelmane is overlooked by Jebel Hayane (7,870 feet), which on a clear day offers a splendid view right across the Rif ■ 24, the Bou Iblane and the peaks of the High Atlas ■ 26.

BEKRITE nestles deep in the forest to the west of the Midelt-Azrou road. The village is famous throughout Morocco for its carpets, which are strikingly decorated with black and white or colored geometric designs. Beyond the high volcanic plateau of Foum Kheneg lies the village of TIMAHDITE where oil shale is mined. Farther to the north there is a winter sports resort on the slopes of Jebel Hebri.

The Souk at Azrou, an etching by Edmond Valès.

AZROU ★

Azrou (4,100 feet) stands on the edge of the most beautiful and best preserved of Morocco's cedar forests ■ 28. There are few impressive architectural sights in Azrou; of the kasbah, constructed in 1684 by Moulay Ismaïl ▲ 233 only ruins remain. But the town is worth a visit for its peaceful atmosphere, its fresh air and its traditional houses, built chiefly in wood. Azrou takes its name from the impressive volcanic rock (the Berber word for rock is *zrou*) which stands at its western entrance. Caves in the area gave the inhabitants protection from the outside world and possibly explain why Azrou remained undiscovered for so long. The Amazir, the town's first known inhabitants, seem to have led an isolated existence, for they had their own language and syntax. Azrou gradually became an important Berber center, however, and the first Moroccan school to teach the shluh (or chleuch) dialect was established here in 1960. Today Arabic is taught. Azrou's convenient position at the crossroads of the significant trade routes between Meknès ▲ 231 and Erfoud ▲ 294, and Fez ▲ 213 and Marrakesh ▲ 259 considerably boosted the town's economy. The focal point of Azrou is the Place Mohammed V, crowded with cafés, shops and arcaded houses with painted wood façades and tiled roofs. Here a large regional market is held, and traders from the Beni M'Guild, the largest Berber tribe in the region, set up their looms in conspicuous positions ● 74. Today the economic life of the town is in fact monopolized by Riffians. Ironworking, wood sculpture, weaving and a variety of other activities take place in workshops clustered around the square, which is also the town's craft center. Prices in the shops there are much lower than in big towns and cities.

AÏN LEUCH

This village may have got its name (Eye of the Wood) from the fact that, from a distance, it resembles an eye set in the forest. It lies in a hollow in the mountain on the track leading to the FORTY SPRINGS OF THE OUM ER RBIA ▲ 148. Further south the springs cascade down the limestone cliffs and collect to form Morocco's longest river. The AGUELMANE AZIGZA ★ (the blue lake) to the west, surrounded by cedars and holm oaks, and bordered by a cliff of red rock, is one of the country's most beautiful lakes.

"Arriving at the souk, the fellah immediately enters an animated world of sights, sounds and smells. The souk is an event which abruptly shatters the silence and isolation of the *douar*, villages and camps."
Jean-François Troin,
Les Souks Marocains

CEDAR FORESTS ■ 28
**OF THE MIDDLE
ATLAS**
Some of the trees in the cedar forests of the Col du Zad are several hundred years old. They reach heights of nearly 200 feet and can be up to 6½ feet in circumference. The most famous of these was the Gouraud cedar near Azrou which measured 33 feet around its base. It was felled at the turn of the century, when it was at least 980 years old.

Olive and cereal plantations in the Khémisset region.

THE "TARAZA"
In the souks storytellers and musicians (far right) mingle with the Zemmour, makers and sellers of *taraza*, wide-brimmed reed or alfa-grass hats with wool embroidery and

multicolored tassels, worn by the horsemen (below).

THE ZAÏANE REGION

The market at Khemisset, in the heart of the Zemmour region, is one of the busiest in northern Morocco. "If you only had time to visit one souk in Morocco, this would be the one to see because it embodies all the others!" wrote Jean-François Troin in *Les Souks Marocains*. The road to Rabat crosses the iron ore mines of Medinette which, on the evidence of tools found there, have been worked since ancient times. Farther south a shortcut runs through villages and souks between Maaziz and Khenifra and crosses the Pays Zaïane, whose administrative center is Tiddas. The region is named after a tribe of Berber warriors who became farmers and stock breeders. The Zaïane, distinguished by their well-trimmed beards and fine mustaches, have a saying: "The mountains are my being, the Oum er Rbia [▲ 148] my boundary and the plain my pasture." Cork-oak and thuja forests give way to the cultivated plateau of Tarmilate, the spa formerly known as Oulmès, where at an altitude of 3,600 feet the hot springs of Lalla Haya rise to temperatures of over 90°F. Below lies the valley of the Oued Marrout, the agricultural region where Moulay Ismaïl built the MARABOUT OF MOULAY BOUAZZA, one of the founders of Sufism, in 1691. Khenifra, known as the "red town" because of the color of the earth on which it was built, lies farther south on the Oum er Rbia. It expanded under Moulay Ismaïl in the 18th century and in the 19th became an active commercial center that was freed from central government control when Hammou ez Zaïani, the Berber chieftain appointed kaïd by Moulay Hassan, took control of the region and developed the town.

IN AND AROUND MARRAKESH

▲ MARRAKESH

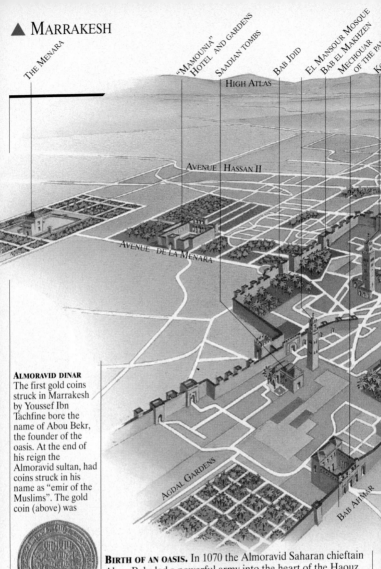

THE MENARA
"MAMOUNIA" HOTEL AND GARDENS
SAADIAN TOMBS
BAB JDID
EL MANSOUR MOSQUE
BAB EL MAKHZEN
MECHOUAR OF THE PAL
KC
HIGH ATLAS
AVENUE HASSAN II
AVENUE DE LA MENARA
AGDAL GARDENS
BAB AHMAR

ALMORAVID DINAR
The first gold coins struck in Marrakesh by Youssef Ibn Tachfine bore the name of Abou Bekr, the founder of the oasis. At the end of his reign the Almoravid sultan, had coins struck in his name as "emir of the Muslims". The gold coin (above) was struck in Marrakesh after his death by his son Ali, in the year 536 of the Hegira (1141), when Marrakesh was becoming an important commercial center.

BIRTH OF AN OASIS. In 1070 the Almoravid Saharan chieftain Abou Bekr led a powerful army into the heart of the Haouz plain at the foot of the High Atlas ■ 26. He set up camp near a small river not far from the rocky outcrop of the Gueliz ▲ 278, which would provide the stone for the construction of his future town. The first palace and the first mosque were built by Abou Bekr. An 11th-century manuscript preserved in the Kairouyine Library ▲ 224 in Fez refers to "Marrakouch," the land of the sons of *Kouch*, black African warriors from Aoudaghost, a large caravan town in Mauretania surrounded by palm trees.

CAPITAL OF THE ALMORAVID EMPIRE. Recalled to the borders of Mauretania and black Africa, Abou Bekr left Marrakesh in the hands of his cousin, Youssef Ibn Tachfine, who promised to make the oasis the Almoravid capital. Saharan tents were soon replaced by *pisé* buildings and Marrakesh grew rich on the gold and ivory brought by the caravans. It became the center of an empire that extended from the Tafilalet to the Ebro, and from the Atlantic Ocean to Algiers. Youssef Ibn Tachfine died in Marrakesh at the age of one hundred in 1106. His son Ali, whose mother was a Christian slave from

MOSQUE
E DU 16 NOVEMBRE
EL BADI PALACE
PLACE DJEMAA EL FNA
LA BAHIA PALACE
BAB DOUKKALA
BEN YOUSSEF MOSQUE
MAJORELLE GARDENS
BEN YOUSSEF MEDERSA
BAB AYLEN
BAB DEBBAGH
BAB EL KHEMIS

OUED ISSIL

🚗 Three days

ABD EL MOUMEN BEN ALI (1130–63)
Abd el Moumen succeeded the religious leader Ibn

Andalusia, became one of the greatest rulers of Morocco. He sent for Andalusian craftsmen to build a new palace and a mosque. The surviving architectural masterpieces built during his reign include the *koubba* el Baroudiyin ▲ 277, the minbar ● 86 of the Koutoubia Mosque and the high ramparts with their monumental gates ▲ 264.

MARRAKESH UNDER THE ALMOHADS. Abd el Moumen, the Almohad sultan from the mountains, captured the town in 1147 ● 54 and destroyed all religious and civil buildings. He had the Koutoubia Mosque (right) ▲ 268 built and the Menara Gardens planted.

Toumert, whose unitarian reform, known as the Almohad reform, had caused unrest in Marrakesh during the reign of Ali Ben Youssef and forced him to retreat into the mountains. Abd el Moumen fought for nine months to take the Almoravid capital. The geographer and cartographer El Idrisi tells how, when the sultan took possession of Marrakesh in 1147, the conquerors pillaged, killed and even sold free men in the name of their faith.

MARRAKESH IN 1646
Engraving (above) made by the Dutch artist Adrian Matham after a visit to the Moroccan capital at the time of its commercial and architectural apogee. Having defeated the Portuguese army (right and far right) Moulay Ahmed el Mansour undertook some extremely fine architectural projects in Marrakesh, including the El Mansour Mosque ▲ 270 and the first Saadian mausoleum ▲ 271.

AN ARABIC CENTER FOR PHILOSOPHY. Abou Youssef Yacoub, the second Almohad sultan, extended the town of Marrakesh, which he wanted to transform into a fine imperial city complete with pleasant gardens (the Agdal Gardens ▲ 266 are among the most beautiful of these). He founded the Arabic center for philosophical studies, which attracted large numbers of scholars and poets to the capital. In the late 12th century Abou Youssef Yacoub's son, Yacoub el Mansour ▲ 163, built a kasbah, an imperial city, palaces, mosques and gardens. The Almohad sultan encouraged trade with Spain, and Marrakesh grew rich on exports of leather, sugar and ceramics ● 80. Leatherwork and sugar refining were the city's two main industries.

DEPOSED BY THE MERINIDS. The beginning of the decline of the Almohad dynasty ● 54, which coincided with the death of Yacoub el Mansour in 1199, initiated the disintegration of the kingdom and the decline of Marrakesh. For fifty years the city suffered as a result of dynastic struggles. In 1269 it lost its status as capital for the first time when the Merinids entered Marrakesh, seized power and transferred the capital to Fez ▲ 216. When a new Fez-Sijilmassa-Gao central Saharan route opened in 1274, and the caravans using the west Saharan route came under the control of the Makil Arabs in 1286, Marrakesh was temporarily deprived of supplies of African gold. This loss hastened the city's physical decay so that, when the Saadians took control in 1522, Marrakesh was a ruined city decimated by famine.

RENAISSANCE. The Saadians settled in the royal residences and made Marrakesh the capital of southern Morocco. Once the Moroccan empire had been re-unified ● 55, it also became the imperial city. In the second half of the 16th century Moulay Abdallah, the great architect of the Saadian dynasty, restored Marrakesh to its former glory. In 1578, following the Battle of the Three Kings ● 55, ▲ 201, Ahmed el Mansour, the Victorious and Golden, used the monies paid as a war indemnity by the Portuguese and gold transported from Timbuktu to embellish it even further. Marrakesh became Morocco's leading city. The Saadian tombs and the now ruined El Badi Palace (the Incomparable) give some idea of the ambitions that this powerful Saadian ruler had for the city. In 1591 an expedition returned from Timbuktu with 3¼ tons of gold which, together with some of the profits from European

SAADIAN TOMBS
At the end of the 16th century the Saadian necropolis (seen above in a painting by Charles Kérivel) contained a number of Saadian mausoleums, one of which housed the tomb of Moulay Ahmed el Mansour. The tomb stands in the Chamber of the Twelve Columns (far right), next to the Chamber of the Mihrab (right), which also contains the tombs of several Alaouite sultans.

exports of sugar produced in the presses of Marrakesh, and "morocco leather", as it was known, was used to find a building program to develop the medina. By the late 16th century Marrakesh had some sixty thousand inhabitants, and its *mellah* became a city housing the largest Jewish community in Morocco. European diplomats and traders flocked to Marrakesh, now at the height of its prosperity.

STAGNATION. During the first half of the 17th century Marrakesh came under threat of attack and began to suffer from famine, rebellions and wars. In 1669 the town was captured by the Alaouite sultan ● *55* Moulay Rachid and, for the second time, the capital was transferred to Fez ▲ *213*. When Moulay Ismaïl ▲ *233* came to power as a result of the accidental death of Moulay Rachid, he chose Meknès as his capital. He continuously tried to stamp out all trace of former dynasties. For Marrakesh this meant the demolition of the El Badi Palace and the encircling of the Saadian tombs within a wall.

MARRAKESH, AN ALAOUITE CAPITAL. In the mid-18th century Mohammed III restored the shrines, mosques ● *86*, gates ● *94*, medersat ● *90* and kasbahs that had been totally or partially destroyed throughout Morocco. For twenty-five years Marrakesh was his capital. He built a new palace, and between 1828 and 1869 laid out new gardens (including the Mamounia Gardens ▲ *266*) and replanted the Agdal and Menara Gardens. In 1873 Moulay Hassan was proclaimed sultan in Marrakesh and he resided there for a year. Luxurious palaces such as the Dar el Bahia ▲ *273* and the Dar Si'Saï were designed and constructed during the reign of Moulay Hassan and his son, Moulay Abd el Aziz.

RESISTANCE. In the late 19th century the French advance in southern Morocco caused unrest in the central and western Sahara. From Marrakesh Moulay Abd el Aziz supported the forces of the Saharan resistance against France. In 1912, the Saharan chieftain El Hiba ▲ *325*, leader of the resistance in the South, waged a campaign to prevent the French protectorates being extended to Marrakesh. He and his forces were stopped in their northward advance at Sidi Bou Othmane ▲ *147* by the army of Colonel Mangin. As a result of a decision by General Lyautey, France's first resident general in Morocco ▲ *141*, Marrakesh finally lost its status as capital. Today it is a major tourist town.

MOULAY ABD EL AZIZ
Moulay Abd el Aziz was proclaimed sultan at the age of six. He ruled under the regency of Ahmed Ben Moussa and did not become involved in government until 1900.

MOULAY HASSAN
On his accession in 1873 Moulay Hassan implemented a policy of fiscal and military reform which, in spite of British support, was a failure.

The ramparts of Marrakesh extend over 6¼ miles and form an impressive clay and chalk *pisé* fortification. The walls, between 26 and 32 feet high, incorporate ten monumental gates in Hispano-Moresque style, some of which have been

> "... The ramparts ... dominated the desert while at the same time prolonging and extending its color."
> Roland Dorgelès,
> *Le Dernier Moussem*

copied in other Moroccan cities. The ramparts were built in the early 12th century and subsequently extended to accommodate the successive developments of the medina at the end of the 12th and during the 18th century. A gate-by-gate tour of the ramparts begins at the PLACE DE LA LIBERTÉ, which lies to the west of the medina. In

BAB DOUKKALA
The Bab Doukkala opens to the north-westard. It was named after the tribes who today live on the Doukkala plain south of El Jadida ▲ *149*.

the north section are the ruins of the BAB EL RAHA with its single surviving bay and, just before the bus station, the BAB DOUKKALA, erected during the reign of the Almoravids. The Bab Doukkala was named after the region to the north of Marrakesh, where the city's leper colony was once situated. The tour follows the road to Fez ▲ *213* for a short distance before reaching the most northerly point of the ramparts.

"VIEW OF THE HIGH ATLAS"
The French artist Lucie Ranvier-Chartier published an illustrated account of the visit she made to North Africa in 1921–3 in the French magazine *L'Art*. It included a number of her sketches and paintings of Morocco, and particularly of Marrakesh, which evoke the light and color of the imperial city dominated by the peaks of the High Atlas ■ *26*.

BAB EL KHEMIS
Flanked by two massive bastions designed to protect the main northeast entrance to the medina, the Bab el Khemis (Gate of the Thursday Market), formerly known as the Fez Gate, opens on to an esplanade where an animal souk is held each week on Thursday.

Donkeys are gradually being replaced by bicycles in the relatively level streets of Marrakesh.

The leaves of the gate are said to have been brought back from Andalusia by a sultan.
BAB DEBBAGH. The five curves of the Bab Debbagh protect the east entrance of the medina, which opens on to the tanners' quarter. Since the 12th century the tanners have been located outside the walls of the medina, near the Oued Issil. This position was chosen so that the tanners should have easy access to water and sufficient space to process their skins, and

so that the pungent smell of their workshops should be kept away from the city. The leatherworkers are found inside the medina, on the other side of the gate. The "morocco leatherwork" of Marrakesh is manufactured according to an age-old tradition renowned the world over. The term was originally applied to Marrakesh leather but its use was later extended to refer to all leatherwork produced in Morocco. The European fashion for Moroccan leather began during the Renaissance, when it was imported primarily for use in book binding. Although the number of industrial tanneries is increasing today, curing ▲ 226 and leatherworking by the traditional methods still continue in the vicinity of the Bab Debbagh.

BAB AYLEN. It was at this gate, named after a Berber tribe, that the Almohads ● 54 were defeated when they tried to capture the town in 1129. It had been built by the Almoravids three years before, at the same time as the first ramparts, during the reign of Ali Ben Youssef, to defend the city against the Almohads.

BAB AGHMAT. The medina's east gate is named after an important village, the former regional capital of the OURIKA VALLEY. The Almohads entered the city through this gate in 1147, following a siege that had caused famine and resulted in the general disaffection of the Christian mercenaries to whom Abd el Moumen had promised safety. Opposite the Bab Aghmat is the *zaouia* of SIDI YOUSSEF BEN ALI, one of the seven patron saints of Marrakesh. He was a leper who died in 1196 and large numbers of pilgrims still come to his tomb. A pilgrimage to the tombs of the city's seven patron saints was instituted by Moulay Ismaïl to restore the religious importance of Marrakesh, which had

❝A *guerrab* or water seller rings his brass bell. Of all the poorly paid jobs in Morocco, this the most picturesque. It is a hard job but needs no apprenticeship. All that is required is a strong back and agile legs. The equipment does not cost much: a copper or brass bowl for Muslims and a tin cup or quite simply an old tin can for Jews. The water is carried in a leather water bottle fitted with a pipe.❞
Henriette Célarié, *Un Mois au Maroc*

declined as a result of the rival pilgrimage of the seven Regraga saints in the Essaouira ▲ 156 region. The annual event proved extremely successful but was strongly opposed in the 18th century by orthodox Muslims, who maintained that, according to the teaching of the Koran, the faithful can only address prayers to God. Today the popular expression "going to the seven men" means "going to Marrakesh".

"CALÈCHES"
This is the best way to see the ramparts and main monuments and sights of Marrakesh.

▲ Marrakesh

A scene from Alfred Hitchcock's
The Man Who Knew Too Much
(1934), shot in the *Mamounia*
Hotel.

THE ROYAL PALACE
A double wall linking
the palace and the
Agdal Gardens
enabled the sultans
and their court to
come and go in
complete privacy.

**THE GARDENS OF
MARRAKESH**
According to El
Idrisi, Ali Ben
Youssef introduced
the *khettara*, a system
of underground water
conduits for
collecting and
channeling spring
water, which made
possible the creation
of gardens such as the
Agdal (right) in
Marrakesh.

❝Later on film
directors would come
and stay at the
Mamounia Hotel,
dream about it and
even go so far as to
give the hotel a
leading role. Alfred
Hitchcock's spy
thriller, *The Man
Who Knew Too Much*
(1934), was set in that
atmosphere of luxury
and confidence
inspired by the hotel.
The couple who
kidnapped the child
would not have
enjoyed the same
credibility had they
been placed in a
different setting. The
Mamounia Hotel
fulfilled the quest for
new images and
perspectives and,
given the wealth of
Islamic art it contains,
it was a natural
choice.❞

André Paccard,
Mamounia

BAB AHMAR. The Bab Ahmar (Red Gate) stands behind the
largest of Marrakesh's cemeteries. It was built by the
Alaouites in the 18th century and, leading directly to the royal
palace, was reserved for the exclusive use of the sultans.
Today, when the King is not in residence, it can be used to get
to the *Mechouar* next to the DAR EL MAKHZEN. This royal
palace was built by the Almohads in the 12th century, rebuilt
by the Saadians in the 16th and finally restored by the
Alaouites in the 17th century. The *mechouar* inside the palace
leads to the AGDAL GARDENS and the GRAND "MECHOUAR"
where, in the late 18th and early 19th centuries, lavish
celebrations were held. In this vast assembly area Marrakesh's
finest horsemen would take part in the fantasias during the
moussem ▲ 339.

AGDAL GARDENS ★. These extensive gardens were built by the
Almoravid sultans in the 12th century to provide shade and a
degree of respite from the desert heat. Irrigation channels
dug by the Almoravids are still used to water the gardens'
many fig, olive, apricot and orange trees ■ 44. The Agdal
Gardens were extended several times
under the Saadians and redesigned in the
19th century. Beside the larger of the
gardens' two lakes (dating from the time
of the Almohads) are the ruins of the
DAR EL HANA, a palace built during the
reign of the Saadians. Standing in the
center of the gardens is a striking pillared
pavilion with openwork walls, a richly
decorated ceiling and a roof covered in
turquoise tiles.

BAB ER ROB. From the BAB IGHLI, standing at the far end of
the Grand *Mechouar*, the Grand Tour of the Ramparts
continues via the Bab Ksiba to the Almohad Bab er Rob
(Gate of the Raisin Juice), which occupied an important
defensive position between the medina and the kasbah, as
a means of controlling the trade in raisin juice syrup (a
sort of aperitif wine extremely popular at the time),

In his retirement Winston Churchill often set up his easel to paint in the gardens of the *Mamounia* Hotel.

Yacoub el Mansour banned the transport of consignments of the liquor into Marrakesh by any other gate. In 1308 the Merinid sultan Abou Thabit had the heads of six hundred decapitated rebels displayed on the leaves of the gate. Today it is still partially walled in and houses a pottery shop ● *80*. In the center of the nearby cemetery stands the Bab ech Charia, built by the Almohads in the 12th century, while the BAB JDID looks down the long Avenue de la Menara. The famous *Mamounia* Hotel is a few hundred yards away.

"MAMOUNIA" HOTEL ★. The *Mamounia* Hotel, one of the most luxurious palaces in the world, was built in 1923 and completely renovated in 1986. Its 32-acre gardens were laid out by a Saadian sultan ● *55* in the 16th century. Today they are planted with olive and orange trees ■ *44* among other varieties of trees and shrubs. The building was named in honor of Sidi Mohammed, who gave the palace to his son, Mamoun. Richard Nixon, Jimmy Carter, Orson Welles, Rita Hayworth, Yves Montand and Catherine Deneuve are just a few of the hotel's famous guests. Winston Churchill used to stay here for months at a time, devoting himself to his favorite pastime: painting. From the Bab Jdid the Grand Tour of the Ramparts continues northward along the best-preserved section of the ramparts before passing the BAB EL MAKHZEN (Gate of the Governor's Palace), which during the reigns of the Almoravids and Almohads ● *54* was reserved for the exclusive use of the sultans. Finally the Boulevard el Yarmouk leads back to the Place de la Liberté, where the tour ends.

The façade of the *Mamounia* Hotel has the classic features of Moorish architecture: columns decorated with ceramics and carved *zellige,* carved and painted wood and traditional arches. The influence of the Moroccan *maalem* (master craftsmen) is very much in evidence, both in the interior and the exterior decoration of the palace. The sun and star motifs of the *zellige* ▲ *173*, the carved wood and stucco and the silks and carpets decorating the private rooms, lounges and reception rooms create a decor redolent of the *Arabian Nights.*

HOTEL
DE
LA MAMOUNIA
TRANSATLANTIQUE
ET
CTM

"DAWN", 1983
The early 1970's marked a turning point in the work of Farid Belkahia, a native of Marrakesh. He began painting abstract asymmetrical symbols and motifs in henna on geometrically shaped pieces of leather colored with natural dyes.

ALMORAVID MINBAR
The minbar ● 87 of the Koutoubia Mosque in Marrakesh was designed in Córdoba in 1120. Inlaid with sandalwood, ebony, ivory and aloe, it was the prototype for the design and decoration of several minbars produced in Morocco between the 12th and 14th centuries.

The Koutoubia minaret seen from the Place Djemaa el Fna in the 1920's.

THE KOUTOUBIA MOSQUE ★

In *Villes impériales* (*Imperial Cities*) the French writer Henri Terrasse said that the Koutoubia Mosque (built by the Almohads ● 54) was probably the most beautifully proportioned mosque in the western Muslim world, as well as being one of the biggest ● 86. He saw it as representative of the Almohad period of Hispano-Moresque art, which combined apparent simplicity with superb craftsmanship and restrained luxury. It is certainly one of the most impressive sights in Marrakesh and is an ideal starting point for those

who want to make a tour of the medina ● 92.

THE MINARET. The Koutoubia minaret ● 88 was begun during the reign of the sultan Abd el Moumen and completed by Yacoub el Mansour. It is both a symbol of the Berber city and a central landmark, and, rising 252 feet into the sky, it towers over the town and its palm groves ■ 42 and stands like a sentinel at the gates of the Sahara. The five-to-one ratio between the height and

the width of the minaret confers a perfect harmony on the tower. A masterpiece of Hispano-Moresque art, it is very similar to the Giralda of Seville. Its pink stone walls are decorated with festooned arches, painted floral motifs and carved tracery. Only a few fragments remain of the blue, turquoise and white frieze that once adorned the top of the minaret. The first of the four copper balls surmounting the lantern ▲ 239 is so small that it is invisible from the ground. The second, 6½ feet in diameter, is huge, and the third and fourth are

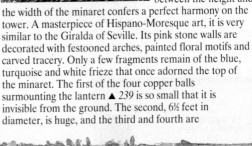

> **"THE FIRST GROUPS OF PALM TREES, THE KOUTOUBIA MOSQUE
> BECOMING MORE CLEARLY VISIBLE AGAINST THE BLUE SKY,
> A RAMPART GATE: AND THEN I AM AT THE ENTRANCE
> OF THE MAMOUNIA HOTEL."** CAMILLE MAUCLAIR

respectively half and three quarters the size of the second.
According to one story the balls of the Koutoubia Mosque
were made from some gold jewelry belonging to the wife of
Yacoub el Mansour ▲ *163* who is said to have offered the
pieces as atonement for having broken the fast of Ramadan
▲ *339* for several hours. The balance of the balls is
supposed to be maintained by the influence of the
planets.

A MOSQUE FACING MECCA. The Koutoubia, or
"Booksellers' Mosque", was named after *kutubiyin*
(sellers of manuscripts) who in the 12th and 13th
centuries gathered to lay out their stalls on the
square in front of the mosque. The original

Koutoubia Mosque was built in 1147 after the conquest
of Marrakesh by Abd el Moumen ▲ *261* but was later
demolished because it was discovered to be incorrectly
positioned in relation to Mecca. Its foundations can still be
seen today to the right of the existing mosque. The second
mosque, built and decorated according to the instructions of
Abd el Moumen on the site of the Almoravid palace, is said
to have been completed in 1199 by Yacoub el Mansour. It has
sixteen parallel, identical naves and a wider central nave.
The Almohad sultan preferred the sobriety and purity of line
characteristic of Andalusian-style decoration to more lavish
Almoravid decoration. The bold and simple geometric,
floral and epigraphic motifs which appear, both outside and
inside the mosque give the building an austere appearance.
The eleven cupolas decorated with *muqarna*, the capitals
and its molded structure make the Koutoubia Mosque the
finest example of Almohad art. Like all Morocco's mosques
the Koutoubia, which is both a place of worship and a
Koranic school, does not admit non-Muslims ▲ *222*. At the
foot of the mosque stands the white *koubba* ● *63*, where the
tomb of Lalla Zohra was placed in the 17th century. Lalla
Zohra was the daughter of a slave who became a religious
leader. The women of Marrakesh traditionally believe that
she was a woman by day and a dove by night and many
dedicate their children to her. These children never eat
pigeons.

"Only part of the vast
Koutoubia Mosque
has survived. But the
minaret has remained
intact and alone
conveys the intensity
of faith experienced
during the reign of
the Almohads. The
minaret's seven,
superimposed stories
symbolize
Marrakesh's seven
patron saints.**"**
Prosper Ricard,
*Les Merveilles de
l'autre France*

THE PALACE GATE
Next to the Bab er
Rob, the Bab Agnaou
leads to the Saadian
tombs. The gate's
characteristically
blue-gray Gueliz
stone is often
reddened by a regular
coating of sand.

AT THE GATES OF THE KASBAH

BAB AGNAOU ★. The Bab Agnaou (Gate of the Hornless
Ram) is one of the oldest and most impressive of the
entrances to the kasbah. Its name comes from the two towers
that once stood on either side of the gate and formed an
offset entrance designed to foil attackers. The sultan Abd el
Moumen built the gate in the mid-12th century, at the same
time as the Koutoubia Mosque ▲ 268. According to a local
story, the stones with which it was constructed were brought
from Andalusia by Muslims driven out of Spain ● 55. It has
red and green sandstone borders decorated with carved Kufic
script reproducing *surah* from the Koran ● 62. Bab Agnaou
was also the gate through which the sultans passed to reach
their palace and on which the heads of executed rebels were
hung.

EL MANSOUR MOSQUE. The street immediately to the right of
the Bab Agnaou leads to the kasbah and the El Mansour
Mosque (also known as the Kasbah Mosque), built in the late
12th century during the reign of the sultan Yacoub el
Mansour. After the explosion of 1569 the mosque was
restored in several stages. In the 16th century it became
known as the "Mosque of the Golden Balls" after the balls
surmounting the lantern of its minaret. Legend has it that
these balls were made, like those of the Koutoubia minaret,
from the jewelry of Bab wife of Yacoub el Mansour. Behind
the crenelated façade, over 260 feet long and immaculately
preserved, is a prayer hall with eleven naves. For centuries its
minaret, delicately decorated with a tracery of lozenges over
green terracotta, and a frieze of colored tiles, stood as a
model of classic architecture.

TOMBS OF THE SAADIAN PRINCES ★

THE KASBAH MOSQUE
The minaret of the
Mosque of the
Golden Balls,
decorated with
tracery on an
emerald-green
background, with a
frieze of colored tiles
above, overlooks the
Saadian tombs and
gardens.

In 1591 the first *koubba* ● 62 of the necropolis of Marrakesh
was built, south of the kasbah. The *koubba* was intended to
house the tombs of the ancestors of the Saadian sultan
Ahmed el Mansour, although Saadian princes had been
buried here since 1557. During the 16th century several
mausoleums were built to receive the tombs of thirteen
Saadian rulers ▲ 55. With its delicate decoration and pure
architectural lines, the necropolis was an outstandingly
beautiful feat of architecture. When Moulay Ismaïl ▲ 233
finally managed to break through the gates and take

possession of the town in 1677, he decided that, rather than raze the entire necropolis, he would preserve the tombs, and he achieved this by building a solid, protective wall around them. The tombs were discovered in 1916 by a group of World War One pilots. They can be reached by an arched side entrance that is linked to the wall of the Mosque of the Golden Balls.

"Koubba" of Lalla Messaouda. In the center of the main chamber of the first building, built by Ahmed el Mansour, stands the finely decorated chapel in which the remains of Lalla Messaouda, mother of the Saadian sultan Ahmed el Mansour ● 55, were laid to rest in 1591. In the courtyard outside the chamber are the tombstones of the dynasty's brave soldiers and loyal servants.

The three chambers of the mausoleum. The Chamber of the "Mihrab", with its solid, carved cedarwood doors and a mihrab ● 86 decorated with small gray marble columns, was originally an oratory. Since the 18th century it has contained Alaouite tombs ● 55. In the center of the Chamber of the Twelve Columns, with a gilt cedarwood cupola supported by twelve columns of Carrara marble, is the tomb of Ahmed el Mansour. The tombs of the Saadian princes' children, wives and concubines are housed in the richly decorated Chamber of the Three Niches.

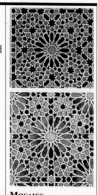

Mosaics
Details (top) of the pattern of colored *zellige* ▲ 173 in the Chamber of the Three Niches, and (above) of the decorative panels in the Chamber of the Twelve Columns.

The walls of the Chamber of the Twelve Columns are decorated with panels of *zellige*. The vaulted cedarwood ceiling, hung with stalactites, is highlighted with color and gold, and the carved tombs are like great ivory caskets. The painting (left) by Gabriel Rousseau shows one of the inscriptions, carved in relief in *zellige*, in the main chamber of the second *koubba* ● 62.

At the end of the 17th century Moulay Ismaïl tore out the marble, onyx, gold and ivory and exotic

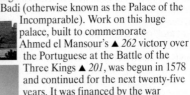

wood from the Dar el Badi (The Incomparable) and used them to build his palaces in Meknès. This demolition process took ten years to complete.

THE MARRAKESH FESTIVAL
For over thirty years the El Badi

Palace has opened its doors to troups of folk dancers, singers and musicians from all the main regions of Morocco. Every year in June hundreds of carpets are laid out in the great courtyard in preparation for these performers and the large audiences they draw.

EL BADI PALACE ★

Behind the Bab Berrima, a gate flanked by massive towers overlooking the Place des Ferblantiers, a passageway between high walls leads to the entrance of the Dar el Badi (otherwise known as the Palace of the Incomparable). Work on this huge palace, built to commemorate Ahmed el Mansour's ▲ 262 victory over the Portuguese at the Battle of the Three Kings ▲ 201, was begun in 1578 and continued for the next twenty-five years. It was financed by the war indemnity paid by the Portuguese ● 55, by gold brought back from Guinea and by sugar produced in the Sous region ▲ 311. Large numbers of European craftsmen were employed to work on the project and the most luxurious materials were imported from black Africa, Italy, France, Spain and India. The Carrara marble used in the palace, so the story goes, was purchased for its weight in sugar. This sumptuous palace was designed for the celebration of festivals on a grand scale and had a total of 360 rooms arranged around a huge inner courtyard with pools and decorative flowerbeds. Every year at the beginning of June a national folk festival is held in the ruins that are all that remain of this former splendor.

EL BAHIA PALACE ★

In the late 19th century, Ba Ahmed, grand vizier to the
sultans Moulay Hassan and Moulay Abd el Aziz, ordered a
magnificent palace to be built. The palace, standing in a
2-acre garden, is a haphazard arrangement of secret luxury
apartments opening on to inner courtyards. For seven years
around a thousand craftsmen from the Fez region worked on
the palace, using the same motifs and materials inside as the
architects had used on the outside of the building. Thus the
carved wood, plaster and stucco of the façade are continued
in the interior decoration. The master of works, seriously
hampered by his weight and small stature, had the palace
built on one level. The only sections of the Dar el Bahia open
to the public are the apartments of the sultan's favorite
concubine, the council chamber with its tiled walls and
illuminated cedarwood ceiling, and the great central
courtyard, paved with marble and decorated with *zellige*
▲ *173*, and fountains. The courtyards, planted with flowers,
were reserved for the sultan's four wives and twenty-four
concubines. During the French protectorate, the palace
was the residence of General Lyautey, France's first
resident general.

DAR SI'SAÏ ★

Since 1912 this Alaouite-style palace, built in the 19th
century by Saïd, brother of the grand vizier
Ba Ahmed, has been the home of the
Marrakesh MUSEUM OF
MOROCCAN ARTS. Here
examples of every type of
the vast array of
southern Moroccan
crafts, from
furniture and
carpets to
weapons and
pottery ● *80*,
costumes ● *78*
and jewelry ● *68*,
are displayed. The
Hispano-Moresque reception
room on the upper floor has a
magnificent cedarwood table and a
bride's chair used during the *selwa*
● *69*. The next room, known as the
women's room, is decorated with
Berber carpets ● *74*. Almost next door
to the Dar Si'Saï is the MAISON
TISKIWIN, which houses part of the
"Matière et Manière" (materials and
techniques) collection belonging to the
art historian Bert Flint. The collection
(of which the other half is in the Musée
d'Agadir ▲ *314*) concentrates mainly on
the rural art of northern Morocco and
perfectly complements the display in the
Dar Si'Saï.

**FRAMES AND CASING
IN THE DAR SI'SAÏ**
The wooden jambs
and leaves of the
interior doors and
windows of the Dar
Si'Saï are decorated
with inlay, carvings
and painted

geometric
decorations. The
polychrome rosette
(above), a legacy of
Merinid art, takes
pride of place.

"MARRAKESH, IN THE SOUK"
Near the Place Rahba Kedima, in a narrow street shaded by bamboo blinds, is the fruit and vegetable souk. The watercolor (center) is by Charles Kérivel.

The Dyers' Souk, by Jean-Félix Bouchor.

THE SLIPPER SOUK
The scene from Yves Allégret's film *Oasis* in which Michèle Morgan, accompanied by Pierre Brasseur, tries on babouches, Moroccan leather slippers, was shot in Marrakesh.

THE MAIN SOUKS

Ideally placed on the Saharan trade routes, Marrakesh was a convenient staging post for caravans and soon developed into a major craft and trading center. Following the fortification of the town under the Almoravids, the traditional weaving ● *75* and tanning ▲ *226* industries thrived. Craftsmen established their various quarters, according to a structured system of corporations, in the central area of the medina. Today the souks of Marrakesh are less distinct. Leaving Place Djemaa el Fna, one comes into an

intricate maze of narrow streets, protected from the sun by slatted awnings.

RUE DU SOUK SMARINE. The Souk Qassabine (basketwork, dried fruit and spices) runs into the Souk Smarine (clothes and material). The original reed blinds of this main thoroughfare were replaced by a modern metal trellis after a devastating fire. Halfway along the street the neon sign of a European shoe shop can be seen, betraying the fact that the modern world has begun to impinge on this timeless society.

PLACE RAHBA KEDIMA ★. The Rue du Souk Smarine leads into the Place Rahba Kedima, where a slave market was held until it was discontinued in 1912. It remains an important commercial site, for it is here that the SOUK GHAZAL (which sells wool) is held early in the morning, while the SOUK EL BTANA (selling skins) fills the square in the early afternoon. There are also a few apothecary shops here and there. The Place Rahba Kedima leads into the SOUK RABIA, the Berber carpet souk, where carpets are auctioned in the latter part of the afternoon, from around 4pm. The SOUK EL KEBIR (leather goods) lies farther along the street, in the area beyond the Souk Rabia. Forking at the SOUK FAGHARINE (ironwork), the street leads to the jewelers' souk and the KISSARIA. Today these covered street markets and galleries with heavy wooden doors are mainly occupied by merchants selling clothes. Standing at the intersection of several streets is the Souk Cherratine (the leatherworkers' souk).

"ON LONG WINTER EVENINGS, IN THE ISOLATED 'DOUARS' ... THE WOMEN WIND THEIR DISTAFF AND SPIN. IT IS THEY WHO WEAVE THE POPULAR GLAOUA AND SEKTANA CARPETS."

HENRIETTE CÉLARIÉ

BEN YOUSSEF MEDERSA
The inner courtyard of the medersa is decorated with *zellige* forming floral motifs

AROUND THE BEN YOUSSEF MEDERSA

BEN YOUSSEF MOSQUE. The medina ● 92 of Marrakesh grew up around the 12th-century mosque that was built to commemorate Sidi Youssef Ben Ali, one of the city's seven patron saints, who, although a leper, was inspired by an unfaltering and unshakable faith throughout his life. Restoration work carried out in the 16th and 19th centuries has left virtually nothing of the original architecture of the mosque. The towering 130-foot stone minaret dominates the city.

BEN YOUSSEF MEDERSA ★. In the next street is the entrance to one of the most beautiful buildings in Marrakesh, the 14th-century Ben Youssef Medersa ● 90. In about 1565 it was entirely rebuilt on the instructions of the sultan Moulay Abdallah and developed into the largest Koranic university in the Maghreb. Its architecture and the subtle use of decoration, achieved through a balanced combination of stucco and mosaic, marble and cedarwood, were influenced by the styles of Moorish Spain. In the inner courtyard, standing on either side of a white marble basin, pillars and carved wooden lintels support two galleries. The prayer hall is softly lit by plaster openwork windows beneath cupolas decorated with *muqarna*. On the second floor thirty-two plainly decorated students' cells open on to a series of small inner courtyards.

SIDI BEL ABBÈS QUARTER

(above). An inscription dedicated to the sultan who founded the medersa reads: "I was constructed as a place of knowledge and prayer by the Prince of the Faithful, the descendant of the seal of the prophets, Abdallah, the most glorious of Caliphs. Pray for him, all ye who enter here, so that his greatest hopes may be realized."

From the medersa a narrow street leads off to the left from the Rue Hart es Soura to the monumental ECHROB or CHOUF FOUNTAIN (Drink and Admire), carved in wood and decorated with Kufic inscriptions. The nearby BAB TAGHZOUT, the gate of the old Almoravid fortifications, marks the entrance to the Sidi bel Abbès Quarter. Sidi bel Abbès, born in Ceuta in 1130, was a cult leader and patron saint of Marrakesh who resolutely championed the cause of the blind. He is buried in the Sidi Marouk cemetery. This old quarter of the medina still contains a number of old *fondouks* ▲ 222, lodging houses used by caravaneers in which the rooms were arranged on two or three levels around a central courtyard reserved for camels.

AROUND THE KOUBBA EL BAROUDIYIN

The cupola of the Koubba el Baroudiyin, with its elegantly
interlaced arches, is the last surviving example of Almoravid
art in Marrakesh. The exterior of the stone and brick *koubba*
● 62, which was not discovered until 1948, is decorated with
rosettes and pointed arches, while the marble interior is richly
carved with floral motifs. Beyond the DYERS' SOUK, with its
brightly colored skeins of material hanging on reed canes,
stands the 16th-century Mosque el Mouassine.

**THE KOUBBA EL
BAROUDIYIN**
The *koubba* once
housed a ritual
ablutions
basin
adjoining
the Ben
Youssef
Mosque.

PLACE DJEMAA EL FNA ★

The Place Djemaa el Fna, the traditional meeting place for
peasants and merchants from the Sous region,
the High Atlas and the South, has become the
heart of Marrakesh. In the words of Jérôme
and Jean Tharaud, "the soul of the South is
here, in the groups of onlookers who, from
morning to night, gather and disperse
around the street performers with the
fluidity of smoke." In the mornings this vast
square, located on the edge of the souk
district and bordered by shops and
workshops, is crowded with fruit and spice
sellers, *guerrab* ▲ 265 with their leather
water bottles and metal drinking cups,
basket sellers, ironmongers and barbers. In
the afternoons come the Gnaoua ▲ 159,
dancers descended from former Guinean
slaves, musicians, story-tellers, snake charmers and
entertainers with performing monkeys. Before starting their
performance, they establish their *halqa* (imaginary circle
blessed by a saint).

"In a matter of
minutes, the vast
square was crowded
with people. Like a
mosque at the hour of
prayer. ... There were
cruel stories of love
and jealousy, of
fabulous treasures
hidden in abandoned
riads [palace gardens]
and found by old
vagabonds and
blind children.
Purses were
stolen, drinking
water sold, and a
huge serpent was
charmed before
your very eyes by
a flute. ... The
many occupations
and countless
ruses devised by
people to earn a
living were
concentrated in
this square where
the simplest of
gestures assumed
an air of mystery.**"**
Augustin Gomez
Arcos,
L'Aveuglon

277

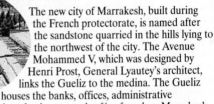

THE GUELIZ

The new city of Marrakesh, built during the French protectorate, is named after the sandstone quarried in the hills lying to the northwest of the city. The Avenue Mohammed V, which was designed by Henri Prost, General Lyautey's architect, links the Gueliz to the medina. The Gueliz houses the banks, offices, administrative organizations, businesses and cafés of modern Marrakesh. The MARCHÉ CENTRAL, selling fruit and vegetables and items made by local craftsmen, is held every morning on the main thoroughfare, halfway between the Place du 16 Novembre and the Place Abd el Moumen Ben Ali, where the terrace of *Le Mirador*, a café, offers a magnificent view of the peaks of the High Atlas.

THE MAJORELLE GARDENS ★. The gardens lie to the north-east of the Gueliz, in a narrow street leading on to the Avenue Yacoub el Mansour, which runs between the Boulevard de Safi and the Avenue el Jadida. These delightful gardens, planted not only with bougainvillea, coconut palms and banana trees, but also with bamboo and palm trees ■ *42*, were laid out in the 1920's by the French artist Jacques Majorelle ▲ *281*. Amid this luxuriant vegetation he built a large studio as well as a number of pergolas and arbors which he decorated in a disconcertingly bright shade of blue. After the artist's death in 1962, the gardens were abandoned but

"As everyone living here knows, scenes of everyday life, scenes of adventure, are captured, by chance ... chance which lies in catching a glimpse of the town, between the veiling and unveiling, between fullness and emptiness or 'absence', as Roland Barthes described the emptiness of the Gueliz in the afternoon, an emptiness which could be applied to the entire town.**"**
Encyclopédie par l'Image

MAJORELLE GARDENS
In 1917 the French artist Jacques Majorelle moved to Marrakesh. His early work there consisted of outdoor paintings. Under the Moroccan sun he sketched scenes of everyday life in the city and in 1921 went on to paint landscapes, including several of the Atlas Mountains. The paintings commissioned later in his career were done in his studio, set among the palms of the Majorelle Gardens.

were restored several years ago by the French couturier Yves Saint-Laurent. Today the studio houses a museum of Islamic art. The sober, geometrical motifs of the Chichaoua carpets ● *74* which are on display there echo the Art Deco architecture of the building itself. One room contains an exhibition of forty or so of Jacques Majorelle's etchings of southern Moroccan landscapes.

THE MENARA ★. From the Bab Jdid a broad avenue runs for about 1¼ miles along the edge of the Hivernage (winter quarters), the district of luxury villas and hotels, before reaching the Menara Gardens, which cover an area of 250 acres and are planted with olive trees. The large central lake, dating from the 12th century, is fed by a network of irrigation channels. At the water's edge a small Saadian pavilion, which was entirely rebuilt in the 19th century, is a breathtaking sight in the evening when it catches the golden rays of the setting sun. The isolated building was used by the sultans for their romantic assignations. There is a story that one of the sultans used to throw his companion of the previous night into the lake at dawn.

THE PALM GROVES. On the outskirts of the city, just before the Oued Tensift bridge on the main Casablanca road, is a narrow road (suitable for cars and calèches) that begins a 14-mile tour of the palm groves. The groves have around 150,000 palm trees and extend over an area of some 30,000 acres. According to legend Youssef Ibn Tachfine pitched a military camp here. In the evening, his soldiers ate dates which they had carried from the pre-Saharan oases and threw away the stones. Some fell into the holes left by lances that had been thrust into the ground, and that was supposedly how the palm groves of Marrakesh were planted. The wells of the *khettara*, the underground water conduits that Ali Ben Youssef (son of the founder of Marrakesh) built to irrigate the plantation, are still visible in places. The principle of the *khettara* (also known as *foggara* in the Figuig region) is to bring the water from the water table to the surface by means of a network of interlinked underground galleries. Because the gradient of these galleries is less than that of the land and the water table, the water rises to the surface like a spring. Over five thousand *khettara* are used to irrigate the Haouz plain of Marrakesh.

THE MENARA PAVILION
The Menara Pavilion, with the snow-covered peaks of the Atlas Mountains rising in the distance, backs on to a huge lake where water sports were once held during the *moussem* ▲ *339*.

"Surrounded by *pisé* walls, a vast olive orchard with symmetrical paths. ... I wandered slowly in a balmy, almost Provençal atmosphere, until I came to a large, clear lake whose waters reflected the simply styled galleries of a pavilion."

Camille Mauclair, *Les Couleurs du Maroc*

▲ MARRAKESH TO OUARZAZATE

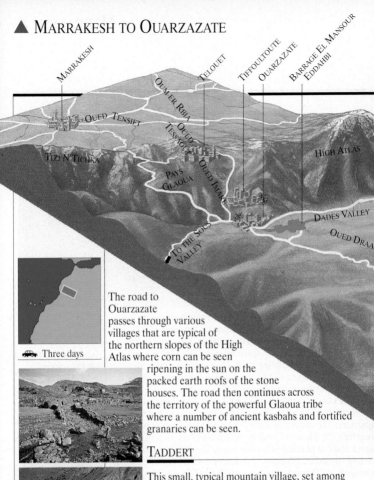

MARRAKESH · OUED TENSIFT · OUM ER RBIA · OUED TESSSAOUT · PAYS GLAOUA · OUED IMINI · TELOUET · TIFFOULTOUTE · OUARZAZATE · BARRAGE EL MANSOUR EDDAHBI · TIZI N'TICHKA · HIGH ATLAS · DADES VALLEY · OUED DRAA · TO THE SOUS VALLEY

🚗 Three days

The road to Ouarzazate passes through various villages that are typical of the northern slopes of the High Atlas where corn can be seen ripening in the sun on the packed earth roofs of the stone houses. The road then continues across the territory of the powerful Glaoua tribe where a number of ancient kasbahs and fortified granaries can be seen.

TADDERT

This small, typical mountain village, set among walnut trees, used to be the first staging post on the caravan route between Marrakesh and Ouarzazate. Today traders still gather here to sell semiprecious stones and fossils found in the mountains. A plaque at the entrance to the village inn informs visitors that in 1939 it was "recommended by the Guide des gastronomes français". On the right, on the road leading toward the Tizi N'Tichka, is the cable car in which consignments of manganese, mined in the Imini basin farther south, are transported.

COL DU TICHKA

The southern (top) and northern slopes (above) of Tizi N'Tichka (Tichka Pass).

ATLAS VILLAGE
The *pisé* buildings of the fortified villages are of different shapes and sizes. The tallest are the *ighrem* (collective granaries).

TIZI N'TICHKA

At an altitude of 7,415 feet TIZI N'TICHKA (Pass of the Pastures) is the highest vehicular pass in Morocco. It links Marrakesh with the pre-Saharan regions, where all roads pass through Ouarzazate. Although they are swept by fierce winds, the stretches of grassland high on the slopes of the High Atlas are generally used as summer pasture. At the end of spring shepherds and herdsmen, who are sedentary farmers, leave their villages, the highest of which are situated at 6,500 feet, and begin their transhumance (the seasonal movement of animals) ■ *50* toward the high pastures.

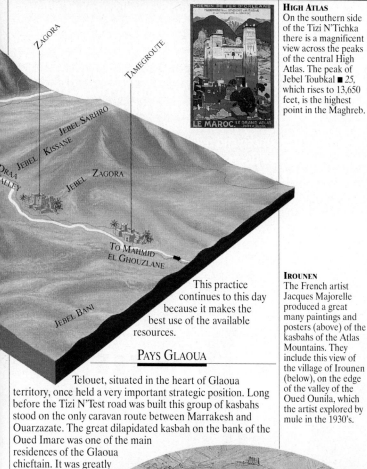

ZAGORA

TAMEGROUTE

JEBEL SARHRO

JEBEL KISSANE

ORAA VALLEY

JEBEL ZAGORA

TO MAHMID EL GHOUZLANE

JEBEL BANI

HIGH ATLAS
On the southern side of the Tizi N'Tichka there is a magnificent view across the peaks of the central High Atlas. The peak of Jebel Toubkal ■ *25*, which rises to 13,650 feet, is the highest point in the Maghreb.

IROUNEN
The French artist Jacques Majorelle produced a great many paintings and posters (above) of the kasbahs of the Atlas Mountains. They include this view of the village of Irounen (below), on the edge of the valley of the Oued Ounila, which the artist explored by mule in the 1930's.

This practice continues to this day because it makes the best use of the available resources.

PAYS GLAOUA

Telouet, situated in the heart of Glaoua territory, once held a very important strategic position. Long before the Tizi N'Test road was built this group of kasbahs stood on the only caravan route between Marrakesh and Ouarzazate. The great dilapidated kasbah on the bank of the Oued Imare was one of the main residences of the Glaoua chieftain. It was greatly enlarged and luxuriously appointed by El Hadj Thami el Glaoui, Pasha of Marrakesh until 1956. This building, a typically Berber structure, was abandoned when the property of the "last of the Atlas chieftains" from Telouet was confiscated. On a wall in the reception hall of the fortress is a frieze of broad silk belts bearing the emblems of families who had previously been courtiers of the powerful El Hadj Thami el Glaoui. Farther south, at the entrance to the fertile valley of the Oued Ounila, stands another Glaoua kasbah, the less prestigious Anemiter kasbah.

281

The Dar Glaoui, the great kasbah of Telouet, surrounded by high, crenelated walls and flanked by square bastions, overlooks the Oued Imare. Built in the 19th century, it was enlarged and extravagantly decorated in order to serve as the residence of Thami el Glaoui. Many buildings have fallen into disrepair, and only two rooms retain their Andalusian-style decoration. The stucco and *zellige,* the painted ceilings and carved doors of the harem and the reception hall give an idea of the kasbah's past splendor.

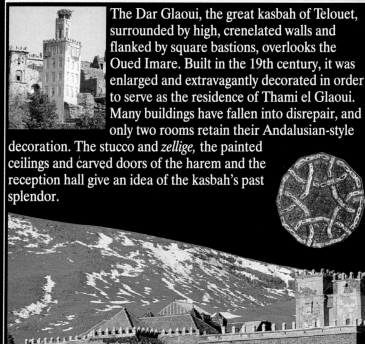

Muqarna (left), honeycomb patterns in plaster or wood, are an imaginative style of architectural decoration. The *zouaq*, or painting on wood (above), is used for geometric, floral motifs on ceilings with exposed beams.

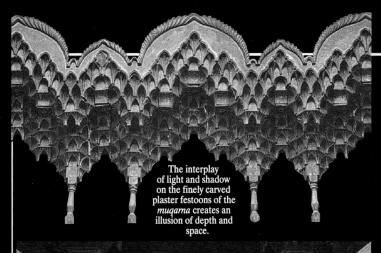

The interplay of light and shadow on the finely carved plaster festoons of the *muqarna* creates an illusion of depth and space.

DECORATION OF THE HAREM
In the former harem (right and below) of the luxurious residence of the Pasha of Marrakesh, the *zellige* ▲ 173 provide a unified decorative scheme.

The *zellige*-covered columns and walls contrast with the white of the stucco work, visually separating it from the dazzling decoration of the painted ceiling. The whole evokes an atmosphere of silence, pleasure and timelessness where the onlooker is drawn into the mesmerizing play of form and color.

CAPITALS
Stucco, finely carved with geometric and floral motifs, decorates the capitals.

CEILINGS
Beams and joists are either coffered or exposed beams. The wooden ceilings are covered with *zouaq* painted with floral, geometric motifs that

echo the patterns and colors of the rooms' upholstery.

Columns (right) are encased in *zellige* and stucco work. Starbursts within a latticework of geometric patterns and fleurons within tracery and "lion's claw" friezes or between the guilloche and knotted borders of *zellige,* produce a counterpoint of lines and colors. The white stucco work above, contrasting with the brilliance of the *zellige,* consists of palm leaves, geometric motifs and intricate floral Kufic calligraphy ● *64.*

Between Telouet and Ouarzazate, the road passes a number of kasbahs and crosses IRHEM N'OUGDAL before reaching Aït Benhaddou. The village is dominated by an *tighremt* (fortified granary) ● *98* that is still in use and open to the public. The thick walls and angled towers of the *pisé* structure, from which the villagers survey their crops and the surrounding area, stands on stone foundations. Inside the *tighremt* the doors of the dwellings are decorated with Berber paintings.

AÏT BENHADDOU. The fortified village of Aït Benhaddou has been classified by UNESCO as one of the world's cultural treasures. It is studded with crenelated towers and its buildings decorated with lozenged motifs and it is considered to be one of the most beautiful villages of its kind in Morocco. A program of restoration work is currently under way to protect the already badly damaged mud houses from further erosion and to encourage the repopulation of the village, which is at present inhabited by just five families.

TIFFOULTOUTE. The kasbah of Tiffoultoute lies about 3 miles north of Ouarzazate. This beautiful structure, built about 250 years ago, used to belong to the Glaoui. It has been very tastefully converted into an inn and its rooms offer travelers a splendid view across the valley of the Oued Ouarzazate and the Jebel Sarhro.

WOMAN FROM TIFFOULTOUTE
Beating out the rhythm of a song on a *bendir*.

"LAWRENCE OF ARABIA"
Scenes from David Lean's film *Lawrence of Arabia* (1962) were shot in the *ksar* of Aït Benhaddou and near Ouarzazate.

OUARZAZATE

The town stands in the middle of an arid plateau that contrasts sharply with the slopes and vegetation of the nearby High Atlas. It enjoys an exceptional climate and occupies a geographic location at the crossroads of the main routes leading to the Draa, Dadès and Sous Valleys. Ouarzazate was built by the French as a garrison in the late 1920's. Today it boasts an international airport, and the tourist and craft industries have expanded rapidly in recent years. The town is also ideally situated in relation to regional trade and is renowned for its pottery ● *80* and carpets ● *74*.

A major cultural center is currently under development. This will be equipped with studios for the many films that are shot on location in the surrounding area. A scene from Bernardo Bertolucci's *The Sheltering Sky* (1990) was shot in the KASBAH TAOURIRT. This former Glaoui residence, situated on the edge of the town on the road to Er Rachidia, is considered to be one of the most beautiful in Morocco. It consists of a maze of luxury apartments, simple *pisé* houses and crenelated towers which are lavishly decorated with geometric motifs. Part of the fortified village is open to the public.

"KSAR" OF AÏT BENHADDOU
Its various quarters are defined in relation to the social hierarchy.

THE DRAA VALLEY

From Ouarzazate the road follows the line of JEBEL TIFFERNINE on the eastern foothills of the Anti Atlas. It winds up the mountain to Tizi N'Tinififft (5,450 feet) and then descends rapidly to Agdz, the tiny administrative center situated at the foot of the rock face of the JEBEL KISSANE. Between here and Zagora the road follows the Oued Draa, with palm groves laid out along the banks and dotted with about fifty kasbahs and *ksour*, many of which are worth a visit. In ancient times the Draa was a permanent river, the longest in Morocco. Today it rises near Ouarzazate and travels for 156 miles before disappearing into the sand.

KASBAH TAOURIRT
The few windows that pierce the *pisé* walls of the Kasbah are decorated with moucharabieh ● 96, which helps to keep the rooms cool. From these windows the women could watch displays taking place in the courtyard, and the master of the house could survey the surrounding area.

THE "CHEICH"
This long muslin scarf keeps out the cold and protects the wearer against sandstorms.

Immediately below its source the Oued Draa cuts a gorge 44 miles long through a fold in the western end of the JEBEL SARHRO. Today the river is bordered by oleanders and acacias and irrigates a narrow oasis where cereals, vegetables ■ *44*, alfalfa and henna ■ *47* are grown. Fruit trees are planted on the middle terraces, while date palms ■ *42* and tamarisk ■ *22* (whose galls are used to produce tan liquor) are cultivated on the high terraces. The fellahin of the Draa Valley were for a long time harassed by the desert nomads, which is why so many *ksour* are protected by high walls and flanked by watchtowers.

TAMNOUGALT. Just outside Agdz, on the left, are the crenelated towers of the *ksar* of Tamnougalt, one of the most picturesque in the region. The village was once the capital of the Mezguita Berbers. Farther south are the walls of the "KSAR" OF IGDAOUN, flanked by high towers shaped like truncated pyramids.

TINEZOULINE. The route crosses an oasis comprising several villages where people from all over the region flock to the weekly market. In the center of the oasis stand the *ksar* and kasbah of Tinezouline. This is one of the most interesting prehistoric sites in the pre-Saharan Maghreb. A stony track (4½ miles in length) leads to falls of black rocks where a number of Libyo-Berber rock carvings representing Iron Age horsemen and hunters can be seen.

IN AND AROUND ZAGORA

THE DRAA VALLEY
In the south (above top), near Zagora, the valley is inhabited mainly by the Roha ed Droua. In the north (above) the Mezguita have settled among the palm groves of Agdz.

This large village, known as the "Gate of the Desert", is an ideal staging post for those intending to travel farther south. In the 16th century Zagora was the point from which the Saadians ● *55*, descendants of the Prophet from Arabia, launched their conquest of the Sous Valley ▲ *311*. They subsequently extended their control as far as Timbuktu. The narrow, winding track leading to the summit of JEBEL ZAGORA situated 3 miles south of the village itself is quite dangerous but those braving it are rewarded with a magnificent view across the Draa Valley, which can be seen from the top. Next to the rocky peak are the remains of a fortified wall that was built in 1056 during the occupation of the Draa Valley by the Berber chieftain Abou Bekr. The road continues toward Tamegroute, passing the PALM GROVES OF AMAZRAOU, where many different kinds of fruit ■ *44* are grown in the gardens and on the terraces. The so-called Jewish Kasbah, which dominates Amazraou, was once occupied by highly skilled jewelers.

TAMEGROUTE.
Tamegroute, surrounded by palm trees, has several mosques with blue-tiled roofs and white minarets. Behind its impressive crenelated

TIMBUKTU
From Timbuktu distances are no longer calculated in miles. The desert overturns the Western concept of time and space. At the end of Zagora's main street, a sign reads "Timbuktu, 52 days" – that is, by camel.

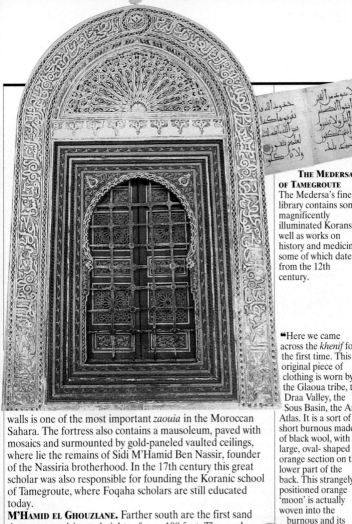

THE MEDERSA OF TAMEGROUTE
The Medersa's fine library contains some magnificently illuminated Korans as well as works on history and medicine, some of which date from the 12th century.

"Here we came across the *khenif* for the first time. This original piece of clothing is worn by the Glaoua tribe, the Draa Valley, the Sous Basin, the Anti Atlas. It is a sort of short burnous made of black wool, with a large, oval- shaped orange section on the lower part of the back. This strangely positioned orange 'moon' is actually woven into the burnous and its edges are decorated with multicolored embroidery. The bottom is edged with a long fringe and the hood has a large black woollen tassel."

Charles de Foucauld

walls is one of the most important *zaouia* in the Moroccan Sahara. The fortress also contains a mausoleum, paved with mosaics and surmounted by gold-paneled vaulted ceilings, where lie the remains of Sidi M'Hamid Ben Nassir, founder of the Nassiria brotherhood. In the 17th century this great scholar was also responsible for founding the Koranic school of Tamegroute, where Foqaha scholars are still educated today.

M'HAMID EL GHOUZLANE. Farther south are the first sand dunes, some rising to heights of over 100 feet. The road soon becomes a corrugated iron track and stops at M'Hamid el Ghouzlane (Plain of the Pazelles), one of the first "Gates of the Desert". The Saharan nomads from the Reguibate tribe, better known as the "blue men" of the desert, sometimes come to the Monday market. The ruined Saadian *ksar* of Ksebt el Allouj was occupied by a small band of Christians who had been converted to Islam and who had captured Timbuktu during the reign of Ahmed el Mansour in the 16th century.

HAMADA DU DRAA ★. Beyond the palm trees lies the Hamada du Draa, a vast, arid limestone plateau. The village elders say that long ago the Oued Draa was inhabited by huge reptiles, probably desert monitors. There is indeed a rock carving of some kind of monster, although its resemblance to a monitor is not immediately obvious. Several projects, including the planting of saplings and erection of palisades, are under way to preserve vegetation and combat the rapid desertification of the region.

OUARZAZATE · BARRAGE EL MANSOUR · SKOURA

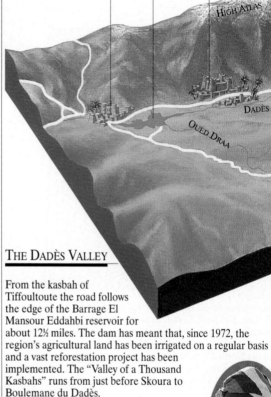

HIGH ATLAS

DADÈS

OUED DRAA

🚗 Three days

"KSOUR"
The *ksar* of Skoura is closed by a monumental gate (above) whose upper section, built with sun-dried mud bricks, is decorated with geometric motifs. The lower section is plain and built of *pisé* (mud and rubble). Like the *ksar* of Amerhidil (above) *ksour* tend to suffer from erosion

THE DADÈS VALLEY

From the kasbah of Tiffoultoute the road follows the edge of the Barrage El Mansour Eddahbi reservoir for about 12½ miles. The dam has meant that, since 1972, the region's agricultural land has been irrigated on a regular basis and a vast reforestation project has been implemented. The "Valley of a Thousand Kasbahs" runs from just before Skoura to Boulemane du Dadès.

SKOURA ★. This fertile oasis, renowned for the cultivation of roses, was founded in the 12th century by Yacoub el Mansour and named after its original inhabitants, the Berbers of the Haskourene tribe (right). Dense palm groves are crossed by a network of tracks running between kasbahs, *ksour* and crops.

AMERHIDIL ★. This fortified residence once belonged to the most powerful family responsible for protecting the village and its lands. Today it is owned by the Sheikh of Amerhidil. A track runs northwards for 15½ miles across the Toundoute region, famous for its salt mines and ocher quarries.

and are sometimes renovated. In the past they were simply abandoned.

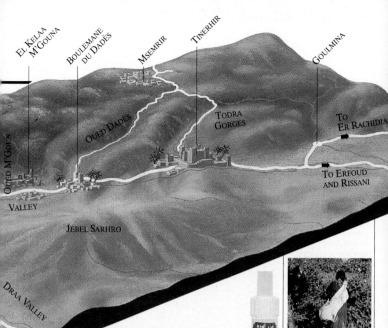

EL KELAA M'GOUNA · BOULEMANE DU DADÈS · MSEMRIR · TINERHIR · GOULMINA

OUED M'GOUN · OUED DADÈS · TODRA GORGES · TO ER RACHIDIA · TO ERFOUD AND RISSANI

VALLEY · JEBEL SARHRO · DRAA VALLEY

El Kelaa des M'Gouna ★.

After running across the TIZI N'TADDERT and past the kasbahs of Imassine and Aït Ridi, the road reaches El Kelaa M'Gouna. The fortress of the M'Goun, built at an altitude of 4,800 feet on the left bank of the Oued M'Goun, consists of a large group of ruined kasbahs whose lavish decorations can still be appreciated. El Kelaa M'Gouna, renowned for its roses, is also the starting point for various trips into the M'Goun mountains. A track leads to the village of Azlag, where about 120 ironsmiths (virtually the entire male population) have formed a cooperative producing traditional daggers in styles ranging from the simplest to the most highly decorated.

THE DADÈS GORGES ★

The administrative center of Boulemane du Dadès, where the houses are built on the mountainside next to the kasbah, stands at the entrance of the magnificent Dadès Gorges. At first the road is bordered by a series of *ksour* and kasbahs, including the kasbahs of Aït Arbi, built at the foot of volcanic rocks, and Tamnalt, known as the "Valley of Human Bodies", where rocks on one of the cliff faces have been eroded into what looks like the soles of human feet! The asphalted road comes to an end at Aït Ali. After the bridges of Aït Aoudinar and Aït Ouffi, the most impressive section of the gorges begins.

ROSE GROWING
A festival of roses is held in El Kelaa M'Gouna in May. To celebrate the new harvest the two hundred workers employed in the rosewater distilleries (below) scatter rose water and petals in profusion. Every year 5,500 tons of petals are used in the two distilleries. It takes just over one ton of petals to produce around two pints of rose water extract,

which is used in small quantities in the manufacture of rose water.

The kasbah of Amerhidil (left).

291

A small hotel-restaurant, surrounded by luxuriant vegetation, near Tinerhir at the entrance to the Todra Gorges.

The steep gorges of the Dadès Valley (right).

BERBER POTTERY
Terracotta pottery, made by local craftsmen, decorated with traditional geometric Berber motifs.

The road winds upward above a deep, vertiginous canyon. There is a story that anyone who ventured into these gorges was either in danger of being killed by the brigands who controlled the route or by the terrifying Atlas lions, the last of which was killed in 1905. Today moufflon live in this peaceful and exceptionally beautiful area, where visitors can go trout fishing or simply wander at leisure. After the village of MSEMRIR, on Aït Atta territory, the track forks left to the villages of Agoudal and Imilchil and right to the Todra Gorges and Tinerhir. The track in the Dadès-Todra direction is difficult and it is advisable to make the trip in the opposite direction (Todra-Dadès). It is also worth obtaining advance information about the general state of the terrain as these mountain tracks are narrow and dangerous, particularly during spring floods.

THE TODRA GORGES ★

At least one full day should be allowed to cover the 87½ miles of mountainous terrain between Tinerhir and Boulemane. From both these points some wonderful excursions can be made into the JEBEL SARHRO and the BOU GAFER RANGES.
TINERHIR. This former military outpost is now a large village of three thousand inhabitants, rising in terraces around a

"The lion population in southern Morocco has inevitably suffered at the hands of man. Local people say that lions became extinct in the area several generations ago."

Paul Bowles

hillock covered with a dense and extensive palm grove. Standing on the banks of the Oued Todra, where olive, pomegranate and orange trees grow, it is one of the most beautiful oases in the region. Next to the ruins of a former Glaoua kasbah, the terrace of the *Hôtel Sarhro* offers an exceptional view across the oasis.

THE GORGES. The road through the Todra Gorges follows the right bank of the river, which is covered with palm trees. About 6 miles from Tinerhir is the SOURCE DES POISSONS SACRÉS (Spring of the Sacred Fish), where fishing is prohibited. According to a local tradition a marabout struck the rock once with his staff to cause the spring to well up, and a second time to fill it with fish. Farther east is the narrowest and most spectacular section of the gorges, where for a distance of 110 yards the narrow corridor between the sheer, towering walls of rock (985 feet high) is only 65 feet wide. The road stops here and a track, difficult in places, leads into the Imilchil region.

IMILCHIL. In this village, in the territory of the Aït Haddidou, will be based the administration of the Parc National du Haut

ALONG THE OUED DADÈS
The Dadès Valley extends over a distance of 94 miles between the High Atlas in the north and the Jebel Sarhro in the south. *Pisé ksour* (above) are dotted along the valley.

MARRIAGE "MOUSSEM"
In September the famous marriage *moussem*, a sort of mass marriage pledge, is held in Imilchil. During the festival the Aït Haddidou perform the *ahaidous*, in the course of which men and women dance side by side to a slow rhythm. The women wear the *taskunt*, a woollen cloak with red, purple or green stripes. Widows wear an *akilous* (pointed bonnet) and young unmarried women cover their hair with a scarf.

Atlas Oriental. One of the main objectives of the park, which is currently being developed in the region of JEBEL ABERDOUZ (10,030 feet), will be to protect a herd of maned moufflon. A tour, preferably taken with a guide, can be made through the attractive palm groves in the southeast to EL HART, a village where traditional methods are still used in pottery and other crafts. The road follows the line of JEBEL TISDAFINE to the *ksar* of TINEJDAD, which stands among the FERKLA PALM GROVES on the territory of the Aït Atta, a warlike tribe who once controlled the region as far as the Draa Valley.

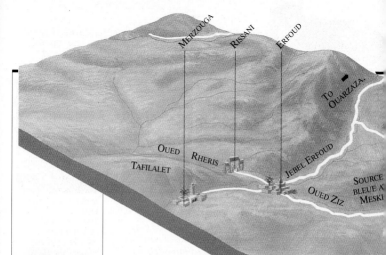

THE TAFILALET ★

🚗 Three days

"In the region of Erfoud alone, there are almost one million palm trees. In their shade the patient Filali peasants cultivate almost all their crops: fruit trees, vegetables and barley. The date is the symbol of the Tafilalet and every year the great traditional date festival is celebrated in October."

Attilio Gaudio,
Maroc saharien

The gate of Erfoud, flanked by two crenelated bastions, is a typical example of Almohad ● *94* architecture.

The Oued Ziz and Oued Rheris run together for a distance of about 15½ miles, irrigating a vast plain that is sometimes referred to as the "Mesopotamia of the Maghreb". From early times the Tafilalet has owed its prosperity to gold brought back from Africa by the caravans and to the cultivation of date palms, the main source of income for the Filali. Today, as a result of persistent drought, the region is producing fewer vegetables, corn and barley, and has declined markedly from the time that Sijilmassa, the first Moroccan city, was founded and that the prestigious Alaouite dynasty began its rise.

ERFOUD. This is one of the largest oases in Morocco, fed by the Oued Ziz and Oued Rheris. A date festival is held here in October. The village, at the foot of JEBEL ERFOUD, was built during the French protectorate as a military outpost and administrative center. It is the starting point for excursions into the first great dunes of the Sahara. The MILITARY FORT OF BORJ EST (East Fort) overlooks the village and offers a splendid view across the date palms, the valley of the Oued Ziz and the desert. About 10 miles further south are the GONIATITE QUARRIES, where a black marble containing goniatite fossils is quarried. A marble mason's yard on the road to TINEJDAD on the outskirts of the village is open to the public.

RISSANI. Enduring a terrible drought in the 13th century, the chieftains of the Tafilalet tribes sent to Arabia for one of the descendants of the Prophet. On his arrival, a spring breeze blew across the mountains and valleys and the long-awaited miracle occurred. It was believed that the divine presence surrounding Hassan the Alaouite had brought back the rains. It was in this way, according to legend, that the ancestor of the Alaouites first came to the Tafilalet and to Rissani, which for eleven centuries was the last staging post on the southern caravan route. The *ksar* was built by Moulay Ismaïl in the 17th century as a residence for his sons and to quash a potential threat to his power. About one mile to the southeast of Rissani stands

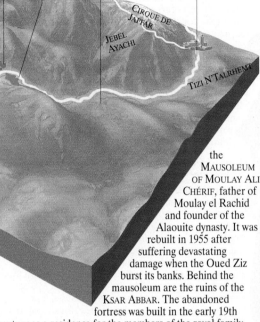

JOULMINA
ER RACHIDIA
BARRAGE HASSAN AL DAKHIL
RICH
MIDELT

CIRQUE DE JAFFAR
JEBEL AYACHI
TIZI N'TALRHEMT

MOULAY ALI CHÉRIF
The founder of the Alaouite dynasty
● *55*, which is still in power today, was laid to rest in 1640 in a beautiful mausoleum decorated with magnificent glazed terracotta. The edifice stands at the center of a sacred compound, next to a mosque with an inner courtyard (below).

the MAUSOLEUM OF MOULAY ALI CHÉRIF, father of Moulay el Rachid and founder of the Alaouite dynasty. It was rebuilt in 1955 after suffering devastating damage when the Oued Ziz burst its banks. Behind the mausoleum are the ruins of the KSAR ABBAR. The abandoned fortress was built in the early 19th century as a residence for the members of the royal family. The fort, originally protected by triple ramparts, cannons and several hundred soldiers, also housed part of the royal treasure. About 3 miles to the southeast the KSAR OF OULAD EL HALIM, known as the "Alhambra of the Tafilalet", was the palace of Moulay Rachid, elder brother of Moulay el Hassan and governor of the region. Notable features of this late 19th-century building include its solid ramparts, its monumental gateway and its decorative brickwork.

SIJILMASSA. The surviving ruins only hint at what Sijilmassa, the first Muslim city in North Africa and the prestigious capital of the Tafilalet, must have looked like. It was founded in around 757 and was an important staging post on the trans-Saharan caravan route, trading in gold, slaves and salt. In the 11th century it is supposed to have had a population of 100,000 and to have been

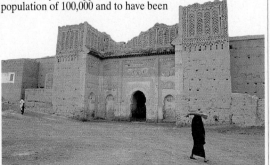

KASBAH OF OULAD EL HALIM
The kasbah of Oulad el Halim has several floors. The rooms on the lower floor were reserved for the watch and those on the middle floor were the communal areas, including granaries, kitchens and living quarters. On the upper floor were the private apartments of the most powerful family in the village.

surrounded by several hundred *ksour*. It was destroyed by the Aït Atta in 1818 during a local war.

MERZOUGA. Less than two hours' journey from Erfoud, the oasis of Merzouga and the DUNES OF THE ERG CHEBBI (some rising to 820 feet) give a foretaste of the breathtaking beauty of the desert. The dunes, so runs a local legend, were created in the course of a punishment inflicted by God on the inhabitants of the old village of Merzouga who, many years ago, refused to give shelter to a woman and her children during a festival. A huge sandstorm blew up and buried the village forever. Since then, every day at midday, the cries of the villagers begging forgiveness can be heard echoing across these vast dunes. On the nearby lake, Dayet Srji, various species of birds, particularly flamingos, can be seen in February and March.

ERFOUD TO ER RACHIDIA

Within the solid *pisé* fortifications of the Maadid *ksar* is an impossibly complicated maze of narrow streets that it is unwise to attempt to explore, unless you are in the company of a guide. Near Borj Yerdi and a few yards from the road are some impressive saltwater geysers rich in iron oxide. At a farm on the other side of the road experiments are being carried out on the reaction of different types of plants to the iron-rich water drawn from this fecund water table. The SOURCE BLEUE at Meski, named after the famous "blue men" who used it as a staging post, rises in a tiny cave in the cliff and spills down into a huge concrete pool near a campsite. Its waters are said to cure barrenness. On Fridays before midday prayer, women come to bathe in the pool and light candles in the cave.

ER RACHIDIA

This town, recently built at the crossroads of the main caravan routes to the Dadès Valley and the Tafilalet, used to be called Ksar es Souk. However, in 1979 it took the name of the Alaouite sultan Moulay Rachid, who left the region in 1666 to depose the Saadian sultan. North of the town, the road follows a picturesque route

HARTANIAT FROM THE ZIZ VALLEY
The women's braided hair is decorated with woollen tassels, silvered ribbons, shells and sometimes charms. Hartaniat women also wear a *ketafiya*, a square of red woollen cloth held in place by brooch fasteners ● 68.

for about 12½ miles along the edge of the emerald-green waters and red-brown shores of the large BARRAGE HASSAN AL DAKHIL (below), which dams the formerly destructive flow of the Oued Ziz and irrigates the extensive palm groves of the Tafilalet to the south. When it was opened in 1971 the dam was given the name of the first Alaouite from Arabia to settle in this valley in 1268. In their oasis village in Arabia, the Alaouite family, descendants of the Prophet, used to receive Moroccans making the pilgrimage to Mecca. One day some of these pilgrims, who were from the Tafilalet, asked Moulay el Kassim, the head of the family, if one of his sons could be their spiritual guide. The patriarch sent for his seven sons and put the same question to each of them in turn: "If someone does you ill, what do you do?" Six out of the seven replied: "I do them ill in return." Only the youngest, Hassan, replied: "I do them good until my good triumphs over their ill." So Hassan was chosen to return to the Tafilalet with the Moroccan pilgrims. Exactly four hundred years later, in 1666, his descendant Moulay Rachid was the first Alaouite to rule Morocco, and the Alouite dynasty, in the person of King Hassan II, is still in power today.

ER RACHIDIA TO FIGUIG

For 250 miles the road between Er Rachidia and Figuig crosses a bare desert landscape, running along the foot of a range of red and black mountains where erosion has exposed the geological strata. The desert road links administrative centers and military outposts such as Boudnib, Bouanane and Bouarfa.

FIGUIG ★. Situated at the foot of the Saharan Atlas, this frontier post on the Algerian border has the largest palm groves in Morocco. It has seven *ksour,* each surrounded by high clay walls, a palm plantation and some sparse vegetable, fruit and cereal plots. Until the turn of the century these *ksour* existed independently of each other and water shortages often led to conflict.

The dunes of the oasis of Merzouga (above), at the edge of the desert.

"KSAR" AND OASIS AT MESKI
The inhabitants of Meski gradually abandoned the *ksar* and settled around the Source Bleue, which irrigates the palm groves.

BARRAGE HASSAN AL DAKHIL
After flooding caused by the Oued Ziz in 1964, a dam (left) was built to control the flow of the Ziz.

THE "CHADOUF"
The *chadouf* (pump

well) was once widely used to irrigate the Ziz Valley. Water is drawn in a goatskin bottle tied to the crosspiece with a length of rope. The system, which today has been replaced by the *foggara*, could only be used to water small areas of land.

The palm groves of Figuig are irrigated by Artesian wells that rise on the Oudaghir plateau. The water is channeled through an extensive network of underground conduits known as *feggaguir*. A rough 20-mile track circles the oasis then climbs to the summit of the JEBEL DJORF, from where there is a splendid view of the palm groves and the surrounding mountains.

ER RACHIDIA TO MIDELT ★

The Ziz Gorges (Gorges of the Gazelles), which are sliced through the imposing rock faces that presage the rise of the High Atlas in the west, are an indication of the former power of the Ziz. As it flowed down the southern slopes of the High Atlas and irrigated the Tafilalet, the river formed the Ziz Valley, with its luxuriant palm groves. Today, as a result of persistent drought, the river is much reduced. The Ziz Gorges form an impressive corridor bordered by a thin line of palms dominated by *ksour* and the beautiful kasbah of Ifri.

THE FOUM ZABEL TUNNEL. Because it was dug by soldiers building the road in 1930, the tunnel also appears on maps as the Tunnel du Légionnaire. There used to be a plaque at the entrance that bore this deadpan explanation: "The mountain blocked our way. The order was given to pass through. The Legion carried out the order."

HAMMAT MOULAY ALI CHÉRIF. The spring, rich in sulfates and magnesium, wells up at a temperature of over 100°F. A small spa, primarily for the treatment of arthritis and rheumatism sufferers, has been established, and visitors can make use of the specially built swimming pool.

RICH. This administrative center, at the foot of Jebel Bou Hamid, is the starting point of a range of difficult tracks that follow the Oued Ziz upstream to the lakes of the High Atlas. One of these tracks, starting from the entrance to the N'Zala Pass, runs for 15½ miles to the *zaouia* of Sidi Hamza, where the library contains a collection of valuable old

The palm groves and gardens of Zenaga, the largest *ksar* in the oasis of Figuig.

books. This ancient place of prayer and study was founded by Sidi Salim, a sage who was reputed to have the powers to make the return trip to Mecca every Friday. A *moussem* is held near his marabout, outside the village, during Aïd Mouloud ● *339*.

IN AND AROUND MIDELT ★

After crossing the Tizi N'Talrehmt (Pass of the She-Camel) the road leads into Midelt, built at the foot of the JEBEL AYACHI, whose summit (12,260 feet) is covered in snow for a large part of the year. Midelt's main sources of income are the beautiful Berber carpets woven in the High Atlas and sold

in the market and the apricots, plums and especially apples grown in the intensively cultivated orchards. A *moussem*, an apple festival, is held at the beginning of October. As you leave Midelt it is well worth visiting the KASBAH MYRIEM, a workshop run by Franciscan nuns where high-quality embroidery ● *76*, carpets ● *74* and Berber blankets, made by local women, are on sale.

THE AOULI LEAD DEPOSITS. The abandoned mining town at the old silver-bearing lead deposits about 15½ miles to the north of Midelt is a truly apocalyptic sight. Tunnels, aqueducts, processing plants and hundreds of houses cling to the sheer rock face of the Aouli gorges, cut by the Oued Moulouya ▲ *256*, the longest of the Moroccan rivers flowing into the Mediterranean.

EXCURSIONS. The best way to reach the natural amphitheater of the CIRQUE DE JAFFAR (6,890 feet) is from the north via Boumia, Tounfite and the Miktane forester's lodge and then back to Midelt. A full day is needed to complete this 50-mile round-trip, which runs across the steppe of the El Arid plateau to the north of the Haute Moulouya basin and then through the cedar forest, to the southwest of Midelt, on the slopes of Jebel Ayachi. It is advisable to inquire in advance about the state of the roads.

"The rivers, streams and springs which flow on the surface of our planet come from two main sources. One of these is fresh water which comes from the clouds and accumulates in the earth, while the other is salt water from the sea which infiltrates the land. There are also riverbeds which are only filled during heavy rains and, in their case, there is no doubt as to how they are formed."
Charles de Foucauld, *Reconnaissance du Maroc*

ZIZ

The Oued Ziz tumbles down the slopes of the High Atlas, winds through the Ziz Gorges and flows into the reservoir of the Barrage Hassan al

Dakhil ▲ *297*. Here women do their washing in the shade of date palms and fruit trees (above).

TAROUDANT

Three days

Three very beautiful one-day excursions start from Marrakesh. The first follows the Ourika Valley and climbs to the winter sports resort of Oukaïmeden, the second takes you to Amizmiz, which lies in the direction of Taroudant, and the third takes in Asni and Tizi N'Test before rejoining the main Agadir-Ouarzazate road.

TO AGADIR

OUED OURIKA
The clear, fast-flowing waters of the Oued Ourika cut through the foothills of the Atlas Mountains and irrigate the Ourika Valley with its green terraces of orchards and crops. The valley is dotted with small *douar* (villages) whose *pisé* houses cluster together on the plateaux or near water.

THE OURIKA VALLEY

The road runs for about 19 miles across the Haouz Plain and then turns off toward the site of ancient Aghmat, an abandoned village founded by the Haoura Berbers before the arrival of Islam ● 62. By the late 10th century it was a rich regional capital but the town was subsequently captured by the Almoravids and gradually declined in importance, as Marrakesh grew. All that remains of the original buildings is the mausoleum of Moatamid Ben Abbad, an Andalusian poet-prince who was taken prisoner during the conquest of Seville in 1091. Back on the main road and about 2 miles to the south of Aghmat, a track leads to Dar Caïd Ouriki, where the busiest souk in the Ourika Valley is held every Monday. Unfortunately the proximity of Marrakesh has meant that it has become something of a tourist spot.

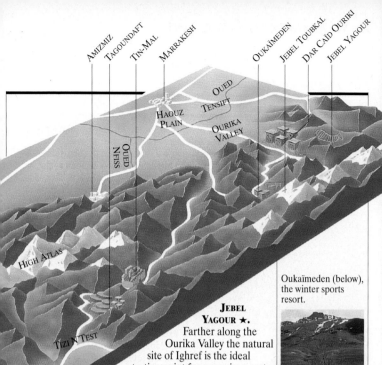

AMIZMIZ • TAGOUNDAFT • TIN-MAL • MARRAKESH • OUKAÏMEDEN • JEBEL TOUBKAL • DAR CAÏD OURIKI • JEBEL YAGOUR

OUED TENSIFT
HAOUZ PLAIN
OUED NFISS
OURIKA VALLEY

HIGH ATLAS

TIZI N'TEST

Oukaïmeden (below), the winter sports resort.

JEBEL YAGOUR ★.

Farther along the Ourika Valley the natural site of Ighref is the ideal starting point for excursions on to the Jebel Yagour. The valley is dotted with villages and at Ighref there is a mosque that overlooks a steep ravine. In Jebel Yagour, over a thousand rock carvings representing weapons, primitive carts, animals and human figures have been discovered.

OUKAÏMEDEN ★. The road turns off to Arhbalou (in the direction of Marrakesh) and leads to the winter sports resort of Oukaïmeden (8,700 feet). The ski lift, which ascends to an altitude of 10,825 feet, is the highest in Africa and, in clear weather, it offers a breathtaking view of the surrounding mountains. Bronze Age carvings can be seen on some of the red sandstone rocks on the edge of the resort. They are identical to carvings found in Europe and support the theory that the two continents were connected during this period.

TO AMIZMIZ

About 6 miles outside Marrakesh, in the direction of Taroudant, lie the *zaouia* of Tamesloht. The *zaouia*, founded in the 16th century by the chérif Abdallah Ben Hussein el Hassani, who was reputed to possess 366 skills, made Tamesloht an important religious center. After passing through Oumnast and skirting the reservoir of the Oued Nfiss dam (Barrage Cavagnac), the road reaches Amizmiz. One of the largest Berber souks is held in Amizmiz on Tuesdays, and the region's plain yet elegant pottery is very much in evidence. In his *Geographical History of Africa* Leo Africanus recorded that the large-grained corn of Amizmiz was the best he had ever seen and that it made perfect flour.

ROCK CARVINGS
Rock carvings of round shields have been discovered at Yagou (center) and Oukaïmeden (bottom). The carvings of cattle (top) were found on rocks near Oukaïmeden.

TIZI N'TEST
The pass of Tizi N'Test dominates the Sous Plain, which stretches for 125 miles between Jebel Siroua and the Atlantic Ocean.

ROAD TO TIZI N'TEST

On a rocky spur in the heart of the Moulay Brahim Gorges stand the village and *zaouia* of Moulay Brahim where a famous annual *moussem* ◆ *339* is held on the occasion of Mouloud, the Prophet's birthday. Moulay Brahim is also renowned as a place of pilgrimage for childless women, who keep alive the local tradition of tying ribbons in the trees in the hope that they will become pregnant when the ribbons work loose.

ASNI. This picturesque Berber village (3,770 feet) lies in the center of the CIRQUE DE TAMARAOUT and is dominated by the towering JEBEL TOUBKAL, the highest peak in the Maghreb (13,650 feet). The village of Imlil lies about 10½ miles from Asni on the edge of the TOUBKAL NATIONAL PARK. It is the starting point for a number of excursions into the High Atlas. The Club Alpin Français has a hotel and three mountain refuges in the park. The Toubkal National Park and the TAGHERGHOUT NATURE RESERVE to the northwest are homes to various species of birds, including golden eagles, vultures, short-toed eagles, falcons, rock doves, Barbary partridges and Alpine choughs, as well as a range of mammals,

OUED NFISS
The valley of the Oued Nfiss crosses the Pays des Goundafi, named after the tribe that once controlled this important route. During the 19th century the Goundafi built a series of strongly fortified kasbahs.

particularly maned moufflons and wild boars. Registered guides take trekkers on foot, or by mule and skis, through the many villages of the valleys or (at higher altitudes) through forests of holm oaks, thuriferous junipers, Atlas cypresses, alyssum and other mountain vegetation. These treks offer an ideal opportunity to take in the magnificent landscapes dotted with *douars* (villages).

OUIRGANE ★. From the Cirque de Tamaraout, the road crosses a low pass and descends to Ouirgane and its salt mines then passes through the gorges of the Oued Nfiss before crossing the Oued Agoundis at Ijoukak. About 2 miles further on, on the right, is Talaa Yacoub, the seat of the Goundafi tribe who ruled the region in the 19th century and controlled traffic on the main route of Tizi N'Test. From the mountain track there is a splendid view across the Argan tree ■ *30* plantation of the Sous Plain below.

Bridge Over a River, an etching by Edmond Valès.

> "THE ARRIVAL OF THE DIFFERENT BROTHERHOODS, WITH THEIR LEADERS, THE MUAQQADDEMIN, THEIR BROTHERS AND THEIR BANNERS … ATTRACTS A MOTLEY CROWD TO THE SHRINE OF MOULAY BRAHIM."
>
> JUAN GOYTISOLO

TIN-MAL ★. This isolated village is one of the most important of Morocco's historic sites. It was the spiritual home of Ibn Toumert ● *54*, ▲ *261*, founder of the Almohad dynasty in the early 12th century. He was an advocate of the strict application of Koranic principles and had many followers in Marrakesh. This concerned the sultan, who had him driven out of the city. Ibn Toumert sought refuge in the mountains, where he gained the support of several tribes in his rebellion against the power of the Almoravids. In 1125 he founded Tin-Mal and wielded absolute power there. His followers were known as the Almohads (Unitarians). He died in 1130, after laying seige to Marrakesh but then leaving his second-in-command, Abd el Moumen, to complete the undertaking. Marrakesh was finally taken in 1147 and as a result Tin-Mal lost its strategic importance. It became a holy town and the treasure house of the caliphs. It was the last pocket of Almohad resistance and was captured and sacked by the Merinids between 1275 and 1276. The fortified MOSQUE ● *54* was built by Abd el Moumen in memory of Ibn Toumert. Despite the damage it has sustained, it is still very beautiful. It consists of nine naves with five aisles and a further two naves with three aisles next to the courtyard. A central aisle leads to the mihrab above which, unusually, the minaret was built.

TAGOUNDAFT. The road continues southward along the banks of the Oued Nfiss and passes beneath the 19th-century KASBAH OF TAGOUNDAFT, built on a rock 330 feet up. The road leaves the Oued Nfiss at Idni where mountain tracks rise steeply to Tizi N'Test (6,890 feet) and then follow the line of the verdant Sous Valley which stretches 125 miles between JEBEL SIROUA in the east and the Atlantic Ocean in the west.

OUIRGANE
The flat roofs of the *pisé* houses of the High Atlas are made of logs and branches covered with earth.

MOSQUE OF TIN-MAL
The ONA Foundation restored this mosque as part of its initiative to preserve the country's Islamic heritage.

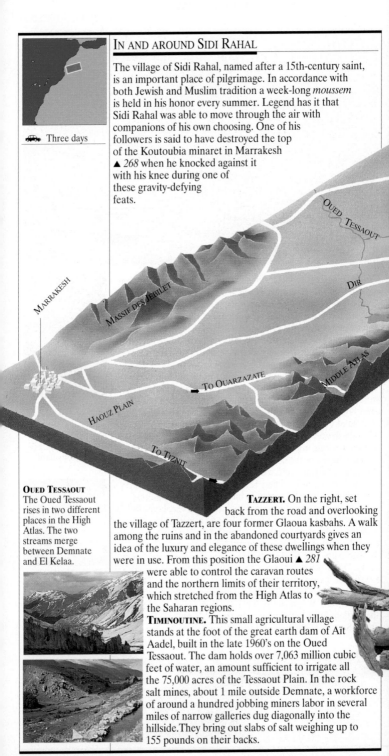

IN AND AROUND SIDI RAHAL

Three days

The village of Sidi Rahal, named after a 15th-century saint, is an important place of pilgrimage. In accordance with both Jewish and Muslim tradition a week-long *moussem* is held in his honor every summer. Legend has it that Sidi Rahal was able to move through the air with companions of his own choosing. One of his followers is said to have destroyed the top of the Koutoubia minaret in Marrakesh ▲ *268* when he knocked against it with his knee during one of these gravity-defying feats.

OUED TESSAOUT
The Oued Tessaout rises in two different places in the High Atlas. The two streams merge between Demnate and El Kelaa.

TAZZERT. On the right, set back from the road and overlooking the village of Tazzert, are four former Glaoua kasbahs. A walk among the ruins and in the abandoned courtyards gives an idea of the luxury and elegance of these dwellings when they were in use. From this position the Glaoui ▲ *281* were able to control the caravan routes and the northern limits of their territory, which stretched from the High Atlas to the Saharan regions.

TIMINOUTINE. This small agricultural village stands at the foot of the great earth dam of Aït Aadel, built in the late 1960's on the Oued Tessaout. The dam holds over 7,063 million cubic feet of water, an amount sufficient to irrigate all the 75,000 acres of the Tessaout Plain. In the rock salt mines, about 1 mile outside Demnate, a workforce of around a hundred jobbing miners labor in several miles of narrow galleries dug diagonally into the hillside. They bring out slabs of salt weighing up to 155 pounds on their backs.

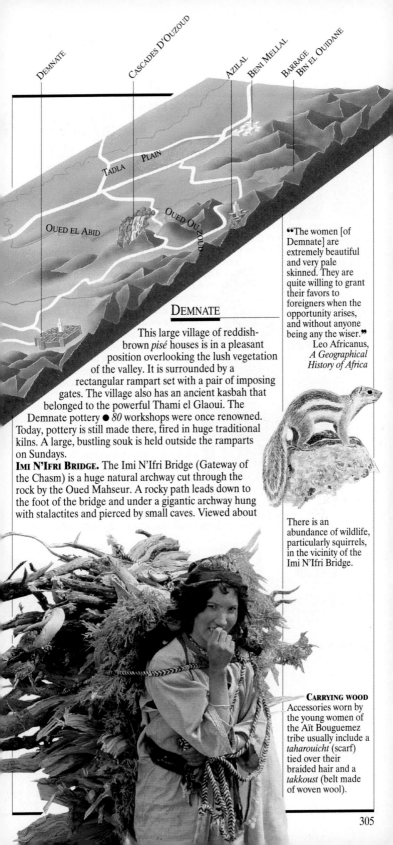

TADLA PLAIN

OUED EL ABID

OUED OUZOUD

DEMNATE

This large village of reddish-brown *pisé* houses is in a pleasant position overlooking the lush vegetation of the valley. It is surrounded by a rectangular rampart set with a pair of imposing gates. The village also has an ancient kasbah that belonged to the powerful Thami el Glaoui. The Demnate pottery ● *80* workshops were once renowned. Today, pottery is still made there, fired in huge traditional kilns. A large, bustling souk is held outside the ramparts on Sundays.

IMI N'IFRI BRIDGE. The Imi N'Ifri Bridge (Gateway of the Chasm) is a huge natural archway cut through the rock by the Oued Mahseur. A rocky path leads down to the foot of the bridge and under a gigantic archway hung with stalactites and pierced by small caves. Viewed about

"The women [of Demnate] are extremely beautiful and very pale skinned. They are quite willing to grant their favors to foreigners when the opportunity arises, and without anyone being any the wiser."

Leo Africanus,
A Geographical History of Africa

There is an abundance of wildlife, particularly squirrels, in the vicinity of the Imi N'Ifri Bridge.

CARRYING WOOD
Accessories worn by the young women of the Aït Bouguemez tribe usually include a *taharouicht* (scarf) tied over their braided hair and a *takkoust* (belt made of woven wool).

305

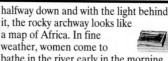

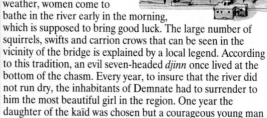

halfway down and with the light behind it, the rocky archway looks like a map of Africa. In fine weather, women come to bathe in the river early in the morning, which is supposed to bring good luck. The large number of squirrels, swifts and carrion crows that can be seen in the vicinity of the bridge is explained by a local legend. According to this tradition, an evil seven-headed *djinn* once lived at the bottom of the chasm. Every year, to insure that the river did not run dry, the inhabitants of Demnate had to surrender to him the most beautiful girl in the region. One year the daughter of the kaïd was chosen but a courageous young man killed the monster before the girl fell into its grasp. The body of the *djinn* decomposed into thousands of worms, each of which transformed itself into a crow.

CASCADES D'OUZOUD. About 13½ miles from Tanaant a road on the left leads to the impressive Cascades d'Ouzoud, one of the most beautiful natural sites in the Middle Atlas. The waters, with their almost permanent rainbow, plunge dramatically through 330 feet into a limestone pool surrounded by a mass of luxuriant vegetation. A pathway shaded by olive trees ■ *44* leads down to the pool at the foot of the falls where bathing is permitted. At the top of the waterfall, just a few yards from the chasm, the water from the falls still turns around a dozen ancient grain mills. At dusk the huge carob trees are filled by families of chattering monkeys, who are particularly fond of the tasty fruit. A hundred or so beige-coated, black-eyed macaques live in the caves in the cliffs. The village of Tanaghmelt beyond the waterfalls consists of a

The Cascades d'Ouzoud (top), the Valley of the Aït Bouguemez (center left), and a guest room in a *ksar* (above).

labyrinth of narrow streets. There is also a narrow and difficult path which leads on to the main Beni Mellal road, via the gorges of the Oued el Abid where the bottom of the breathtaking canyon, 1,970 feet below, is sometimes invisible.

AZILAL. This large garrison village is the point of departure for a range of excursions into the M'Goun mountains. Shepherds from the oases come up to this rather isolated region in summer, leading their flocks to greener pastures at higher altitudes. The track forks about 17½ miles from Aït Mehamed, the right fork leading down the valley of the Aït Bouguemez to Agouti, via Jebel Azourki, the Lac d'Izourar and a series of *ighrem*. The left fork leads up to the Tizi N'Ilissi, then down again to the *Zaouia* Ahansal. From here the route proceeds along the edge of an impressive forest of dead trees to the cliffs (2,625 feet) of the "Cathédrale des Rochers" (Cathedral of the Rocks) and Tilougguite before continuing to Ouaouizarht and then Beni Mellal via the Barrage Bin el Ouidane. Bin el Ouidane (Between the Oueds), 935 feet long and 436 high, is the largest dam in Morocco. It was built in 1948 and its 9,230-acre reservoir holds enough water to irrigate the entire cereal crop of the Tadla Plain. Its hydroelectric power station supplies the region's electricity.

THE VILLAGE OF IMELGHAS, AS SEEN BY TITOUAN LAMAZOU
The navigator Titouan Lamazou was born in Casablanca in 1955 and spent his childhood in Tétouan (hence his nickname "Titouan"). A year (1981–82) spent in the High Atlas inspired several paintings and drawings, including those of the village of Imelghas (above and below).

❝The *tamesriyt*, the Arabic word for guest room, is a shrine dedicated to hospitality. In some houses the head of the family keeps it locked and it is only opened for important guests or on special occasions.❞
Titouan Lamazou,
Sous les toits de terre

EXCURSIONS IN THE CENTRAL HIGH ATLAS
There are various ways of exploring the mountains of the High Atlas, but a minimum amount of equipment and organization are necessary. Local guides and porters familiar with the region can be hired. Berber porters cooking donuts around a camp fire (top left), canoeing down the Oued Tessaout (above left) and a party of hikers (right) at Idrabaken in the Azilal region.

Berber porters on Jebel Tifferdine (11,810 feet), on the south face of Jebel M'Goun.

BENI MELLAL

This large agricultural town at the foot of Jebel Tassemit (7,372 feet) has one of the highest rates of population growth in Morocco. The ramparts were built in 1688 by Moulay Ismaïl. He also built a kasbah, but it has been restored so many times that it is now of little architectural interest. A souk, where Berber blankets are sold, is held here every Tuesday. Beni Mellal stands in the center of a huge orchard of orange, fig and olive trees ■ *44* irrigated by the Barrage Bin el Ouidane. A delightful 6-mile walk passes through olive groves to the spring of Aïn Asserdoun (Spring of the Mule), surrounded by large gardens. About half a mile from the spring the ruined *borj* of Ras el Aïn offers a splendid view over the town, the olive groves and the fertile Tadla Plain.

AGADIR

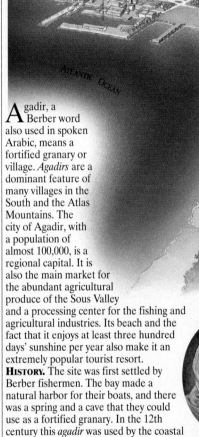

To Essaouira

Port · Old Kasbah · Boulevard Mohammed V · Avenue des Armées

Atlantic Ocean

🚗 One day

AGADIR

CREST OF THE AGADIR AREA
Goats feed on the branches of an argan tree ■ *30* under the watchful eye of a shepherd.

SIDI MOHAMMED BEN ABDULLAH (1757–90)
In 1760, to punish the rebellious inhabitants of the Sous region for rebelling against his authority, the Alaouite sultan Sidi Mohammed Ben Abdullah closed the port of Agadir. Its decline was to the advantage of Mogador (modern Essaouira ▲ *158*), which now became the center for European trade.

The mosque of the old Kasbah (below), built in the 16th century and destroyed in the earthquake of 1960.

A gadir, a Berber word also used in spoken Arabic, means a fortified granary or village. *Agadirs* are a dominant feature of many villages in the South and the Atlas Mountains. The city of Agadir, with a population of almost 100,000, is a regional capital. It is also the main market for the abundant agricultural produce of the Sous Valley and a processing center for the fishing and agricultural industries. Its beach and the fact that it enjoys at least three hundred days' sunshine per year also make it an extremely popular tourist resort.

HISTORY. The site was first settled by Berber fishermen. The bay made a natural harbor for their boats, and there was a spring and a cave that they could use as a fortified granary. In the 12th century this *agadir* was used by the coastal Ksima tribe, and between 1325 and 1470 European maps referred to it as Porto Meseguinam (Port of the Ksima). Portuguese sailors made it a center for fishing and arms smuggling. A small Berber fort, Agadir el Arbaa, was built on the shore and gave its name to the first Saadian fortifications. In 1505 a Portuguese nobleman, Joâo Lopez de Sequeira, built a small fort at the foot of the

CENTRAL MARKET
TOURIST OFFICE
AGADIR MUSEUM
BOULEVARD HASSAN II
BOULEVARD DU 20 AOÛT
ROYAL PALACE

TO THE AIRPORT

hill overlooking the bay to control access to the port. In 1513 Manuel I, King of Portugal, took over the fort, extended it and installed a garrison. Santa Cruz de Cap de Gué ("do Cabo de Aguer" in Portuguese) controlled the overland and maritime gold and slave routes to the Sudan and Guinea. At the same time the region's tribal confederation assembled near the marabouts of the Chadiliya-Jazouliya brotherhood, allies of the Maqil Arabs. A holy war led by the Saadian *chorfa* (princes) was waged against the invaders. On March 12, 1541, after a six-month siege, Guttere de Monroy, the governor of Agadir, surrendered to the sultan Mohammed Sheikh.

BIRTH OF A MAJOR PORT. In the 17th century the Saadians ● *55* were ousted by the Alaouite dynasty. The Berber Tazeroualt dynasty rebelled against the authority of the Alaouites and took control of the Sous region. Under the Berbers, Agadir became a major port, where European cloth and corn were exchanged for gold from Guinea and sugar from the Sous. In the 18th century the Alaouites re-established their authority and closed the port of Agadir, symbol of Sous independence.

FRANCO-GERMAN RIVALRY. Agadir became the subject of dispute once again in 1911 when Kaiser Wilhelm II, King of Prussia and Emperor of Germany, tried to set up a naval

WILHELM II
In July 1911 the German emperor sent the cruiser *Panther* into the bay of Agadir.

"COURRIER SUD"
"Mail will land Agadir 21.00, take off for Cabo Juby 21.30, land there with Michelin bomb stop. Cabo Juby to prepare usual flares stop. Order remain in contact with Agadir. Signed: Toulouse. From the Cabo Juby observatory, in mid-Sahara, we were watching the trail of a distant comet."
Saint-Exupéry

LIGNES AÉRIENNES
G. LATECOERE

France
Espagne
Maroc

SERVICE POSTAL AÉRIEN ENTRE LA FRANCE ET LE MAROC

TRANSPORT DE PASSAGERS ET MESSAGERIES

▲ AGADIR

In 1992 a naval repair yard was installed in Agadir, one of the busiest fishing ports in Morocco.

By 1960 Agadir, known as the "Nice of Morocco", was already a thriving tourist resort. That year the earthquake destroyed 80 percent of the city in a matter of seconds, while the neighboring town of Inezgane remained intact. Near the port only the *koubba* ● *63* of the marabout Sidi Bouknadel withstood the tidal wave caused by the earthquake.

base on the Moroccan coast in an attempt to establish a German presence in the region. Joseph Caillaux, the French premier, negotiated an agreement with Germany under which France ceded part of the Congo to Germany in return for control of Morocco. When French troops entered Agadir in 1913 the city had less than one thousand inhabitants.

THE AGE OF AIRMAIL. In the 1930's Agadir was an important staging post on the routes flown by the French airmail company, the Compagnie Générale Aéropostale. It was here that the French pilots Antoine de Saint-Exupéry and Jean Mermoz landed before flying on to Cap Juby and Villa Cisneros (modern Tarfaya and Dakhla ▲ *327, 328*), from where they took off to cross the Atlantic. On evenings when the "Paris taxi" was due bonfires were lit as markers on a hastily improvised landing strip. A coastal telephone line between Agadir and Port-Lyautey also helped open up the city to the outside world. Economic activity began with fishing and agriculture. A large number of port and food canning plants were built and Agadir soon rivaled Safi ▲ *153* as the world's leading sardine port.

THE 1960 DISASTER. On February 29, 1960, at 11.47 pm an earthquake shook Agadir, killing over fifteen thousand people and destroying most of the houses in the city. Mohammed V ● *57* declared that, although fate had chosen

> "THE SKY ABOVE WAS OBSCURED BY FIRE. THE SAND
> FLOWS BETWEEN THE STONES WERE FILLED WITH A
> MILKY LIGHT."
>
> CLAUDE OLLIER

THE KASBAH
The citadel, on the hill overlooking the bay of Agadir, was built by Mohammed Sheikh in 1540. The ramparts were restored after the 1960 earthquake. It is an ideal spot from which to watch the sun set over the sea.

AVENUE MOHAMMED V
The Avenue Mohammed V, Agadir's main thoroughfare, runs north-south across the city, cutting it in two. On one side is the modern city center and, on the other, the tourist district along the bay.

to destroy the city, the faith and determination of the inhabitants would rebuild Agadir. By 1962 a new town was rapidly developing, with a harbor and industrial complexes in

the northern part of the city, and residential districts and hotels along the 6-mile beach. Today Agadir's hotels can accommodate twenty thousand tourists. It is Morocco's leading tourist center.

THE PORT ★. Agadir, Morocco's leading fishing port, has around twenty canning and freezing factories. Its main exports are early vegetables and fruit, canned foods and ore. Fish auctions take place every afternoon in the fish market, and delicious fried fish is sold nearby in small open-air restaurants.

"VALLÉE DES OISEAUX". This little zoo (The Valley of the Birds) is located in a gully that cuts across the Avenue Mohammed V and Avenue Hassan II, bisecting the city. Birds from all over the world are kept in aviaries that authentically imitate their natural habitats.

THE KASBAH ★. The citadel atop a hill 775 feet high looks down on the city and out over the Atlantic Ocean. It was built by Mohammed Sheikh in 1540 as a base from which to lay siege to Agadir and was later used as a defense against attacks from the Portuguese. Two hundred years subsequently it was strengthened by Moulay Abdallah, who installed a garrison of two thousand men. All that remained standing after the 1960

Besides birds, species of local fauna that can be seen in Agadir's zoo (left) include maned mouflon and macaques.

313

THE BAY OF AGADIR
The new commercial port, in the foreground, is separated from the beach by a jetty.

Beautiful shells can be picked up for next to nothing from vendors on the beaches or along the coast road.

A wide range of spices from Morocco and other countries are offered for sale in Agadir's central market.

earthquake were sections of the ramparts (which have been partially rebuilt) and the main gateway, where an inscription in Dutch, a vestige of the Dutch trading center established here in 1746, reads "Fear God and obey the King".

A MODERN CITY. The new city of Agadir, modern and simply laid out, was built farther south to minimize damage in the event of another earthquake. Green spaces and broad avenues separate the city's various districts. Among the best examples of modern architecture are the post office, a successful combination of concrete and cedarwood, the elegant lawcourts, the primary school in the Avenue des Forces-Armées-Royales and the fire station, with its conspicuous training tower.

THE AGADIR MUSEUM. The museum, in Agadir's theater complex, opened in 1992. It is devoted to the culture and folk art of the Sous Valley and the Saharan regions, and houses the other half of the Bert Flint collection on display in the Maison Tiskiwin in Marrakesh ▲ 273. The costumes, jewelry, carpets, furniture, musical instruments and tools in the collection were gathered together by the Dutch-born art historian Bert Flint, who has lived in Morocco since 1957.

A TOURIST CENTER. Agadir's tourist accommodation is continually increasing as more new hotels are built. A new seaside resort known as Palm Bay is being developed near the beach. It will include hotels, holiday villas, a conference center, a casino, sports facilities and a school of hotel management. Although the main attraction of Palm Bay is its long soft sand beach bordered by eucalyptus, pines and tamarisks, the Agadir region also has much to offer in the way of beautiful scenery and interesting places to visit.

IMMOUZER DES IDA OUTANANE

About 72 miles north of Agadir a road leads off to the right and winds over 15 miles of mountainous terrain, through landscapes ranging from plateaux and valleys to gorges and mountains. In the mixed vegetation argan trees ■ 30 and *doum* (dwarf) palms ■ 42 predominate.

> "THE BEAUTY OF THE DAY WAS INTENSELY PURE AND ALL ITS RADIANCE SEEMED TO RISE FROM THE DEEP BLUE OF THE SEA."
>
> JOSEPH KESSEL

ARGAN TREES
A vast argan forest, comprising some twenty million trees, covers an area of 27 square miles between Essaouira and Agadir. Although the forest is state-owned, common law grants each family the right to own a few trees. The trees are divided into inheritances (two for a son and one for a daughter) like plots of land, which leads to extreme fragmentation. An unwritten law prohibits one family's goats from climbing another family's trees, particularly when they are in flower.

In the middle of this natural botanical garden, known locally as the Vallée du Paradis, is Immouzer, where white houses cluster around a palm grove. This is the "capital" of the Ida Outanane, a confederation of Berber tribes who until 1927 remained independent of the central government and the authority of the great *kaïds*. Beekeeping is one of the region's main economic activities and a honey festival is held in Immouzer at the beginning of May. Thyme and wild lavender honey is mixed with argan oil and ground almonds to make *amlou*, a delicacy given to newlyweds. Some hives are cylindrical in shape and about 8 inches in diameter. They are made of woven reeds covered with clay, and are set in a wall. About 2 miles outside Immouzer, near the source of the Oued Tinkert, waterfalls cascade down a rock face that limestone deposits have turned white. The falls are known as the Voile de la Mariée (Bride's Veil).

THE COAST ★

The coast road between Agadir and Essaouira ▲ *156* runs behind the beaches of TAMRAKHT and TARHAZOUTZ, past the CAP RHIR LIGHTHOUSE and on to the village of Tamri on the Asif Aït Ameur estuary, where there are extensive banana plantations. The valley is covered with euphorbia ■ *22*, which was named after Euphorbus, the doctor of Juba II, King of Mauretania (modern Morocco and western Algeria)

Camel driver from the Agadir region (far left).

THE CAP RHIR LIGHTHOUSE
From a height of 1,180 feet, the slopes of the High Atlas fall steeply to the Atlantic Ocean at Cap Rhir.

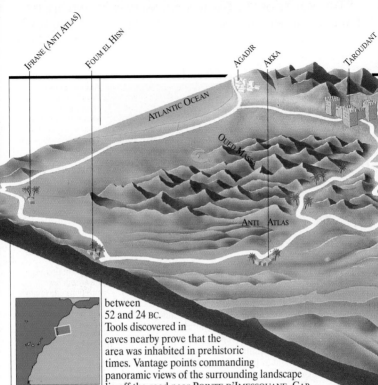

IFRANE (ANTI ATLAS) · FOUM EL HISN · ATLANTIC OCEAN · AGADIR · AKKA · TAROUDANT · OUED MASSA · ANTI ATLAS

🚗 Three days

MARKET AT TAROUDANT
The abundant produce of the orchards of the Sous Valley is sold in the market at Taroudant. Ibn Hauqal, the 10th-century geographer, marveled at the size and fertility of the Sous el Aqsa, the prosperity of the inhabitants and the abundance of food grown there, and remarked that fruit characteristic both of

cool and warm climates was grown there.

between 52 and 24 BC.
Tools discovered in caves nearby prove that the area was inhabited in prehistoric times. Vantage points commanding panoramic views of the surrounding landscape lie off the road near POINTE D'IMESSOUANE, CAP TAFELNY and the MARABOUT OF SIDI KAOUKI, a saint with remarkable healing powers who was said to be able to make barren women fertile. A *moussem* ◆ *339* is held here in mid-August. Halfway between Agadir and Taroudant, the road passes through OULED TAIMA. This small town, known locally as "44" because it lies 44 kilometers (27½ miles) from Agadir, has become a sort of new town. Many of its rich red, blue-shuttered houses were built by Moroccans working in Europe. The combine harvesters sometimes seen in the main street reflect the agricultural wealth of the Sous region. A souk is held here every Tuesday. Outside the town cornfields, orange groves, greenhouses full of tomatoes and banana plantations stretch as far as the eye can see.

TAROUDANT ★

Taroudant, which stands at the entrance to the Sous Valley and the High Atlas, is off the main tourist routes. However, with its red ramparts surrounded by gardens, eucalyptus, olive, pomegranate and palm trees, it is very picturesque. Although it is known as "little Marrakesh", the pace of everyday life there is far removed from the bustle of the real Marrakesh.
A REBEL STRONGHOLD. In the 11th century Taroudant was the capital of a small kingdom. It was annexed by the Almoravids in 1056, was independent under the Almohads and was destroyed by the Merinids ● *54* in 1306. It reached its apogee during the 16th century under Mohammed Sheikh, who made it his capital and the base for his military offensives against the Portuguese in Agadir ▲ *310*. During this period Taroudant was renowned for the abundance and quality of its produce, which included sugar, cotton and rice, and it became an important caravan

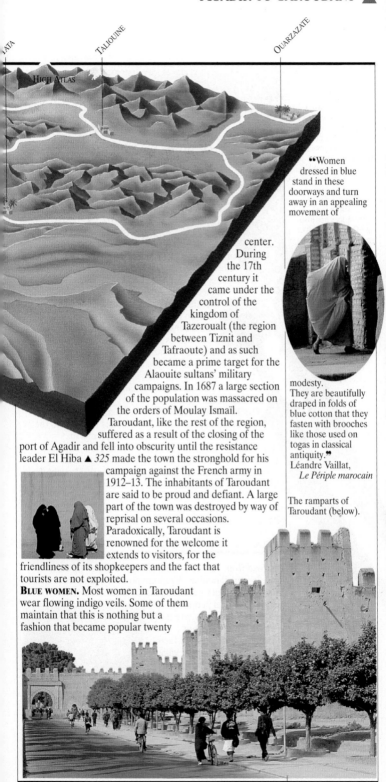

IATA   TALIOUINE   OUARZAZATE

HIGH ATLAS

center. During the 17th century it came under the control of the kingdom of Tazeroualt (the region between Tiznit and Tafraoute) and as such became a prime target for the Alaouite sultans' military campaigns. In 1687 a large section of the population was massacred on the orders of Moulay Ismaïl.

Taroudant, like the rest of the region, suffered as a result of the closing of the port of Agadir and fell into obscurity until the resistance leader El Hiba ▲ *325* made the town the stronghold for his campaign against the French army in 1912–13. The inhabitants of Taroudant are said to be proud and defiant. A large part of the town was destroyed by way of reprisal on several occasions. Paradoxically, Taroudant is renowned for the welcome it extends to visitors, for the friendliness of its shopkeepers and the fact that tourists are not exploited.

BLUE WOMEN. Most women in Taroudant wear flowing indigo veils. Some of them maintain that this is nothing but a fashion that became popular twenty

❝Women dressed in blue stand in these doorways and turn away in an appealing movement of modesty. They are beautifully draped in folds of blue cotton that they fasten with brooches like those used on togas in classical antiquity.❞
Léandre Vaillat,
Le Périple marocain

The ramparts of Taroudant (below).

The Place Assarag (right), lined with arcades, is the starting point for a visit to the souks of Taroudant, a local center for traditional crafts. Silver jewelry, one of the town's specialties, is sold by weight. Leather goods, engraved limestone, saffron and a whole host of other spices are also on offer, as are silver and copper daggers.

or thirty years ago. But it is also the color of the "Blue Sultan" ▲ 325, and is associated with the famous "blue men" of the desert (whose skin is stained by the indigo dye of their clothing) and with the days when Taroudant was a busy caravan town.

THE RAMPARTS. Five monumental gates set in the ramparts of Taroudant open on to the medina, where a maze of narrow streets gives the visitor a taste of the pace of Moroccan city life. Just outside the ramparts is the impressive *Hôtel Gazelle d'Or*, a former hunting lodge built by a French baron at the turn of the century.

THE PLACE ASSARAG. This busy square is the heart of Taroudant, former capital of the Sous region, and the meeting place for Roudanis (the inhabitants of Taroudant), who gather in cafés there in the evening. A narrow street leads to the souks, which although relatively small are as animated and varied as those of Marrakesh.

AROUND TAROUDANT. About 19 miles southeast of Taroudant is the oasis of Tiout, with its old kasbah. From here a fairly rough track runs south for around 25 miles to the village of Amagour, in the foothills of the Anti Atlas.

TAROUDANT TO OUARZAZATE

The road from Taroudant to Ouarzazate passes through Aoulouz and Taliouine, departure points for treks of several days up the extinct volcano of Jebel Siroua (10,843 feet). In summer the local people go up into the mountains, where they live in *azib,* or makeshift sheepfolds, one or two of their number remaining in the village to guard the *agadir,* which contains each family's wealth. The area has a harsh climate, and snow falls on the high slopes of the Anti Atlas. This is why the *akhnif* ● 78, a burnous made of thick, black wool decorated with colored embroidery, is a typical item of clothing in the region.

Off the main roads and vehicular tracks, donkeys and mules are the only means of transport in the mountains.

TALIOUINE. The best Moroccan saffron comes from near Taliouine. It is harvested at the beginning of winter, and picked before sunrise so that the flowers do not wilt. The stigma (three pistils) of each hand-picked flower are pinched off with the fingernails and put into wooden boxes to dry. This expensive spice is of course an ingredient of Moroccan cooking, but is also used as an antispasmodic drug and as makeup to be worn during festivals.

TAZENARKT. The town was described by Charles de Foucauld in 1883 as "the home of the *khenif* (carpet), where the entire population is occupied in weaving and embroidery". Today Tazenarkt is the headquarters of a large cooperative for carpets made in the surrounding mountain villages. A track leads over two passes, the Tizi Taguergoust (5,360 feet) and the Tizi N'Timlaine (3,904 feet), and then forks east (left) toward Adgz and the Draa Valley and south (right) to Foum Zguid and Jebel Bani. The main road continues to Ouarzazate.

SOUTH OF TAROUDANT ★

After crossing the Anti Atlas, a minor road hugs the contour of the southern slopes as it makes its way toward the Atlantic Ocean. It passes through the modest *ksar* ● *98* (6,250 feet) of Igherm, where craftsmen make weapons and copper vessels, then reaches Tata, a large oasis surrounded by some thirty *ksour*. Three tributaries merge and the river flows into the Draa Valley, on the other side of Jebel Bani.

AKKA. It was near Akka that, in 1511, Abou Abdallah Mohammed Mobarek, local leader of the Jazouliya brotherhood, appointed the Saadian chieftain of the Draa region, Mohammed Ben Ahmed el Qaïm, leader of the holy war. Today Akka is the main village in an oasis consisting of about ten *ksour* where a sweet variety of date known as *bousekri* grow.

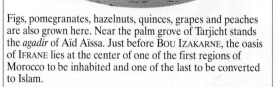

Figs, pomegranates, hazelnuts, quinces, grapes and peaches are also grown here. Near the palm grove of Tarjicht stands the *agadir* of Aïd Aïssa. Just before BOU IZAKARNE, the oasis of IFRANE lies at the center of one of the first regions of Morocco to be inhabited and one of the last to be converted to Islam.

Women from the Tata region gather for a *moussem* ◆ *339,* an annual festival held in honor of a saint. The Maa el Aïnine *moussem* (above) is held in July.

ROCK CARVINGS
Thousands of rock carvings of antelopes, elephants, cattle and two-wheeled carts have been discovered at various sites in the region, particularly near Foum el Hisn (about 4 miles from Icht) and Akka. These carvings indicate that around

3000 BC hunters in the locality had become herdsmen and also prove that lakes existed in the Sahara at that time.

The inhabitants of the province of Ouarzazate depend almost entirely on agriculture. Every available plot of land (left) is under cultivation.

319

🚗 Three days

The quickest way to get from Agadir to Marrakesh is via Chichaoua where the Agadir-Chichaoua road joins the main Essaouira-Marrakesh road. About 50 miles from Agadir the road passes the BARRAGE DE TAMZAOURT, whose waters irrigate 8,750 acres of the fertile Sous Plain. An area of several hundred acres around the lake is currently being reforested.

ARGANA

Squat, thorny argan trees grow by the thousands everywhere, casting their irregular

Hives like these can produce between 8½ and 10½ pints of honey per year.

"She was wearing a lot of jewelry: a necklace, a bracelet, a headband tied round her long braided hair intertwined with lengths of wool. ... In contrast to the brilliance of her jewelry, young Mina was simply dressed."
Henriette Célarié
Un mois au Maroc

shadow over the rocks to which they cling, and flourishing where nothing else can, not even weeds or cacti. The odd-looking argan trees ■ 30 are in fact the only type of vegetation to be seen between Agadir and the turning to the village of Argana, but at that point they disappear completely and are replaced by thujas and junipers. From Argana a very rough track initially running parallel to the road leads upward into the foothills of the High Atlas, crossing Tizi Maachou (5,577 feet) and rejoining the main road about 9 miles before Immi N'Tanoute, not far from a site where some impressive fossils of prehistoric animals, including brontosauruses and giant frogs and toads, can be seen, set in the rock face. They date from a time when this part of North Africa was still a vast swamp, before the Atlas Mountains were formed.

An agame

CAP RHIR

AGADIR

ATLANTIC OCEAN

CHICHAOUA

This busy town stands at the crossroads of the main Essaouira-Marrakesh and Agadir-Marrakesh

routes. The region is inhabited by the Ouled Bou Sbaa, incorporating members of the Maqil Arab tribe who have been resident in the Maghreb since the 13th century. The Merinids, who attempted to conquer them, managed to drive them out of the Tafilalet and the Draa Valley, and in the late 14th century they settled in the northern High Atlas. They are expert weavers and make the famous Chichaoua carpets. In the 1930's the French established a workshop in Chichaoua in an attempt to encourage the use of natural dyes. At the same time they introduced a new, much less ornate style of carpet that was better suited to European taste.

SUGAR. Approximately 2 miles outside Chichaoua, on the road to Chemaïa, stand the remains of an aqueduct which during the 16th century fed a large sugar mill. Throughout the reign of the Saadians, sugar was an inestimable source of wealth and was even used as a form of currency in certain circumstances. To give one example, the marble the Saadians used for the magnificent royal palaces of Marrakesh was imported from Carrara in Tuscany (Italy) and was paid for in sugar, pound for pound. Several aqueducts were required to irrigate the sugarcane plantations which, like the fourteen sugar mills, were owned by the ruling powers and run either by Europeans or Jews. The majority of the huge workforce consisted of slaves. Sugar was exported to Italy, France and England but competition from the West Indies and Brazil, combined with the conflicts that marked the end of the Saadian dynasty, brought about the decline and disintegration of the sugar industry.

Chichaoua carpets ● *74* are woven with one or two motifs in black against a dark red background. The patterns represent people or animals, usually a goat and a snake.

THE DANCERS OF IMMI N'TANOUTE This troupe (left) is performing a mixed *ahouach* ● *70*. The men play the *bendir* and clap their hands while the women dance.

321

▲ Agadir to Tiznit via Tafraoute

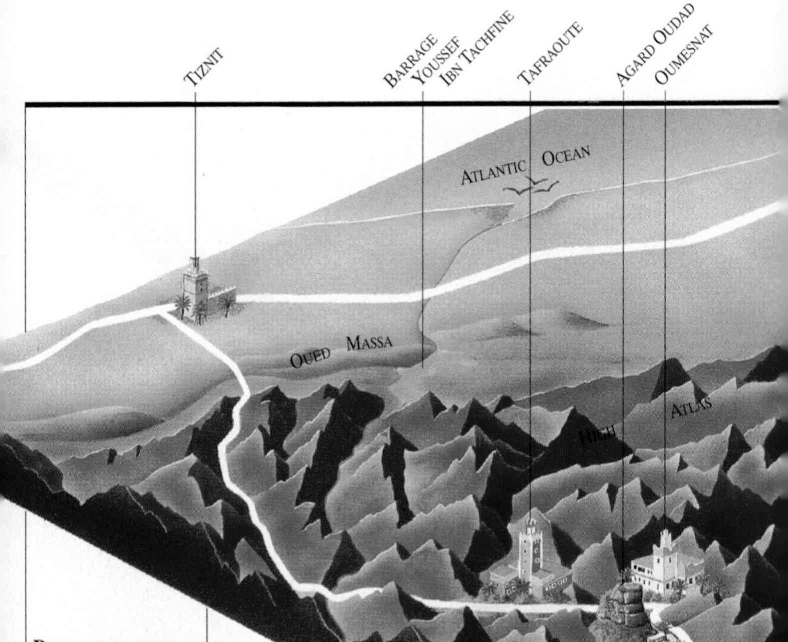

Tiznit
Barrage Youssef Ibn Tachfine
Tafraoute
Agard Oudad
Oumesnat
Atlantic Ocean
Oued Massa
High Atlas

Decorated doors
The doors of the old houses are made of wood, often walnut, decorated with geometric motifs. More modern doors are made of brightly painted metal.

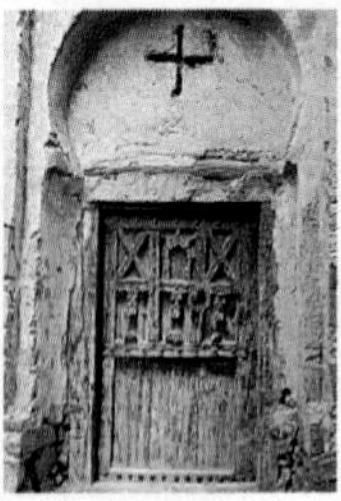

The road between Agadir and Tiznit crosses one of the most interesting regions in southwestern Morocco. It is a landscape of huge granite boulders interspersed with palm groves. Between the end of January and mid-February, when the almond trees are in bloom, it is a truly spectacular sight. An almond blossom festival involving all kinds of folkloric events takes place in February. Day and night, a large number of trucks, buses and taxis pass between Inezgane and Aït Melloul, making it one of the busiest routes in Morocco. After Aït Baha, an important agricultural center, the road climbs up into the Anti Atlas and crosses the Ilali region, famous for its *agadirs.* The *agadir* of Tioulit, a fortress on a rocky spur to the right of the road, is open to the public. Fortified granaries

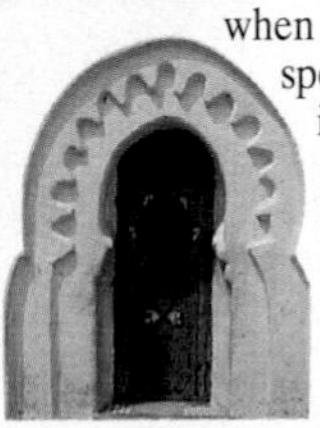

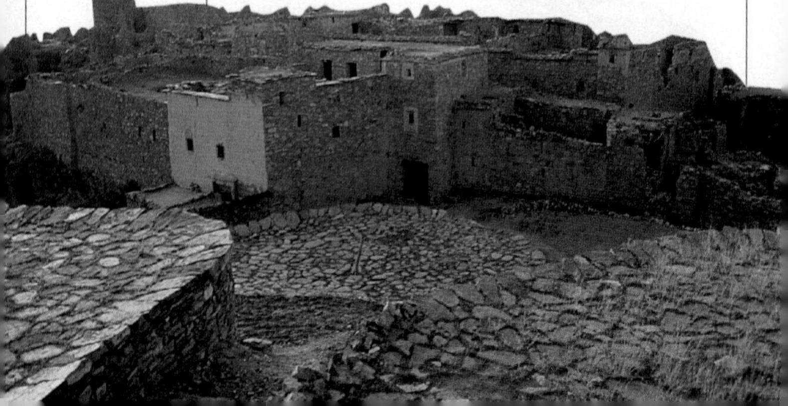

(*agadir* or *irghrem* depending on the dialect) are part of the landscape in the Maghreb. Whether as fortified villages, as in the Draa Valley, or as fortified oasis villages, they served the same purpose: to gather individual property under one common protective roof to prevent looting. The rules governing the *agadir* were contained in a common law whose authority sometimes covered an entire region. The 17th Ajarif charter, for example, applied to the granaries of the whole of the western and central Anti Atlas.

TAFRAOUTE

At an altitude of 3,937 feet, Tafraoute stands in the center of a cirque (a bowl-shaped formation) where outcrops of the pink granite have been weathered into rounded boulders and piled up in finely balanced, acrobatic formations. The town is surrounded by palm and olive groves and almond orchards. It is the regional capital of the Pays des Ameln, a tribe of Chleuch Berbers renowned for their highly developed sense of business. Many of the men have moved into the large towns and cities of Morocco and other countries where they own mainly grocers' shops. As a result the villages are inhabited chiefly by women, children and old people, who survive by harvesting almonds and working in the fields. Once they have earned enough money the men return home and usually build a house. These traditionally square, stone buildings rendered in pink ocher are built around a central courtyard and have a low-angle tower and narrow windows bordered in white.

Two days

ALMOND BLOSSOM FESTIVAL
The festival is held in February, when the pink and white almond trees are in bloom. Many sightseers come to Tafraoute at this time of year for this

splendid folk festival, featuring performances by the best dance troupes in the region and acrobats from nearby Sidi Ahmed and Moussa.

An abandoned kasbah (left) on the mountain road between Aït Baha and Tafraoute. The threshing area is in the foreground.

323

In the heart of the High Atlas, about one mile south of Tafraoute (above), is the village of Agard Oudad (right). It lies at the foot of a group of strangely shaped red granite rocks known locally as "The Finger" or "Napoleon's hat".

OUMESNAT
Many houses in the village, which are typical of the traditional houses of the Vallée des Ameln, have been restored by Moroccans working in Europe.

A track near Tafraoute leads to the

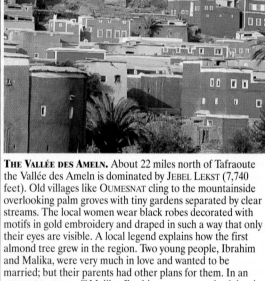

THE VALLÉE DES AMELN. About 22 miles north of Tafraoute the Vallée des Ameln is dominated by JEBEL LEKST (7,740 feet). Old villages like OUMESNAT cling to the mountainside overlooking palm groves with tiny gardens separated by clear streams. The local women wear black robes decorated with motifs in gold embroidery and draped in such a way that only their eyes are visible. A local legend explains how the first almond tree grew in the region. Two young people, Ibrahim and Malika, were very much in love and wanted to be married; but their parents had other plans for them. In an attempt to carry off Malika, Ibrahim set up an ambush but it went wrong and he was killed and buried on the spot. Malika ran away and was never seen again. Every year white flowers fall from a tree that sprang up in that place, its roots entwining the body of Ibrahim. This tree, an almond tree, is said to be Malika.

OUED MASSA

Beyond Tafraoute the landscape is arid until the road branches off to AÏT BELFA. Here a minor road leads to the estuary of the Oued Massa and the MARABOUT OF SIDI RBAT. A town (possibly the ancient city of Massa) is supposed to be buried beneath the sands of this barren landscape. According to legend it was from this beach that, in the 7th centuryAD, Okba Ibn Nafi, the Arab conqueror of the Magrheb, rode his horse into the sea to demonstrate that he had carried his conquest in the name of the Prophet to the ends of the earth. Massa was

"Blue Stones", a group of pink rocks that the Belgian artist Jean Verame painted blue in 1984.

commercially active in the 11th century, when it was frequented by the Genoese. In the 15th century the Portuguese set up a trading center here and an important religious community was founded by the prince El Jazouli. Two hundred years later Massa's importance was supplanted by that of Agadir. In 1991 the area around the Oued Massa estuary became the Sous Massa National Park, a nature and wildfowl reserve covering an area of 32,500 acres. It is located partly inland and partly on the coast and is home to many species of birds, amphibians and reptiles. It can be visited from Agadir in a single day's outing.

TIZNIT

The town of Tiznit was built by the sultan Moulay Hassan in 1881 during an extensive campaign to bring the tribes of the region under his control and drive out the Europeans. As a result of European trade it expanded rapidly and, because of its position midway between Paris and Dakar, was the starting point for overseas routes flown by the French airmail company, the Compagnie Générale Aéropostale.

EL HIBA. The town of Tiznit is closely associated with Moroccan resistance to the Treaty of Fez. In 1912, only a few days after Morocco had become a French protectorate, it was here that Ahmed el Hiba, then aged about 35, had himself proclaimed sultan at the mosque of Tiznit and launched his campaign against the authority of France. El Hiba, also known as the "Blue Sultan" because he wore the blue robes of the nomads, rallied the people of the Sous Valley to his cause and set up his headquarters at Taroudant. He reached Marrakesh and came face to face with Colonel Mangin's troops but was forced to withdraw to the extreme south of the region. He died in 1919, without having been able to relaunch his offensive.

CITY CENTER. The Bab Oulad Jarrar, Tiznit's main gate, is set in 4 miles of crenelated rampart walls made of pink *pisé*. The polygonal *mechouar*, surrounded by shops and workshops with striped blinds, is the heart and commercial center of Tiznit. Silver Berber jewelry for sale in the nearby jewelers' souk is often decorated with the hand of Fatima ● 66, an ancient talismanic motif signifying that the wearer is protected by the Prophet's daughter. The motif is also used in tattooing and on the walls of houses. Daggers and swords with elaborately carved scabbards are a specialty of the craftsmen of Tiznit. North of the *mechouar* is the Great Mosque, with a minaret rather unusually surmounted by waterspouts on which, so it is said, rest the souls of the departed.

LALLA TIZNIT. Near the mosque is the Lalla Tiznit spring. Like the town, it is named after a woman, who repenting her sins, became a marabout (saint) and is said to have lived on this spot.

SOUS MASSA NATIONAL PARK
Half the world's population of bald ibis (above) live in this remarkable nature reserve. The best time to visit the park is in winter, when tens of thousands of migrating birds gather. In summer flamingos, herons and great cormorants, as well as wild boar and many other animals, can be seen there. The vegetation consists mainly of euphorbia (above center) and acacias, which are planted to stabilize sand dunes.

The Great Mosque of Tiznit (left).

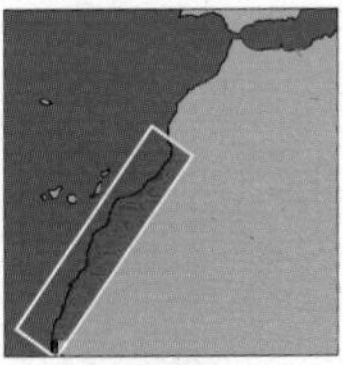

🚗 Four days

About 102 miles south of Tiznit lies the Plage d'Aglou. A walk of 2 miles along the beach leads to a tiny natural port where caves hollowed out of the rocks are used by the fishermen. The coast road passes through the village of GOURIZIM, perched high above the sea, and runs behind the beautiful beach at the foot of the BORJ OF MIRLEFT.

SIDI IFNI

The town of Sidi Ifni stands on a rocky plateau 165 feet above the Atlantic. The Spaniards took it over in the 15th century to control the route to the Canary Islands. They were driven out by the Saadians in 1524 but returned four hundred years later. The town was restored to Morocco in 1969 but has retained its 1930's Spanish colonial style.

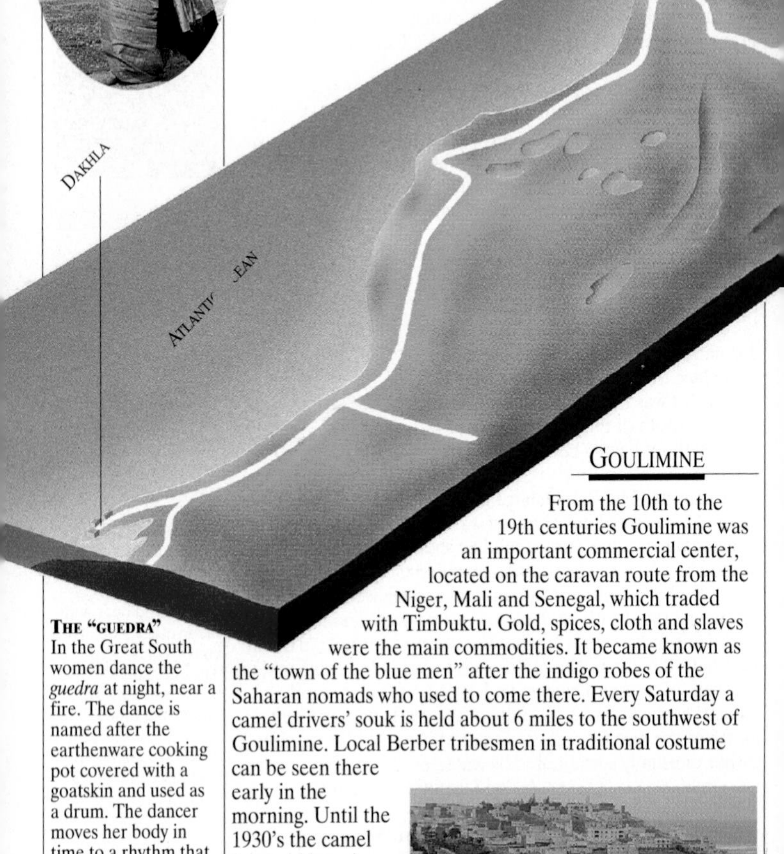

CAP JUBY

TARFAYA

DAKHLA

ATLANTIC OCEAN

GOULIMINE

From the 10th to the 19th centuries Goulimine was an important commercial center, located on the caravan route from the Niger, Mali and Senegal, which traded with Timbuktu. Gold, spices, cloth and slaves were the main commodities. It became known as the "town of the blue men" after the indigo robes of the Saharan nomads who used to come there. Every Saturday a camel drivers' souk is held about 6 miles to the southwest of Goulimine. Local Berber tribesmen in traditional costume can be seen there early in the morning. Until the 1930's the camel fair held here in July was the largest in the Sahara and, in its heyday, up to forty thousand

THE "GUEDRA"
In the Great South women dance the *guedra* at night, near a fire. The dance is named after the earthenware cooking pot covered with a goatskin and used as a drum. The dancer moves her body in time to a rhythm that gets faster and faster until she faints.

Sidi Ifni (right).

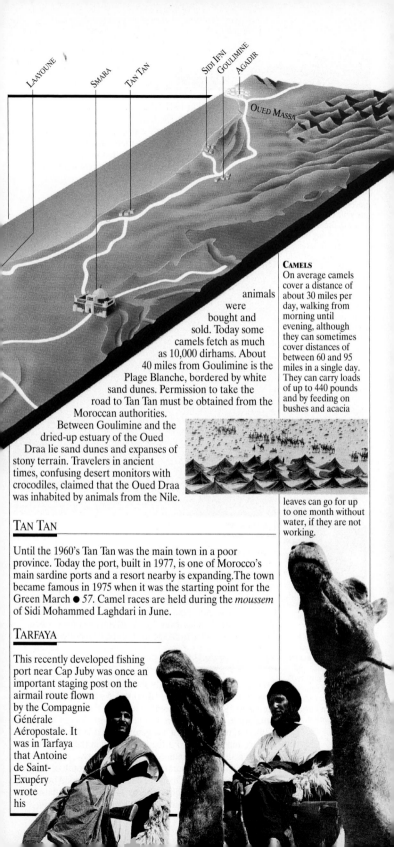

LAAYOUNE   SMARA   TAN TAN   SIDI IFNI   GOULIMINE   AGADIR

OUED MASSA

CAMELS

On average camels cover a distance of about 30 miles per day, walking from morning until evening, although they can sometimes cover distances of between 60 and 95 miles in a single day. They can carry loads of up to 440 pounds and by feeding on bushes and acacia

animals were bought and sold. Today some camels fetch as much as 10,000 dirhams. About 40 miles from Goulimine is the Plage Blanche, bordered by white sand dunes. Permission to take the road to Tan Tan must be obtained from the Moroccan authorities.

Between Goulimine and the dried-up estuary of the Oued Draa lie sand dunes and expanses of stony terrain. Travelers in ancient times, confusing desert monitors with crocodiles, claimed that the Oued Draa was inhabited by animals from the Nile.

leaves can go for up to one month without water, if they are not working.

TAN TAN

Until the 1960's Tan Tan was the main town in a poor province. Today the port, built in 1977, is one of Morocco's main sardine ports and a resort nearby is expanding. The town became famous in 1975 when it was the starting point for the Green March ● 57. Camel races are held during the *moussem* of Sidi Mohammed Laghdari in June.

TARFAYA

This recently developed fishing port near Cap Juby was once an important staging post on the airmail route flown by the Compagnie Générale Aéropostale. It was in Tarfaya that Antoine de Saint-Exupéry wrote his

"The blue men
advanced along the
invisible track,
towards Smara, freer
than any being on this
earth. Around them,
as far as the eye could
see, were the moving
crests of the dunes,
those constantly
changing waves of
space. The bare feet
of the women and
children left a light
imprint in the sand
that was immediately
erased by the wind.**"**
J.-M.G. Le Clézio

In Smara the kasbah
of Maa el Aïnine
(above) included an
unfinished mosque
(of which the circular
cupola, arcades and
pillars have survived),
a library, a Koranic
school, grain silos, a
hammam and living
accommodation.

novel *Courrier Sud* in 1927. The landscape also provided the
inspiration for his work *The Little Prince*. The road then
crosses vast arid, mostly sandy expanses of terrain. This is the
heart of the territory of the "blue men". Today the way of life
of these nomadic desert tribes is threatened, their flocks are
decreasing and they are becoming increasingly sedentary.

LAAYOUNE

Laayoune, founded by the Spaniards in the 1930's, is the
economic capital of the region. The town receives large
subsidies from the Moroccan government, which is keen to
develop this part of the western Sahara, restored to Morocco
after General Franco's death in 1975. The port is used as a
transit port for phosphates and is linked to the mines of
Boukra, over 60 miles away, by an automatic conveyor belt.
The beach, 15 miles from the town, is heavily polluted.

THE SAHARAN PROVINCES

SMARA. The seat of the brotherhood founded in 1887 by sheik
Maa el Aïnine (father of El Hiba) ● *325* was attacked by the
French in 1913 and occupied for a day by the Spaniards.
BOUJDOUR. This provincial capital is situated near Cap
Boujdour, which Catalan navigators passed in the 14th
century and where the Portuguese landed in the 15th century.
Fishing is the town's main commercial activity.
DAKHLA. The fishing port of Dakhla, on the mouth of the Rio
de Oro (renamed the Oued el Fouch), was founded by the
Spaniards in 1884 as Villa Cisneros. Given the abundance of
fish along this Atlantic coast, it has a promising future.

PRACTICAL
INFORMATION

BY AIR

From Great Britain: Scheduled flights depart from Heathrow and Gatwick. Charter flights, which also depart from Manchester, are

available to the main resorts.
From the US: Connecting flights to destinations in Morocco depart from London, Paris, Brussels, Frankfurt and Madrid.

ferries to Tangier and Ceuta depart from Algeciras, Málaga and Almeria in Spain, from Sète in France and from Gilbraltar. There

are six or seven sailings daily from Algeciras. The crossing takes 2 hours and costs £10–£21 (US $15–$30) per person. There are two sailings a week from Sète to Tangier. The crossing takes 38 hours and costs

FORMALITIES

A full passport is required. A visa is not necessary for US and UK nationals. Visitors can stay for three months. If you wish to extend your stay, apply to the local police department. If you take your own car to Morocco, you will need your driver's license and international insurance. If you intend to hire a care there, take your driver's license and a credit card.
No vaccinations are compulsory for Morocco, but for tourists intending to visit the desert or the Atlas Mountains, a vaccination against hepatitis A is advised.

BY TRAIN AND FERRY

Continental trains run from London Victoria via France and Spain.

BY CAR AND FERRY

To drive to Morocco, cross to France or northern Spain. Cars can be transported on overnight trains through Europe.

FERRIES

Passenger and car

about £140 (US $210) per person. Rates for cars range from about £45 ($67) (from Algeciras) to around £170 ($255) (from Sète), and about £15 to £65 ($22 to $98) for motorcyles. An inclusive return ticket from Britain to Morocco is the best value.

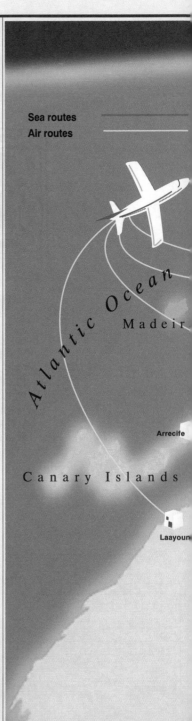

Sea routes
Air routes

Atlantic Ocean

Madeir

Arrecife

Canary Islands

Laayoun

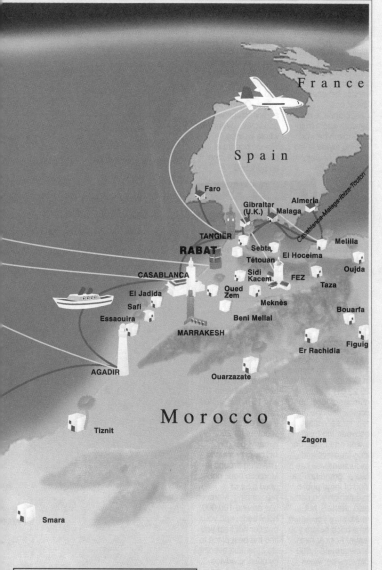

Cost and length of journey airport-city center by taxi		
Casablanca	19 miles	150 DH
Rabat	6 miles	50 DH
Tangier	9 miles	75 DH
Fez	9 miles	75 DH
Agadir	17 miles	130 DH
Marrakesh	4 miles	30 DH

BY TRAIN

The ONCF (railroad company) runs between all major towns and cities in Morocco. The network consists of an express shuttle service between Rabat and Casablanca, a rail network and a train-and-coach network serving towns in the south (particularly Essaouira and Agadir) and on the Mediterranean coast (Tetouan and Nador). For example the journey from Fez to Agadir via Marrakesh (470 miles) takes 12 hours, including 4 hours by coach between Marrakesh and Agadir (170 miles). On the train-and-coach network, one ticket covers the whole journey. Tickets bought at the station do not have to be punched.

AUTHORIZATION TO VISIT THE SOUTH
If you want to visit the Great South (the area beyond Dakhla), you have to apply to the Ministry of the Interior in Rabat for official authorization.

BY ROAD

The national bus network CTM (Compagnie des Transports du Maroc) in Casablanca (tel: 02 25 29 01) and a number of local bus companies operate regular services between the main towns and cities. For long journeys and excursions you can hire a "grand taxi", a kind of large public taxi (which you can also charter), but make sure you agree on a price before you leave! For car hire allow around 1,000 dirhams per week and an additional 150 dirhams per day. For motorcycle hire allow around 300 dirhams per day.

CITY TRANSPORT
In towns and cities you can hire a "petit taxi" for between 10 and 15 dirhams. You can also hire bicycles for 60 dirhams and scooters for 250 dirhams per day.

INTER-CITY TRAVEL
Traveling around in Morocco does not need a lot of preplanning. Morocco has around 100,000 hotel beds, and your hotelier will help you find the best place to stay the next evening by offering advice and booking a room for you in advance.

Road	P27
Motorway	
O.N.C.F. (railway)	
T.N.R (Express train)	
Coach and rail link	

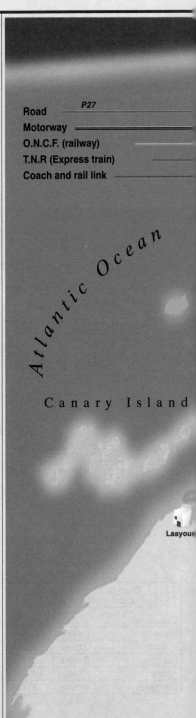

Atlantic Ocean

Canary Island

Laayou

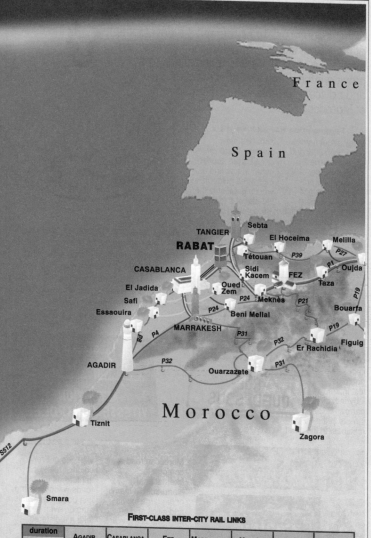

France

Spain

Morocco

TANGIER
RABAT
Sebta
El Hoceima
Melilla
Tétouan
Sidi Kacem
FEZ
Oujda
CASABLANCA
Oued Zem
Meknès
Taza
El Jadida
Beni Mellal
Bouarfa
Safi
P24
P21
Essaouira
MARRAKESH
P31
P32
Figuig
Er Rachidia
AGADIR
Ouarzazate
P31
Tiznit
Zagora
Smara

FIRST-CLASS INTER-CITY RAIL LINKS

duration / price	AGADIR	CASABLANCA	FEZ	MARRAKESH	MEKNÈS	RABAT	TANGIER
AGADIR						8 h 30 * / 210 DH	
CASABLANCA			3 h 30 / 121.50 DH	2 h 30 / 92 DH	3 h 30 / 99 DH	50 mn / 32 DH	4 h / 143.50 DH
FEZ		3 h 30 / 121.50 DH		6 h 30 / 212.50 DH	1 h / 20.50 DH	3 h 30 / 87 DH	3 h / 117 DH
MARRAKESH		2 h 30 / 92 DH	6 h 30 / 212.50 DH		5 h 30 / 190.50 DH	3 h 30 / 123.50 DH	6 h 30 / 234 DH
MEKNÈS		3 h 30 / 99 DH	1 h / 20.50 DH	5 h 30 / 190.50 DH		2 h 30 / 66.50 DH	3 h 30 / 96.50 DH
RABAT	8 h 30 * / 210 DH	50 mn / 32 DH	3 h 30 / 87 DH	3 h 30 / 123.50 DH	2 h 30 / 66.50 DH		3 h / 109.50 DH
TANGIER		4 h / 143.50 DH	3 h / 117 DH	6 h 30 / 234 DH	3 h 30 / 96.5 DH	3 h / 109.50 DH	

* Train-and-coach service: train from Rabat and coach to Agadir.

333

◆ FINDING YOUR WAY AROUND

You will soon get used to finding your way around in this country of cultural, linguistic and climatic contrasts. To encourage the development of the tourist industry the Moroccan government has set up special tourist organizations that provide information and offer practical help and advice to enable you make the most of Morocco.

FINDING YOUR WAY AROUND TOWN

Many street names have been changed since Moroccan independence. Although the pre-1956 street signs may have a more attractive appearance they are particularly uninformative and do not help you find your way around. Signposts in the new districts of larger towns and cities are in French and Arabic. However, no matter how careful you are, it is virtually impossible not to get lost in the labyrinth of narrow streets in the medinas. In the most

popular tourist districts refuse offers of help from "tourist hunters" and find a registered guide. If you do get lost in the old part of a town, ask a young boy to show you the way and don't forget to thank him for his help by offering him a few dirhams.

GUIDES

Registered guides are pleasant and efficient. They are licensed by the Ministry of Tourism and wear an official identity disk. Don't hesitate to call on their services if you want to visit the town or do some shopping in the souks. To hire a guide allow between 100 and 150 dirhams per day.

ROAD SIGNS

Moroccan road signs conform to international standards. In many of the large towns and cities and on main roads signs are usually in both French and Arabic. In rural areas the few signs in French that you will see are

vestiges of French colonial rule. Don't venture off the main roads without having first bought a reliable map or, even better, take a registered guide with you, who will also be able to act as an interpreter if necessary.

These old street signs may be picturesque, but they are also uninformative, out-of-date and misleading.

BASICS

Your hotel is a real mine of information and the hotel staff will often provide more practical help and advice than you will find at the local Tourist Office. If you ask, your hotelier will find you a guide, suggest suitable trips and interesting places to visit and even book hotel rooms in advance for the next stage of your journey. Hotel shops cater to tourists and usually stock such things as souvenirs, pieces of traditional handicraft and antiques. Prices tend to be higher than in town or in souks, but you may be able to get a bargain by haggling.

ELECTRICITY

Some wall sockets in Morocco are only suitable for low-voltage appliances. Take care and check with your host or hotelier. Two-pin round plugs are the norm.

OPENING HOURS

Museums are open from 9am to 12 noon and from 3pm to 5.30pm. Shops are usually open from 9.30am to 1pm and from 3pm to 7.30pm. Banks and offices, open 8am to 3.30pm, do not close at lunchtime during the summer. The time in Morocco is Greenwich Mean Time, five hours ahead of New York.

NEWSPAPERS

The *International Herald Tribune* and the previous day's edition of English newspapers are available in most large towns and cities. The Sunday edition of *L'Opinion*, the French-language daily, carries a supplement in English. *El Alaam* (The Flag) and *El Anneba* (The News) are two of Morocco's Arabic-language daily papers.

CLIMATE

Differences between night and day temperatures can be extreme. The contrast between full sun and a cool house or shaded street can also be dramatic.

RAINFALL AND HOURS OF SUNSHINE

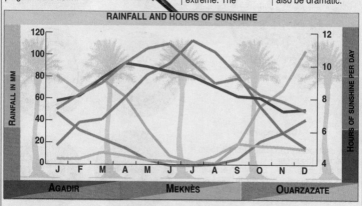

AGADIR   MEKNÈS   OUARZAZATE

ANNUAL TEMPERATURES

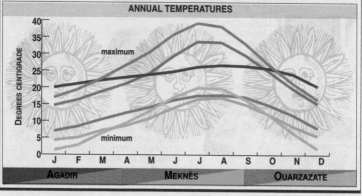

AGADIR   MEKNÈS   OUARZAZATE

Although Arabic is the national language in Morocco, French is spoken in most towns and cities. Banks and most businesses accept credit cards.

CURRENCY

In early 1994 the pound was worth 14 dirham (DH) and the US dollar 9.6 dirham. Currency consists of 100, 50 and 10 dirham notes and 5, 1, 0.10 and 0.05 dirham coins. It cannot be obtained outside Morocco. All airports have bureaux de change.

CASH POINTS

A few cash points can be found in the larger towns and cities. Banks are generally open from 8.15am to 11.30am and from 2.15pm to 4.30pm. Opening hours are shorter during Ramadan and longer during the summer, when banks do not close at lunchtime. Major credit cards are accepted in most hotels, restaurants and antique shops.

WARNING

The dirham cannot be exchanged for foreign currency and cannot be taken out of the country. All local currency must be spent in Morocco or changed at the airport before you leave. Use your credit card for purchases wherever possible.

COST OF TELEPHONE CALLS

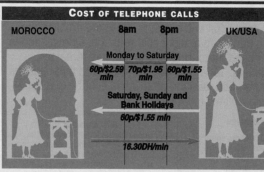

MOROCCO   8am   8pm   **UK/USA**

Monday to Saturday

60p/$2.59 min   70p/$1.95 min   60p/$1.55 min

Saturday, Sunday and Bank Holidays

60p/$1.55 min

16.30DH/min

DIALLING CODES
Casablanca: 02
Settat: 03 (Beni Mellal, El Jadida)
Marrakesh: 04 (Essaouira, Ouarzazate, Safi)
Fez: 05 (Er Rachidia, Meknès)
Oujda: 06 (Nador, Figuig)
Rabat: 07 (Kénitra, Salé, Sidi Kacem)
Laayoune: 08 (Agadir, Tan Tan)
Tangier: 09 (Al Hoceima, Tétouan)

TELEPHONES

Since 1989 15 percent of public spending in Morocco has been devoted to improving the telecommunications system. All main towns and cities have direct dialling.

MAKING A CALL
To make a local call (within the same town or area) dial the appropriate six-figure number. To call a town in another area, dial the prescribed code for that area (for example, the code for Rabat is 07) followed by the number. To call Britain from Morocco dial 00 44. To call Morocco from Britain dial 010 212 followed by the second figure of the area code (if calling Rabat, dial 7) and then the six-figure number you are trying to reach. To call the US from Morocco dial 011 212 followed by the second figure of the area code and the number.

THE SPEAKING CLOCK
Dial 17

POSTAGE

Postage on a letter from Morocco to Britain is 4.80DH, or 5DH to the US. Postage to Morocco from Britain is 41 pence, or $0.50 from the US.

SOME PRICES

1 ROOM: 196 DH (***) TO 3000 DH (*****)

1 MEAL: 15 DH (SANDWICH) TO 350 DH (MEAL + CABARET)

MUSEUM: 10 DH

COFFEE: 2 DH (IN A CAFÉ) TO 15 DH (IN LARGE HOTELS)

CAKES AND PASTRIES: 5 TO 7 DH

PETROL: 7 DH PER LITER (¼ GALLON)

1 WEEKEND AT THE HOTEL "LA MAMOUNIA", MARRAKESH: 7,000 TO 9,000 DH (INCLUDING FLIGHT)

TOUR "THE IMPERIAL CITIES IN A WEEK": 7,000 TO 8,000 DH (INCLUDING FLIGHT)

Morocco is a friendly and welcoming country but living there means respecting its laws, traditions and customs. Religion, architecture, dress and trade are part of an ancient culture that has developed in a harsh environment and, furthermore, one that has remained unchanged for centuries. Today Morocco is still a land that beckons the intrepid adventurer, although the great Atlas and the awesome Sahara are no longer entirely untamed.

MONEY AND BUSINESS

Attitudes to money in Morocco are quite different from those in the Western world. Charity is one of the duties of all good Muslims and a service rendered deserves a reward, no matter how small. In Moroccan towns if someone helps you park your car or keeps an eye on it for you in your absence, it is customary to thank him by giving him a few dirhams. Similarly it would be discourteous not to give a *bakchich* to the boy who showed you the way out of the medina ● *92* when you'd lost your way.

HAGGLING

This is an intrinsic part of the Moroccan way of life. The vendor's main objective is not necessarily to negotiate a final price, which both parties often know in advance, but more to take the opportunity of making the buyer's acquaintance. If the vendor agrees to lower his price (and similarly if the buyer accepts an increase), it is an acknowledgment

of the time spent and the pleasure gained from the negotiation. Conversation is by no means restricted to the transaction in hand. Quite often the vendor will, in the course of the conversation, offer his customer mint tea in an attempt to

win him over. Today haggling usually goes on only in the souks of the medina. When you go there don't hesitate to enlist the help of an official guide. He will probably steer you in a particular direction to the stalls of his friends, but what they have to offer is likely to be just as interesting as the goods on the stalls anywhere else in the market and with his guidance you will be less likely to end up paying over the odds for a magnificent white elephant!

REFRESHMENT

Drink only bottled or boiled water. Never drink from springs or streams and don't accept fresh fruit or ice cubes, which may have been washed in or made from contaminated water and might cause you serious stomach problems.

PRECAUTIONS

Although you are unlikely to be bitten by a poisonous snake, it is always wise to carry an antivenin in the desert ■ *36* and the Atlas Mountains ■ *26*. If you are camping ◆ *346* make sure you clear the area around your tent. It's worth shaking out your shoes in the morning in case a scorpion or a sand viper has crept in there during the night. Don't forget that the Atlas are high mountains near the tropics and that where their eastern slopes end, the Sahara begins. The air is sharp and dry. A protective cream and some kind of headgear are precautions against sunburn and sunstroke. In an emergency, dial 15 for first aid.
If you are driving and decide to go off the beaten track,

remember to take an ample supply of water, spare wheels and a can of gasoline. Drive especially carefully at night, as obstacles and vehicles may not be particularly well marked.

SOME ADDITIONAL ADVICE

As a general rule non-Muslims ▲ *222* may not enter mosques. There are a few specific exceptions. Always ask permission before taking photographs of people in the street. If you are speaking French use "vous" when speaking to adults, even if they use "tu". Although Moroccans tend not to use "vous" they are aware of its use and implications for European French speakers.

Women are advised to dress in a restrained manner. Short, tight-fitting or low-cut clothes are not suitable. Remember that, although the days may be hot, evenings and nights are very chilly, so pack a few warm clothes.

The mint tea ceremony

> "FEZ WITH YOUR NIGHTS OF RAMADAN! NIGHTS OF RAMADAN!
> WHATEVER MAY BEFALL, I WILL REMAIN FAITHFUL TO THE
> MEMORY OF MY ENCHANTED CITY!"
>
> AHMED SEFRIOUI

Festivals

	J	F	M	A	M	J	J	A	S	O	N	D
TAFRAOUTE												
Almond blossom festival	●											
BENI MELLAL / AL HOCEIMA												
Cotton festival			●									
EL KELAA DES M'GOUNA (OUARZAZATE)												
Festival of roses				●								
SEFROU (FEZ)												
Cherry harvest					●							
IMMOUZER DES IDA / OUTANANE (AGADIR)												
Honey festival						●						
AL HOCEIMA												
Festival of the sea						●						
AGADIR												
Festival of oranges						●						
IMMOUZER DU KANDAR (FEZ)												
Festival of apples and pears							●					
ASILAH												
International music festival							●					
MEKNÈS												
Festival of fantasias								●				
MARRAKESH												
National folklore festival								●				
ILMICHIL												
Marriage "moussem"								●				
TISSA (FEZ)												
Festival of the horse									●			
ER RACHIDIA / ERFOUD												
Date festival									●			
BERKANE (FEZ)												
Festival of clementines												●

RELIGIOUS FESTIVALS

FIRST DAY OF MOHAREM: MUSLIM NEW YEAR

ACHOURA: 10TH DAY OF THE MONTH OF MOHAREM

AÏD ES SEGHIR: THE ENDING OF THE FAST OF RAMADAN

AÏD EL KEBIR: 70 DAYS AFTER AÏD ES SEGHIR

MOULOUD: FESTIVAL OF THE PROPHET'S BIRTH

PUBLIC HOLIDAYS AND FESTIVALS

	J	F	M	A	M	J	J	A	S	O	N	D
NEW YEAR'S DAY	1											
NATIONAL DAY	11				23							
FEAST OF THE THRONE			3									
LABOR DAY					1							
YOUTH DAY							9					
OATH OF ALLEGIANCE OF OUED ED DAHAB								14				
FESTIVAL OF THE REVOLUTION, THE KING AND THE PEOPLE								20				
GREEN MARCH DAY											6	
INDEPENDENCE DAY											18	

339

Morocco is divided into four main regions: the coast (fishing and processing industries), the plains and plateaux of the northwest (agriculture and commerce), the Rif and Atlas mountains (livestock and forestry) and the desert (oasis crops and mining industries).

A YOUNG, URBAN POPULATION

Over 50 percent of the population of Morocco is under the age of 21. Four million young Moroccans attend school, but in this developing economy 31 percent of 15- to

POPULATION DISTRIBUTION IN 1992	
CASABLANCA	2.8 million
RABAT - SALÉ	1.1 million
FEZ	0.7 million
OUJDA	0.6 million
MARRAKESH	0.6 million
Total	5.8 million
OTHER TOWNS	7.2 million
RURAL AREAS	13 million

24-year-olds living in urban areas are unemployed. An exodus of between 100,000 and 300,000 people per year from rural areas is swelling the population of towns and cities. But this growth is not equaled by a comparable increase in the number of jobs. The resulting discrepancy is severe. According to a census taken in 1982 57.5 percent of Morocco's industrial employment is centered in Casablanca alone.

AGRICULTURE, LIVESTOCK AND FISHING

Morocco's agricultural foodstuffs industry supplies the home market while, at the same time looking to overseas trade. The industry has not succeeded in its aim of making Morocco self-sufficient in food since two commodities still have to be imported: grain and sugar. This despite, or possibly because of, the quality of Moroccan confectionery. The Moroccans are in fact the world's greatest consumers of sugar, each person getting through 68 pounds per year. Programs of mechanization and irrigation, together with more intensive production methods, have already improved the average yield per acre and an ambitious schedule of dam construction should provide the water and energy necessary for further modernization. The results of this policy are striking: 12 percent of the land produces 25 percent of the crops and 80 percent of the agricultural produce sold abroad. These exports consist mainly of citrus fruit ■ 44, wine and fish products ■ 48. They are the main

source of Morocco's foreign income, in spite of the falling off in demand caused by Spain and Portugal, two of Morocco's traditional customers, joining the European Community. As well as being self-sufficient, small family farms growing crops and raising livestock help to keep the home market supplied. Forestry fulfills a similar role, with homegrown wood currently providing 40 percent of Morocco's domestic energy requirements. The fishing industry, which concentrates on exploiting the sardine shoals off the Moroccan coast, has created an important subsidiary industry – canning. Fishing is considered to be the country's third major natural resource, after agriculture and mining, although it only employs 130,000 people.

Two faces of traditional craftsmanship: the cobbler and the goldsmith.

MINING AND INDUSTRY

For many years Morocco exported its raw materials to the developed countries. Since independence, however, industry has served local demand. Today Morocco is the world's leading producer and exporter of phosphates, and the revenue this generates is being used to finance an ambitious and forward-looking industrial development program in the refinery, chemical and agricultural sectors. Today the industries that are geared to an international market, such as carpets, clothing, leather and electronic assembly, are those requiring a large work force. Some 85 percent of Morocco's textile production is exported (althought the raw materials for this industry are imported). In 1990, the industrial sector accounted for 17.5 percent of Morocco's GDP.

CRAFTS AND COMMERCE

Although the traditional crafts industry has run into difficulties, partly because of competition from certain other sectors of industry, producing and marketing crafts products is still central to the Moroccan economy.

The crafts business, in which one-third of the working population is employed, is geared to serving a dense network of markets and retailers. The sector has great growth potential and this has drawn investment away from industry and exports, hampering their development. This means that much of Morocco's economic activity is not affected by fluctuations in the international markets, but the country's weak industrial base limits its ability to buy or manufacture the amount of machinery necessary for real economic expansion. However, the fruits of that traditional craftsmanship, ranging from carpets to jewelry, can be seen in abundance in the souks of Morocco.

TRANSPORT AND COMMUNICATION

In recent years almost one-quarter of government spending has been devoted to the systematic development of transport and communications infrastructures in Morocco. The network of roads and railroads established during the French protectorate mainly to transport raw materials to the ports, is gradually being extended. Today Morocco's main economic centers are connected by a tightly knit road and rail network and by a modern and efficient system of telecommunications.

Morocco's sardine ports are the largest in the world.

Royal Palace, Rabat.

Bab el Mansour, Meknès.

If you have a week to spend in Morocco, you can travel around on a variety of different itineraries. Tours of the Imperial Cities, a journey across the Atlas Mountains or a trip to the Great South can be made in groups or individually. The tour of the Imperial Cities described here includes a stay in the four imperial cities of Marrakesh, Rabat, Meknès and Fez, and a visit to Casablanca, economic capital of Morocco. If you start your tour in Marrakesh, you can go on to Rabat via Casablanca.

DAY ONE

MORNING.
The best way to get the feel of Casablanca in a few hours is to set out on foot from the Place des Nations-Unies ▲ *141* and walk toward the Marché Central ▲ *140*, along Casablanca's most picturesque streets. The shops and stalls sell a range of traditionally made craft items as well as locally grown fruit ● *45*, vegetables ● *44* and spices ● *46*. Walk through the Quartier Habbous, past the Royal Palace and then along the corniche, from where there is a truly splendid view. The Boulevard de la Corniche is bordered by cafés and restaurants as far as the resort of Aïn Diab. The restaurant *A ma Bretagne* ▲ *140*, ◆ *363* serves some of the finest cuisine in Morocco.

AFTERNOON.
Rabat can be reached in less than an hour along the freeway. From the esplanade of the Hassan Tower you can admire the minaret of the unfinished mosque ▲ *170* and the Mohammed V Mausoleum ▲ *170*, and catch the changing of the guard. Although you will not be able to go inside, the Dar el Makhzen (Royal Palace) ▲ *174* should be seen from the outside and from there you can also take in the Merinid tombs of the Chellah Necropolis ▲ *171*.

EVENING.
The rooms of the *Hôtel Safir* ◆ *380* overlook the Oued Bou Regreg and Salé ▲ *175*. Dinner at the *Dinarjat* is recommended.

DAY TWO

MORNING.
Don't leave Rabat without visiting the Kasbah of the Oudayas ▲ *166*, the Andalusian gardens and the Oudaya Museum ▲ *168*, ◆ *378*. Allow yourself time at the end of the morning to wander through the streets and do some leisurely shopping in the antique shops and bazaars. Among the antiques sold in the fascinating Rue des Consuls ▲ *166*, lined with old houses, you will find beautifully written and illuminated Korans ● *62*, which in good condition will cost at least 1,000 dirhams. Korans bound in gold-stamped leather can cost anything from 10,000 to 15,000 dirhams.

AFTERNOON.
Meknès, founded in the 17th century and the former capital of Moulay Ismaïl, is 80 miles away, about an hour's drive from Rabat. On arrival, take a walk round the medina ▲ *240*, where you can see the Bab el Mansour ● *94*, ▲ *239*, one of the most beautiful gates in Morocco and the Bou Inania Medersa ▲ *222, 241*. Late afternoon is the best time to visit the Imperial City ▲ *236* and the Moulay Ismaïl Mausoleum ▲ *238*, ◆ *374*.

EVENING.
Those staying at the *Hôtel Transatlantique* ◆ *374* will have an enchanting view of the medina at night.

The ancient city of Volubilis.

The Bab Bou Jeloud stands between Fez el Jdid and Fez el Bali.

In the Middle Atlas.

DAY THREE

MORNING.
Before going on to Fez, which is approximately 40 miles from Meknès, visit Moulay Idriss ▲ 250. The nearby ruins of the Roman city of Volubilis ▲ 243 stretched out at the foot of Jebel Zerhoun ▲ 242 are extremely impressive and make a fascinating tour. In Fez, the delightful *Hôtel Palais Jamaï* ◆ 369 situated near the Bab Guissa in Fez el Bali offers visitors the opportunity of staying in a former palace. Today this splendid building is richly decorated in Hispano-Moresque style.

DAY FOUR

MORNING.
It is best to make an early start if you are visiting the medina ▲ 221 of Fez. You can wander at leisure among the pedestrians and mules (no vehicles are allowed inside the medina) and watch bakers, potters, coppersmiths and a host of other craftsmen at work. It will take you an hour to reach the historic Kairouyine Mosque ▲ 224, which you can view from the outside, and to visit the Bou Inania ▲ 222 and Attarine ▲ 224 medersa. Then, after inspecting the splendid fountain decorated with *zellige* and the 17th-century *fondouk* ▲ 223 in the Place Nejjarine, sample the Fasi specialities of the *Dar Saada* ◆ 367.

AFTERNOON.
If you decide to spend the afternoon in Fez el Jdid, don't forget to take your camera! The three gleaming gilt-bronze doors of the Royal Palace ▲ 218 and the facades of the houses in the *mellah* ▲ 218 are well worth capturing on film. Leave time in the late afternoon, when it is not so hot, to visit the colorful Tannery Quarter ▲ 226. Stop at the Dar Nejjarine, a former palace, that today houses a display of old and modern carpets, some of which are for sale. In the evening you can take the air while you stroll along the ramparts and enjoy the splendid panoramic view ▲ 230 over the medina and new town.

DAY FIVE

If you don't know the Middle Atlas ■ 28, you may want to take a whole day to drive from Fez to Marrakesh. The road follows a very attractive route through the most beautiful cedar forests ▲ 257 in Morocco and it is worth stopping in Ifrane ▲ 251, Azrou ▲ 257 and Khenifra ▲ 258. In summer you will come across a good many hikers in the area. The Middle Atlas is ideal for picnics, and you will have a choice of spots with stunning views, but don't be surprised if you are invited to eat with the local people! In the afternoon carry on to Kasba Tadla and Beni Mellal at the foot of the Jebel Tassemit ▲ 307. You will have covered 300 miles by the time you catch sight of the ramparts of Marrakesh ▲ 260, aptly named "Pearl of the South".

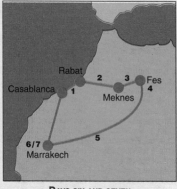

DAYS SIX AND SEVEN

You could follow the itinerary outlines on the preceding pages for a weekend in Marrakesh. Before you leave bid the city a final farewell by joining the groups of spectators in the Place Djemaa el Fna ▲ 277. For a few dirhams you can watch *chleuch* dances or the acrobatic performances of the followers of Si Ahmed or Moussa. The square is taken over by fire-eaters, story-tellers and *guerrab* ▲ 265. It will only take you a few minutes to get to the airport, which is situated 4 miles from the city center ◆ 330.

The village of Aït Boulhi, perched on the western slopes of the central High Atlas.

Rock carving on Jebel Rat.

Muleteer in the central High Atlas.

Hiking, horse riding, "ski-mule" mountaineering, para-jumping, hang gliding and white water rafting are just some of the many tourist adventure packages currently being developed. It is advisable to ask for information from registered mountain guides or from Moroccan or other tourist agencies specializing in this type of organized or tailor-made holiday. The various types of accommodation include hostels, bed and breakfast in local houses, mountain refuges, tents and bivouacs. In spring and summer you may even decide to sleep under the stars!

TREKKING

Following the many winding mule tracks that run through the mountains is an ideal way of discovering the little-known face of Morocco.

WESTERN HIGH ATLAS
A two- to six-day circuit starts at Tazzitount or the Pont d'Amellougi and crosses the Plateau du Yagour ▲ 301, where some very interesting rock carvings can be seen.

CENTRAL HIGH ATLAS
This is undoubtedly one of the most beautiful itineraries from Marrakesh ▲ 259. It takes between four and six days to reach Tabant via the Tizi N'Tichka pass ▲ 280 and the villages of Megdaz, Ichbaken and Abachkou. There are a number of possible alternative routes via the Tessaout Gorges ▲ 304 and the valleys of Aït Mallat and Aït Boulhi. The track crosses high-altitude *oueds* passing

through verdant landscapes dotted with *pisé* villages.

JEBEL SARHRO
This itinerary, on the edge of the Sahara, is ideal for those seeking solitude. It starts from Ouarzazate ▲ 286, near Iknioun, and traverses the lunar landscapes and eery rock formations of the Anti Atlas ■ 24, taking you across vast expanses of sand and red earth.

EASTERN HIGH ATLAS
If you enjoy walking you will like the Plateau des Lacs route around Jebel Ayachi (12,300 feet) ■ 26. The trek lasts between three and four days.

THE RIF
The Rif Mountains, rising to a height of 6,500 feet above the Mediterranean, are covered with cedars, holm oaks and heather ■ 28. They offer almost unlimited scope for trekkers.

TREKS ON HORSEBACK OR BY CAMEL

Exploring the plains and mountains of the Middle, High or Anti Atlas on horseback or by camel is an option that offers endless possibilities and is also an absolutely ideal way of discovering Morocco and meeting its hospitable inhabitants. There are no restrictions on traveling in this way. Although there are very few organized holidays of this type in Morocco, it is sometimes possible to hire pack mules in mountain villages. Camel treks are mainly organized from centers in Marrakesh, Essaouira ▲ 156, and Agadir ▲ 310. The more adventurous traveler may decide to join a caravan.

"SKI-MULE" TREKKING

Winter, up to the beginning of spring, is an ideal time to enjoy a "ski-mule" package, complete with mountain porters, on the Jebel Toubkal ▲ 302, ■ 26 and Jebel M'Goun ▲ 291 where there is usually plenty of snow. The "Grande Traversée des Atlas Marocains" (Great Trek Across the Moroccan Atlas), which takes thirty to forty days, can be divided into units of four to six days and is suitable for all levels of competence. Only experienced skiers should tackle the Toubkal route.

MOUNTAINEERING AND ROCK-CLIMBING

The Jebel Toubkal ▲ 302 is accessible to mountaineers year-round. More experienced climbers start their ascent from one of the five refuges located above 11,500 feet, and particularly from Tazarhart (13,000 feet). The sport of mountaineering originated in the High Atlas and today there are a number of exciting routes in the Aoui (or Aroudane) Mountains, the Taghia Gorges and Cirque, the Todra Gorges ▲ 292, the Jebel Sarhro ▲ 292 and the Jebel Fengour. A mountaineering school, the first to be established in Morocco, has been set up in the Valley of the Aït Bouguemez in the central High Atlas ▲ 305.

The gorges of the Asif N'Timedhras in the central High Atlas.

Overnight gîte and mountain guide on the road to Azilal.

CROSS-COUNTRY SKIING

From the end of December to the end of February cross-country skiers can explore the Mediterranean slopes of the Rif Mountains ■ 24 and the Middle and the High Atlas and particularly the cedar forests of the Middle Atlas ■ 28, between Ifrane ▲ 251 and Khenifra ▲ 258. Mischliffen and Jebel Hebri, at a mean altitude of 6,500 feet near Ifrane and Azrou, are the best-equipped centers. Above 9,800 feet the slopes of the Middle Atlas fold mountains are suitable for cross-country skiing between December and May. In the region of the Aït Bouguemez, in the central High Atlas ▲ 306, the route taking in Tabant and the Lac d'Izourar is very popular with lovers of sport.

SKI SLOPES

Ski slopes have been opened up in the cedar forests of the Middle Atlas and near the winter sports resorts of Mischliffen and Jebel Hebri. The resort of Oukaïmeden ▲ 301 (High Atlas), about 47 miles from Marrakesh, has the highest ski lift in Africa and the finest ski slopes in Morocco.

PARA-JUMPING AND HANG GLIDING

Para-jumping is a good way of bypassing tedious descents when hiking or cross-country skiing in the mountains. The central High Atlas has a number of takeoff sites, particularly on the northern slopes (the southern slopes tend to be affected by sandstorms). Hang gliding in the more isolated regions is more difficult because of the problem of carrying so much heavy equipment, although mules can be used to carry it up the mountains.

FRESH-WATER FISHING

The rivers, waterfalls and mountain lakes near the tourist resorts of Beni Mellal ▲ 308, Marrakesh, Ouirgane ▲ 302, Ifrane, Azrou ▲ 257 and Khenifra in the High and Middle Atlas offer fishing enthusiasts unrivaled scope for catching fine trout, pike, pike-perch, shad and eels in a beautiful natural setting.

CANYONING, WHITE WATER RAFTING AND CANOEING

For those seeking a more exhilarating type of holiday, canyoning, white water rafting and canoeing open up the wilder side of the Moroccan landscape. But do remember that this is a country where certain rivers swell rapidly after rain: this can easily take you by surprise if you are not well-prepared. It is also advisable to take a guide with you. Starting from the *zaouia* of Ahansal ▲ 307 or from Tabant, a choice of four-day itineraries will take you either through the sweep of the eastern canyons (the gorges of Tazart, Taghia and Tafraoute) or through the western canyons (the gorges of Jorro and the Tessaout ▲ 304 Pass). From Marrakesh ▲ 259, Azilal ▲ 307, Ifrane ▲ 251 and Khenifra ▲ 258, the *oueds* of the High ■ 26 and Middle Atlas offer a range of truly remarkable descents, covering up to 90 miles on the Ahansal and Melloul. The Oum er Rbia ▲ 148 has a 37½-mile white-water rafting course, which is negotiable throughout the year.

ADDRESSES

ALGÉRIATOURS
Villa Ourida
Quartier Saadia
MARRAKESH
Tel: 04 43 47 93
Hiking and cross-country skiing.

ATLAS SAHARA TREKS
72, rue de la Liberté
MARRAKESH
Tel: 04 44 93 50
Hiking, cross-country skiing, white water rafting-canyoning.

AZOURKI RANDONNÉES
81, av. Mohammed V
AZILAL
Tel: 03 45 83 32
Hiking and cross-country skiing.

DYNAMIC TOURS
34, boulevard Zerktouni
CASABLANCA
Tel: 02 20 26 82
Hiking, cross-country skiing and canyoning.

IMILCHIL VOYAGES
416, boulevard Mohammed V
BENI MELLAL
Tel: 03 48 90 60
Hiking and fishing

RIBAT TOURS
3, avenue Moulay-Rachid
RABAT
Tel: 07 76 03 05
Hiking, cross-country skiing, canyoning, white water rafting, climbing, para-jumping and mountain biking.

UNITOURS MAROC
127, avenue Mohammed V
MARRAKESH
Tel: 04 43 11 96
Camel trekking.

◆ MOROCCO IN THE MOVIES

Morocco has much to offer movie directors: guaranteed sunshine throughout the year, a wide and varied range of landscapes, well-preserved architectural features and large numbers of extras. The Lumière brothers were the first to use this natural setting when they made *Le Cavalier marocain* (*The Moroccan Horseman*), the first short movie shot in Morocco, in 1897. Although Western directors tend to use the country primarily as a backdrop, from 1959 onward it became an integral part of movies made by Moroccan directors.

AN IDEAL SETTING

Many foreign film directors have used the Moroccan landscape to evoke settings with an Oriental flavor. Several scenes have been shot in Morocco for movies that are actually set in another country.

EL JADIDA.
The Portuguese cistern ▲ *151* was the setting for the love affair between Diane and Prince Selim of Arabia in Arthur Joffe's *Harem* (1985).

AÏT BENHADDOU.
For *The Jewel of the Nile* (1986), Lewis Teague shot Jack Colton's (Michael Douglas) plane in front of the kasbah gate of Aït Benhaddou.

ESSAOUIRA.
In *Othello* (1950), Orson Welles used the *Skala* ▲ *158* to represent the ramparts of the island of Cyprus. Many other Western film directors have brought the wide-open landscapes of Morocco to the big screen.

THE TODRA GORGES.
David Lean chose the magnificent Todra Gorges ▲ *292* as the setting for the stirring Jordanian ambush in *Lawrence of Arabia* (1962).

THE DADÈS VALLEY.
In Franco Zeffirelli's *Jesus of Nazareth* (1976) the Dadès Valley ▲ *290* provided the setting for Herod's massacre of the innocents in Galilee.

THE ATLAS MOUNTAINS.
John Huston shot the "Tibetan" sequences of *The Man Who Would Be King* (1975), starring Sean Connery and Michael Caine, in the Atlas Mountains.

MOROCCO AND COLONIAL CINEMA

Moroccan towns and cities provided an ideal setting for the colonial themes that became popular with foreign scriptwriters during the French protectorate and after Moroccan independence in 1956.

TANGIER.
Daniel Schmid used the fascinating, almost mythical image of 1920's Tangier as the setting for the mysterious and tortured nights of the young diplomat in *Hecate* (1982).

MARRAKESH.
The narrow streets of the medina ▲ *274* provided a natural labyrinth for the pursuits in Alfred Hitchcock's *The Man Who Knew Too Much* (1956).

The sequence from Claude Chabrol's "Marie-Chantal contre le Docteur Kha" (1965), in which Marie Laforêt tries to shake off Russian and American spies, was shot in the Ben Youssef Medersa ▲ 276 in Marrakesh (left).

348

A scene from Arthur Joffe's "Harem" (1985) (above).

Bernardo Bertolucci's "The Sheltering Sky" (1990) was shot near Ouarzazate ▲ 286.

MOROCCAN REALISM

The first Moroccan films were shot in 1959 and were mainly shorts and documentaries. Unlike their Western counterparts, who

MOVIE THEATERS

Morocco's 250-odd movie theaters are concentrated mainly in the major towns and cities and in tourist centers. A ticket costs 2 dirhams.

tended to use Morocco to provide an exotic setting, Moroccan directors wanted to reflect the sociological and ethnic reality of their country. *El Chergui* (1970), shot in Tangier by Moumem Smihi, depicts the customs and beliefs of a people, while Souheil Ben Barka's *Les Mille et une*

mains (*A Thousand and One Hands*) (1972) denounces the abuses of Moroccan society in an examination of working conditions in the business sector of Marrakesh. *Ibn as Sabil* or *Le Grand voyage* (*The Great Journey*) (1980) is an analysis of Moroccan society. Its director Abd er Rahmane Tazi uses the journey of Omar, who is driving a truckload of dates from Inezgane (in the south) to Tangier, to highlight the many social and geographical contrasts between the north and south of the country. *Le Coiffeur du quartier des pauvres* (*Neighborhood Barber*) (1985) offers another view of Moroccan society in which Mohammed Reggab depicts the everyday life, the rituals, human relationships, and living and working conditions, of people living in the working-class districts of Casablanca.

Carpet from Rabat.

Straw hat from Khémisset.

Morocco has managed to preserve the skills of its traditional craftsmen, which have been handed down from generation to generation. An enormous range of traditionally made items, from the rustic to the more elaborate, can be bought all over Morocco. The most conspicuous tend to be carpets, basketwork, jewelry, leatherwork and woodwork.

CARPETS
The size and design of Moroccan carpets are usually related to their intended use and position in the home. Their value is determined by the number of knots or strands of warp and weft forming the foundation fabric. There is also a difference between town and tribal carpets. The best-known in the "town" category are the predominately red Rabat carpets ▲ 162 with their Oriental-style designs. According to one story, a piece of Oriental carpet, dropped by a stork in the courtyard of a house in Rabat, was copied by the women who found it. Tribal or Berber carpets are made of thick knotted wool and feature geometric, often latticework designs in

a harmonious combination of colors. They fall into four main categories: the carpets of the Middle Atlas ▲ 74, with a colored ground typical of Meknès ▲ 232 or black and brown motifs against a white background characteristic of the Taza region ▲ 252; the thin, finely textured carpets of the High Atlas; the Haouz carpets of Marrakesh, known as Chichaoua ▲ 321 carpets, characterized by human, animal and insect motifs; and the carpets of eastern Morocco which have predominately blue and green designs against a dark red background.

EMBROIDERY
The art of embroidery is particularly well developed in the towns and cities of northern Morocco, notably Fez, Meknès, Rabat, Salé, Chechaouen, Tétouan and Azemmour. Because they have been subject to

different influences, each town has developed a particular style and technique characterized by choice of color, decorative motifs and types of stitches. Fez ▲ 214 is famous for its silk embroidery on linen and cotton, aleuj ● 76 (gold thread on silk) and tsel (cotton and satin voile decorated with metallic thread). Meknès ▲ 232 is renowned for its warm colors embroidered on muslin, while Rabat ▲ 162 uses a wide range of decorative motifs that are the legacy of Muslim Spain. Work from Salé ▲ 175 is recognized by its geometric, floral and even architectural motifs and Azemmour ▲ 148 by brightly colored threads worked on

strips of white or unbleached linen used as hangings and curtain trimmings.

BASKETWORK
This popular traditional craft produces a wide range of articles for everyday use. Dwarf palms ● 43, rushes and reeds are the most widely used materials. Tasseled hats from Khémisset ▲ 258, garden furniture and lampshades are particularly eye-catching, and large, lightweight baskets are ideal for carrying your purchases on the return flight.

Copper tray.

The blue and white pottery of Fez.

MARQUETRY

Most of the splendid marquetry seen throughout Morocco comes from Essaouira ▲ *156*. Tables, armchairs, chess boards, caskets and jewel boxes are made of thuja and inlaid with ivory, mother-of-pearl, citrus wood, orange wood and ebony.

COPPER AND BRASS

Moroccan metalwork includes iron, bronze and especially copper and brass. Marrakesh and Fez are the two main centers where it is made and sold. A wide range of decorative and functional objects, such as copper trays and ewers inlaid with silver,

teapots, cooking pots, pots and pans, vases and caskets, are offered for sale in souks.

LEATHER

Leatherwork is very much in evidence throughout Morocco. Whereas it was previously limited to saddles, book bindings and babouches, it now includes poufs, cushions, bags, suitcases, belts and clothes. Fez and Marrakesh vie with each other for the monopoly on decorative leatherwork. Men's babouches are in white and yellow leather while women's are made of leather or material. It is advisable to compare, feel, smell and try the weight of babouches before you buy.

JEWELRY

City jewelry is usually made of elaborately worked gold and is sometimes set with precious stones. It is made by craftsmen grouped in specialist quarters within major towns and cities such as Fez ▲ *214*, Meknès ▲ *232*, Tangier ▲ *180*, Tétouan ▲ *190*, Rabat ▲ *162*, Salé ▲ *175*, Essaouira ▲ *156* and Marrakesh ▲ *260*. Rural or Berber jewelry is traditionally made of silver and varies from the simple to the elaborate. Ouarzazate ▲ *286*, Tazenakht ▲ *319* and Talouine ▲ *318* are renowned for their burnished silver jewelry. Generally speaking the value of the jewelry is measured by its weight, regardless of the quality or the amount of work involved. Daggers are often decorated like jewelry and the curved Khenjar and Koumiya are the most common. The straight-bladed

Sboula are mainly found in the Oujda region.

POTTERY

The two main centers of pottery manufacture in Morocco are Fez ▲ *214*, renowned for what used to be known as "Fez blue" (similar to "Delft blue") pottery, and Safi ▲ *153*, which imitates Fez pottery in different colors, largely green, yellow and brown. Meknès ▲ *232*, Rabat ▲ *162*, Azemmour ▲ *148*, Marrakesh ▲ *260* and Taroudant ▲ *325* also produce their own particular versions of unglazed, glazed and painted pottery. In fact every region, from the Sous to the Rif via the valleys of the High Atlas, has its own type of pottery, usually handmade from red clay. Its simplicity is governed by practical necessity and it consists mainly of vessels designed to hold or preserve food. The interior is sometimes glazed and decorated with geometric and symbolic patterns.

◆ USEFUL WORDS AND PHRASES

COMMON EXPRESSIONS

YES: naam, iyeh
NO: la
PLEASE: min fadlak
THANK YOU: shoukran
SORRY/EXCUSE ME: afouan
GOOD MORNING: sbah el-khir
GOOD EVENING: msa el-khir
GOODBYE: bes-slama
TODAY: el-youm
TOMORROW: ghedda
YESTERDAY: el-bareh
PROHIBITED: memnou
I AM ENGLISH: ana inglis
I AM AMERICAN: ana americano
I DO NOT UNDERSTAND: ma nefhamch
CAN YOU HELP ME?: yemken lek tsaadni?
INFORMATION: istiilamat
WHAT TIME IS IT?: chhal, es-saa?

DAYS OF THE WEEK

MONDAY: el-tnine
TUESDAY: et-tlata
WEDNESDAY: el-arbaa
THURSDAY: el-khemis
FRIDAY: ej-jemaa
SATURDAY: es-sebt
SUNDAY: el-hadd

MONTHS OF THE YEAR

JANUARY: yennayer
FEBRUARY: febrayer
MARCH: maras
APRIL: abril
MAY: mayou
JUNE: younyou
JULY: youlyouz
AUGUST: ghoucht
SEPTEMBER: shoutanbir
OCTOBER: oktober
NOVEMBER: nouanbir
DECEMBER: doujanbir

SEASONS

WINTER: ech-chetoua
FALL: el-khrif
SPRING: er-rbii
SUMMER: es-sif

NUMBERS

ONE: wahad
TWO: zouj
THREE: tlata
FOUR: arbaa
FIVE: khamsa
SIX: setta
SEVEN: sebaa
EIGHT: tmenia
NINE: tesaa
TEN: achra
ONE HUNDRED: mia
ONE THOUSAND: alf

FAMILY

FATHER: bou
MOTHER: om
SON: ben
DAUGHTER: bent
SISTER: okht
BROTHER: kho
AUNT: amma
UNCLE: khal

TRAVEL

BUS: hafila
AIRPLANE: tayara
LUGGAGE: mataa
TICKET: tadkira
CHANGE: sarf
CONNECTION: morasala
CUSTOMS: diouana
STATION: mahatta
PLATFORM: rasif
PORTER: hammal
TRAIN: qitar
SUITCASE: haqiba
DEPARTURE: dahab
ARRIVAL: wousoul
DELAY: taakhkhor
TRAVEL AGENCY: ouikalat asfar
PETROL/GAS STATION: mahattat benzine

FINDING YOUR WAY AROUND

WHERE IS...?: fin...?
IS IT NEAR?: ouach qrib?
IS IT FAR?: ouach biid?
ON THE LEFT: aala shmal
ON THE RIGHT: aala limine
STRAIGHT ON: nichan
SOUTH: janoub
NORTH: shamal
EAST: sharq
WEST: gharb

GETTING AROUND

PETROL/GAS: benzine
PUMP UP: nfokh
OIL: zit
HIRE: kra
BRIDGE: qantra
GATE: bab
WHEEL: jarrara
ROAD: triq
TAXI: taxi
CAR: sayara

AT THE HOTEL

HOTEL: otil
ROOM: bit
KEY: meftah
SHOWER: douche
WASH BASIN: lafabo
TOILETS: mirhad
BREAKFAST: ftor
BATHROOM: hammam
TOWEL: fota
SHEET: izar
BLANKET: ghta
PILLOW: ousada
WHERE IS THE NEAREST HOTEL?: fin el-otil elli qrib bezzef men hna?
CAN YOU SHOW ME A GOOD HOTEL?: yemken lek touerri-li shi otil mezien?
I HAVE RESERVED A ROOM: qbat ouahad el-bit

I WOULD LIKE A ROOM: bghit ouahad el-bit
SHOW ME THE ROOM: weerili el-bit
WHAT DOES IT COST?: chhal el-taman?
PLEASE WAKE ME: naouadni min fadleq

AT THE RESTAURANT

RESTAURANT: mataam
MENU: qaimat el-makla
BILL: el-hsab
LUNCH: el-ghda
DINNER: el-acha
WATER: el-ma
WINE: ech-chrab
GLASS: kas
PLATE: tabsil
KNIFE: mouss
FORK: chouka
SPOON: maalqa
BREAD: khobz
BUTTER: zabda
OLIVES: zitoun
CHEESE: jban
SALAD: chlada
VEGETABLES: khoudra
MEAT: lham
MUTTON: khouf
BEEF: bagri
POULET: djaj
PORK: hallouf
FISH: hout
DESSERT: halwa
BISCUITS: baskaouita
FRUIT: fakia
ICE-CREAM: talj
COFFEE: qahoua
TEA: ataï
CAN I HAVE THE BILL PLEASE?: lehsab men fadlek?

VISITS

VISIT: ziara
OPEN: meftouh
CLOSED: mesdoud
TICKET OFFICE/WINDOW: choubbak
TICKET: tadkira
TOWN: medina
QUARTER: haiy
HOUSE: dar
GARDEN: hadiqa
THEATER: masrah
MOVIE THEATER: sinima
MUSEUM: mathaf
GALLERY: riwaqa

AT THE POST OFFICE

WHERE CAN I TELEPHONE?: fin yemken ndaouer el-tilifoun?
POST OFFICE: el-barid
POSTAGE STAMP: tabac baridi
TELEPHONE: tilifoun
TELEGRAM: barqiya

EMERGENCIES

POLICE: chourta
FIRE BRIGADE: itfaiyoun
INFIRMARY: machfa
HOSPITAL: moustachfa
PHARMACY: saidaliya

DOCTOR: tbib
PLEASE CALL THE DOCTOR: tlob el-tbib min fadlak

SHOPPING

BUREAU DE CHANGE: maktab es-sarf
PRICE: el-taman
HOW MUCH IS IT?: chhal?
IT'S TOO EXPENSIVE: ghali bezzef
BAKER: khabbaz
PATISSERIE: maqtfa
GROCER'S: biqala
BUTCHER'S: majzara
PHOTOGRAPHER'S: matjar souar
TOBACCONIST'S: tabgh
BOOKSHOP: maktaba
NEWSPAPER STAND: kachk el-jarayid
NEWSPAPER: jarida
BOOK: ktab
ANTIQUES DEALER: tajir athariyat
JEWELER: sayigh
WHAT TIME DOES THE SHOP OPEN?: ach men saa yeftah el-matjar?
WHAT TIME DO YOU CLOSE?: fuqach tseddou?
WHERE CAN I FIND ...?: fin yemken nelqa ...?

MATERIALS

GOLD: dhab
SILVER: fedda
IRON: hdid
BRONZE: bronz
COPPER: nhas
TERRACOTTA: tin tayeb
EARTHENWARE: fakhkhar
SILK: hrir
COTTON: qton
SYNTHETIC: tarkibi
WOOL: sof

COLORS

WHITE: biad
BLACK: khal
RED: hmar
GREEN: khdar
BLUE: zrak
YELLOW: sfar
ORANGE: bourtouqali
PINK: wardi
PURPLE: zbibi, banafsaji

CLOTHES

TROUSERS/PANTS: serwal
JACKETS: sodra
SHIRT: qamija
SKIRT: joubba
DRESS: foustan
SOCKS: tqacher
SHOES: sabbat
BELT: hazzama

TRADITIONAL ITEMS

CARPET: zarbiya
POTTERY: fikhara
DISHES: tbasil
POTS: qlalesh
CARAFES: ghraref

USEFUL ADDRESSES

☀ VIEW
C CITY CENTER
⌂↔ ISOLATED
◍ LUXURY RESTAURANT
◑ TYPICAL RESTAURANT
○ BUDGET RESTAURANT
🏨 LUXURY HOTEL
⌂ TYPICAL HOTEL
⌂ BUDGET HOTEL
P CAR PARK
🚗 SUPERVISED GARAGE
⬒ TELEVISION
⌂ QUIET
🏊 SWIMMING POOL
▭ CREDIT CARDS
⚘ REDUCTION FOR CHILDREN
✖ NO ANIMALS
♫ MUSIC
🎺 LIVE BAND

◆ CHOOSING A HOTEL

- ♦ < 200 DH
- ♦♦ 200–400 DH
- ♦♦♦ 400–800 DH
- ♦♦♦♦ > 800 DH

	PRICE	VIEW	TERRACE, GARDEN, SWIMMING POOL	AIR CONDITIONING	RESTAURANT	FURNISHINGS – DECORATION	TELEVISION	HAMMAM	CONFERENCE ROOM(S)	NO. OF ROOMS
AFOURAR										
HÔTEL TAZERNOUNT ****	♦♦♦	●	●	●	●	●	●	●		139
AGADIR										
AGADIR BEACH CLUB ****	♦♦♦	●	●	●	●	●	●	●	●	350
AL MADINA PALACE ****	♦♦	●	●	●	●	●	●	●	●	206
HÔTEL ADRAR ****	♦♦		●					●	●	174
HÔTEL ALI BABA ***	♦♦		●		●	●				105
HÔTEL AMADIL ****	♦♦♦	●	●	●	●	●			●	324
HÔTEL ANEZI ****	♦♦	●	●	●	●		●		●	254
HÔTEL EUROPA SAFIR *****	♦♦♦	●	●	●	●	●	●	●		240
HÔTEL OASIS ****	♦♦		●		●		●			132
HÔTEL OUMNIA ***	♦♦♦		●		●				●	180
PLM LES DUNES D'OR ****	♦♦		●	●	●				●	450
HÔTEL SAHARA *****	♦♦♦		●	●	●		●		●	277
HÔTEL SHERATON AGADIR ****	♦♦♦		●	●	●		●			195
HÔTEL TAFOUKT ****	♦♦		●	●	●		●			135
HÔTEL TRANSATLANTIQUE ****	♦♦		●	●	●		●		●	208
SUD BAHIA ***	♦♦		●	●	●	●				246
ASILAH										
HÔTEL EL-KHAIMA ***	♦		●		●					74
BENI MELLAL										
HÔTEL CHEMS ****	♦♦		●	●	●					77
HÔTEL OUZOUD ****	♦♦		●	●	●					60
CASABLANCA										
HÔTEL BASMA ****	♦♦		●				●			117
EL-MOUNIA ****	♦♦				●		●	●		79
HOLIDAY INN, CROWN PLAZA *****	♦♦♦♦		●	●	●	●	●		●	150
HYATT REGENCY *****	♦♦♦♦		●	●	●	●	●	●	●	229
HÔTEL IDOU ANFA ****	♦♦♦		●	●	●		●	●	●	222
HÔTEL MOUSSAFIR ***	♦		●	●	●		●			105
HÔTEL SAFIR *****	♦♦♦		●	●	●		●		●	311
HÔTEL SHERATON *****	♦♦♦♦		●	●	●		●	●	●	304
HÔTEL SUISSE ****	♦♦	●	●	●	●		●	●		192
RÉSIDENCE CLUB TROPICANA ****	♦♦	●	●	●	●					62
RIAD SALAM, HÔTEL LE MÉRIDIEN *****	♦♦♦	●	●	●	●	●	●	●	●	150
CHECHAOUENE										
HÔTEL ASMA ***	♦	●	●		●					94
HÔTEL DE CHAOUEN ****	♦♦	●	●		●					37
AL HOCEIMA										
HÔTEL EL-MAGHREB EL-JEDID ***	♦				●					40
HÔTEL MOHAMMED V ****	♦♦	●	●		●					34
HÔTEL QUEMADO ***	♦	●	●		●					102
EL JADIDA										
HÔTEL DOUKKALA ****	♦♦		●		●					78
LE PALAIS ANDALOUS ***	♦♦		●	●	●					36
ERFOUD										
HÔTEL SALAM ****	♦♦		●	●	●					98
ER RACHIDIA										
HÔTEL PLM RISSANI ****	♦♦		●	●	●					60
ESSAOUIRA										
HÔTEL DES ÎLES ****	♦♦		●		●					66
HÔTEL TAFOUKT ***	♦				●	●			●	40
HÔTEL VILLA MAROC ***	♦♦	●	●							15
FEZ										
HÔTEL DE FÈS *****	♦♦♦		●	●	●					285
HÔTEL LES MÉRINIDES *****	♦♦♦	●	●	●	●	●	●		●	79
JNAN PALACE *****	♦♦♦♦		●	●	●	●	●		●	193
MOUSSAFIR HOTEL ***	♦		●	●	●					83
PALAIS JAMAI *****	♦♦♦♦		●	●	●	●	●			136
PLM VOLUBILIS ****	♦♦		●	●	●					120
HÔTEL SALAM ZALAGH ****	♦♦		●	●	●			●	●	77
MARRAKESH										
HÔTEL AGDAL ****	♦♦		●	●	●					130
HÔTEL AMALAY ***	♦		●	●	●					35
HÔTEL ATLAS ASNI ****	♦♦		●	●						304
HÔTEL ES-SAADI *****	♦♦♦	●	●	●	●				●	152

	PRICE	VIEW	TERRACE, GARDEN, SWIMMING POOL	AIR CONDITIONING	RESTAURANT	FURNISHINGS – DECORATION	TÉLÉVISION	HAMMAM	CONFERENCE ROOM(S)	NO. OF ROOMS
Hôtel Farah Safir *****	♦♦♦♦		●	●	●		●	●	●	293
Hôtel Les Idrissides *****	♦♦			●	●				●	341
Hôtel Issil **	♦		●	●		●				
Hôtel Kenza ***	♦♦		●	●	●			●		87
Hôtel Le Marrakech ***	♦♦		●	●	●				●	350
Hôtel de La Ménara **	♦		●	●	●					100
Hôtel N'Fis ***	♦♦♦	●	●	●	●		●	●	●	284
Hôtel Oudaïa **	♦		●	●	●					92
Hôtel Palmariva	♦♦♦		●	●	●		●		●	340
Hôtel Pullman Mansour Eddahbi *****	♦♦♦♦		●	●	●		●	●	●	441
Hôtel Résidence de la Roseraie			●		●		●		●	30
Hôtel Semiramis Le Méridien *****	♦♦♦		●	●	●		●		●	182
Siaha Safir ***	♦♦		●	●	●			●		287
Hôtel Tafilalet ***	♦♦		●	●	●					83
Hôtel Tichka ***	♦♦♦		●	●	●	●				138
Hôtel Le Tikida ***			●	●		●				
Imperial Borj *****	♦♦♦		●	●	●	●	●		●	217
La Mamounia *****	♦♦♦♦		●	●	●	●	●	●	●	232
Moussafir Hotel **	♦	●	●	●	●		●			103
Palmeraie Golf Palace	♦♦♦♦		●	●	●		●	●	●	316
MEKNÈS										
Hôtel Transatlantique *****	♦♦	●	●	●	●		●			120
Hôtel Volubilis **	♦		●	●						37
MOHAMMEDIA										
Hôtel Miramar *****	♦♦♦	●	●	●	●		●		●	188
Hôtel Samir ***	♦♦		●	●	●				●	146
OUARZAZATE										
Hôtel Bellère ***	♦♦		●	●	●					287
Le Berbère Palace *****						●				220
Hôtel club Karam ***	♦♦		●	●	●		●	●	●	147
PLM Azghor ***	♦♦		●	●	●					109
Hôtel Riad Salam *****	♦♦♦		●	●	●	●	●			70
Hôtel Tichka ***	♦♦		●	●	●					164
OUJDA								●		
Hôtel Moussafir **	♦		●	●	●	●				
RABAT										
Hôtel Le Belère ***	♦♦			●	●					90
Hôtel Chellah ***	♦♦			●	●					117
Hôtel Moussafir **	♦			●	●				●	60
Hôtel Les Oudayas **	♦♦			●						35
Rabat Hyatt Regency *****	♦♦♦♦	●	●	●	●	●	●	●	●	220
Hôtel Safir *****	♦♦♦	●	●	●	●	●	●		●	200
Hôtel de La Tour Hassan KTH *****	♦♦♦♦		●	●	●		●		●	148
Hôtel Yasmina **	♦♦			●	●					55
SAFI					●					
Hôtel Atlantide **	♦	●		●	●				●	48
Hôtel Safir ***	♦♦		●	●	●				●	90
TANGIER										
Grand Hôtel Villa de France **	♦	●	●		●					60
Hôtel Les Almohades *****	♦♦♦	●	●	●	●			●	●	150
Hôtel El-Minzah *****	♦♦♦	●	●	●	●		●	●	●	100
Hôtel El-Oumnia **	♦♦		●	●	●					100
Hôtel Intercontinental *****	♦♦♦	●	●		●		●	●	●	125
Hôtel Rif ***	♦♦	●	●		●				●	130
Hôtel Shéhérazade ***	♦♦	●	●		●				●	146
Hôtel Solazur ***	♦♦		●		●				●	360
TAROUDANT										
La Gazelle d'Or *****	♦♦♦♦		●	●	●	●		●		23
Hôtel Salam ***	♦♦		●	●	●	●		●		75
TÉTOUAN										
Hôtel Safir ***		●		●	●				●	99
TIZNIT										
Kerdous Hotel	♦♦	●	●	●	●		●			38
ZAGORA										
Hôtel Reda Doumia PLM ***	♦♦♦	●	●		●				●	155
Hôtel Timsouline ***	♦♦		●	●	●			●	●	180

◆ CHOOSING A RESTAURANT

Price key:
♦ < 200 DH
♦♦ 200–300 DH
♦♦♦ > 300 DH

	PRICE	VIEW	TERRACE, GARDEN	MOROCCAN SPECIALTIES	FISH AND SEAFOOD	TRADITIONAL SETTING	CABARET, ENTERTAINMENT
AGADIR							
La Corniche	♦♦♦				●		
Le Président	♦♦♦				●		
Restaurant de l'hôtel Sahara	♦♦♦			●		●	
Yacht Club	♦				●		
CASABLANCA							
Les Ambassadeurs Hôtel Holiday Inn	♦♦♦						●
A ma Bretagne	♦♦	●			●		
El-Bahia Hôtel Holiday Inn	♦♦			●		●	●
El-Mounia	♦♦			●		●	
La Broche	♦						●
Le Cabestan	♦♦	●			●		
Douira	♦♦♦			●		●	
Le Fellini	♦♦						
Imilchil	♦		●				
Le Kim Mon	♦♦						
La Mer	♦♦	●			●		
Le Petit Rocher	♦♦				●		●
Restaurant du Port de pêche	♦				●		
Le Prétexte	♦♦	●					
La Réserve	♦♦	●					
Le Tajine	♦♦			●		●	
La Taverne du Dauphin	♦				●		
Wong Kung	♦						
EL JADIDA							
La Marquise	♦				●		
Restaurant Français	♦				●		
FEZ							●
Al-Safia Palais Jamaï	♦♦♦			●		●	
L'Ambra	♦♦			●			
Astor	♦						
La Cheminée	♦			●			
Dar Saada	♦			●		●	
Dar Tajine	♦♦			●		●	●
Le Firdaous	♦	●	●				
Mirty's (Chez Claude)	♦						
Le Nautilus	♦♦				●		
Au Palais de Fès	♦			●		●	
Au Palais Mnebhi	♦♦♦			●		●	
Yan Tsé	♦				●		
MARRAKESH							
Bahia	♦			●			
La Belle Époque	♦♦						
Le Casher Hôtel Pullman Mansour Eddahbi	♦♦			●			●
Chez Ali	♦			●		●	
Chez Jack Line	♦						
Dar Es Salam	♦			●		●	
Douirya	♦♦			●		●	
La Jacaranda	♦♦					●	
Jardin des arts	♦					●	●
La Maison Arabe	♦♦			●			

	PRICE	VIEW	TERRACE, GARDEN	MOROCCAN SPECIALTIES	FISH AND SEAFOOD	TRADITIONAL SETTING	CABARET, ENTERTAINMENT
LE MAROCAIN Hôtel La Mamounia	◆◆◆			●		●	
L'OASIS	◆◆	●	●	●		●	●
PALAIS GHARNATTA	◆			●		●	●
LE PAVILLON	◆◆				●	●	
RIAD	◆			●		●	
LA TRATTORIA	◆						
TUIZRA	◆◆			●			
VILLA ROSA	◆◆		●			●	
MEKNÈS							
BELLE VUE Hôtel Transatlantique	◆◆	●					
LA CASE	◆						
LE DAUPHIN	◆◆			●	●		
L'HACIENDIA	◆◆						
ISMAÏLIA Hôtel Transatlantique	◆◆			●			
OUARZAZATE							
CHEZ DIMITRI	◆						
COMPLEXE DE OUARZAZATE	◆	●	●	●		●	●
ES-SALAM	◆			●			
KASBAH DE TIFOULTOUTE	◆	●		●		●	
LE MIMOSA	◆						
RABAT							
LE CRÉPUSCULE	◆						
LE DINARJAT	◆◆◆			●		●	●
LE DRAGON D'OR	◆						
EL-ANDALOUS Hôtel Rabat Hyatt Regency	◆◆			●			●
EL-MANSOUR Hôtel de la Tour Hassan	◆			●		●	●
L'ENTRECÔTE	◆◆						
L'ÉPERON	◆◆				●		
FUJI	◆◆						
LE GOÉLAND	◆◆				●		
LE JUSTINE'S Hôtel Rabat Hyatt Regency	◆◆◆				●		
LA KOUTOUBIA	◆			●			
LA MAMMA	◆						
LE MANDARIN	◆						
LES MARTINETS	◆◆		●				
OUAZZANI	◆	●		●		●	
LA PAGODE	◆						
PIZZERIA NAPOLI	◆						
LA PLAGE	◆	●				●	
LE VERT GALANT	◆◆						●
TANGIER							
LE DÉTROIT	◆◆	●		●			
EL-KORSAN Hôtel El-Minzah	◆◆◆	●		●		●	●
LE GAGARINE	◆						
MARHABA	◆			●		●	●
LE MARQUIS	◆◆				●		
LE NAUTILUS	◆◆				●		
ROMERO	◆				●		●
TAMASCOUS	◆◆			●			●
TÉTOUAN							
LE ZARHOUN	◆			●		●	●

357

1 CLUB SANGHO **2** HÔTEL MARHABA **3** HÔTEL OASIS **4** HÔTEL TAFOUKT **5** HÔTEL AFERNI **6** HÔTEL ALI BABA **7** HÔTEL EUROPA SAFIR

AGADIR

GENERAL INFORMATION

MOROCCAN EMBASSIES
49, Queen's Gate Gdns
London SW7 5NE
Tel. 071 581 5001

1601 21st Street, NW
Washington DC 20009
Tel: 202 462 7979

BRITISH EMBASSY
17, bd de la Tour
Hassan
Rabat
Tel. 72 09 05

AMERICAN EMBASSY
2, avenue Marrakesh
Rabat
Tel. 76 22 65/76 22 62

There are British and
American consulates at
Casablanca (p. 361)
and Tangier (p. 381)

MOROCCAN NATIONAL TOURIST OFFICES
205, Regent Street
London W1R 7DE
Tel: 071 437 0073

20 East 46th Street
New York, NY 10017
Tel. 212 557 2520

TRANSPORT

BY AIR
ROYAL AIR MAROC
205, Regent Street
London W1R 7DE
Tel: 071 439 8854
or New York
Tel: 212 750 6077
The only airline that flies
directly to Morocco

BRITISH AIRWAYS
Information inquiries
Tel: 081 897 4000
(London area)
0345 222 111
(rest of UK)
GIBRALTAR AIRWAYS
081 897 4000
(London area)
0345 222 111
(rest of UK)

BY TRAIN AND FERRY
SOUTHERN FERRIES
179, Piccadilly
London W1 9DB
Tel: 071 491 4968
FRENCH RAILWAYS
179, Piccadilly
London W1V 9DB
Tel: 0891 515477
COMARIT FERRY
(VOYAGES WASTELLS)
7, rue du Mexique

Tangier (Morocco)
Tel. (09) 93 12 24
SNCM FERRYTERRANÉE
61, bd des Dames
13002 Marseille
Tel. 91 56 30 30
or 91 56 30 10

TOUR OPERATORS
CLUB MÉDITERRANÉE
106–110, Brompton
Road
London SW3 1JJ
Tel: 071 581 1161
HAYES & JARVIS
152, King Street
London W6 0QU
Tel: 081 748 0088
KUONI TRAVEL
Kuoni House

Dorking
Surrey RH5 4AZ
Tel: 0306 743000

A comprehensive list of
tour operators and
special-interest
holidays in Morocco is
available from the
Moroccan National

Tourist Offices in
London (071 437 0073)
or New York (212 750
60 77).

AFOURAR

DIALING CODE
03

ACCOMMODATION

HOTEL TAZERNOUNT
Main Fez-Marrakesh
road
Tel. 44 01 01
*Garden (7½ acres),
hammam, horse riding,
excursions, keep fit,
tennis courts, disco.*

AGADIR

DIALING CODE
08

USEFUL INFORMATION

HOSPITAL
Route de Marrakech
Tel. 82 24 77

TOURIST OFFICES
Immeuble (building) A,
Place du Prince
Héritier Sidi
Mohammed
Tel. 82 28 94
Av. Mohammed V
Tel. 84 06 95

TRANSPORT

AIRPORT
AGADIR-INEZGANE
6 MILES S./E. OF
AGADIR
Tel. 83 14 18

TRAVEL AGENTS
FM TOURS
INTERNATIONAL
Av. Hassan II
Immeuble Rachdi
Tel. 82 00 45
FOUR SEASONS TRAVEL
AGENCY
Rue des Administrations
publiques
Tel. 82 19 80
Tlx 818 25

GLOBUS
119, av. Hassan II
Tel. 82 13 59
Tlx 81 895
MENARA TOURS
341, av. Hassan II
Tel. 82 11 08
Tlx 817 13
OLIVE BRANCH TOURS
125, av. Hassan II
Tel. 82 52 97
Tlx 82 627
SAHARA TOURS
Av. du Général Kettani
Tel. 82 16 30
Tlx 81 688

CAR HIRE
ADVENTURE CARS
Place des Taxis

industrial district
Tel. 82 16 55
AFRIC CAR
Av. Mohammed V
Tel. 84 07 50
AGADIR VOITURES
Immeuble Baraka
Rue de Paris
Tel. 82 24 26
AUTOS CASCADES
Av. Hassan II
Tel. 82 37 81
AVIS
Av. Hassan II
Tel. 84 03 45
BUDGET
Av. Mohammed V
Tel. 84 07 62
HANSALOC
Chez Globus

Av. Hassan II
Tel. 82 14 39
HORIZON CARS
Immeuble Assima
Av. Hassan II
Tel. 82 03 03
INTERRENT
Av. Mohammed V
Tel. 84 03 37
L.V.S.
52, av. Hassan II
Tel. 82 38 22
LOTUS CARS
Bungalow Marhaba
Hôtel
Tel. 82 18 52
MIETWAGEN
Rue Comte Hubert
Giraud
Tel. 82 47 37
PYRAMIDES CARS
Hôtel Sud Bahia
Tel. 82 37 41
STAR CARS
Hôtel Les Almohades
Tel. 82 32 33
TOURING CARS
Immeuble Marrakchi
Av. Moulay Abdallah
Tel. 82 03 03

CULTURE

KASBAH:
built in 1954,
overlooking the town.
Magnificent view.
Open daily.

RESTAURANTS

LES ARCADES
1, rue Allal Ben
Abdallah
Tel. 82 37 06
Open for lunch and
dinner
*Fine international
cuisine.*
100 DH–200 DH.
⌨

**RESTAURANT-BAR
LA CORNICHE**
On the promenade
and seafront
Tel. 84 09 41
Open for lunch and
dinner
*Dinner and cabaret.
Specialties:
fish, seafood,*

*lunch-time salads.
100–350 DH.*
⌨ 🏊 🅿

LE PRÉSIDENT
Hôtel Europa Safir
Bd du 20 Août
Tel. 82 12 12
Open for dinner
*Gastronomic restaurant.
Specialties: fish and
seafood".
200–350 DH.*
⌨ 🅿

**RESTAURANT DE
L'HÔTEL SAHARA**
Av. Mohammed V
Tel. 84 06 60
Open for dinner
*Luxurious and
sophisticated
setting. Upper price
range.
150–350 DH.*
🏨 ⌨

YACHT-CLUB
Port area
Tel. 82 30 95
Open for lunch and
dinner
*Relaxed atmosphere
and rapid service.
Specialties: fish,
seafood.
50–200 DH.*
⌨ 🅿

ACCOMMODATION

AGADIR BEACH CLUB
B.P. 310
Tel. 84 43 44
Fax 84 08 63
*Four restaurants, grill,
brasserie, bars,
swimming pool in
garden setting, sauna,
conference room, direct
access to the sea.
500 DH.*
🏨 🏠 📠 ☐ 🏊 �car
⌨

AL MADINA PALACE
Bd du 20 Août
Tel. 84 53 53
Fax 84 53 08
*Lounges, piano-bar,
conference room,
restaurant with*

*panoramic view,
hammam.*
🏨 🏊 🏊 ⌨

HÔTEL ADRAR
Bd Mohammed V
Tel. 84 04 37
Fax 84 05 45
*Small hotel with tennis
courts, sauna, horse
riding, conference room.
314 DH.*
🏠 🏠 ☐ 🏊 �car ⌨

HÔTEL AFERNI
Av. du Général Kettani
Tel. 84 07 30
Tlx 827 56
*Modest hotel, not
suitable for tourists.
196 DH.*
🏠 ⧈ �car ⌨

HÔTEL ALI BABA
Bd Mohammed V
B.P. 380
Tel. 82 33 26
Fax 84 12 47
*Restaurant, nightclub,
shop, tennis courts.*
🏠 🏊 �car ⌨

**HÔTEL LES
ALMOHADES**
Bd du 20 Août
Tel. 84 02 33
Fax 84 01 30
*Holiday complex: horse
riding, tennis courts,
nightclub, movie theater.
Service unreliable.
311 DH.*
🏨 🏠 📠 ☐ 🏊 �car
⌨

HÔTEL AMADIL
Rue de l'Oued Souss
Tel. 84 06 20
Fax 82 36 63
*Restaurant, nightclub,
conference room, tennis
courts Direct access to
the beach.
430 DH.*
🏠 📠 ☐ 🏊 �car
⌨

HÔTEL ANEZI
Av. Mohammed V
B.P. 29
Tel. 84 09 40
Fax 84 07 13
*Tennis courts,
shop, nightclub.
Restaurant with
panoramic view over
Agadir.
320 DH.*
🏠 🏊 ☐ 🏊 �car
⌨

HÔTEL ARGANA
Av. Mohammed V
Tel. 84 00 70
Fax 84 05 64
Restaurant, solarium

and nightclub are
among the facilities on
offer.
181 DH.
🏠 🏊 �car ⌨

HÔTEL EUROPA SAFIR
Bd du 20 Août
Tel. 82 12 12
Fax 82 34 35
Luxury hotel.
🏨 ☐ 🏊 �car ⌨

HÔTEL MARHABA
Av. Mohammed V
B.P. 346
Tel. 82 26 70
Tlx 816 25
Restaurant, shop, disco.
🏨 🏊 �car ⌨

HÔTEL OASIS
Av. Mohammed V
Tel. 84 33 13
Fax 84 42 60
*Moroccan-Swiss hotel.
Air conditioning, heated
swimming pool, TV,
Moroccan restaurant in*

a kaïdal tent, fitness
club, jacuzzi, disco,
mini-golf, tennis courts.
359 DH (tax and
breakfast incl.).
🏨 🏊 ⌨ 🎵

HOTEL OUMNIA
Rue de l'Oued Souss
Resort center.
Tel. 84 03 52
Tlx 818 71
*Small resort center:
nightclub, conference
room, tennis, shop.
Access to beach.
290 DH.*
🏠 🏠 📠 🏊 �car ⌨

PLM LES DUNES D'OR
Resort center.
Tel. 84 01 50
Fax 84 05 74
*Holiday and sports
complex. Hotel
overlooks the beach.
685 DH.*
🏨 🏠 📠 ☐ 🏊 �car
⌨

**PLM LES
OMMAYYADES**
Bd du 20 Août
Resort center
Tel. 84 09 17
Fax 84 22 01
*Swimming pool, tennis
courts, conference room
(seating for 20),*

LA GAZELLE D'OR
TRANSPORTS

hairdresser. Quality
hotel.
655 DH (full board).

HÔTEL SAHARA
Bd Mohammed V
Tel. 84 06 60
Fax 84 07 38
*Luxury hotel, efficient
service. Restaurants,
nightclub, conference
rooms, movie theater,
tennis courts.*
570 DH.

**HÔTEL SHERATON
AGADIR**
Bd Mohammed V
B.P. 339
Tel. 84 32 32
Fax 84 43 79
*Restaurant, nightclub,
shop, tennis courts,
chalets.*
500 DH (breakfast incl.).

HÔTEL SOLMAN
Av. Hassan II
Tel. 84 45 65
Fax 84 59 95
196 DH.

SUD BAHIA
Rue des
Administrations
publiques
Tel. 84 07 41
Fax 84 08 63
*Restaurant, bar, shop.
Pleasant atmosphere.
258 DH.*

HÔTEL TAFOUKT
Bd du 20 Août
Tel. 84 07 27
Fax 84 09 71
*Air conditioning,
restaurant over
swimming pool,
exotic gardens.
Direct access to
beach.*

**HÔTEL
TRANSATLANTIQUE**
Av. Mohammed V
Tel. 84 21 10
Fax 84 20 76
*Very tasteful, traditional
décor. Two restaurants,
grill, keep fit, tennis
courts, shops.
314 DH.*

**CLUB BORJ
EDDAHAR**
Bd du 20 Août
Tel. 84 09 28
*Tennis courts,
swimming pool,*

*international restaurant,
nightclub. Pleasant
surroundings, near the
sea.
400 DH.*

CLUB DE LA CASBAH
Bd du 20 Août
Tel. 84 09 50
Tlx 817 34
*Beach, tennis courts,
shop, movie theater,
nightclub, bar,
restaurant. Only 8
rooms with en suite
bathrooms. Pleasant
location, friendly service
(full board).
403 DH.*

CLUB MÉDITERRANÉE
Rue de l'Oued Souss
Tel. 84 06 01
Tlx 810 25
*Pleasant surroundings.
Beach, shops,
hairdresser.
4630 DH per week.*

CLUB SANGHO
Av. Mohammed V
Tel. 84 03 42
Fax 84 01 19
*Pleasant décor but
mediocre service.
Beach, tennis courts,
bar, restaurant
(full board).
600 DH.*

CAMP SITE
Opposite the
Hôtel ETAP, on the Bd
Mohammed V.

DIALING CODE
09

TRANSPORT

AL HOCEIMA AIRPORT
10½ miles from Al
Hoceima, along the Rif
coast

TRAVEL AGENTS
KETAMA VOYAGES

146, bd Mohammed V
Tel. 98 21 73
Tlx 43 001
LA MÉDITERRANÉE
47, bd Mohammed V
Tel. 98 23 76
Tlx 43 642

ACCOMMODATION

**HÔTEL EL-MAGHREB
EL-JEDID**
Bd Mohammed V
Tel. 98 25 04
Tlx 436 31
*Restaurant, bar.
196 DH.*

HÔTEL MOHAMMED V
Place de la Marche-
Verte
Tel. 98 22 33
Tlx 436 39
*Magnificent view over
the bay of Al Hoceima.
Friendly welcome.
Restaurant, nightclub,
tennis courts, beach.
268 DH.*

HÔTEL QUEMADO
Plage de Quemado
Tel. 98 23 71
Fax 98 33 14
*Hotel by the sea with
chalets, restaurant,
nightclub, tennis courts,
shops.
182 DH.*

ACCOMMODATION

HÔTEL EL-KHAIMA
Route de Tanger
Tel. 91 74 28
*Hotel by the sea.
Restaurant, bar, tennis
courts.
196 DH.*

DIALING CODE
03

FOR THE GOURMET

**SALON DE THÉ
EL AFRAH**
Place Afrique
*Excellent patisserie and
fruit juices.*

**SALON DE THÉ
AZOUHOUR**
241, av. Mohammed V
*Closed at lunchtime
Beautiful interior décor.*

ACCOMMODATION

HÔTEL CHEMS
1 mile outside Beni
Mellal
Route de Marrakech
Tel. 48 34 60
Tlx 248 91
*Restaurant, bar, tennis
courts, nightclub.
262 DH.*

HÔTEL OUZOUD
Route de Marrakech
Tel. 48 37 52

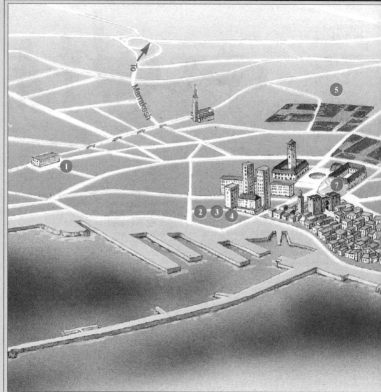

Tlx 247 41
Restaurant, bar, tennis
courts, shop.
262 DH.

CASABLANCA

DIALING CODE
02

USEFUL
INFORMATION

BRITISH CONSULATE
60, bd d'Anfa
Tel. 22 16 53

AMERICAN CONSULATE
8 bd Moulay Youssef
Tel. 22 41 49

TOURIST OFFICES
55, rue Omar Slaoui
Tel. 22 11 77
98, bd Mohammed V
Tel. 22 14 31

POST OFFICE
Bd de Paris,
On the corner of Av.
Hassan II

TRANSPORT

MOHAMMED V
AIRPORT
(Information)
AIR FRANCE
Tel. 33 91 10
IBERIA
Tel. 33 92 60
ROYAL AIR MAROC
Tel. 33 91 00

AIRLINES
AIR AFRIQUE
Tour des Habbous
15, av. des F.A.R.
Tel. 31 83 79
AIR FRANCE
15, av. de l'Armée
royale
Tel. 29 30 30

GIBRALTAR AIRWAYS
(and BRITISH AIRWAYS)
Tour Atlas
57, Place Zellaga
Tel: 32 18 62
ROYAL AIR MAROC
44, rue des F.A.R.

Tel. 31 11 22
Airport
Tel. 36 16 20

BOAT
COMANAV
(COMPAGNIE MAROCAINE

DE NAVIGATION)
43, av. de l'Armée
royale
Tel. 31 20 50

COACH
CTM (COMPAGNIE DES
TRANSPORTS DU MAROC)
303, bd Brahim
Roudani,
Tel. 25 29 01

TRAIN
ONCF
Casa-port
Tel. 22 30 11
Casa-voyageurs

Tel. 24 38 18

TRAVEL AGENTS
CLUB MÉDITERRANÉE
30, av. des F.A.R.
Tel. 31 99 11
FM TOURS
63, bd d'Anfa
Tel. 26 14 85
FM TOURS
INTERNATIONAL
23, bd Girardot
Tel. 30 21 46
Tlx 27 805
GLOBUS VOYAGES
35, rue de Foucauld
Tel. 26 42 03
Tlx 21 651
OLIVE BRANCH TOURS
76, rue de Foucauld
Tel. 22 39 19
Tlx 21 651
OVERSEAS TRAVEL
3, rue Branly
Tel. 27 76 21
Tlx 21 665
SAFIR VOYAGES
39, rue de Foucauld
Tel. 27 45 45
Tlx 21 903
SAHARA TOURS
Tour Atlas, place
Zellaqa
Tel. 30 48 11

CASABLANCA

To the airport →

To El Jadida →

Bd Mouley Youssef

8
6
9 10

TOURISME MAROCAIN WATA
8, bd Emile Zola
Tel. 30 40 22
Tlx 27 054
TRANSALPINO MAROC
98, av. Mers Sultan
Tel. 27 00 96
Tlx 21 638
VOYAGES PAQUET SA
65, av. de l'Armée royale
Tel. 31 19 41
Tlx 210 19
VOYAGES WASTEELS
Place Pierre Sémard.
Bâtiment ONCF (ONCF Building)
Tel. 24 47 93
Tlx 25 793
WAGONS-LITS TOURISME MAROC (DISCOVER MOROCCO)
5, av. des F.A.R.
Tel. 27 14 . 81
Tlx 240 27

CAR HIRE

ASSAD TOURS
10, rue Nolly
Tel. 26 83 71
ATIS CAR
217, bd Brahim Roudani

Tel. 25 81 44
AVIS
19, av. des F.A.R.
Tel. 31 11 35
AZUR RENT
138, bd Rahal El Meskini
Tel. 31 65 37
BUDGET RENT A CAR
Tour des Habbous
Av. des F.A.R.
Tel. 31 40 27
CAR LOC
95, rue Allal Ben Abdallah
Tel. 31 78 96
CHEMS CAR
63, bd d'Anfa
Tel. 36 65 48
EUROPCAR-INTERRENT
Tour des Habbous
Av. des F.A.R.
Tel. 31 37 37
EXPRESS LOCATION
246, bd Mohammed V
Tel. 30 78 47
G. RENAISSANCE CAR
3, rue Dumont dUrville.
Tel. 30 03 01
HERTZ-STARC
25, rue Foucault
Tel. 31 22 23
INTER LOC
34, avenue Hassan

Sghir
Tel. 31 66 53
INTER-VOYAGES
Hôtel Hyatt-Regency
Tel. 26 12 34
INTERVOYAGES
4, av. des F. A. R.
Tel. 22 22 50
LOCASOM
Km 12, Autoroute de Rabat
Tel. 35 18 12
MAG-TOURS
5, rue Nolly
Tel. 22 39 90
SCAL AVIS
71, av. des F.A.R.
Tel. 31 44 51
SAFLOC
77, av.

Hassan Ier
Tel. 27 69 47
SAUDIA CAR
26, rue Tazi
Tel. 22 02 57
SOUMIA CAR
129, av. Hassan Ier
T. T. M.
33, rue de Foucauld
Tel. 22 27 69

RESTAURANTS

LES AMBASSADEURS
Hôtel Holiday Inn
Rond-point Hassan II
Tel. 29 49 49
Open for lunch and dinner.

363

Closed Sundays.
*Candlelit dinners,
gastronomic menu.
Background music,
pianist. Specialty:
French cuisine.*
200–350 DH.
▭ P

A MA BRETAGNE
Sidi Abderrahman
Tel. 36 21 12
Open for lunch and
dinner
Closed Sundays
*Fine cuisine, beautiful
décor, good service.*
200–300 DH.
▭ ☀ P

LA BROCHE
132, rue de Gay Lussac
Tel. 27 25 99
Open for lunch and
dinner
*Specialty: meat
dishes.*
100–200 DH.
▭

LE CABESTAN
Phare d'El Hank
Tel. 39 11 90
Closed Sundays
*Pleasant, comfortable
surroundings. View over
the sea. Excellent
cuisine.
Specialties: fish,
seafood.*
150–250 DH.
▭ ☀ P

DOUIRA
Hôtel Royal Mansour
27, av. des F.A.R.
Tel. 31 30 11
Open from 7.30pm
Closed Sundays
*Excellent Moroccan
cuisine, top-quality
service.* 150–350 DH.
⌂ ▭ P

EL-BAHIA
Hôtel Holiday Inn
Rond-point Hassan II
Tel. 29 49 49
Open for dinner
Closed Mondays
*Oriental singing and
dancing. Specialty:
Moroccan cuisine.*

EL-MOUNIA
95, rue du Prince
Moulay Abdallah
Tel. 22 26 69
Open for lunch and
dinner
Closed Sundays
*Traditional décor.
Specialty: Moroccan
cuisine.*
100–250 DH.
▭

LE FELLINI
36, rue Moussa
Ibn Noussair
Tel. 20 45 25
*Italian cuisine.
Specialty: fresh pasta.*
150–250 DH.

IMILCHIL
Rue Vizir Tazi
Tel. 22 09 99
Open for lunch and
dinner
Closed Sundays
Specialty: Moroccan
cuisine.
100–200 DH.
▭

LE JARDIN
Bd de la Corniche
Tel. 39 13 13
Open for lunch and
dinner
Closed Mondays
*Specialty: international
cuisine.*

LE KIM MON
160, av. Mers Sultan
Tel. 26 32 26
*Specialty: Asian cuisine,
the best in Casablanca.*
120–250 DH.
▭

LA MAMMA
Corner of the Bd Biarritz
and the Bd de la
Corniche
Tel. 39 15 58
Open for lunch and
dinner
*Traditional Italian
setting.*
75–200 DH.
▭

LA MER
Phare d'El Hank
Tel. 36 33 15
Open for lunch and
dinner
Closed Sundays
*Splendid view. Good
cuisine and good
service. Specialties:
fish, shellfish.*
150–250 DH.
▭ ☀ P

LE PETIT ROCHER
Phare d'El Hank
Tel. 36 45 13
Closed Sundays
*Specialties: fish,
seafood.*
150–250 DH.

**RESTAURANT
DU PORT DE PÊCHE**
Fishing port,
Casablanca
Tel. 31 85 61
Closed during
Ramadan
*Brasserie atmosphere.
Patronized by artists
and journalists.
Specialties: fish,
seafood.*
50–150 DH.
⌂ ▭ P

LE PRÉTEXTE
Complexe du Dawliz
Bd de la Corniche
Tel. 39 14 32
Closed Friday, Saturday
and Sunday lunchtimes.
*French nouvelle
cuisine.*
▭ P

LA RÉSERVE
Bd de la Corniche
Tel. 36 71 10
Open for lunch and
dinner
Closed Saturdays
*Good family
cuisine.*
150–250 DH.
▭ P

RETRO 1900
Centre 2000
Gare Casa Port
Tel. 27 60 73
Closed Sunday
French cuisine.

LE TAJINE
Centre 2000
Tel. 27 64 00
*Traditional setting and
atmospheric music.
Specialties: méchoui,
couscous, pastilla.*
100–250 DH.
▭

**LA TAVERNE
DU DAUPHIN**
115, bd Houphouât-
Boigny
Tel. 22 12 00
Open 11am–3pm
and 7–11pm
Closed Sundays
*Friendly brasserie
atmosphere.
Specialities: seafood*

and fresh fish.
60–200 DH.
▭

IL VENEZIANO
90, rue Jean Jaurès
Tel. 29 50 03
Open for lunch and
dinner. Closed
Sundays
*Good cuisine.
Specialties: pasta,
pizza.*
100–200 DH.
▭

LE WONG KUNG
Hyatt Regency Hotel
Tel. 26 12 34
Closed Sunday
evenings and Mondays
*Specialty: Asian
cuisine.*
100–200 DH.

FOR THE GOURMET

PÂTISSERIE BENNIS
2, rue Fkih el Gabbas
Quartier des Habbous
Tel. 30 30 25
*Excellent but
expensive Moroccan
patisserie.*

**PÂTISSERIE
LA NORMANDE**
213, bd Mohammed V
Tel. 31 17 52
*Patisseries made with
butter.*

ACCOMMODATION

HÔTEL BASMA
35, av. Hassan Ier
Tel. 22 33 23
Tlx 228 29
*Modest hotel,
unsuitable for a long
stay or holidays.*
292 DH.
⌂ C ▯ 🖬 ▭

HOLIDAY INN,
Crown Plaza
Rond-point Hassan-II
Tel. 29 49 49
Fax 29 30 29
*Hotel with three
restaurants, nightclub,
three conference
rooms.*
1300 DH.
🏨 C ▯ ⚲ 🚗 ▭

HYATT REGENCY
Place Mohammed V
Tel. 26 12 34
Fax 22 01 80
*Three restaurants
(Italian, Asian and
Moroccan). Conference
rooms. Nightclub,
squash, sports
hall.*
2000 DH.
🏨 C ▯ ⚲ 🚗 ▭

HÔTEL IDOU ANFA
85, bd d'Anfa
Tel. 26 40 04
Fax 20 00 29
*Three restaurants,
piano-bar with
panoramic view, sauna,
two fully equipped
conference rooms
(seating for up to 230
people).*
450 DH.
🏨 C ⚱ ▯ ⚲
🚗 ▭

HÔTEL EL KANDARA
44, bd d'Anfa
Tel. 26 15 60
Fax 22 06 17
*Three restaurants, two
conference rooms*
390 DH.
🏨 C ▯ ⚲ 🚗 ▭

EL-MOUNIA
24, bd de Paris
Tel. 20 32 11
Tlx 239 14
*Restaurant, bars,
nightclub, sauna.*
218 DH.
⌂ C ▯ 🚗 ▭

HÔTEL MOUSSAFIR
Av. Bahmad
Place de la Gare des
voyageurs
Tel. 40 19 84
Fax 40 07 99
*Recently built, clean
hotel. Traditional décor.
International restaurant,
barbecue, cafeteria, bar,
Moroccan lounge.
Committee room
(seating for 20).*
196 DH.
🏨 C ▯ ⚲ 🚗 ▭

**RÉSIDENCE CLUB
TROPICANA**
Bd de la Corniche
Tel. 36 75 95

*Hotel on the water's
edge. Not
recommended in winter,
pleasant in summer.
Restaurant with
panoramic view.*
314 DH.
⌂ ⌂ ⚱ ⚲ 🚗 ▭

RIAD SALAM
Hôtel le Méridien
Bd de la Corniche
Aïn Diab
Tel. 39 22 44
Fax 39 13 45
*On the sea front.
Institute of
Thalassotherapy. Four
restaurants, five
conference rooms.*
660–900 DH.
🏨 ⌂ ⚱ ▯ ⚲ 🚗
▭

**HÔTEL ROYAL
MANSOUR**
27, av. des F.A.R
Tel. 31 30 11
Fax 31 25 83
*Trusthouse Forte. Three
restaurants, four
conference rooms.*
2100 DH.
🏨 C ▯ ⚲ 🚗 ▭

HÔTEL SAFIR
160, av. des F.A.R.
Tel. 31 12 12
Fax 31 65 14
*Two restaurants,
nightclub (cabarets),*

*sauna, five conference
rooms.*
800 DH.
🏨 C ▯ ⚲ 🚗 ▭

HÔTEL SHERATON
100, av. des F.A.R.
B.P. 15870
Tel. 31 78 78
Fax 31 51 37
*Three restaurants
(French, international
and Oriental), nightclub,
squash, gym club,
hammam, sauna.
Six conference rooms.*
1900 DH.
🏨 C ▯ ⚲ 🚗 ▭

**AUBERGE DE
JEUNESSE**
(Youth Hostel)
6 place Amiral-Philibert
Tel. 22 05 51
Closed 10am–12 noon

CAMP SITES

CAMPING OASIS
Av. Mermoz
Tel. 25 33 67

**CAMPING
INTERNATIONAL**
Les Tamaris
10 miles from the coast
road to Azemmour

CHECHAOUENE

FOR THE GOURMET

PÂTISSERIE MAGOU
Av. Hassan II
*Delicious bread and
patisserie.*

ACCOMMODATION

HÔTEL ASMA
Sidi Abdelhamid
Tel. 98 60 02
*Restaurant, shop, bar.
Beautiful setting.*
196 DH.
⌂ C ⌂ ⚲ 🚗 ▭

HÔTEL DE CHAOUEN
Outa El Hamam
Tel. 98 63 24
*Small, clean hotel.
Beautiful setting.
Bar, restaurant.*
262 DH.
⌂ C ⚲ 🚗 ▭

EL JADIDA

DIALING CODE
03

TRANSPORT

CAR HIRE
RISSANI
Club Hôtel de

Doukkala Salam
Tel. 34 37 37

RESTAURANTS

LA MARQUISE
Place Mohammed V
Open for lunch and
dinner
*French cuisine. ·
Specialties: fish,
seafood.*
100–200 DH.
▭

FRENCH RESTAURANT
Place Mohammed V
Open for lunch and
dinner
*Specialties: fish,
seafood, grilled meat,
salads.*
100–200 DH.

ACCOMMODATION

HÔTEL DOUKKALA
Av. de la Ligue Arabe
Tel. 34 37 37
Tlx. 780 14
*Hotel by the sea. Fish
and seafood restaurant.*
232 DH.
⌂ ⌂ ⚲ 🚗 ▭

LE PALAIS ANDALOUS
Bd du Docteur Lanouy
Tel. 34 37 45
Tlx 780 01
*Attractive hotel.
Average service.
Restaurant, bar.*
⌂ C 🚗 ▭

ER RACHIDIA

DIALING CODE
05

ACCOMMODATION

HÔTEL PLM RISSANI
Route d'Erfoud
B.P. 3
Tel. 57 21 86
Fax 57 25 85
Modern hotel,

restaurant, bar,
nightclub.
280 DH.

ESSAOUIRA

DIALING CODE
04

CULTURE

SIDI MOHAMMED BEN ABDALLAH MUSEUM
Rue Derb Laalouj
Open 9am–12noon and
2.30–6pm
Closed Tuesdays
*Andalusian and
traditional musical
instruments. Jewelry,
weapons, traditional
costumes.*

ACCOMMODATION

HÔTEL DES ILES
Bd Mohammed V
Tel. 47 23 29
Fax 47 24 72
*Restaurant, bar,
nightclub, conference
room.*
280 DH.

HÔTEL TAFOUKT
98, bd Mohammed V
B.P. 38
Tel. 47 25 05
Tlx 710 22
*Modest hotel.
Restaurant, shop.*
183 DH.

HÔTEL VILLA MAROC
The medina
*Hotel in a beautiful,
traditional residence.
Good cuisine.*
250 DH.

FEZ

DIALING CODE
05

USEFUL INFORMATION

HOSPITAL
Quartier Dar el
Khemis
Tel. 62 51 92

TOURIST OFFICES
Place de la Résistance
Tel. 62 62 97
Place Mohammed V
Tel. 62 47 69

TRANSPORT

FEZ SAÏS AIRPORT
8 miles from Fez on the
Imouzzer road
Tel. 62 47 12

TRAIN
ONCF
Tel. 62 50 01

TRAVEL AGENTS
RAM
54, av. Hassan II
Tel. 204 56
WAGONS-LITS
Rue de la Liberté

Immeuble Grand Hôtel
Tel. 62 29 58
Tlx 51 622

CAR HIRE
AVIS
50, bd Chefchaouen
Tel. 62 67 46
BUDGET
Bureau Grand Hôtel
Bd Chefchaouen
Tel. 62 09 19
EUROPCAR-INTERRENT
41, av. Hassan II
Tel. 62 65 45
GOLD CAR
2, bd Mohammed V
Tel. 62 04 95
HERTZ
Bureau Hôtel de
Fès
Av. des F.A.R.
Tel. 62 28 12
MAROC-CAR
53, rue Compardon
Tel. 62 53 76
POPULAIRE-CAR
1380, bd Mohammed V
Tel. 62 38 98
STOP-CAR
7, rue Larbi Kerrat
Tel. 62 26 03
ZEIT
35, av. Mohammed

Slaoui
Tel. 62 55 10

CULTURE

MUSÉE D'ARMES
Borj Nord
Open 9am–12 noon
and 3–6pm
Closed Tuesdays.
*Remarkable collection
of weapons displayed
inside a 16th-century
fortress.*

MUSEUM OF MOROCCAN ARTS
Dar Bartha Palace
Place de l'Istiqlal
Open 9am–12 noon
and 3–6pm
Closed Tuesdays and
national and religious
holidays.
*Large collection of
ancient pottery,
astrolabes (dating
from 11th to 17th
century), fine
examples of Fez
gold-thread
embroidery, Korans
and carpets.*
10 DH.

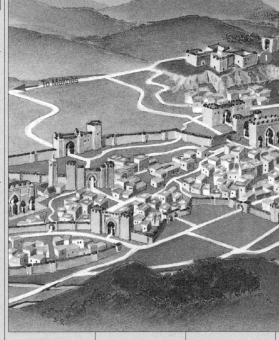

To Meknès

FEZ

To Chechaouche

RESTAURANTS

AL-SAFIA
Palais Jamaï
Bab Guissa
Tel. 63 43 31

Open for dinner only
*Traditional setting,
Andalusian atmosphere
and music. Very good
service. Specialty:
Moroccan cuisine.
150–350 DH.*
① ▭ **P**

L'AMBRA
47, rue d'Immouzzer
Tel. 64 16 87
Open for dinner

*Advisable to book in
advance. Traditional
Moroccan cuisine. Slow
service. Jeweler's shop.*
① ▭ **P**

ASTOR
18, av. Slaoui
Tel. 63 38 96
*Traditional Jewish,
Moroccan and
international cuisine.
100–200 DH*
▭

LA CHEMINÉE
6, rue de l'Indonésie
Tel. 62 49 02
Open for lunch and
dinner
Closed Sunday
*Wide choice of menu
and excellent service.
Specialties: hors-
d'oeuvres, traditional
Moroccan and French
cuisine.
75–150 DH.*
▭

DAR SAADA
Souk el Attarine
Fès el Bali
Tel. 63 33 43

*Installed in a former
carpet shop. Attractive
décor. Specialty:
Moroccan cuisine.
80–150 DH.*
▭

DAR TAJINE
15, Ross Rhi
Tel. 63 41 43
Open for dinner
Dinner-cabaret
*Excellent décor.
Specialties: tajines,
confits.
100–250 DH.*
① ▭ **P**

LE FIRDAOUS
Bab Guissa
Tel. 63 43 43
Open for lunch and
dinner
*Tourist menu. Good
cuisine. Entertaining
cabaret. Specialties:
kebabs, Moroccan
salads, tajines.
75–150 DH.*
① ▭ **P**

**MYRTY'S
(CHEZ CLAUDE)**
4, rue de Taza

Tel. 62 63 45
Open for lunch and
dinner
*Very reasonable
cuisine. Specialties:
French cuisine, red
meat, fish "en sauce".
75–150 DH.*
▭

LE NAUTILUS
Av. Hassan II
Tel. 62 50 72
Open for lunch and
dinner.
*Quiet restaurant. Good
quality cuisine and
service. Specialties:
French cuisine, meat
and fish "en sauce."
100–250 DH.*
▭

**AU PALAIS
DE FÈS**
16, rue Boutouil

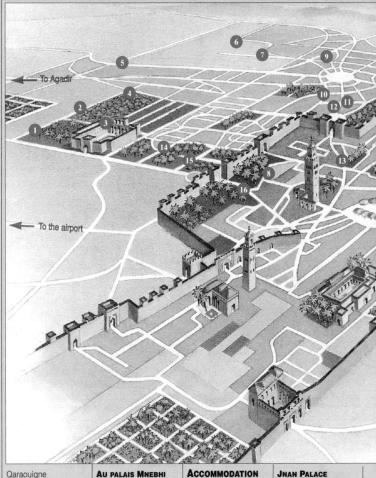

To Agadir

To the airport

Qaraouigne
Tel. 62 47 07
Open for lunch and dinner
Restaurant and bazaar. Good, affordable cuisine. Specialties: kebabs, Moroccan cuisine.
75–150 DH.
○ ⊡ 🅿

AU PALAIS MNEBHI
Talaa Seghira
Tel. 63 38 93
Closed certain days of the week. Advisable to book in advance.
Attractive, traditional setting. High quality local cuisine. Specialties: Moroccan cuisine.
50–350 DH.
◐ ⊡ 🅿

YAN TSÉ
23, rue Erytheria
Tel. 62 14 85
Open for lunch and dinner
Good Chinese cuisine (adapted for local tastes and ingredients). Friendly service.
50–120 DH.
⊡

ACCOMMODATION

HÔTEL DE FÈS
Av. des F.A.R.
Tel. 62 30 06
Fax 62 04 86
Suites designed by A. Paccard. Olympic swimming pool, conference room. Very good menu.
525 DH.
🏛 C ▭ ⌂ 🚗
⊡

GRAND HÔTEL
Bd Chefchaouni
Tel. 62 55 11
Tlx 516 31
Modest hotel, with reasonable French cuisine. Nightclub, conference room.
196 DH.
⌂ C 🚗 ⊡

JNAN PALACE
Av. Ahmed Chaouki
Tel. 65 22 30
Fax 65 19 17
Tlx 510 31
International hotel (air conditioned rooms with en suite bathroom and TV), tennis courts, four restaurants (Moroccan, Italian, international, gastronomic), conference centre (seating for 1300), English bar, tea rooms, swimming pool, tennis courts, extensive grounds.

HOTEL LES MÉRINIDES
Borj Nord
Tel. 64 60 40
Fax 64 52 25
Tlx 519 89 and 518 35
Air conditioned rooms

MARRAKESH

DIALING CODE
08

USEFUL INFORMATION

BUREAU DU TOURISME DU SAHARA
Av. Moulay Abd el Aziz
Tel. 42 24

TRANSPORT

AIRPORT HASSAN I
Tel. 89 33 46

BOAT
COMANAV
7, av. Hassan II
Tel. 22 41 06

CAR HIRE
MASSIRA CAR
Av. de La Mecque
Tel. 32 16
RAM
7, place bir Anzarane
Tel. 22 40 71
ESSALAM
Charia Mecque
Tel. 39 56
LAAYOUNE
7, Chari el Barid
Tel. 47 44
MAATALLAH
Sahat Dchira
Tel. 38 89
OULED ABDELLAH
Sahat Dchira
Tel. 39 19
SAQUIA EL HAMRA
Charia Mecque
Tel. 36 67

DIALING CODE
04

USEFUL INFORMATION

HOSPITAL
Tel. 44 80 11

TOURIST OFFICES
Place Abd el Moumen Ben Ali
Tel. 44 89 06
176, bd Mohammed V
Tel. 43 20 97

TRANSPORT

MÉNARSA AIRPORT
Tel. 43 43 38

BY AIR
AIR STAR (TAXI PLANE)
33, rue Loubnane Guéliz
Tel. 43 55 02

---

with en suite bathroom and TV. Two restaurants (Moroccan and international). Very fine décor. Loggia with magnificent view over the medina of Fez. Two bars (one with panoramic view), swimming pool.

MOUSSAFIR HOTEL
Av. des Almohades
Tel. 65 19 02 08
Fax 65 19 09
International restaurant, barbecue, terrace overlooking the garden.
196 DH.

PALAIS JAMAÏ
Bab Guissa
Tel. 63 43 31
Fax 63 50 96

Prestigious hotel-palace. Luxury rooms. Andalusian garden. Excellent Moroccan cuisine.
680–950 DH.

PLM VOLUBILIS
Av. Allal Ben Abdallah
Tel. 62 11 26
Tlx 519 40
Rooms overlooking the garden. Nightclub.
290 DH.

HÔTEL SALAM ZALAGH
Rue Mohammed Diouri
Tel. 62 28 10
Tlx 519 75
Residential district. International restaurant, sauna, nightclub,

conference room.
234 DH.

HÔTEL SOFIA
3, rue du Pakistan
B.P. 2098
Tel. 62 42 65
Tlx 519 50
Conference room, nightclub, restaurant.with international cuisine.
285 DH.

CAMP SITES

CAMPING ALFA
Angle Roland Frejers, Rue Hansali
Tel. 62 16 64

CAMPING DU DIAMANT VERT
On the Aïn Chkeff road

TRAVEL AGENTS

COMANAV VOYAGES
149, av. Mohammed V
Tel. 43 02 65
Tlx 72 903

DISCOVER
213, av. Mohammed V
Tel. 43 34 25

FM TOURS
221, av. Mohammed V
Tel. 44 60 66
Tlx 74 871

FOUR SEASONS
213, av. Mohammed V
Tel. 43 23 99
Tlx 72 947

GLOBUS VOYAGES
213, av. Mohammed V
Tel. 43 09 97
Tlx 72 947

MÉDITOURS
79, av. Zerktouni Appt. 5

MENARA TOURS
41, rue de Yougoslavie

Guéliz
Tel. 44 66 54
Tlx 729 26

OLIVE BRANCH TOURS
Hôtel Palais el Badia
Av. de la Menara
Tel. 44 88 81
Tlx 72 953

ONCF
Hôtel Mamounia
Tel. 44 89 81
Tlx 720 18

ORANGE TOURS
245, av. Mohammed V
Tel. 43 46 82
Tlx 74 003

OVERSEAS TRAVEL
213, av. Mohammed V
Tel. 43 22 31
Tlx 74 868

PALM INTER TOURS
Bab Doukkala
Immeuble Habbous
Tel. 44 60 15

PANAFRICAN TOURS
183, av. Mohammed V
Tel. 44 69 83

RAM
Bd Mohammed V
Tel. 43 43 38

SAFIR VOYAGES
Hôtel Safir
Tel. 43 46 26
Tlx 720 26

SAHARA TOURS
128, av. Mohammed V
Tel. 43 00 62
Tlx 72 966

WAGON-LIT TOURISME
122, av. Mohammed V
Tel. 43 16 87
Tlx 74 868

CAR HIRE

ATLANTICA CAR
213, av. Mohammed V
Tel. 43 21 01

AVIS
137, av. Mohammed V
Tel. 43 37 23

AZUR RENT
221, bd Mohammed V
Tel. 43 10 95

BERNOV
24, rue Yougoslavie
Tel. 44 81 52

BUDGET
213, av. Mohammed V
Tel. 43 46 04

CHEM'S
Place de la Liberté
Tel. 44 87 81

CONCORDE CARS
Av. Mohammed V
Tel. 44 61 29

EUROPCAR-INTERRENT
63, bd Zerktouni
Tel. 43 12 28

F.S.T. CAR
213, immeuble Maâlal
Av. Mohammed V
Tel. 43 23 99

HAOUZ CAR
88, av. Mohammed V
Tel. 44 82 35

HERTZ
154, av. Mohammed V
Tel. 43 46 80

IFIS CAR
Rue Mauritania
Tel. 43 03 10

INTER RENT
63, bd Zerktouni
Tel. 43 12 28

MEDLOC
Av. Hassan II
Immeuble Habbous F
16
Tel. 44 98 80

SAFLOC
221, bd Mohammed V
Tel. 44 63 58

SOUMIA CAR
37, bd Mansour
Eddahbi
Tel. 43 42 58

TOURIST CAR
Bd Zerktouni
Tel. 484 52

CULTURE

DAR SI'SAÏ
Rue Dar Graoua
Open 8.30am–12 noon
and 2.30–6pm
*Fine collection of
various traditional
items from southern
Morocco, displayed in a
late 19th-century
palace.*

MAJORELLE GARDENS
900 yards northwest of
the Bab Doukkala
Open 9am–12 noon and
2–6pm
*Luxuriant vegetation
with several species of
birds.*

MENARA GARDENS
About 1 mile from the
Bab el Jdid
*Large lake built by the
Almohads in the
12th century,
surrounded by gardens
and extensive orchards.
Extremely pleasant at
sunset.*

AGDAL GARDENS
Near the Dar el
Makhzen and the
Mechouar.
*Gardens redesigned
in the 19th century.
Pleasant walk among
the fruit trees.*

LA BAHIA PALACE
Rue Bab Rhemat
Open 8.30am–12 noon
and 2.30–6pm
*Guided tour. Pleasant
walk through the
gardens.*

EL BADI PALACE
Place des Ferblantiers
Open 8am–6pm
*Ruins of a 17th-century
palace where the
annual festival of
Moroccan folklore is
held.*

THE SAADIAN TOMBS
Place Yacoub el
Mansour
Open 8–12 noon
and 2pm–6pm
*Guided tours. Entrance
through the outer wall.*

RESTAURANTS

BAHIA
11, Riad Zitoun,
Idid Medina
Tel. 44 13 51
Open for lunch and
dinner
*Tourist restaurant.
Unreliable quality.
Specialty: Moroccan
cuisine.*
90–150 DH.
◐ ⊟ ℗

LA BELLE ÉPOQUE
5, rue Sourya
Tel. 44 64 20

Open for lunch and
dinner
*Two air-conditioned
rooms. Good service
and good French
cuisine.*
120 or 250 DH.
⊟

LE CASHER
Hôtel Pullman Mansour
Eddahbi, av. de France
Tel. 44 80 43
Closed Fridays
*Advisable to book in
advance. Good cuisine,
excellent service.
Specialty: Jewish
cuisine.*
150–300 DH.
⊟ ℗

CHEZ ALI
After the Pont de Tensift
(Tensift Bridge)
Tel. 30 77 30
Open for lunch and
dinner
*Pleasant, traditional
setting. Live folk music,
fantasia. Unreliable
quality. Tourist
restaurant. Specialty:
Moroccan cuisine.*
120 DH.

CHEZ JACK LINE
63, av. Mohammed V
Tel. 44 75 47
Open for lunch and
dinner
*Atmospheric music in
the evening.
Specialties: French and
Italian cuisine.*
75–200 DH.
⊟

DAR ES SALAM
170 bis, Riad Zitoun
Kedim Medina
Tel. 44 32 73
Open for lunch and
dinner.
*Traditional setting.
Specialty: Moroccan
cuisine.*
100–200 DH.

DOUIRYA
14, Derb el Jdid
(Mellah)
Tel. 44 28 02
Open for lunch and
dinner
*Friendly service in a
traditional setting. Good
Moroccan cuisine.
Advisable to book in
advance.*
100–250 DH.
◐ ⊟

L'HIBISCUS
255, rue de l'Hôpital
Tel. 44 99 48

Open for lunch and dinner
International cuisine. Quiet setting.
100–200 DH.

LA JACARANDA
32, bd Zerktouni
Tel. 44 72 15
Open for lunch and dinner. Closed Tuesdays
Rustic setting. Good French cuisine but unreliable service. Specialties: red meat, regional dishes. Advisable to book in advance.
200–300 DH.

JARDIN DES ARTS
6–7 Akioud Semlalia
Opposite l'Hôtel Amine
Tel. 43 11 31
Open for lunch and dinner.
Gallery restaurant: exhibitions of Moroccan artists' work. Specialty: international cuisine.
100–200 DH.

LA MAISON ARABE
Derb Ferrane
Tel. 42 26 04
Open for dinner
Dinner-cabaret, exotic setting. Essential to book in advance. Specialty: Moroccan cuisine.
150–300 DH.

LE MAROCAIN
Hôtel La Mamounia
Av. Bab el Jdid
Tel. 44 89 81
Open for dinner
Traditional décor. Very good Moroccan cuisine. Specialty: Moroccan cuisine.
150–350 DH.

L'OASIS
5½ miles outside Marrakesh
Route de Casablanca, B.P. 586
Tel. 43 03 68
Open 11am—midnight
Exotic walk. Dinner-cabaret with son-et-lumière. Specialty: Moroccan cuisine.
100–300 DH.

PALAIS GHARNATTA
5–6, Derb el Arsa
(Riad Zitoun)

Tel. 44 52 16
Traditional setting. Specialty: Moroccan cuisine.
100–200 DH.

LE PAVILLON
Rue Ibn Hanbal
Tel. 43 26 07
Open for lunch and dinner
Pleasant fireside area. Specialties: meat, fish.
150–250 DH.

RIAD
11, rue Dar Dou
Arset el Maach
Tel. (04) 42 54 30
Open for lunch and dinner
Traditional setting, friendly service. Pleasant in the evening. Specialty: Moroccan cuisine.
100–200 DH.

LA TRATTORIA
179, rue Md el Bequal
Tel. 43 26 41
Open for lunch and dinner
Specialty: fresh pasta.
80–200 DH.

TUIZRA
361, Bab Agnaou
Near the Saadian Tombs
Tel. 44 10 28
Open for lunch and dinner
Pleasant atmosphere. Specialty: Moroccan cuisine.
100–250 DH.

VILLA ROSA
Av. Hassan II Guéliz
Tel. 43 08 32
Open for lunch and dinner
Luxury décor, garden. Specialties: Italian cuisine, fish.
150–250 DH.

LE YAOURT
79, rue Sidi Ahmed

Soussi
Tel. 31 01 58
Moroccan cuisine. Magnificent setting.
500–700 DH.

ACCOMMODATION

HÔTEL AGDAL
1, bd Zerktouni

Tel. 43 36 70
Fax 43 12 39
Very reasonable hotel.
314 DH.

HÔTEL LES ALMORAVIDES
Arset Djnane Lakhdar
Tel. 44 51 42
Fax 44 31 33
Restaurant, tennis courts, shop, folk evenings.
234 DH.

HÔTEL AMALAY
Av. Mohammed V
Tel. 43 13 67
Tlx 720 50
Small, clean hotel. Reasonable food.
196 DH.

HÔTEL AMINE
Semlalia
Tel. 43 49 53
Tlx 729 11
Restaurant, bar, shop.
262 DH.

HÔTEL ANDALOUS
Av. Kennedy
Tel. 44 82 26
Fax 44 71 95
Tlx 748 02
Swimming pool, bar, international and Moroccan restaurant. Popular with groups.

HÔTEL ATLAS ASNI
Av. de France
Tel. 44 70 51
Fax 43 33 08
Attractive hotel, nightclub, conference room, tennis courts.
390 DH.

HÔTEL CHEMS
Av. Hoummane el Fetouaki
Tel. 44 48 13
Tlx 720 08
Bar, shop, restaurant.
262 DH.

HÔTEL ES-SAADI
Av. el Quadissia
Tel. 44 88 11
Fax 44 76 44
Splendid grounds, conference room, nightclub. Good French cuisine.
755 DH.

HÔTEL FARAH SAFIR
Av. du Président Kennedy
Tel. 44 74 00
Fax 44 87 30
Tlx 720 59
Restaurant, conference room, nightclub, hammam, tennis courts, horse riding.
1000 DH.

HÔTEL IBN BATTOUTA
Av. Yacoub el Marigny
Tel. 43 41 45
Tlx 740 51
Restaurant, bar.
196 DH.

HÔTEL LES IDRISSIDES
Av. de France
Tel. 44 87 77
Fax 44 67 23
Restaurant, nightclub, shop, tennis courts.
380 DH.

371

IMPÉRIAL BORJ
Av. Ech Ouhada
Tel. 44 73 22
Fax 44 62 06
Extremely attractive hotel, opened in 1990. Original interior architecture. Restaurants, conference room, nightclub. Bar overlooking swimming pool.
755 DH.

HÔTEL ISSIL
Circuit de la Palmeraie
Tel. 30 91 92
Fax 30 43 76
Tlx 728 53
Small, recently built hotel with attractive exterior décor, swimming pool, air-conditioned rooms.

HÔTEL KENZA
Av. Yacoub el Mansour
Tel. 44 83 30
Tlx 740 92
Fax 43 53 86
Restaurant, nightclub, shop. Keep fit club, hammam. Children under 12 free.
314 DH.

LA MAMOUNIA
Av. Bab el Jdid
Tel. 44 89 81
Fax 44 46 60
Sumptuous hotel, built in 1923 and renovated in 1986. Restaurants, bars, theme rooms, limousines.
1100–3000 DH.

HÔTEL LE MARRAKECH
Place de la Liberté
B.P. 761
Tel. 43 43 51
Fax 43 49 80
Very reasonable hotel, nightclub, small conference room, swimming pool

To Rabat

(heated in winter).
314 DH.

HÔTEL DE LA MÉNARA
Av. des Remparts
Tel. 44 98 14
Tlx 729 05
Renovated in 1991. Exotic setting. Friendly service and very reasonable cuisine.
196 DH.

MOUSSAFIR HOTEL
Av. Hassan II
Place de la Gare
Tel. (04) 43 59 29
Fax (04) 43 59 36
Recently built, all mod. cons. International restaurant, barbecue,

Moroccan lounge, bar.
196 DH.

HÔTEL N'FIS
Av. de France
Tel. 44 87 72
Tlx 720 86
Hotel-club built in traditional Marrakshi style. Rooms overlook beautiful grounds. Nightclub, tennis courts, sauna, conference room.
600 DH.

HÔTEL OUDAÏA
147, rue Mohammed el Beqal
Tel. (04) 44 85 12
Fax (04) 44 87 51
Pleasant service. Unpretentious, clean hotel. Good cuisine. Swimming pool (heated in winter).
196 DH.

HÔTEL PALMARIVA
4 miles, Route de Fès
Tel. 44 91 49
Fax 44 91 50

Hotel-club with full board. Buffet lunch and dinner. Events organised throughout the day and evening. Children's playground. Gym center. Golf practise range, mini golf course, horse riding.
600 DH.

PALMERAIE GOLF PALACE
Circuit de la Palmeraie
B.P. 1488
Tel. 30 10 10
Fax 30 50 50
Golf, swimming pool, restaurants. Extensive grounds. Luxury international complex.

HÔTEL PULLMAN MANSOUR EDDAHBI
Av. de France
Tel. 44 80 43
Fax 44 90 82
Restaurants, nightclubs, conference center (seating for 5,000), central swimming pool, Jewish restaurant.
1140 DH.

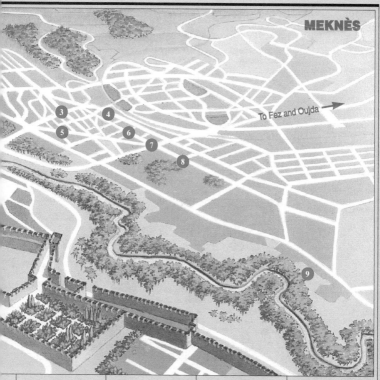

MEKNÈS

To Fez and Oujda →

HÔTEL RÉSIDENCE DE LA ROSERAIE
B.P. 769
Tel. 43 20 93
Fax 43 20 95
Tlx 728 08
A pleasant stop in the Val d'Imigane, 37½ miles from Marrakesh. Menu recommended.

HÔTEL SAHARA INN
Semlalia
Tel. 43 43 88
Tlx 750 51
Shops, restaurant, disco.
262 DH.
🏛 🏠 🖥•• 🛥 🚗 ▭

HÔTEL SEMIRAMIS LE MÉRIDIEN
Route de Casablanca
Tel. 43 13 77
Fax 44 71 27
Restaurant, nightclub, conference room, tennis courts, swimming pool.
620 DH.
🏛 🏠 🖥•• ▢ 🛥 🚗

HÔTEL SIAHA SAFIR
Av. Kennedy
Tel. 44 89 52
Fax 44 69 27

Chalets, tennis courts. Modest hotel. Pleasant, good cuisine.
340 DH.

HÔTEL SMARA
Bd Zerktouni
Tel. (04) 43 41 50
Fax 740 43
Unpretentious, clean hotel. Near the Place Djemaa el Fna.
133 DH.
🏠 🅲 ▭

HÔTEL TACHFINE
18, bd Zerktouni
Tel. 44 71 88
Tlx 720 89
No restaurant.
196 DH.
🏠 🅲 🚗 ▭

HÔTEL TAFILALET
Av. Abdelkrim El Khattabi
Tel. 44 98 18
Fax 44 75 32
Charming, family hotel. Clean, lots of flowers. Sophisticated French cuisine. Good Moroccan cuisine. Pleasant, friendly staff.
280 DH.
🏠 🏠 🛥 🚗 ▭

HÔTEL TICHKA
Av. de Casablanca
Tel. 44 87 10
Tlx 748 55
Delightful hotel, pleasant friendly service.
610–710 DH.
🏛 🏠 🛥 🚗 ▭

HÔTEL LE TIKIDA
La Palmeraie
B.P. 1585 Daoudiate
Tel. 30 90 99
Fax 30 93 43
Tlx 727 77
Charming, small hotel in garden setting. Swimming pool.

HÔTEL TROPICANA
Semlalia
Tel. 44 74 50
Fax 44 74 58
Restaurant, nightclub, shop.
350 DH.
🏠 🖥•• 🛥 🚗 ▭

CLUB SANGHO
Daoudiyat
Tel. 30 90 90
Fax 30 91 26
Stands in a palm grove. Two swimming pools (one with a waterfall).

Children's mini club. Beautifully décorated. Full board.
600 DH.
🏠 🏠 🖥•• 🛥 🚗 ▭
🏃

AUBERGE DE JEUNESSE
(Youth Hostel)
Rue el Jahid
Tel. 43. 28 31

MUNICIPAL CAMP SITE
Av. de France
Tel. 44 60 85

SPORTS

GOLF CLUB DE LA PALMERAIE
Les Jardins de la Palmeraie
Eighteen-hole golf course, with lakes, designed by the American architect Robert Trent Jones. Superb club house with excellent facilities.

MEKNÈS

DIALING CODE
05

373

USEFUL INFORMATION

HOSPITAL
Tel. 52 11 34

TOURIST OFFICES
Place Administrative
Tel. 52 44 26
Esplanade de la Foire
Tel. 52 01 91

TRANSPORT

MÉZERGUES AIRPORT
Tel. 52 29 04

TRAIN
ONCF
Tel. 52 06 89

TRAVEL AGENTS
RAM
7, av. Mohammed V
Tel. 52 09 63
WAGONS-LITS
1, rue de Ghana
Tel. 52 19 95
Tlx 410 90
WAGONS-LITS TOURISME
Bd Mohammed V
Tel. 25 20
WASTEELS
Av. Mohammed V
Tel. 249 66

CAR HIRE
BUDGET
Gare ONCF.
Tel. 27 01
HERTZ
Av. Houmane el
Fetouaki
Tel. 28 38
MAROC VOYAGES
Av. Allal Ben Abdallah.
Tel. 39 93
STOP-CAR
3, rue Essaouira
Tel. 42 50 61
ZEIT
4, rue Antissade
Tel. 42 59 18

CULTURE

DAR JAMAÏ PALACE
Place el Hedim
Tel. 53 08 63
Open 9am–12 noon
and 3pm–6pm.
Closed Tuesdays
*19th-century palace
built by the vizier Jamaï.
Fine collection of
traditional pieces made*

by craftsmen from the
city and region of
Meknès.

MOULAY ISMAÏL MAUSOLEUM
Open 9am–12 noon
and 3pm–6pm
Closed Friday mornings
*One of the few Muslim
monuments open to
non-Muslims. It
comprises the mosque
and tomb of Moulay
Ismaïl, and several
open courtyards.
Admission is free, but a
tip for the curator is
appreciated.*

KOUBBA EL KHAYATINE
*The Koubba leads into
the vast underground
storage chambers
known as the Christian
prison.*
10 DH.

BOU INANIA MEDERSA
Open 9am–12 noon and
3–6pm
Visits morning and
afternoon.
*Built in the mid-14th
century. Its four arcades
rest on the neighboring
houses and support an
open cupola.*
10 DH.

KOUBBA OF SIDI MOHAMMED BEN AÏSSA
(strictly no admittance)
*The koubba of the
founder of the Aïssonas
Brotherhood is located
in the city's oldest
Muslim cemetery.*

RESTAURANTS

BELLE VUE
Hôtel Transatlantique
Rue el Mérinyine
Tel. 52 50 50
Open for lunch and
dinner
*The smartest restaurant
in Meknès. Excellent
service, good cuisine.*
150–300 DH.

LA CASE
8, bd Moulay Youssef
Tel. 52 40 19
Open for lunch and
dinner
*Friendly service.
Specialties: French
cuisine, family menus.*
100–200 DH.

LE DAUPHIN
5, av. Mohammed V
Tel. 52 34 23
Open for lunch and
dinner
*Varied menu. Good
service.
Specialties: fish "à la*

*marocaine" and "à la
française".*
100–250 DH.

L'HACIENDA
Route de Fès
Tel. 52 10 92
Open for lunch and
dinner
*Swimming pool and
nightclub. Very popular
with the Meknassi.
Specialties: Spanish
cuisine, paëlla.*
100–200 DH.

ISMAÏLIA
Hôtel Transatlantique
Rue el Mérinyine
Tel. 52 50 50
Open for dinner only
*Excellent Moroccan
restaurant.*
150–300 DH.

LE MÉTROPOLE
On the corner of the Av.
Hassan II
Tel. 52 25 76
Open until 10pm
*More of a café than a
restaurant.
Specialties: grilled
kebabs, kemia
(Morrocan salads).*
30–70 DH.

ACCOMMODATION

HÔTEL BAB MANSOUR
38, rue Emir Abd el
Kader

Tel. 52 52 39
Tlx 419 39
*Small hotel, but
reasonable service.
Nightclub: chikhate
or disco.*
196 DH.

HÔTEL RIF
Rue d'Accra
Tel. 52 25 91
Tlx 410 39
*European and
Moroccan restaurants
(Oriental dancer or
gnaoua troupe during
the summer season).
Swimming pool in an
enclosed area with little
sun. Bar, nightclub.*
314 DH.

HÔTEL TRANSATLANTIQUE
Rue el Mérinyine
Tel. 52 50 50
Fax 52 00 57
*The most attractive
hotel in Meknès.
Magnificent gardens
and view. Tennis courts.
Restaurants renowned
for their Moroccan
cuisine.*
400 DH.

HÔTEL VOLUBILIS
45, av. des F.A.R.
Tel. 52 01 02
*Center of the new town
Modest hotel. Friendly
service.*
196 DH.

HÔTEL ZAKI
Bd el Massira
Tel. 52 09 90
Tlx 410 79
*Pleasant setting but
service leaves a lot to
be desired. Two
restaurants, sauna,
conference room.
Nightclub.*
314 DH.

AUBERGE DE JEUNESSE
(youth hostel)
Av. Oqba Ben Nafie
Tel. 52 46 98

CAMPING INTERNATIONAL AGDAL
Near the royal stables
of Moulay Ismaïl,
about 1 mile from the
center, on the Rabat
road.

MOHAMMEDIA

DIALING CODE
03

ACCOMMODATION

HÔTEL MIRAMAR
Rue de Fès
Tel. 32 20 21
Fax 32 46 13
Pleasant hotel for leisure activities, near the golf course and the sea. Tennis courts, nightclub, conference room, casino.
600 DH.

HÔTEL SAMIR
Bd Moulay Youssef
Tel. 31 07 70
Fax 32 33 30
Near the sea. Tennis courts, restaurant, bar, nightclub, conference room.
175 DH.

CAMP SITES

CAMPING MOHAMMEDIA-ZENATA (LORAN)
4½ miles from Mohammedia, near the sea.

CAMPING OUBAHA
At Mansouriah, 3 miles from Mohammedia.

NADOR

DIALING CODE
06

TRANSPORT

AIR
RAM
Corner Bd Mohammed V
Tel. 60 38 46

TRAIN
ONCF
87, bd Prince Sidi Mohammed
Tel. 60 47 60
Tlx 65 699

ACCOMMODATION

HÔTEL RIF
Av. Youssef Ben Tachfine
Tel. 60 65 35
Tlx 657 52

HÔTEL RYAD NADOR
Av. Mohammed V
B.P. 60
Tel. 60 77 15
Fax 60 77 19

OUARZAZATE

DIALING CODE
04

USEFUL INFORMATION

POST OFFICE
Av. Mohammed V
Tel. 88 24 51

HOSPITAL
Tel. 88 24 44

TOURIST INFORMATION
Av. Mohammed V
Casbah de Taourirt
Tel. 88 24 85

TRANSPORT

TAOURIRT AIRPORT
Tel. 146 ou 148

TRAVEL AGENTS
HOLIDAY SERVICES
Av. Mohammed V
Tel. 88 29 97
KSOURS VOYAGES
Place 3 Mars
Tel. 88 28 40
MOROCCO SAGA
C.G.I.
Tel. 88 23 59
PALMIER VOYAGES
Place de la Poste
Tel. 88 26 17
TOP VOYAGES
Hôtel Karam
Tel. 88 36 45

CAR HIRE
BUDGET
Av. Mohammed V
Résidence Warda.
Tel. 88 28 92
DAMI CAR
Place 3 Mars
Tel. 88 30 63
HERTZ
Av. Mohammed V
Tel. 88 20 84
INTER RENT
EUROPCAR
Place 3 Mars
Tel. 88 20 35
MIRRAGE
Place 3 Mars
Tel. 88 32 26
STOP CAR
Bd Mohammed V

CULTURE

WEAVERS' COOPERATIVE
Place Mohammed V
Open 8am–12 noon and 2pm–6pm
Manufacture and sale of carpets from Ouzguita. A wide range of ceramics and stone sculpture.

KASBAH OF TAOURIRT
Toward Boulemane du Dadès
Open 8am–6pm
Former Glaoua residence, traditional kasbah used for folk festivals and events. Splendid view from the terrace.

RESTAURANTS

CHEZ DIMITRI
Av. Mohammed V
Tel. 88 26 53
Open for lunch and dinner
Ouarzazate's first post office, built in 1928 and converted into a restaurant, where the seating is poor but the food is good.
60 DH.

COMPLEXE DE OUARZAZATE
Near the camp site, on the outskirts of Ouarzazate on the Tinerghir road.
Tel. 88 31 10
Open for lunch and dinner
Near the old municipal swimming pool. You can eat in Berber tents near the pool. Magnificent setting, excellent service. Folk entertainments in the evenings from September to June.
90–150 DH.

KASBAH OF TIFOULTOUTE
Route de Zagora. First village on the right, in the direction of Tifoultoute.
Tel. 88 28 13
Open for lunch and dinner
One of the finest settings in Morocco. Former Glaoua kasbah, situated on a rocky outcrop, high above the oued and palm grove.

375

RABAT

To Meknès

Basic accommodation.
Specialties: Moroccan
cuisine, tajines.

LE MIMOSA
175, place Anzarane
av. el Mouakama
Tel. 88 31 15
*Very friendly service.
Very pleasant
restaurant, good menu
and good value for
money.*
50–85 DH.

ACCOMMODATION

HÔTEL LE BELLÈRE
Tel. 88 28 03
Fax 88 22 23
*Hotel with swimming
pool, tennis courts,
shop, hairdresser,
nightclub. Snack-bar by
the swimming pool and
international restaurant.*
314 DH.

LE BERBÈRE PALACE
Rue Mansour Eddahbi
Tel. 88 30 77
Fax 88 30 71
*Quiet hotel, peaceful
atmosphere, car park.*

HÔTEL CLUB KARAM
Bd du Prince Moulay
Rachid
Tel. 88 25 22
Tlx 748 26
*Large new hotel with
restaurant, nightclub,
conference room, horse
riding, tennis courts.
Excursions available.
Rooms overlooking
beautiful gardens.*

PLM AZGHOR
Bd du Prince Moulay
Rachid
Tel. 88 26 12
Tlx 720 23

*Restaurant, bar, shops,
disco.*
314 DH.

PLM ZAT AÏT KDIF
Aït Gief
Tel. 88 25 21
Fax 88 20 64
*Restaurant, bar,
shop, tennis courts,
disco.*

HÔTEL RIAD SALAM
Rue Mohammed
Diouri
Tel. 88 22 06
Fax 88 26 27
*Attractive hotel that
looks like a kasbah.
Restaurant, bar, video,
tennis courts, horse
riding.*
500 DH.

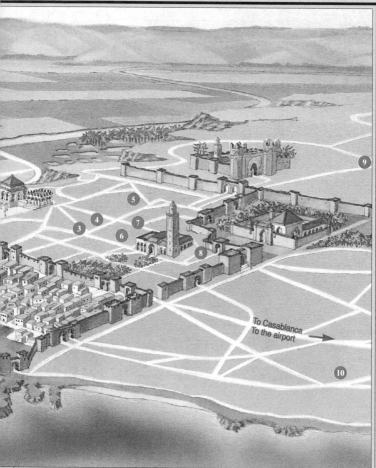

To Casablanca
To the airport →

HÔTEL TICHKA
Bd Mohammed V
Tel. 88 22 06
Tlx 740 49
*Small, friendly hotel
with restaurant, bar
and garden.*

CLUB MÉDITERRANÉE
Bd Moulay Rachid
Tel. 88 26 50
Fax 88 28 14
*Holiday village with
evening entertainment
and a wide range
of sporting and
other tourist
activities.*

OUJDA

DIALING CODE
06

TRANSPORT

AIRPORT
Les Angads (9½ miles
outside Oujda)
Tel. 68 32 61

TRAIN
ONCF
Tel. 68 27 01

TRAVEL AGENTS
EUROPA VOYAGES
17, Bd Zerktouni, corner
of Rue Moulay Ahmed
Laghrari
Tel. 68 26 27
Tlx 61 600
MAROC VOYAGE
TOURISME
110, bd Allal Ben
Abdallah
Tel. 68 39 93
WAGONS-LITS TOURISME
Av. Mohammed V
Tel. 68 25 20

ACCOMMODATION

**HÔTEL
MOUSSAFIR**
Place de l'Unité
Africaine
*Small, comfortable
hotel.*
196 DH.

RABAT

DIALING CODE
07

**DIRECTORY
ENQUIRIES**
16

USEFUL
INFORMATION

BRITISH EMBASSY
17, bd de la Tour
Hassan
Tel. 72 09 05

HOSPITAL
Tel. 77 28 71

TOURIST OFFICES
22, av. d'Alger
Tel. 72 12 52
Rue Patrice Lumumba
Tel. 72 32 72

TRANSPORT

AIRPORT
Rabat Salé
Tel. 76 73 93

AIR
AIR FRANCE
281, av. Mohammed V
Tel. 76 88 04
ROYAL AIR MAROC
Av. Mohammed V
Tel. 76 97 00

TRAIN
ONCF
Rabat-Agdal

Tel. 77 23 85
Rabat-Ville
Tel. 76 73 53

TRAVEL AGENTS
AFRIC VOYAGES
(tickets)
28 bis, av. Allal Ben
Abdallah
Tel. 76 96 46
AFRIC VOYAGES
(travel enquiries)
Résidence el Minzah
Rue el Kahira
Tel. 70 96 42
Fax 70 22 07
RAM
Corner of Av.
Mohammed V and Rue
el Emir Moulay Abdallah
Tel. 76 97 00
RAINBOW TRAVEL
1, rue Derna
Tel. 70 25 79
SAFIR VOYAGES
Hôtel Safir
Tel. 73 10 93
Tlx 32 086
WAGONS-LITS
Av. el Emir Moulay
Abdallah
Tel. 76 96 25
Tlx 31 671

CAR HIRE
INTER-RENT
25 bis, rue Patrice
Lumumba
Tel. 72 23 21
AVIS CAR
7, Zankat Abou Faris
el Marini
Tel. 76 79 59
BUDGET CAR
Gare ONCF
(center)
Tel. 76 76 89
CITER
Résidence el Minzah
Rue el Kahira
Tel. 72 27 31
Tlx 31 618
EUROPCAR
Hôtel Hyatt Regency

Tel. 77 02 18
EUROPCAR INTERRENT
25, rue Patrice
Lumumba
Tel. 72 23 28
HAPPY LOC
Rue Abou Faris
el Marini
Tel. 72 49 01
HERTZ
291, bd Mohammed V
Tel. 76 92 27
HOLIDAY CAR
1 bis, av. Ibn Sina.
Agdal
Tel. 77 13 51

IFIS CAR
30, rue Oqba
Agdal
Tel. 77 72 42
MARATHON CAR CIE
78, av. Allal Ben
Abdallah
Tel. 70 07 98
NORTH CAR
1, rue Tabarya
Tel. 72 48 18
OLYMPIA
1, rue Tanta
Av. Allal Ben Abdallah
Tel. 76 80 92
PACIFIC CAR
11, rue de Baghdad
Tel. 76 55 65
Fax 76 79 17
ROAD CAR
32, av. Omar Ibn

Khattab Agdal
Tel. 77 50 60
SALÉ LOC
8, rue Moulay
Rachid
Tel. 72 09 98
VISA CAR
9, rue Beit Lahm
Av. Moulay Youssef
VOYAGE OMAR
425, av. II
Tel. 73 80 34
WAFA CAR
17, av. Moulay Youssef
Passage Hatim
Tel. 76 11 78

CULTURE

**RABAT
ARCHEOLOGICAL
MUSEUM**
23, rue el Brihi
Tel. 76 22 31
Open 8.30am–12 noon
and 2.30–6pm
Closed Tuesdays and
public holidays
*Extensive collection of
prehistoric and later
objects from
excavations throughout
Morocco.*

**NATIONAL CRAFT
MUSEUM**
6, bd Tarik el Marsa
Open during office
hours.
*Carpets, jewelry,
ceramics, embroidery.
Fine examples of
modern Moroccan
craftsmanship.*

OUDAYAS MUSEUM
Place Souk el Ghezel
Tel. 73 15 12
Open 8.30am–12 noon
and 2.30–6pm
Closed Tuesdays and
public holidays
*Silks and embroidery,
Berber jewelry and
musical instruments
displayed in the royal
residence of Moulay
Ismaïl.*

**MOHAMMED V
MAUSOLEUM**
Admission free
*Visitors must be
properly dressed
Opposite the Hassan
Tower. The Mausoleum
commemorates the
sultan who enabled
Morocco to achieve
independence.*

**MOHAMMED V
MUSEUM**
9am–6pm daily.
*The museum traces the
history of the Alaouite*

*dynasty from the 17th
century to the present
day.*

HASSAN TOWER
9am–6pm daily.
*All that remains of
the mosque which was
originally begun in
1196.*

**CATHÉDRALE
DE SAINT-PIERRE**
9am–noon, 3–6pm daily.
*Next to the Great
Mosque.
Consecrated in 1921
and today the diocesan
church of the
Archbishop of Rabat.*

THE MEDERSA (SALÉ)
9am–noon, 3–6pm daily.
*From the easily
accessible roof of the
medersa, there is a
magnificent view across
the terraced roofs of the
city.*

RESTAURANTS

LE CRÉPUSCULE
10, rue Laghouat
Tel. 73 24 38
*Young clientele.
Specialties: pancakes,
pizzas, salads.*
75–200 DH.
⌂ 🖂

LE DINARJAT
6, rue Belgnaoui
Medina (av. Al Alou).
Tel. 70 42 39
*Excellent Moroccan
cuisine in an attractive
setting. The best
Moroccan restaurant in
Rabat. A man with a
lantern escorts
customers through the
medina at night.*

LE DRAGON D'OR
Behind the Souissi
supermarket

Tel. 75 55 77
Open for lunch and
dinner. Closed
Sundays.
*Good Asian cuisine, but
poor service.
Specialties: soups,
donuts.
75–150 DH.*

EL-ANDALOUS
Hôtel Rabat Hyatt
Regency
Tel. 77 12 34
*Good cuisine. Cabaret
every evening.
150–250 DH.*

EL-MANSOUR-HASSAN
Hôtel de la Tour
26, av. du Chellah
Tel. 73 38 15
Tlx. 327 88
*Traditional setting and
cabaret. Good cuisine.
Specialties: couscous,
tajines, pastillas.
100–200 DH.*

L'ENTRECÔTE
74, av. Gouled Oumeir
Agdal
Tel. 77 11 08
Open 12 noon–7.30pm
Closed Sundays
*Excellent international
cuisine. Fresh pasta
and quality cuts of meat.
Very good service.
Specialties: fresh pasta,
meat cooked over a
wood fire.
150–300 DH.*

L'ÉPERON
8, av. Jazaïr
Tel. 72 59 01
Closed Sundays
Open for lunch and
dinner
*Pleasant setting but
quality unreliable. Good
meat dishes.
Specialties: fish,
seafood and salads.
100–200 DH.*

FUJI
2, av. Michlifen Agdal
Tel. 67 35 83
Open for lunch and
dinner
*Good Japanese cuisine.
Specialties: sushi,
sashimi, yakitori.
80–252 DH.*

LE GOÉLAND
9, rue Moulay Ali
Chérif
Tel. 76 88 85

Open for lunch and
dinner. Closed Sundays
*Excellent service.
Fresh produce.
Excellent cuisine.
Specialties: seafood,
fish, shellfish.
150–300 DH.*

LE JUSTINE'S
Hôtel Rabat Hyatt
Regency
Tel. 77 12 34
Open for lunch and
dinner. Closed Sunday
lunchtimes.
*Luxurious and
sophisticated setting.
Wine list offers a good
selection of French
wines. Specialty: fish.
200–350 DH.*

LA KOUTOUBIA
Rue Pierre Parent
Tel. 76 01 25
Open 11am–3pm and
7–11pm.
*Moroccan and
traditional cuisine. A la
carte and set menus.
Friendly atmosphere.
Quality unreliable.
Specialty: Moroccan
cuisine.
75–200 DH.*

LA MAMMA
6, rue Tanta
Tel. 76 37 29
Open for lunch and
dinner
Closed Sundays
*Rustic setting, rapid
service, reasonable
cuisine. Specialties:
pizza, meat, pasta.
75–150 DH.*

LES MARTINETS
7, av. Imam Malik
Tel. 75 20 44
Open for lunch and
dinner
*Pleasant garden. Good
French family cuisine.
150–250 DH.*

OUAZZANI
Place Ibn Yacine
Agdal
Open until 9pm
*The best kebabs in
Rabat. Traditional
setting. Unpretentious,
clean restaurant. No
alcohol. Specialties:
meat kebabs, Moroccan
salads, soups, tajines.
50–150 DH.*

LA PAGODE
13, rue Bagdad
Tel. 76 33 83
Open for lunch and
dinner
Closed Sundays
*Good Asian cuisine.
Service quite slow.
75–150 DH.*

PIZZERIA NAPOLI
8, rue Moulay
Abd el Aziz
Tel. 76 38 02
*New restaurant, clean
and pleasant. Parking
difficult at lunchtime.
Specialties: pizza
cooked over a wood
fire, pasta.
70 or 150 DH.*

LA PLAGE
Plage de Rabat
Tel. 72 31 48
Open for lunch and
dinner. Closed
Sundays
*Service mediocre and
quality inconsistent.
Large terrace with
splendid view.
Specialties: seafood,
fish.
100–200 DH.*

LE VERT GALANT
Corner of Rue Atlas and
Rue Sébou Agdal
Tel. 77 42 47
Open for lunch and
dinner. Closed Sundays
*Good French cuisine in
a pleasant setting.
Guitarist in the evening.
Specialties: sweet-
breads, kidneys cooked
in Madeira, fillet of duck.
100–250 DH.*

FOR THE GOURMET

**AU CHOCOLAT
CHAUD**
21, av. Tadla
Tel. 75 83 67
*Patisserie, bakery,
tea rooms: viennoiserie,
fruit tarts, Moroccan
patisserie.
Excellent.*

AU DÉLICE
Av. Mohammed V
Tel. 70 97 35
Patisserie.

**PÂTISSERIE
JOHARA**
7, rue Asfi
Tel. 76 29 66
*Specialty: Moroccan
patisserie.*

PATACHOU
76, galerie Kay's
Sahat Rabia El Adaouia
Agdal Rabat
*Delicious French
patisserie.*

ACCOMMODATION

HÔTEL BELÈRE
33, av. Moulay Youssef
Tel. 76 99 01
Tlx 317 93
*Bar and nightclub.
320 DH.*

HÔTEL CHELLAH
2, rue d'Ifni
Tel. 76 40 52
Tlx 316 15
*International
restaurant.
314 DH.*

HÔTEL MOUSSAFIR
Rue Abd er Rahman
El Ghafiki
Rabat Agdal
Tel. 77 49 01
*Recently built,
clean hotel with
traditional décor and
all mod. cons.
International restaurant,
barbecue overlooking
garden.
196 DH.*

1 HÔTEL INTERCONTINENTAL
2 GRAND HÔTEL VILLA DE FRANCE
3 HÔTEL EL-MINZAH
4 HÔTEL TANJAH
5 AFRICA HÔTEL
6 HÔTEL REMBRANDT
7 HÔTEL RIF
8 HÔTEL SHÉHÉRAZADE
9 HÔTEL LES ALMOHADES
10 HÔTEL EL-OUMNIA
11 HÔTEL SOLAZUR

To the airport

To Rabat

HÔTEL LES OUDAYAS
4, rue de Tobrouk
Tel. 70 78 20
Fax 310 40
Small, unpretentious and clean.
274 DH.

RABAT HYATT REGENCY
Aviation Souissi
B.P. 450
Tel. 77 12 34
Fax 77 24 92
Near the Dar es Salam golf course. Four restaurants (one of which is Moroccan). Piano-bar, Andalusian gardens, sports hall, several tennis courts, golf practise range.
1450–1550 DH.

HÔTEL SAFIR
Place Sidi Makhlouf
Tel. 73 21 17
Tlx 328 73
A particularly noisy hotel. Tennis courts,

conference rooms.
800 DH.

HÔTEL DE LA TOUR HASSAN
26, av. du Chellah
Tel. 73 38 15
Fax 72 54 08
Two restaurants. Nightclub, conference room, tennis courts.
1100 DH.

HÔTEL YASMINA
Corner of Rue El Mérinyine and Rue Makka.
Tel. 72 20 18
Fax 72 21 00
Recently built. Clean, unpretentious hotel. International restaurant.
279 DH.

YOUTH HOSTEL
34, rue Marrassa
Tel. 72 57 69
Open every day
7.30–10am

12 noon–3pm and
7pm–midnight

CAMPING DE TEMARA
Temara plage, on the Casablanca coast road, 9´ miles outside Rabat

SAFI

DIALING CODE
04

USEFUL INFORMATION

TOURIST OFFICE
Rue Imam Malik
Tel. 46 45 43

TRANSPORT

ONCF
Tel. 46 33 75

CULTURE

DAR EL BAHR
North entrance of the old port
Château de la Mer, built in the 17th century by the Portuguese to

protect the north entrance of the old port.

LA KECHLA
Guided tour one or two hours, mornings and afternoons.
16th-century Portuguese fortress overlooking the roofs of the medina. Its monumental gate opens onto a mechouar (assembly area), a palace and an oratory.

ACCOMMODATION

HÔTEL ATLANTIDE
Rue Chaouki
Tel. 46 21 60
Tlx. 717 24
Small, centrally located hotel. Restaurant, bar, friendly service.
196 DH

HÔTEL SAFIR
Av. Zerktouni
Tel. 46 42 99
Tlx 710 71

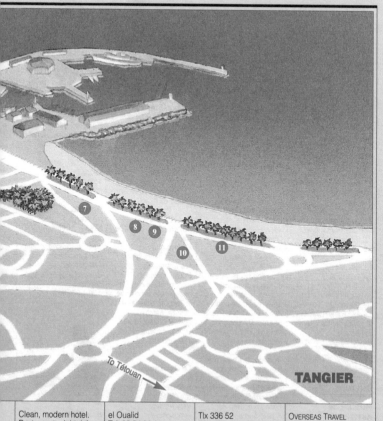

Clean, modern hotel.
Restaurant, nightclub,
tennis courts, beach.
Pleasant setting.
314 DH.
⌂ ⌂ 🎾 ⊃ 🚗
▭

TANGIER

DIALING CODE
09

**USEFUL
INFORMATION**

**AMERICAN
CONSULATE**
29, rue Achouak
Tel. 93 59 04

BRITISH CONSULATE
9, rue Amérique du Sud
Tel. 93 59 04

POST OFFICE
Bd Mohammed V
Tel. 93 26 06

TOURIST OFFICES
29, bd Pasteur
Tel. 93 82 49 29
11, rue Khalid Ibn

el Oualid
Tel. 93 54 86 11

TRANSPORT

**BOUKHALEF SOUAHEL
AIRPORT**
Tel. 93 51 29

BY AIR
GIBRALTAR AIRWAYS
(and British Airways)
83 rue de la Liberté
Tel. 93 58 77
ROYAL AIR MAROC
Place Mohammed V
Tel. 93. 55 01

BY BOAT
COMANAV
43, rue Abou Inane
el Marini
Tel. 93 26 49
Tlx 330 46
COMARIT FERRY
7, rue du Mexique
Tel. 93 12 20
Tlx 338 98
COMPAGNIE LIMADET
FERRY
13, rue Prince Moulay
Abdallah
Tel. 93 29 13

Tlx 336 52
TRANSMÉDITERRANEA
31, av. de la Résistance
Tel. 94 11 01
Tlx 330 05

BY TRAIN
ONCF
Tel. 93 12 01

TRAVEL AGENTS
GLOBUS VOYAGES
3, av. Youssoufia
Tel. 94 29 05
Tlx 339 34
MENARA TOURS
7, rue du Mexique
Tel. 380 12
OLIVE BRANCH TOURS
11, rue Omar Ibnou el
Hass
Tel. 93 80 83

OVERSEAS TRAVEL
AGENCY
45, av. Mohammed V
Tel. 93 72 68
PAQUET VOYAGES
21, av. d'Espagne
Tel. 93 42 23
Tlx 33 007
RAM
Place de France
Tel. 93 47 22
SAHARA TOURS
54, rue el Moutanabi
Passage Bestofol
Tel. 93 54 79
Tlx 39 619
WAGONS-LITS TOURISME
86, rue de la Liberté
Tel. 93 16 40
Tlx 33 65

CAR HIRE

ADIL CAR
84, bd Mohammed V
Tel. 94 22 67

AVIS
54, bd Pasteur
Tel. 93 30 31

BEST CARS
128, av. dEspagne
Tel. 94 38 98

BUDGET
79, av. du Prince
Moulay Abdallah
Tel. 93 79 94

CITER
Airport Boukhalef

EUROPCAR INTERRENT
Immeuble Coficom
87, bd Mohammed V
Tel. 93 82 71

HARRIS
1 bis, rue Zerktouni
Tel. 94 21 58

MOROCCAN HOLIDAYS
23, rue Rembrandt
Tel. 93 54 93

SALAM CARS
13, rue Antaki
Tel. 94 10 73

STARC HERTZ
36, av. Mohammed V
Tel. 93 33 22

TANGER RATES CAR
7, rue Omar Ibn
El Hass
Tel. 93 39 53

TOURIST CARS
84, bd Mohammed V
Tel. 93 54 93

CULTURE

MUSEUM OF ANTIQUITIES

Dar el Makhzen
Medina. Open
9–11.45am and 3–6pm:
9am–3pm in summer
Closed Tuesdays
Opening hours vary
during Ramadan.
*Prehistoric and Roman
Morocco. History of
Tangier.*

FORBES MUSEUM OF MILITARY MINIATURES

Rue Shakespeare
Tel. 93 96 06
Open 10am–5pm
*115,000 toy soldiers
donated by Malcolm
Forbes, displayed in the
former Mendoubia.*

*Interesting
presentations of various
great historical events.*

MUSEUM OF MOROCCAN ARTS

Dar el Makhzen
Medina
Open 9–11.30am and
3–6.15pm. Summer
opening: mornings only,
closed Tuesdays
*Pottery, basket work,
cloth from northern
Morocco, weapons,
Rabat carpets. Bound
and illuminated books,
silks, jewelry, painted
wood.*

DAR EL MAKHZEN (ROYAL PALACE)

In the medina,
near the Kasbah
Open 9–11.45am
and 3–5.30pm
Summer opening:
9am–3.30pm
Opening hours vary
during Ramadan
Closed Tuesdays
*Magnificent tiled and
marble columns, interior
garden. Décorated in
the style of a royal
palace.*

AMERICAN LEGATION

9am–noon, 3–6pm.
*Permanent exhibition of
works by various artists
(Stewart Schurch,
Lecouteux, Ben Ali
R'bati) and ancient
maps (Mercator, Leo
Africanus, Ortelius).*

GROTTOES OF HERCULES

6 miles outside Tangier.
Open daily.
*These natural,
limestone caves are
flooded at high tide.
According to legend,
Hercules rested here
after accomplishing his
labors.*

RESTAURANTS

LE DÉTROIT

In the Kasbah
Tel. 93 80 80
Good quality

*Moroccan cuisine.
Magnificent view across
the Bay of Tangier and
the Straits of Gibraltar.
100–250 DH.*
⌨ ⛰

EL-KORSAN

Hôtel el-Minzah
85, rue de la Liberté.
Tel. 93 87 87
Open from 8pm
Closed Monday
*Cabaret three times per
week: Tuesdays,
Fridays and Sundays.
Oriental dancing and
live folk music.
Sophisticated,
traditional setting. The
best Moroccan cuisine
in Tangier. Specialties:
pastilla, méchoui,
tajines, couscous and
local patisserie.
150–350 DH.*
⌨ 🅿

LE GAGARINE

28, rue Abou Alaa
al Maani
Tel. 93 45 31
*Very friendly
atmosphere.
Specialties: inter-
national, Russian and
East European cuisine.
90 DH.*
⌨

MARHABA

In the Kasbah
Tel. 93 76 43
Open 9am–11pm
*Traditional setting. Live
folk music in the
evenings.
Specialty: Moroccan
cuisine.
50–150 DH.*
⌨

LE MARQUIS

18, rue el Baghtouri
Tel. 94 11 32
Open 12 noon–8pm
Closed Sundays
*Simple setting. Quiet,
sophisticated
atmosphere. French
cuisine.
Specialties: fish (sole,
fillet of John Dory,
turbot), desserts.
150–250 DH.*
⌨

LE NAUTILUS

Rue Ibn Oualid
Tel. 93 11 59
*French cuisine. Simple,
quiet setting. Quality
service. Specialties:
grilled fish, fish "en
sauce."
100–250 DH.*
⌨

ROMERO

12, rue du Prince
Moulay Abdallah
Tel. 93 22 77
*Spanish cuisine, setting
and atmosphere.
Friendly service.
Specialties: paëlla, fish,
shellfish.
100–200 DH.*
⌨

SAN REMO

15, rue Ahmed Chaouki
Tel. 93 84 51
*Italian cuisine, simple
but good. Specialties:
fresh pasta, desserts.
75–150 DH.*
⌨

TAMASCOUS

Rue du Prince Moulay
Abdallah
Tel. 93 47 30
*Quality Moroccan
cuisine. Dinner and folk
cabaret. Very good
atmosphere and
service. Specialty:
Moroccan cuisine.
150–250 DH.*
⌨

FOR THE GOURMET

LA ESPANOLA

Rue de la Liberté
Patisserie.

SALON ROXY

30, rue Allal Ben
Abdallah
*Patisserie, 1950's
décor.*

LA HELADERCA COLONNA
27, rue Allal Ben Abdallah
Patisserie.
Specialty: ice cream.

ACCOMMODATION

AFRICA HOTEL
17, rue Moussa Ben Nouar
Tel. 93 55 11
Tlx 336 47
314 DH.
⌂ 🄲 ⌁ 🚗 ▭

AHLEN VILLAGE
3 miles on the Rabat road
Tel. 94 30 00
Tlx 330 95
Tennis courts, nightclub, conference room. Small, pleasant but unfortunate location.
258 DH.
⌂ ⌁ 🚗 ▭ 🕴

HÔTEL LES ALMOHADES
Av. des F.A.R.
Tel. 94 03 30
Fax 94 63 71
Opposite the beach. Two restaurants, tennis courts, sauna, conference room, nightclub.
340–460 DH.
⌂ 🄲 ☀ ⌁ 🚗 ▭ 🕴

HÔTEL EL-MINZAH
85, rue de la Liberté
Tel. 93 87 87
Fax 93 45 46
Rooms overlooking the sea are more expensive but recommended. Very good cuisine. Very pleasant wine bar. Mini golf, tennis courts, table tennis, darts.
460–575 DH.
🏨 🄲 ⌂ ☀ ▢ ⌁ ▭ 🕴

HÔTEL EL-OUMNIA
Av. L. van. Beethoven
Tel. 94 03 66
Tlx 330 90
International restaurant, conference room.
314 DH.
⌂ 🄲 ⌁ ▭ 🕴

GRAND HÔTEL
Villa de France
143, rue de Hollande
Tel. 93 14 75
Magnificent view over the Kasbah and the Bay of Tangier. The hotel has a prestigious past, as the artist Henri

Matisse stayed here. Minimal comfort.
196 DH.
⌂ 🄲 ☀ ⌁ 🚗 ▭

HÔTEL INTERCONTINENTAL
Park Brooks
Tel. 93 60 53
Fax 93 79 45
This is not part of the international Intercontinental chain. Two restaurants (European and Moroccan), sauna, nightclub and conference room. Situated in the new town.
445–620 DH.
🏨 🄲 ⌂ ▢ ⌁ 🚗 ▭ 🕴

HÔTEL PASSADENA
Half a mile, Route de Tétouan
Tel. 94 59 15
Tlx 336 47
Near Tangier's industrial district. Recommended for business trips.

HÔTEL REMBRANDT
Bd Mohammed V
Tel. 93 78 70
Fax 330 40
Small rooms, décorated in a combination of local and European styles. Not recommended for long stays.
263–350 DH.
⌂ 🄲 ⌁ ▭ 🕴

HÔTEL RIF
Av. d'Espagne

Tel. 93 59 08
Tlx 330 79
Overlooking the sea Very good swimming pool, tennis courts, nightclub, conference room and international restaurant.
280 DH.
⌂

HÔTEL SHÉHÉRAZADE
Av. des F.A.R.
Tel. 94 05 00
Tlx 330 83

Overlooking the beach. Nightclub and international restaurant.
258 DH.
⌂ 🄲 ☀ ⌁ 🚗 ▭

HÔTEL SOLAZUR
Av. des F.A.R.
Tel. 94 01 64
Fax 94 52 86
The hotel was taken over and converted by the American millionaire Malcolm Forbes. Two restaurants (Moroccan and international),

tennis courts, conference room.
314 DH.
⌂ 🄲 ☀ ⌁ 🚗 ▭ 🕴

HÔTEL TANJAH
6, bd Mohammed V
Tel. 93 33 00
Fax 93 43 47
Small, roof-top swimming pool with magnificent view.
289–400 DH.
⌂ 🄲 ☀ ⌁ 🚗 ▭

AUBERGE DE JEUNESSE
(Youth Hostel)
8, rue Antaki
Tel. 94 61 27

CAMPING TINGIS
Av. Sidi Mohammed
(going toward Malabata)

CAMPING

LE MIRAMONTE
Route Marshan
Tel. 93 71 33
Admissions: Open 8am–12 noon and 3–8pm

DIALING CODE
08

TRANSPORT

CAR HIRE
STARS CARS
99 bis, Bab Zergane
Tel. 85 25 13

FOR THE GOURMET

PATISSERIE EL OUARDA
Place Talmaklat
French and Moroccan patisserie.

ACCOMMODATION

LA GAZELLE D'OR
Tel. 85 20 39
Fax 85 25 37
Closed August.
Delightful luxury hotel. Tennis courts, horse riding, hammam, shops, nightclub.
1525 DH.
🏨 ⌂ ☐ ⌁ 🚗 ▭

HÔTEL SALAM
B.P. 258
Tel. 85 23 12
Fax 85 26 54
Very attractive hotel in a former palace. Traditionally décorated rooms opening onto a luxurian patio. Sauna, tennis courts, horse riding, conference room.
311 DH.
🏨 ⌂ ☐ ⌁ 🚗 ▭

TRANSPORT

TRAVEL AGENTS
AGENCE DE VOYAGES BENNANI
Pl. de l'Indépendance
Tel. 67 33 07

DIALING CODE
09

USEFUL INFORMATION

TOURIST INFORMATION
Tel. 41 44 07
Av. Mohammed V
Tel. 41 12 30

TRANSPORT

SANIAT R'MEL AIRPORT
4 miles outside Tétouan
Tel. 96 55 01

383

TRAVEL AGENTS

AGENCE SOLEIL ET MER
Rue Moukaouma
Tel. 96 58 16
HIBA MAROC-VOYAGES
23, rue Mohammed V
Tel. 96 42 24
INTERCONTINENTAL
Rue Moukaouma
Tel. 96 58 16

MAROC CONSEIT-
VOYAGES
9, rue du 10 mai
Tel. 96 58 32
RAM
5, av. Mohammed V
Tel. 96 20 60

CAR HIRE

ESSALAM
Charia Mecque
Tel. 96 39 56
ZEIT WAGEN
3, av. Moulay Abbes
Tel. 96 59 83

CULTURE

MUSEUM OF MOROCCAN ARTS

Bab el Oqla
Open 9am–12noon and
2–6pm. Closed
Tuesdays and public
holidays
*Fine display of regional
crafts in a magnificent
Hispano-Moresque
building.*

ARCHEOLOGICAL MUSEUM

Open 9.30am–12 noon
and 2.30–5.30pm
Closed Sunday
*Large number of
mosaics and objects
excavated at
archeological sites*

*in northern Morocco.
10 DH.*

SCHOOL OF TRADITIONAL ARTS AND CRAFTS

Open 9am–12 noon and
2.30–5.30pm
Closed Tuesdays and
Saturdays

*For over 50 years,
the school has been
teaching skills such
as weaving, mosaics
and painting.
Landscaped garden,
with various plants and
flowers.*

RESTAURANTS

LE ZARHOUN

Bd Mohammed Ben
Larbi Torres
Open for lunch and
dinner
*Typically Moroccan
setting (décor, music
and atmosphere).
Limited choice but good
cuisine.
65–110 DH.*

ACCOMMODATION

HÔTEL SAFIR

Route de Ceuta
Av. Kennedy
Tel. 97 01 44
Tlx 436 50
*Restaurant, nightclub,
conference room, tennis
courts.*
⌂ ⌂·· ⌲ 🚗 ▭

TIZNIT

DIALING CODE
08

TRANSPORT

TRAVEL AGENTS

ESSAHARA VOYAGES
16–17, av. du 20 Août
Tel. 86 25 12
SOUSS TOURISME
7, av. du 20 août.
Tel. 86 22 78
TIZNIT VOYAGES
59, place du
Mechouar
Tel. 86 21 17

ACCOMMODATION

KERDOUS HOTEL

Col du Kerdous,
34 miles fom Tiznit, On
the road from Tiznit to
Tafraout . B.P. 326 Tiznit
(3,600 feet)
Tel. 86 20 63
*Air-conditioned rooms,
restaurants, bar,
swimming pool.
275 DH.*

ZAGORA

DIALING CODE
04

CULTURE

FORTRESS

Open daily.
*Outside the town, on
the track to Tamegroute.
Recommended at
sunrise and sunset.
Magnificent view over
the Oued Draa, the
palm groves and the
desert.*

ACCOMMODATION

HÔTEL REDA DOUMIA PLM

Route de Mahmid
Tel. 84 72 49
Fax 84 70 12
*Restaurant, bar, shop,
tennis courts.*
⌂ ⌂ ⌲ 🚗 ▭

HÔTEL SALAM

Route de Rissani
Tel. 55 66 65
Fax 57 65 22

*Restaurant, conference
room, tennis courts.
314 DH.*
⌂ ▭ ⌲ 🚗 ▭

HÔTEL SIJILMASSA

Tel. 57 65 22
*Attractive, recently
modernised hotel, with
splendid view over the
palm groves.
Restaurant, bar,
swimming pool.* ⌲
⌂ ⌂ ⌂·· ⩍ ⌲
🚗 ▭

HOTEL TIMSOULINE KTH

Tel. 84 72 52
Restaurant, bar, shop.
⌂ ⌂ ⌲ 🚗 ▭

AGADIR

The Kasbah	◆ 360	Open every day.
Vallée des oiseaux (zoo)		Near Avenues Mohammed V and Hassan II.

ESSAOUIRA

Sidi Mohammed Ben Abdallah Mus.	◆ 365	9am–12 noon/2.30–6pm. Closed Tuesdays.

FEZ

Musée d'armes	◆ 366	9am–12 noon/3–6pm.
Museum of Moroccan Arts	◆ 366	Closed Tuesdays and national and religious holidays.

MARRAKESH

Dar Si'Saï, Museum of Regional Art	◆ 370	8.30am–12 noon/2.30–6pm.
Majorelle Gardens	◆ 370	9am–12 noon/2–6pm.
Menara Gardens	◆ 370	9am–6pm.
Agdal Gardens	◆ 370	9am–6pm.
La Bahia Palace	◆ 370	8.30am–12 noon/12–6pm.
El Badi Palace	◆ 370	8am–6pm.
Saadian Tombs	◆ 370	8am–12 noon/2–6pm.

MEKNÈS

Dar Jamaï Palace	◆ 374	9am–12 noon/3–6pm. Closed Tuesdays.
Moulay Ismaïl Mausoleum	◆ 374	9am–12 noon/3–6pm. Closed Friday am.
Koubba el Khayatine	◆ 374	Admission: 10 DH.
Bou Inania Medersa	◆ 374	9am–12 noon/3–6pm. Admission: 10 DH.
Koubba of Sidi Mohammed Ben Aïssa	◆ 374	No admission.

OUARZAZATE

Weavers' cooperative	◆ 375	8am–12 noon/2–6pm.
Kasbah of Taourirt	◆ 375	8am–6pm.

RABAT

Archeological Museum	◆ 378	8.30am–12 noon/2.30–6pm. Closed Tuesdays and public holidays.
National Craft Museum	◆ 378	Open office hours.
Oudayas Museum	◆ 378	8.30am–12 noon/2.30–6pm. (3–6pm in summer.) Closed Tues. and public holidays.
Mohammed V Mausoleum	◆ 378	Admission free. Proper dress essential.
Mohammed V Museum	◆ 378	9am–6pm.
Hassan Tower	◆ 378	9am–6pm.
Cathédrale Saint–Pierre	◆ 378	9am–12 noon/3–6pm.
Medersa (Salé)	◆ 379	9am–12 noon/3–6pm.

SAFI

Dar el Bahr	◆ 380	9am–12 noon/3–6pm.
La Kechla	◆ 380	One– or two–hour guided tours mornings and afternoons.

TANGIER

Museum of Antiquities	◆ 382	9am–11.45am/3–6pm (9am–3pm in summer).
	◆ 382	Closed Tuesdays.
Forbes Museum of Miniatures	◆ 382	10am–5pm.
Museum of Moroccan Arts	◆ 382	9–11.30am/3–6.15pm (mornings only in summer) Closed Tuesdays.
Dar el Makhzen (Royal Palace)	◆ 382	9–11.45am/3–5.30pm. (9am–3.30pm in summer).
American Legation	◆ 382	9am–12 noon/3–6pm.
Grottoes of Hercules	◆ 382	Open every day.

TÉTOUAN

Museum of Moroccan Arts	◆ 384	9am–12 noon/2–6pm. Closed Tuesdays and public holidays.
Archeological Museum	◆ 384	9.30am–12 noon/2.30– 5.30pm. Closed Sun.
School of Traditional Arts & Crafts	◆ 384	9am–12 noon/2.30–5.30pm. Closed Tues./Sat.

ZAGORA

Fortress	◆ 384	Open every day.

APPENDICES

◆ FURTHER READING

.ESSENTIAL ◆ READING ◆

◆ MAXWELL, Gavin: *Lords of the Atlas*
◆ HARRIS, Walter: *Morocco that was*

◆ GENERAL ◆

◆ BARBOUR, Nevill: *Morocco*, Thames & Hudson, London, 1965.
◆ BERGIER, P. and F.: *A Birdwatcher's Guide to Morocco* Prion, Huntingdon, 1990.
◆ *De l'Empire romain aux villes impériales – 6000 ans d'art au Maroc*, Paris-Musée, 1990.
◆ CAMPS, G: *Les Berbéres: mémoire et identité*, Errance, Paris, 1987.
◆ BURCKHARDT, Titus: *Fez – City of Islam*, Islamic Texts Society.
◆ DENNIS, L. and L.: *Living in Morocco*, Thames and Hudson, London.
◆ GROVE, Lady Agnes: *Seventy-one Days Camping in Morocco*, Longmans, Green & Co., London, 1902.
◆ LANDAV, Rom: *The Kasbahs of Morocco*, Faber, London, 1969.
◆ MELVILLE, Jennifer and McBEYS, James: *Morocco*, HarperCollins, London, 1991.
◆ PARKER, Richard: *Islamic Monuments in Morocco*, Baraka Press, Virginia, 1981.
◆ PICKENS, S. and SAHAROFF, P: *Les Villes Imperiales du Maroc*, ACR, Paris, 1990.
◆ PULSIFER, Gary (ed.): *Paul Bowles by his friends*, Peter Owen Publishers, 1992.
◆ STUART, Graham H.: *The International City of Tangier*, Stanford University Press, 1955.
◆ TALABOT, M.: *A Marrakesh et dans le Sud marocain*, Hachette, Paris, 1988.
◆ *The Atlas Mountains*, Cicerone Press.
◆ TOUSSAINT-MEDINE, S.: *Mémorial de Meknès*, Tougui, 1990.
◆ TROIN, D: *Les Souks Marocains*, Édisud, Aix-en-Provence, 1975.

◆ VAIDON, Lawdom: *Tangier: A Different Way*, Scarecrow Press, New Jersey, 1977.
◆ WINTER, G. and KOCHMAN, W.: *The Rogue's Guide to Tangier*, Tangier, 1986.
◆ ZURFLUH, Jean Michel: *Casablanca*, Soden, Casablanca, 1988.

◆ FOOD ◆

◆ CARRIER, Robert: *A Taste of Morocco*, Century, London, 1988.
◆ WOLFART, P.: *Good Food from Morocco*, John Murray, London.

◆ HISTORY ◆

◆ ABUN NASR, J.M.: *A History of the Maghreb*, 1971.
◆ ANDERSON, Eugene M.: *The First Moroccan Crisis*, Archon Books, Hamden, Conn., 1966.
◆ ASSAYAG, Isaac, J.: *Tanger ... une siècle d'histoire*, Tangier, 1981.
◆ BAREA, Arturo: *The Forging of a Rebel*, Fontana, London, 1984.
◆ BOVILL, E.W.: *The Golden Trade of the Moors*, Oxford University Press, 1968.
◆ CABOT BRIGGS, L.: *Tribes of the Sahara*, 1960.
◆ CLOUDSLEY-THOMPSON, J.L. (ed.): *Sahara Desert*, Pergamon Press, Oxford, 1984.
◆ FLINT, John E. (ed.): *The Cambridge History of Africa*, Cambridge University Press, 1976.
◆ HARRIS, Walter: *Morocco That Was*, Eland Books, London, 1983.
◆ JULIEN, C.A.: *Histoire de l'Afrique du Nord*, Hachette, Paris, 1982.
◆ LANDAU, Rom and SWAAN, Wm: *Morocco*, Elek Books, London, 1967.
◆ LE TOURNEAU, Roger: *La Vie Quotidienne à Fès en 1900*, Hachette, Paris, 1965.
◆ LEGUIL, A.: *Contes berbères de l'Atlas de Marrakech*,

L'Harmattan, Paris, 1988.
◆ MAALOUF, A.: *Léon l'Africain*, Lattes, Paris, 1986.
◆ MAXWELL, Gavin: *Lords of the Atlas. The Rise and Fall of the House of Glaoua 1893–1956*, Century, London, 1985.
◆ MOKHTAR, G. (ed.): *General History of Africa*, UNESCO/Heinemann, Paris/London, 1981.
◆ PERRY, J.: *Les Sables roses d'Essaouira*, Calmann Levy, Paris, 1990.
◆ PORCH, Douglas: *The Conquest of Morocco*, Jonathan Cape, London, 1986.
◆ RONDEAU, D.: *Tanger*, Quai Voltaire, Paris, 1987.
◆ SERHANE, A.: *Les Enfants des rues etroites*, Éditions du Seuil, Paris, 1986.
◆ WOOLMAN, David S.: *Rebels of the Rif*, Oxford University Press, 1969.

◆ GUIDES ◆

◆ BIDWELL, Margaret and Robin: *Morocco: The Traveller's Companion*, Tauris, London and New York, 1992.
◆ GLEN, Simon: *Sahara Handbook*, Lascelles, London, 1990.
◆ KINNINMONTH, Christopher: *The Traveller's Guide to Morocco*, London, 1987.
◆ Lonely Planet *Maghreb Survival Kit*
◆ McLACHLAN, A. and K. (eds): *North African Handbook, with Moorish Southern Spain*, Trade and Travel, Bath, 1993.
◆ *Morocco*, Nagel's Encyclopedia Guide, Geneva, 1969.
◆ *Morocco*, Blue Guide, A & C Black, London and W.W. Norton, New York, 1992.
◆ *Maroc*, Hachette Guides Bleus, Paris, 1987.
◆ *Morocco*, Insight Guides, APA, London, 1989.

◆ ISLAM ◆

◆ AHMED, (S. Akbar): *Discovering Islam: Making Sense of*

Muslim History and Society, Routledge, London, 1988.
◆ BANNERMAN, P.: *The Essential Teaching of Islam*, Rider, 1987.
◆ BOSWORTH, C.E.: *The Islamic Dynasties*, Edinburgh, 1980.
◆ GUILLAUME, Alfred: *Islam*, Penguin Books, Harmondsworth, 1956.
◆ HUGHES, T.P.: *Dictionary of Islam*, repr. London, 1988.
◆ CRONE, Patricia, and COOK, Michael: *The Making of the Islamic World*, Cambridge, 1977.
◆ GUMLEY, Frances, and REDHEAD, Brian: *The Pillars of Islam: An Introduction to Islamic Faith*, BBC Books, London, 1990.
◆ *Islam in Perspective: A Guide to Islamic Society, Politics and Law,*. Royal Institute of International Affairs, 1988.
◆ ROGERS, J.M.: *The Spread of Islam*, Oxford, 1976.
◆ SYED BARAKAT AHMAD: *Introduction to Qu'ranic Script*, Curzon, London, 1984.

◆ ART ◆

◆ ADNAN, E.: *L'Artisanat Créateur – Maroc*, Dessain et Tolra/Almadaviss, Paris/Casablanca, 1983.
◆ ARAMA, M.: *Le Maroc de Delacroix*, Éditions du Jaguar, Paris, 1987.
◆ ARAMA, M.: *Intinéraires marocains: Regards de peintres*, Éditions du Jaguar, Paris, 1991.
◆ ARAMA, M.: *Regards croisés*, Éditions du Jaguar, Paris, 1992.
◆ ATASOY, N. et al.: *The Art of Islam*, UNESCO/Flammarion, Paris, 1990.
◆ BARTHES, Roland: *Incidents*, Éditions du Seuil, Paris, 1987.
◆ BARTHÉLEMY, A. and BALMIGERE, G.: *Tazra: tapis et bijouz de Ouazarte*, Édisud, Paris, 1991.
◆ BARBOUR, Neville: *Morocco*, Thames and Hudson, London, 1965
◆ BESANCENOT, J.: *Costumes du Maroc*,

Édisud, Aix-en-Provence, 1988.
◆ BOUKOBZA, A.: *La Poterie Marocaine*, OFP, Paris, 1987.
◆ BREND, Barbara: *Islamic Art*, British Museum Press, London, 1991.
◆ DUMUR, G.: *Delacroix et le Maroc*, Herscher, Paris, 1988.
◆ FEHERVARI, G.: *Islamic Pottery*, London, 1973.
◆ FINLAYSON, Iain: *Tangier: City of the Dream*, HarperCollins, London, 1992.
◆ FONTAINE, I.: *Henri Matisse: 1904–1917*, Éditions du Centre Pompidou, Paris, 1993.
◆ GIRARD, X.: *Matisse: une Splendeur inouïe*, Gallimard, Paris, 1993.
◆ HAYES, John R.: *The Genius of Arab Civilization*, Phaidon, London, 1976.
◆ Hoag, J.D.: *Islamic Architecture*, New York, 1977.
◆ HEDGECOE, John and SAMAR DAMLUJI, Salma: *Zillij – The Art of Morocco*, Garnet.
◆ HUBEL, R.J.: *The Book of Carpets*, New York, 1970.
◆ LOVICONI, A. and BELFOTAH, D.: *Regards sur la faïence de Fès*, Édisud, Aix-en-Provence, 1991.
◆ MICHELL, George (ed.): *Architecture of the Islamic World: its History and Social Meaning*, Thames and Hudson, London, 1978.
◆ POCHY, Y. and TRIKI, H.: *La Médersa de Marrakech*, EPA, Paris, 1990.
◆ QUIROT, O.: *Eugène et le Sultan: le voyage du peintre Delacroix au Maroc*, Biro, Paris, 1990.
◆ SCHNEIDER, P.: *Matisse*, Flammarion, Paris, 1993.
◆ SIJELMASSI, Mohammed: *Fés Cité de l'Art et su Savoir*, ACR Editions, Paris, 1991.

◆ **LANGUAGE** ◆

◆ *Arabic Phrase Book and Travel Pack* (with cassette) BBC Books, London, 1993.
◆ *Breakthrough Arabic: The Complete Introductory Course for Colloquial Arabic*, Macmillan, London, 1992.
◆ *Teach Yourself Quick and Easy Arabic* (with cassette): Langenscheidt/Hodder, 1992.

◆ **LITERATURE** ◆

◆ BLUNT, Wilfrid: *Black Sunrise*, Methuen, London, 1951.
◆ BOWLES, Jane: *The Collected Works of Jane Bowles, with an Introduction by Truman Capote*, Peter Owen, London,1984.
◆ BOWLES, Jane: *Out in the World: Selected Letters 1935–1970*, Black Sparrow Press, Santa Barbara, 1985.
◆ BOWLES, Paul: *Without Stopping*, Peter Owen, 1972.
◆ BOWLES, Paul: *Let it Come Down*, Arena, London, 1985.
◆ BOWLES, Paul: *Their Heads are Green*, Peter Owen, London 1985.
◆ BOWLES, Paul: *A Hundred Camels in the Courtyard*, City Lights Books, San Francisco, 1986.
◆ BOWLES, Paul: *The Spider's House*, London.
◆ BRADSHAW, Jon: *Dreams that Money Can Buy*, Morrow, New York, 1985.
◆ BURROUGHS, William: *The Naked Lunch*, Paladin, London, 1986.
◆ CANETTI, Elias: *The Voices of Marrakesh*, Marion Boyars, London, 1978.
◆ CAPOTE, Truman: *A Capote Reader*, Hamish Hamilton, London, 1986.
◆ CAPOTE, Truman: *Answered Prayers*, Plume, New York, 1988.
◆ CHOUKRI, Mohammed (trans. P. Bowles): *For Bread Alone*, Grafton, London, 1987.
◆ COLETTE: *Places*, Peter Owen, London, 1970.
◆ CROFT-COOKE, Rupert: *The Caves of Hercules*, W.H. Allen, London, 1974.
◆ DAVIDSON, Michael: *The World, The Flesh and Myself*, Quartet, London, 1977.
◆ DILLON, Millicent: *A Little Original Sin: The Life and Work of Jane Bowles*, Virago, London, 1988.
◆ EPTON, Nina: *A Journey Under the Crescent Moon*, Victor Gollancz, London, 1949.
◆ FINLAYSON, Iain: *Tangier, City of the Dream*, HarperCollins, London, 1992.
◆ GROVE, Lady Agnes B.: *Seventy-One Days Camping in Morocco*, Longman, Green & Co.,London, 1902.
◆ HERBERT, David: *Second Son*, Peter Owen, London, 1972.
◆ HUGHES, Richard: *In the Lap of the Atlas: Stories of Morocco*, Chatto & Windus, London, 1979.
◆ KENNEDY, Sylvia: *See Ouazazarte and Die: Travels Through Morocco*, Scribners, London 1992,.
◆ KRITZECK, James (ed.): *Anthology of Islamic Literature*, Penguin Books, London, 1964.
◆LANDAU, Rom: *Invitation to Morocco*, Faber, London, 1950.
◆ LANDAU, Rom: *Portrait of Tangier*, Robert Hale, London, 1952.
◆ LEARED, Arthur: *Morocco and the Moors*, Sampson Low, London, 1891.
◆ LITHGOW, William: *Rare Adventures and Painfull Peregrinations 1614–32*, James MacLehose, Glasgow,1906.
◆ LOTI, Pierre: *Morocco*, Werner, 1990.
◆ MAUGHAM, Robin: *The Wrong People*, Heinemann, London, 1970.
◆ MAYNE, Peter: *A Year in Marrakesh*, London, Eland Books.
◆ MAYNE, Peter: *The Alleys of Marrakesh*, John Murray, London,1953.
◆ MORGAN, Ted: *Rowing Towards Eden*, Houghton, Mifflin, New York, 1981.
◆ MORGAN, Ted: *Literary Outlaw: The Life and Times of William S. Burroughs*, Henry Holt & Co., New York, 1988.
◆ MRABET, Mohammed: *The Beach Café & The Voice*, Black Sparrow Press, Santa Barbara, 1980.
◆ MRABET, Mohammed: *Marriage With Papers*, Tombouctou Books, Bolinas, 1988.
◆ MRABET, Mohammed: *Look and Move On*, Peter Owen, London, 1989.
◆ MRABET, Mohammed: *M'Hashish*, Peter Owen, London, 1988.
◆ MRABET, Mohammed: *The Chest*, Tombouctou Books, Bolinas, 1983.
◆ MRABET, Mohammed: *Love With a Few Hairs*, Arena, London, 1986.
◆ NEWBY, Eric: *On the Shores of the Mediterranean*, Picador, London, 1984.
◆ ORTON, Joe: *The Orton Diaries* (ed. John Lahr), Methuen, London, 1986.
◆ RIGO DE'RIGHI, Eleanor: *Holiday in Morocco*, Foulis, London, 1935.
◆ RONDEAU, Daniel: *Tanger*, Quai Voltaire, Paris, 1987.
◆ SAINT-EXUPERY, Antoine de: *Wind, Sand and Stars*, Heinemann, London, 1939.
◆ SAWYER-LAUÇANNO, Christopher: *An Invisible Spectator*, Bloomsbury, London, 1989.
◆ SEFRIOUI, Ahmed: *Morocco*, Hachette, Paris, 1956.
◆ SITWELL, Sacheverell: *Mauretania: Warrior, Man and Woman*, Duckworth, London, 1940.
◆ TWAIN, Mark: *Traveling with the Innocents Abroad*, University of Oklahoma Press, 1958.
◆ WHARTON, Edith: *In Morocco*, Century, London, 1984.

Bernard. *Agama*, drawing by Jean Chevalier. *Young Arab girl in finery*, photo Brahim Tazi.
321 *Chichaoua carpet*, photo A.Ermont, © MAAO. *Chichaoua carpet*, photo A.Ermont, © MAAO. *Folk troupe*, photo Brahim Tazi.
322 *Marabout near Tafraoute*, photo Gérard Degeorge. *Door of house near Tafraoute*, photo Gérard Degeorge. *Between Tafraoute and Aït Baha*, photo Yvan Travert.
323 *Riding on a donkey*, drawing by Jean Chevallier. *Almond blossom festival*, photo Christian Occuli.
324 *Tafraoute*, photo Yvan Travert. *idem* . *Oumesnat*, photo Gérard Degeorge. *Blue stones*, photo Yvan Travert.
325 *Great Mosque of Tiznit*, photo Brahim Tazi
326 *Sidi Ifni*, photo Brahim Tazi. *Guedra*, photo Pierre Bernard.
327 *Beach at Sidi Ifni*, photo Brahim Tazi. *Tents*, photo Pierre Bernard. *Blue men*, photo Pierre Bernard.
328 *Laayoune*, photo Brahim Tazi. *Dunes*, photo Brahim Tazi. *Mosque at Smara*, photo Brahim Tazi. *Ruins of Mausoleum mosque, Smara*, photo Brahim Tazi.
330 *Plane, ferry*, photo êditions Voyages.
332 *Signpost*, photo Monsigny. *Coach*, photo Pierre Bernard. *Road signs*, photo Guy Léger.
334 *Guide's identity disk*, photo G. Léger. *Street sign, road signs*, photo G. Léger. *Key ring*, photo P. Léger. *Street signs*, photo P. Léger. *Milestone*, photo P. Léger. *Electric plug*, photo P. Léger. *Newspapers*, photo P. Léger. *Road signs*, photo P. Bernard. *Road signs*, photo B. Monsigny.
336-7 *Phone booth*, photo P. Bernard. *Letter box*, photo P. Léger. *Cash dispenser*, photo G. Léger.
340-1 *Olive hall, metalworker*, photos P. Léger. *Cobbler*, photo P. Bernard. *El Ksiba*, photo F. Busnel.
342-3 *Hôtel La Mamounia*, photo P. Bernard. *National folklore festival, Marrakesh*, photo Tazi. *Majorelle Gardens, Koubba el Baroudiyine*, photo G. Léger.
344-5 *Meknès, Volubilis, Middle Atlas*, photo F. Busnel. *Fez*, photo P. Léger. *Rabat*, photo Guy Léger.
346-8 *Rock carving, Jebel Rat*, photo Suzanne Searight. *Berber porter, Asif N'Timedhras gorges*, photo R. Richebé. *Overnight gâte, trekkers*, photo B. Tazi.
348-9 *Marie-Chantal contre le docteur Kha, The Sheltering Sky, Harem*, © Cahier du Cinéma Coll.
350-1 *Fez pottery, tray*, photo P. Bernard. *Carpet*, Khémisset hats, photo P. Léger.
329-408 Ills by Maurice Pommier. Maps by Emmanuel Calamy. Graphics by Paul Coulbois.

In some cases, we have been unable to trace the owners and publishers of some of the photographs and illustrations used. They are requested to make themselves known to us.

Acknowledgments:

Excerpt from Nina Epton *A Journey under the crescent moon* © 1949 by Victor Gollancz Ltd. Reprinted by kind permission of the author (UK and US).

Excerpt from Colette *Places* © 1970 by Peter Own Ltd. Reprinted by permission of Peter Own Ltd.

Excerpt from Peter Mayne *The alleys of Marrakesh* © 1953 by John Murray. Reprinted by permission of John Murray (Publishers) Ltd

Excerpt from Mohammed Mrabet *Look and Move on* © 1989 by Peter Own Ltd Ltd. Reprinted by permission of Peter Owen Ltd.

Excerpt from Paul Bowles *Their heads are green and their hands are blue* © 1953 by Peter Own Ltd Ltd. Reprinted by permission of Peter Owen Ltd.

Excerpt from Sacheverell Sitwell *Mauretania Warrior, Man and Woman* © 1940 by Duckworth. Reprinted by permission David Higham Associates Ltd.

◆ A ◆

ABD/ABID: slave, servant
AGADIR: fortified granary (or IGHREM)
AHIDOUS: Berber dance
AHOUACH: performance of dances and songs
AIN: spring
AIT: son of
AKER: red makeup
ALEM/OULEMA: scholar, wise man
ALEUJ: Christian
ANZET OR ANZIO: squirrel
ARBA: four, Wednesday
AROUSA: young bride
ATTARINE: perfumiers, spice sellers
AYA/AYAT: verse of the Koran

◆ B ◆

BAB: gate
BABOUCHE: leather slippers used as shoes
BARAKA: blessing
BEN/BENI: son of
BENDIR: type of drum
BETOUM: pistachio tree
BIR: well
BLED: country
BORJ: tower, bastion
BOU: father of
BOULGHOUR: ground corn
BULBUL: sparrow
BURNOUS: woolen cloak

◆ C ◆

CADI: juge according to Koranic law
CHADOUF: pump well
CHEICH: muslin scarf
CHERGUI: south-easterly wind
CHÉRIF: descendant of the Prophet
CHIKHATE: female dancer, musician
CHORFA: descendants of the Prophet

◆ D ◆

DAR/DOUAR: house
DAHR: royal decree
DAYA: freshwater lake
DERBOUKA: terracotta drum
DIFFA: ceremonial meal
DIRHAM: Arab currency
DJELLABA: long shirt with hood
DJIHAD (JEHAD): holy war
DJINN: good or evil spirit
DOUAR: an encampment or permanent village

◆ E ◆

EMIR: prince
ERG: dunes of the Sahara

◆ F ◆

FANTASIA: equestrian spectacle
FARAJIYA: cotton garment worn over a kaftan
FELLAH: peasant
FIBULA: Berber brooch fastener
FLIJ: woven band forming part of tent
FQIH: scholar
FONDOUK: warehouse with accommodation
FOUTA: piece of cloth

◆ G ◆

GANDOURA: sleeveless garment
GELLOUCH: type of pot
GHAYTA: Berber oboe
GHARBI: westerly wind
GHOTAR: type of dish
GORRAF: type of pitcher
GOURBI: cottage
GUEDRA: Sous region dance
GUEMBRI: two- or three-stringed lute

◆ H ◆

HARAM: sacred precinct, prayer hall
HABBOUS: possessions bequeathed to a religious foundation
HAD: first, Sunday
HADDADINE: ironsmiths
HAIDOU: Berber dance
HAIK: piece of cloth worn by women
HAJJ: Pilgrimage to Mecca or person who has made the pilgrimage
HAMMAM: Moorish baths
HARTANI/HARATINE: black slave
HARIRA: soup
HARQUS: paint used instead of tattooing
HEGIRA: Beginning of the Muslim era
HENDIRA: woolen blanket used as cloak
HENNA: dye
HERIR: silk
HZAM: belt

◆ I ◆

IGHREM: fortified granary
IMAM: Muslim prayer leader
IZAR: sheet

◆ J ◆

JAMAA: mosque
JAMMOUR: ornamental feature on a minaret
JEBEL: mountain
JOBBANA: cheese pot

◆ K ◆

KAABA: black stone of Mecca
KAFTAN: long robe
KAÏD: someone responsible for an administrative district, leader
KASBAH: the fortified district of a town
KHABIA: type of jar
KHALKHAL: anklet
KHAMSA: five
KHATIB: orator, speaker
KHAYAT/KHAYATINE: tailor
KHETTARA: system of undergound water conduits (known as FOGGARA/FEGGAGUIR in the Figuig region)
KOHL: powder of antimony sulfide
KISSARIA: craftsmen's and merchants' district
KOUBBA: shrine, dome
KSAR/KSOUR: fortified village

◆ L ◆

LALLA: (female) form of address or saint

◆ M ◆

MADAIJ: pearl necklace
MAHAKMA: courthouse
MAKHZEN: government
MARABOUT: saint
MASRAF: secondary canal
MECHOUAR: esplanade, assembly area
MEDERSA: Koranic school, students' residence
MEDINA: town
MELLAH: Jewish quarter
MENDOUB: representative
MINBAR: pulpit
MIHRAB: niche indicating the direction of Mecca
MOKHAZNI: soldier of the Sultan's guard
MOUCHARABIEH: carved wood panel
MOULAY: lord
MOULOUD: festival commemorating the birth of the Prophet or a saint
MOUSSEM: annual pilgrimage to the tomb of a saint
MUEZZIN: man who calls the Faithful to prayer from the top of the minaret

◆ N ◆

NASKHI: type of writing
NBAIL: hinged bracelet
NEJJAR/NEJJARINE: cabinetmaker
NIRA: reed flute

◆ O ◆

OUED: river
OUCHCHENE: jackal

◆ P ◆

PISÉ: mud and rubble

◆ Q ◆

QALAA: citadel
QARQAB: metal castanet
QIBLA: direction of Mecca
QOUAQEB: type of wooden shoe
QUS: bow (for stringed instrument)

◆ R ◆

RAS EL HANOUT: special blend of spices
REBAB: stringed instrument (rebec)
RHASSOUL: clay used for washing hair
RIBAT: military monastery

◆ S ◆

SALAT: prayer
SAWM: fast
SEBT: seven, Saturday
SEGUIA: secondary canal
SELHAM: burnous
SELWA: presentation of a bride
SERDAL: head band
SHAHADA: Muslim profession of faith
SHEIKH: chieftain, elder
SIDI: (male) form of address
SKALA: rampart walk
SKIFFA: offset entrance to a house
SOUK: market
SURAH: verse of the Koran
STUCCO: plaster- and lime-based rendering

◆ T ◆

TAARIJA: tambourine
TAJ: tiara
TAJINE: traditional Moroccan dish
TARBOOSH: fez
TAWARZA: latex tree
TCHAMIR: shirt
TEBILAT: tambourines
TIT: source, spring
TIZI: mountain pass
TLATA: three, Tuesday
TNIN: two, Monday

◆ Z ◆

ZAKAT: tax imposed by the Koran
ZAOUIA: brotherhood, religious center
ZARBIA: carpet
ZELLIGE: elaborate tile mosaics

INDEX